LAND, FAMILY AND INHERITANCE IN TRANSITION

Aerial view of Kibworth Harcourt, 1947

LAND, FAMILY AND INHERITANCE IN TRANSITION

KIBWORTH HARCOURT 1280–1700

CICELY HOWELL

Sometime Fulford Research Fellow,
St Anne's College, Oxford
and Research Fellow in Agrarian History,
Department of English Local History, Leicester

CAMBRIDGE UNIVERSITY PRESS

Cambridge
London   New York   New Rochelle
Melbourne   Sydney

Published by the Press Syndicate of the University of Cambridge
The Pitt Building, Trumpington Street, Cambridge CB2 1RP
32 East 57th Street, New York, NY 10022, USA
296 Beaconsfield Parade, Middle Park, Melbourne 3206, Australia

© Cambridge University Press 1983

First published 1983

Printed in Great Britain at The Pitman Press, Bath

Library of Congress catalogue card number: 82-17827

British Library Cataloguing in Publication Data

Howell, Cicely
Land, family and inheritance in transition.
1. Kibworth Harcourt (Leicestershire)—History
I. Title
942.5'44   DA670.L50

ISBN 0 521 24631 8

This book is dedicated to
EVERYMAN

Contents

(Frontispiece: British crown copyright: RAF photograph)

Figures

Maps

Tables

Acknowledgements

During its twelve years in preparation this book has been forwarded on its way by treble that number of scholarly, encouraging, patient and critical minds. It was my great privilege to be trained in the use of medieval estate documents by Trevor Aston and he it was who first directed my attention away from lords to peasants. From other former students of Aston I received not only encouragement but also specialised advice, in particular from Dr Thomas Charles-Edwards, also from Dr Paul Hyams and Dr Rosamond Faith. As the work carried me forward into the early modern period Dr Joan Thirsk became my supervisor. To her my debt is beyond measure: always available, encouraging, critical, attentive to detail. Not only was I permitted to draw upon her immense erudition but also upon her seemingly boundless circle of colleagues and pupils for their special-ised skills, foremost among them being Dr Christopher Currie on vernacular architecture and Giles Harrison on farm accounts.

Dr Eric Stone, Mr Aston, Mr Wernham and Dr Urry initiated me into the skills of palaeography and for a year I spent my days in Merton College Library transcribing and abstracting the Kibworth material. In this I was helped and advised by Dr J. R. L. Highfield and more particularly by Mr J. B. Burgass whose tiny office accommo-dated five bundles of Kibworth rolls at a time. But all was not work, for good food, good conversation and good friends were found first at my own college, Lady Margaret Hall, with the aid of a grant from the SSRC, and later at St Anne's and Holywell Manor as Fulford Research Fellow. Pleasurable indeed were field trips to Kibworth where I stayed in the Manor House by the courtesy of the then tenant, Mr J. E. Bartlett, and where I made many friends including Mr F. B. Aggas and Mr W. Yates to whose active collaboration and hospitality the book owes much. Bert Aggas not only allowed me to make use of his work on the Roman site on Banwell Furlong, the thirteenth-century mill and the enigmatic Mound, but he also measured the Paddocks

Farm House for me and helped prepare the drawings. The labour of many weeks in the Leicester Record Office was lightened by the courtesy, efficiency and friendly interest of the staff, to be matched only by the staff of the Bodleian.

When I made these trips to Kibworth little did I suspect that having submitted the thesis in 1974 I would spend three years in Leicester as Research Fellow in Agrarian History in the Department of English Local History. While at Leicester I was working on the Cambridgeshire Hundred Rolls and did little more than take my students out to Kibworth for fieldwork on wintry Wednesday afternoons. Now I am at Cambridge and working on Somerset and I owe it to Dr Margaret Spufford and Dr Jack Ravensdale that the Kibworth material has been reworked into a book. But for their persistent prodding and the encouragement of the Cambridge University Press I would never have embarked upon the rigours of seeing a book into print. At this point Professor Sir Michael Postan lent the full weight of his enthusiasm to the project, and to him is owed the section on diet – following kitchen experiments on the fermentation of barley and the baking of barley bread. It has indeed been a privilege and a pleasure to have worked with him. My especial thanks are also due to Professor E. A. Wrigley and Dr R. S. Schofield for their advice on the demography of the early modern period and for allowing me to make use of their collected data on mortality in the Kibworth region, also to Dr R. M. Smith for his meticulous examination of and advice on the medieval demography of Kibworth and to John Milton of Imperial College, London, who handled the mathematical aspects of the work.

Lastly, I have to thank Mrs Brenda Hutt who typed the thesis, Mrs Dorothy Franklin who typed the book, Mrs Susan Gell who did the art work, and Stephen Barr and Chris Lyall Grant who steered the manuscript into print. I should also acknowledge those scribes of the past, Robert Heyne, Robert Godyer, Dominus John Godwyn, and Peter Sargiant, for in the written word are the generations brought together.

C.H.

Abbreviations

Depositories

BM	British Museum
Bodl.	Bodleian Library, Oxford
HMC	Historical Manuscripts Commission
Leics. Museum	Leicester Museums and Art Gallery, Department of Archives
LRO	Leicestershire Record Office
MM	Merton College Muniments
NRO	Northamptonshire Record Office
PRO	Public Record Office
Cal. Pat.	Calendar of Patent Rolls
Cal. IPM	Calendar of Inquisitions Post Mortem
Inq. Misc.	Calendar of Inquisitions, Miscellaneous

Books and Journals

Ag.HR	*Agricultural History Review*
Am.HR	*American Historical Review*
Annales	*Annales Economies, Societies, Civilisations*
BIHR	*Bulletin of the Institute of Historical Research*
Ec.H	*Economic History*
Ec.H.Jl.	*Economic History Journal*
Ec.HR	*Economic History Review*
Ec.HS. Occ. Papers	*Economic History Society. Occasional papers*
Ec.Jl.	*Economic Journal*
EHR	*English Historical Review*
Med.Arch.	*Mediaeval Archaeology*
P & P	*Past and Present*
Scand. Ec.HR	*Scandinavian Economic History Review*
TLAS	*Transactions of the Leicestershire Archaeological Society*
TRHS	*Transactions of the Royal Historical Society*

Books and Journals (cont)

VCH	*The Victoria History of the Counties of England 1900–*
Yorks.Bull.Econ. and Soc.Resc.	*Yorkshire Bulletin of Economic and Social Research*

In quotations from original documents abbreviations have been expanded where possible, the extensions being indicated by brackets. Errors of spelling or grammar have not been corrected and not usually especially noted.

The spelling of surnames has been standardised, except in direct quotations or where the reader is referred to a specific document, in which cases the form used in the particular document is reproduced unaltered.

1

Kibworth Harcourt: its geography and early history

The manor and civil parish of Kibworth Harcourt lies about nine miles south-east of Leicester on the main road from Leicester to Market Harborough. The parish, roughly triangular in shape and 1475 acres in extent, occupies part of a ridge running from south-west to north-east and forming the watershed, at a height of 350–450 feet, between the head-waters of the River Sence to the north-west and the tributary streams of the Welland to the south-east (*VCH Leics.* V: 78).

Like so many Leicestershire villages, it lies on the spring line where heavy boulder clay gives way to glacial deposits of sand and gravel lying over impermeable rock. As can be seen on maps 1 and 2, the sand-filled basin of impervious lower lias was in fact too marshy a site for the village, which lies on the edge of the boulder clay to the west of it. Numerous wells,[1] sunk to the underlying gravels, provided the village with an ample water supply (Richardson 1931). To the north and west the village arable and pasture extended over fertile boulder clay. To the south-east lay lower lias with its characteristic drainage problems and most of this area was kept under permanent pasture. The village is one of the best sited in the region, a strong argument for its antiquity *vis-à-vis* its neighbours. The whole region, which is shown in map 1, has been described by R. M. Auty as 'the best fatting pasture of the Eastern region [of Leicestershire] and possibly of England' (Auty in Stamp 1937: 254ff).

The village has been fortunate in its communications. Today the A6 links it with Leicester and Market Harborough. In 1726 this road became a turnpike road and in 1744 the first coach from London to Leicester via Northampton and Dunstable passed through Kibworth, ushering in a period of prosperity for its five hostelries. The first mail coach used the route in 1785, and in 1810 a by-pass was made through Hall Close in order to avoid the narrow right-angle corner of the village street and its difficult gradient; thus the older part of the village has been spared the noise and grime of modern traffic.

1

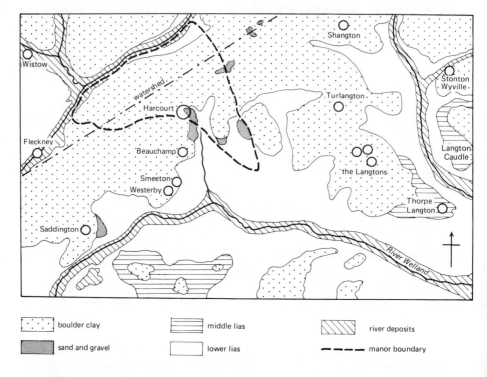

Map 1 The geological situation of Kibworth Harcourt and the neighbouring villages
Source: Geological Survey of G.B. Section of Solid and Drift Sheet 170 (1963)

However, the old turnpike road was itself a relatively new road, which had probably developed out of a chain of inter-village tracks in the later twelfth century to link the new township of Market Harborough, founded in 1160–70, with Leicester (Hoskins 1965: 53–67). Before this period the principal road had been the east–west one linking the village with the market town of Hallaton in the east and running westwards through Wistow, Kilby and Countesthorpe to Cosby. By the sixteenth century and possibly earlier, the road was known as the Cole Pit Way (see below p. 24fn).[2] At Cosby one branch ran north-east to the Coalville area, the other ran eastwards to the Bedworth coal pits in Warwickshire. A still earlier track, known as the Ridgeway, ran into the village at Cole Bridge Ford, followed the southern headland of Banwell Furlong and then struck north-east towards Carlton Curlieu. This may have been a section of the conjectured Jurassic Way, which ran from the Wiltshire downs to the

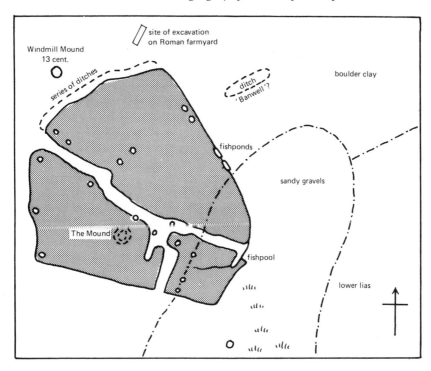

Map 2   Sketch map of Kibworth Harcourt to show the spring line and archaeological features

Yorkshire wolds in pre-Roman times (*VCH Leics.* III: 57, 60).* Not far east of the village ran the Roman road from Leicester to Colchester known as the Via Devana and locally as the Gartree Road (Bellairs 1893: 292–8, 357–64, map p. 357).

In spite of its advantageous position, half way between the market towns of Market Harborough and Glen Magna, Kibworth Harcourt never became a market centre. Kibworth Beauchamp secured this privilege for reasons which have probably more to do with the activities of the Harcourt and Beauchamp families at higher levels than with geographical convenience. However, there was a market

---

* The skeletal remains of at least four individuals and associated artefacts from a Beaker burial (1800–1700 BC) were discovered at Smeeton Westerby in 1975. SP 671911.

on most days of the week at one or other of the local villages within walking distance, where small surpluses of grain, butter and cheese could be bought and sold. The emphasis should be laid on the exchange of *small* surpluses, since with the exception of St Mary's Abbey, Leicester, demesne farms in the country were small and not market orientated (Hilton 1947: 80–2), while the profit margin on peasant holdings was so small, as we shall see later, that purchases of more than a few bushels of grain or pounds of cheese would have been rare. Indeed, the Kibworth situation would support R. H. Britnell's contention that the proliferation of markets between 1200–1349 was more closely related to the growth of local trade between food producers, craftsmen and tradesmen than to developments in international or inter-regional trade, or to the growth of the landlord's household expenditure. 'Landlords', Britnell suggests, 'founded

```
━━━━━━━━  roads in existence before 1086
━ · ━ · ━ ·  roads in existence before 1100
━ ━ ━ ━  roads in existence before 1200
━ ━ ━ ━ ━  modern roads, date of origin unknown
▬▬          village shape in 1835
```

the earliest known date for a market charter is indicated where known

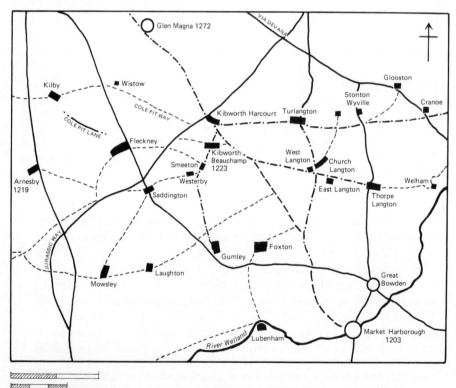

Map 3a   Minor roads around Kibworth Harcourt

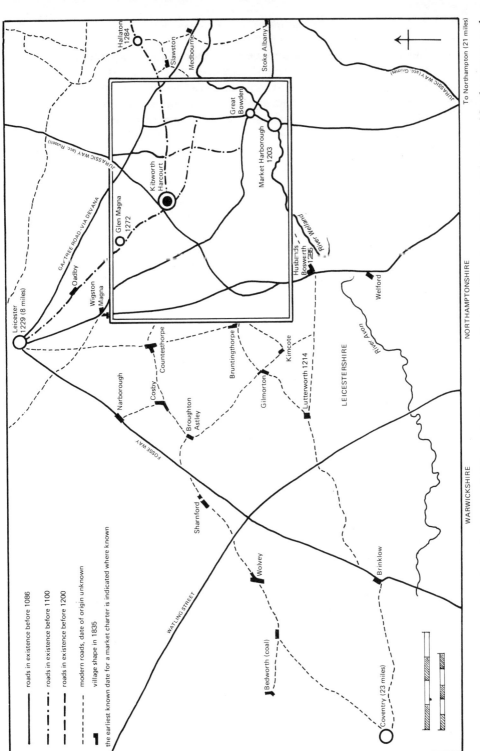

Map 3 The road system and markets around Kibworth Harcourt, and their position in relation to Leicester, Northampton and Coventry

small, unambitious markets perhaps more to accommodate the poor than for profit' (Britnell 1981: 209–21). One of the arguments put forward for the absence of large-scale demesne farming in Leicester-shire is the poor transport system. Before McAdam, the heavy clays of the county had always made road haulage difficult and given the competitive edge to livestock husbandry. However, the difficulties are not insuperable and in a recent seminar paper Professor Sir Michael Postan has argued that with road transport costs at 1.2 pence per ton mile in the thirteenth century, the haulage of medium- and high-value commodities, such as wheat and wool, over distances of up to thirty miles was not disproportionately high.[3] By contrast, Postan argues, the increase in labour and haulage costs in the fifteenth century and the fall in agricultural prices led to a decline in long-distance haulage and to the decay of the road system. The argument put forward in the sixteenth century that Leicestershire was 'too far remote from any means of exportation of corn'[4] may not have been equally true of the thirteenth century; the road system *may* have been more fully used in the pre-plague period. However, the winter conditions of roads in a clayland region would have restricted haulage to summer and autumn and necessitated the drying and storing of grain over winter. This is what St Mary's Abbey did, but until we have evidence of other landlords storing grain for summer transport the argument cannot be substantiated. The fact remains that demesne farms in Leicestershire were small and were for the most part parcelled out for rents.

By the sixteenth century specialised markets were developing rapidly in the region. Market Harborough had become famous for its cattle, horse and sheep markets. Northampton specialised in horses and in leather goods; Coventry in cattle; Leicester in cheese, leather goods and wool (Clarkson 1966: 25–9; Everitt in Thirsk 1967: 466–589). The absence of a grain market is noticeable. Lying beyond the influence of the London market, Leicestershire corn prices were marginally lower than in the South Midlands, as was the value of arable land. By contrast, the value of pasture land was appreciably higher; fallow pasture, for example, was valued at 20 shillings the acre in Leicestershire as against a mere 5 shillings the acre in Oxfordshire (Havinden 1965). By the sixteenth century there was certainly no market at Kibworth but the number of shopkeepers had increased from a draper, two broggers and a doctor in the thirteenth century to a weaver, a tailor, a shoemaker, a butcher, a baker, a brewer and a carpenter. In both the medieval and the early modern period there was a long-distance carter.

The early history of the manor

Conspicuous in the village is a conical, flat-topped mound some 16 yards in diameter at the top and 122 yards in circumference at the base, while the height in the slope is 18 yards, vertical height 9 feet. So large a man-made feature cannot be lightly dismissed. It should be able to shed some light on the origin of the settlement, or at least upon its development. However, the Mound, as it is called, is extraordinarily reluctant to yield its secrets; not only is it difficult to get experts to agree as to its measurements, but opinion differs as to its origin and function – it could be either an early Roman barrow or a medieval motte.

Apart from a short stretch on its north side, the mound is surrounded by a ditch measuring 9 feet wide and 5 feet deep in the south-west. It was excavated in 1863 by Sir H. Dryden and measured and planned in 1965 by Mr A. Aggas and Mr G. Yates.[5] Dryden's plans survive but they are uninformative without the notes, which are now lost.[6] A somewhat incoherent account of his work appeared in the *Transactions of the Leicestershire Archaeological Society* for 1863, in which it was reported that the mound in Hall Close, together with 'an elevated barrow connected with it', had been excavated. The 'elevated barrow' was almost certainly that 'considerable barrow' which Nichols described in 1778 as lying to the north-west of the village (*VCH Leics.* I: 275; Nichols 1790: 639). This was excavated recently by Aggas and Yates and proved to be the site of the thirteenth-century windmill. The Mound itself has proved more baffling. According to the *Leicester Journal* for Friday, 7 August 1863, the mound had first been excavated in 1836 or thereabouts when a trench was cut into its western side. In 1863 a second trench was cut, this time from north to south. Traces of both trenches can be seen today, and neither cut through the centre. According to the newspaper report, the

> depth of the cutting was in the centre eight to nine feet. About five feet deep was found a layer of black soil and what sometimes appeared ashes and burnt wood. In this layer were found bones, teeth and one or two pieces of Roman pottery. On a level with the same layer a pavement of large stones about four feet by two was discovered. A bone bodkin was also found and an iron candlestick. At a depth of from eight to nine feet there was a regular layer of black soil; looking as if that was the old natural ground, and the above made up ground.

According to a note on Dryden's plan, the pavement was found, not in the mound, but near the hedge some 70 feet from the ditch on the east side. It was 4 feet 6 inches under the surface and a second pavement was found a further 4½ feet below the first. Dryden's plan shows the Mound as round, on Mr Aggas's plan it is oval.

One cannot draw firm conclusions from such garbled accounts. According to the *Leicester Chronicle* for Saturday, 8 August, 1863, the Reverend Edward Trollope of Leasingham, whose views were evidently held in high esteem, gave it as his opinion that the mound was 'a ring barrow, and probably that of a Roman military officer or agricultural colonist'. The evidence does indeed suggest a Roman barrow, an unusually large one, on what is known to have been the site of a Roman settlement, but Mr Dunning found the evidence inconclusive[7] (Dunning and Jessup 1936: 37–53). In his opinion, the mound is too large for a Roman barrow, and seems to have been altered at some later date, possibly to provide part of the earthworks of a medieval manor house. Dr V. R. Webster felt it was more probably a medieval motte than a Roman tumulus.[8] Both these distinguished archaeologists had only the plans of Dryden and Aggas to work on and the garbled accounts in the *Transactions* and the local press. To take the suggestion that it was part of a medieval manor house first: this seems unlikely because the village in the medieval period was always a member of a far-flung estate, was never the *caput* of the Honor and was never held by a mesne tenant. Consequently, there was no need for a manor house. The bailiff occupied a modest building with a garden and dovecote to the north of the main street[9] (see below pp. 125–6). However, the mound may have been used as a motte at some time. Approached from the north-west it lies *below* the general level of the settlement, but to the south-east the land falls away gently to the marshy area on the boundary with Kibworth Beauchamp. Therefore, from a strategic point of view, the mound was quite well sited to repulse attack from the south-east, and may have been part of a system of defences in association with the series of ditches further to the north-west. As such it may well have formed a link in the Danish chain of 'burhs' to the south-west of Leicester commanding the Welland frontier (Hoskins 1935–7: 94–109), or have been hastily erected during the disturbances of Stephen's reign. However, the narrowly restricted value of the site, capable of repulsing attack from the south-east only, suggests the utilisation of an earthwork already in existence, such as a burial mound of Roman or pre-Roman origin, given the Roman finds the excavators associated with it. In which case, the settlement at Kibworth was already 'old' in Saxon times and was associated with some fairly important personage. The number of Roman villas identified in the immediate vicinity testifies to the advanced degree of Romanisation of the area, and though no more than the *yard* of the Roman villa/farm at Kibworth has been excavated, it is sufficient evidence to justify the association of a burial mound with a Roman or Romano-Celtic villa, at least as a possibility (see below p. 82). However, whether Celt or Roman, the villa owner would have employed Celtic labourers, slave or free. With the decline of direct Roman influence, either the local Celtic community or a group of Anglian settlers ploughed over the site of the Roman buildings and established a village immediately north of the mound, between the mound and the ditches, an area easily converted into a burh. The situation of Kibworth Harcourt: on the Ridgeway, on a spring line, on a Roman site, in an area extensively cleared and settled in the Roman period, if not earlier, makes it very improbable that the site was deserted for long, if at all, during the interval between the withdrawal of the legions and the settlement of the Saxons, although the field names are for the most part Saxon (Roberts 1977: 78–81). Fortunately, Scandinavian attitudes towards family land are so similar to those of the Welsh that it is not of critical importance to the thesis developed in chapter ten to establish a firm conclusion with regard to the Celtic or Anglian origin of the community. If, however, the settlement had been established *de novo* around a Danish burh or medieval motte, then the customs *may* have been of a hybrid complexion and of questionable use in interpreting the development of custom in relation to the regional economy. The difference between estate custom and indigenous custom is as yet an unexplored field and may turn out to be unimportant, but it should not be forgotten, hence our interest in the origin of the Mound: it may have been a burial mound later adapted to purposes of defence, or it may have been commissioned as a motte in the early medieval period. If the former, then we have a non-military origin for the settlement; if the latter, we can be certain that the settlement pre-dated the mound and its military character is not of importance to the social structure and development of the village.

By 1066 Kibworth Harcourt formed one of a group of manors held by a certain Aelric, the son of Meriet, a freeman. The estate was considerable, and all of it seems to have passed to Robert de Veci (*VCH Leics.* I: 323), with the exception of a group of manors in Kesteven which one Baldwin held in 1086 but which, it was claimed, had been granted by Aelric to Westminster Abbey.[10] Thus the Veci estate in 1086 consisted of Wolvey and Nether Whitacre in Warwickshire, Braybrooke in Northamptonshire, Great Steeping, Caythorpe, Friston, Normanton, Willoughby, Brandon, *Suanitone* and *Hechintune* in Lincolnshire and, in Leicestershire, 14 carucates at Gilmorton, 12 carucates at Kibworth Harcourt, 10 at Newton Harcourt, 6¼ at Shenton, 4 at Kilworth, at Gumley and at Husband's Bosworth, 3¾ at Thorpe Langton, and 2 at Shangton, a total of 59 carucates in Leicestershire alone, with 47 ploughs. Robert de Veci kept only the two Harcourts in his own hand, the rest of the Leicestershire estates he subinfeudated to mesne tenants.

According to the Leicestershire survey made in 1130, one Ansketil was holding the de Veci manors in Gartree Hundred, namely, Kibworth Harcourt, Shangton and Thorpe Langton (Slade 1956: 14, 95). Unfortunately, the remaining manors were not included in the Leicestershire Survey, nor in the Lindsey Survey of 1115–18 (Round 1909: 181ff). G. F. Farnham and H. Round were of the opinion that this Ansketil was Anchetil de Harcourt, the son of Robert and grandson of Anchetil de Harcourt (Farnham 1927: 104–5). The second Anchetil begot William, who begot Robert who married Isabel of Stanton in Oxfordshire. Their grandson, Richard, married Arabella, daughter of Saer de Quincy. Richard died in 1258 leaving two sons, William who held the Bosworth fee and in whose line it descended until 1509 when it was sold, and Saer, the younger son who received Kibworth Harcourt (Wedgewood 1914: 187–210). Saer married Agnes de Segeville[11] and they had two sons, Richard and Simon.[12] Saer supported the cause of Simon de Montfort and forfeited his lands in 1265;[13] they were granted to Saer's overlord, William Mauduit, Earl of Warwick.[14] In 1267, however, Saer received the king's pardon and by October 1268 the manor had been returned to him by Mauduit's widow, the Countess Alice.[15] But Saer's finances continued in disarray and at some date between 1267 and 1269 he conveyed the manor to John le Ferrun of London, perhaps as a security for debt.[16] Meanwhile, Walter of Merton, Bishop of Rochester and Chancellor of England, was engaged in the purchase of property for the endowment of his new college, the present site of which, in Oxford, he purchased in 1268 (Henderson 1899). In 1269 Walter opened negotiations for the acquisition of Kibworth Harcourt by buying out John le Ferrun's interest in the manor,[17] and also that of a Jew named Cok, son of Cresse, who might otherwise have claimed an interest on account of Saer's debts to him.[18] In 1270 Walter paid Saer £400 for the manor,[19] and in 1271 Saer granted the manor to Walter of Merton, saving only to himself an annual payment of 20s for the advowson, View of Frankpledge and all suits of court, customs and exactions.[20] It seems that Walter's original intention was to add the entire manor of Kibworth Harcourt to the corpus of estates belonging to his college. In his second charter, that of 1270, he mentions Kibworth among the several other estates he had assigned to the college and he makes a particular provision out of it in a memorandum at the end of the charter. Moreover, both Richard, Earl of Warwick, and Richard, son and heir of Saer de Harcourt, assert the founder's concession of the manor to the college: Warwick in 1272 and Harcourt in his composition made with the college in 1284 (Osborne 1870: 222–4). However, in 1276 Walter granted a rent charge of 8 marks to his sister Edith, wife of Thomas Tayllard,[21] and another of 4 marks to Roger, son of Edith Tayllard,[22] and when he died in 1277 he was still possessed of the manor. His heirs were three of his sisters, Christina de Wortynges (wife of Thomas Worting of the Basingstoke area), Agnes de Ewelle (wife of Gilbert de Ewelle), Edith (wife of Thomas Tayllard) and three of his nephews, Peter de Clyve (son of Walter's sister, Alice), Alan de Portemuwe – Portsmouth – (son of Walter's sister, Matilda) and Richard Olyver (another nephew).[23] The estate was divided between the six heirs in the manner indicated in table 1.

An extent of Saer de Harcourt's land, made for exchequer purposes in 1265, gives the following description of the estate:

> One messuage and 9 virgates of land in demesne worth £7 12 0d.
> 18½ virgates of land in villeinage, each virgate being worth 16s per annum.
> Rents from free tenements and cottars amounting to 38s 10d per annum.
> Fixed rent from 1 virgate free land worth 6s 8d per annum.
> One mill worth 26s 8d per annum in rents.
> A render of 4 capons at Christmas worth 6d.
> Total value of the manor, £26 0s 8d per annum.[24]

(Not included are the 10 virgates held of Harcourt by the Apetoft family.)

The extent tallies with the rentals and surveys made by Merton College in the thirteenth and fourteenth centuries,[25] and included the entire estate bar the Apetoft holding. Comparison of the extent with table 1 shows that the estate had been shared out among the heirs leaving nothing to the college except the administrative duties of appointing to the living, holding the View of Frankpledge and the court baron and presumably collecting the rents. Faced with this burdensome and potentially costly arrangement, the college seems to have lost no time in reaching the decision to buy out the heirs. From the point of view of the villagers this was, in retrospect, a momentous decision. The village had always been a closed one, and the division into six portions threatened to turn it into an open village and to expose it to the anarchic tendencies and consequent poverty which too often attended the removal of good lordship, and which characterised Kibworth Beauchamp by the sixteenth century. The decision

Table 1. *Distribution of rents among the six beneficiaries of Walter of Merton's grant, 1270*[a]

Holder	Demesne	Bond	Free and cottage rents	Manorial buildings
Portsmouth	land in 3 fields	2½v.	1½v. + 1 rod + 2 placea	4 capons, share in dovecote and mill, etc.
Ewelle	2 virgates	2½v.	2 cots + 1 placea	6s 8d share in dovecote and fishponds
Oliver⎱ Clive⎰	3 + x virgates	6½v.	5¼v. + 1 placea + 8 acres	13s 4d, double share in dovecote, etc.
Worting	2 virgates	2½v.	4s 1½d	–
E. Tayllard	1 virgate	2½v.	1 cot. + 2 placea + 55s 0¾d	–
R. Tayllard	–	2½v.	–	–
TOTALS	8 + x virgates	19v.	3 cots, 6 placea, 8¼ acres, 6¾v., 59s 2¼d	Assized rent of 20s, mill, 4 capons dovecote, fishponds, Hall Close

[a] Cf. appendix 1 for 1279 version in the Hundred Rolls.

of Merton to re-establish unity restored the protection of seigniorial control. Whether Merton offered *good* lordship remains to be seen.

In the same year as the partition, 1278, Peter de Clive sold his share for 13 marks and the education of his two sons at Oxford, they being provided with a reasonable allowance of food and clothing, one cap and gown a year, two pairs of linen *pannorum*, six pairs of socks and three pairs of shoes *si tanto indigeant*.[26] In the same year Richard Oliver sold his share at twelve years' purchase for 66 marks.*[27] In 1279 Robert and William de Ewelle, son of Agnes de Ewelle, released their share to Merton, for what sum we are not told.[28] At about the same time Alan de Portsmouth released his share,[29] and at some date soon after 1283 Thomas, son of Christina de Worting, transferred his share at ten years' purchase for 60 marks.[30] The Tayllard lands seem to have formed part of the dower land of Agnes, widow of Saer de Harcourt, and they did not come into the hands of the college until her death in 1309.[31] In 1284 Robert and Richard Withside gave up their interest in 2 bovates and 2 messuages for 100s; this land had been granted to William Withside of Thorp in 1263 by Saer de Harcourt.[32]

The college was now in possession of that portion of Kibworth Harcourt which Saer de Harcourt had exploited directly in 1265, but there remained a block of 10 virgates which William de Harcourt, Saer's grandfather, had granted to Laurence d'Apetoft in the first quarter of the thirteenth century (MM 3094). This estate was subsequently held at farm by William, priest of Aylestone, then by John del Haye, later by John le Ferrun and finally it came to be held in fee by Walter of Merton. The negotiations surrounding this final transfer in fee were protracted. In 1295 a certain William of Ingwardby and his wife Audrey granted the estate to two Fellows of the college, Henry de Fodringeye and Robert Gerneys de Candevere (MM 2935). When they in turn attempted to transfer the property to the college (MM 2868, 2898, 2916–18, 2921, 3017) their right to do so was challenged by the Earl of Warwick, on the ground that the transfer contravened the Statute of Mortmain (MM 2984, 3021). In February 1300–1 Edward I licensed the transfer to the college, the Statute notwithstanding; Fodringeye and Candevere released the estate in consideration of £100, at the king's command; and the college appointed Robert of Glen and Roger Foxton of Glen to act as its attorneys and to take possession of the property (MM 2921, 2868). The Earl was not the immediate lord of the fee and had no right to appropriate the estate; nevertheless, having entered it in 1298 he refused to relinquish it until five days before his death in 1315, when he acknowledged that he

---

* Ten years' purchase was more usual at this period. Evidently a university education was valued at 26 marks.

had unjustly evicted Fodringeye and Candevere and enjoined obedience to the college upon the tenants of the estate (MM 2919, 2920).
Rents received from the Apetoft estate were entered upon the reeve's
account roll for the first time in 1316–17 (MM 6220); and the last stage
in this lengthy and expensive transfer was completed in 1323 when
Thomas, the 'son' and heir of Laurence d'Apetoft, released his rights
in the estate (MM 8959). It is not clear how William of Ingwardby had
come to be associated with the property in the first place; and his is
not the only foreign name. Burton's transcript of the 1279 Hundred
Rolls describes one Hubert de Told as being in possession of $2\frac{1}{2}$
carucates (10 virgates) which can only refer to the Apetoft estate.*

The stage is now set. To this already ancient settlement, well
acquainted with the rule of Belgic, Celtic, Roman, Saxon and early
Norman lordship, what influence for good or ill would an Oxford
college bring?

---

* For a transcript of the Hundred Roll entry see appendix 1. Comparison of the
transcript with the rentals as set out in chapter 2 will indicate how inaccurate was the
description of the manor as reported to the commissioners in 1279.

2

Land and tenants

Apart from the 1265 extent, which is an exchequer document, only two groups of deeds have survived from the Harcourt period: three deeds relating to 2 bovates of land granted to Robert Wytside of Thorp in 1263 (the occupiers of the land being Robert, son of William the Reeve and William of Langton)[1] (see appendix 2) and two deeds concerning the grant of half a virgate and 8 acres to Robert son of Richard the Parson of Elynhole, by Richard of Harecourt (the occupier in this case being Robert the son of Matilda) for a rent of 1½ lb of pepper and all services.[2]

Therefore, the scene does not fully unfold until the 1270s and 1280s with a bundle of rentals, terriers and memoranda drawn up for the Warden and Fellows. The college had not only to discover who its tenants were, what lands they held and for what rent, but it had also to allocate these rents equally between the six heirs to the estate: a task which involved a thorough enquiry into almost every aspect of estate management. Eventually a single rental for the whole manor was drawn up (MM 6370, 6371), a list of all the men in tithing was made, and a system of recording the proceedings of the courts and the accounts of the bailiff was inaugurated. Unfortunately, the working documents and even the rentals themselves are undated, but by comparing the names of the rent payers with the names mentioned in the court rolls, which are dated, and with the lists of witnesses to dated deeds we are able to date them to within a decade. In 1286, for example, the demesne was farmed out for an annual rent of £12 16s,[3] the rental numbered MM 6371 records a similar sum, the rental MM 6370 gives an earlier, lower figure, and was therefore probably drawn up before 1286. But MM 6371 cannot have been made much later than 1286 because so many of the names on it also appear in the tithing list, which was made in 1280. An *inquissicio cartae* was ordered in 1290[4] and MM 6371 may have been a part of, or result of, the enquiry. In the interests of clarity the most legible of the early

Table 2. *Free and customary tenants at Kibworth Harcourt c. 1280–90*

FREE TENEMENTS

1 WILLIAM DE PEKE*	3 virgates	rent 8s

(*MM 6370*. Henry Parson* held this for 10s. Cf. *MM 2869, 2896*)
(*MM 6369*. William de Pecco held this for 10s.)

2 WILLIAM DE REYNES*	½ virgate	3 capons +

(*MM 2867, 2895, 6239*.)   services
(*MM 6377c*) (His tenants *c.* 1315†   58 *Robert Swan*   (described)
                                       59 *William Heyne*
                                       60 *William Atte Cross*
                                       61 *Roger Ferour*
                                       62 *William Osborne*
                                       63 *Alice Heyno*
                                       64 *Adam Sybile*
                                        9 *John Sybile**
                                       65 *Stephan* and *Roger de Pek, brothers*
                                       66 *John de Reynes*
                                       67 *Amabil Heyne*)

3 NICHOLAS POLLE*	½ virgate	1s
4 ROBERT SHARON*	1 virgate	1s 1d
5 NICHOLAS FABER*	1 virgate (Apetoft land)	6s 8d
6 RICHARD SON of ROGER	1 virgate	2s

(Agnes de Harcourt's reeve)

7 HENRY POLLE*	½ virgate	1s
8 HENRY BOTON*	½ virgate	6s 1½d
8 HENRY BOTON*	¼ virgate	9d

(Life lease. *MM 2897*)

9 JOHN SYBILE*	¼ virgate	9d

(aged 12, 1290–3)   (William de Langton's
                                       11 acres. *MM 6374*
                                       6373h, 2867, 3017)

His tenant: 64 *Adam de Kibworth (Sybile)*
(*MM 6374, 6373h, 6239, 6242*)   5½ acres   9d
(Adam's tenants *c.* 1315†:   65 *Roger Pek*
                                       58 *Roger Swan*
                                       66 *Roger Hildesley*
                                        3 *Nicholas Polle**
                                       63 *Alice Heyne*
                                       60 *William Atte Cross*
                                       67 *Roger Polle*
                                       68 *Matilda Bonde*
                                       69 *Dom. John Godwyn*)

Remaining tenants on the Langton land:
                                       65 *Richard de Pek* [*Roger*]
                                       58 *Robert Swan*
                                       63 *Alice Heyne*
                                       66 *Roger Hildesley*
                                       64 *Adam Sybile*

9 JOHN SYBILE	1 messuage	rent 3s

(*MM 6367* John Sybile *per aula* Henry Parson 1s 6d + 1 lb pepper)

		Rent	Works
10 WILLIAM BRON*	1 messuage	rent 1d	
11 ALICE and MATILDA STERRE, sisters	1 ploughshare	rent 4d + ½[?]	

CUSTOMARY TENEMENTS

		Rent	Works
12 JOHN POLLE	½ virgate	6s 9d	3s 4d
13 HUGH MAGISTER*	½ virgate	6s 7½d	3s 4d
14 WIDOW SCOLATE*	½ virgate	6 1½d	3s 4d
15 ROBERT son of REGINALD (HEYNE) *ALIAS* ROBERT AD FONTEM* (*MM 6370* describes the services owed)	1 virgate	12s 3d	13s 4d
9 JOHN SYBILE (aged 12, 1290–3)	½ virgate	6s 6d	3s 4d
16 BEATRICE SYBILE (floruit 1298)	½ virgate	6s 1½d	3s 4d
17 WILLIAM son of ROBERT* (Sybile)	½ virgate	6s 0½d	3s 4d
18 WILLIAM son of the REEVE* (William Heynes)	1 virgate	11s 10½d	6s 8d
19 JOHN son of the REEVE	½ virgate	7s 2½d	3s 4d
20 RADULF, REEVE	½ virgate	7s 2½d	3s 4d
21 ROGER JOYE*	½ virgate	6s 9d	3s 4d
22 HUGH BONDE	½ virgate	6s 3½d	3s 4d
23 JOHN GODYER	½ virgate	7s 0½d	3s 4d
24 HUGH GODWINE*	½ virgate	6s 4½d	3s 4d
25 RADULF CARTER*	½ virgate	6s 10½d	3s 4d
26 JOHN son of WALTER	½ virgate	6s 0d	[torn]
27 ROGER WADE*	½ virgate	6s 3d	3s 4d
28 ALOT WYGEN*	½ virgate	6s 1½d	3s 4d
29 ROBERT MICHOL	½ virgate	5s 6s	3s 4d
30 HUGH HARCOURT*	½ virgate	5s 9d	3s 4d
31 ROBERT WADE*	½ virgate	6s 1½d	3s 4d
32 ROBERT LE COUN'	½ virgate	6s 1d	3s 4d
33 WILLIAM SISSOR*	½ virgate	6s 3½d	3s 4d
34 NICHOLAS son of JOHN	½ virgate	6s 3d	3s 4d
35 EMMA GILBERT	½ virgate	6s 1½d	3s 4d
36 HUGH SILVESTRE*	½ virgate	7s 1d	3s 4d
37 NICHOLAS THORN (AD SPINAM)	1 virgate	12s 6d	6s 8d
38 NICHOLAS LE YONGE	½ virgate	5s 6½d	3s 4d

TOTAL 15½ virgates for £9 3s 8¾d in rents and £6 10s 0d in commuted works. (NB The rents of numbers 18, 20, 23, 37, 39 were allocated to the Tayllard revenue.)

COTTAGES

39 ROBERT TRITURATOR	1 toft	2s
40 ALICE GODWINE	1 toft	2s
41 ROBERT LE BROCHAR*	1 toft	2s
42 ROBERT LE MEDICO* (*MM 6388* manumitted 1289)	1 toft	2s
43 WILLIAM LE BROCHAR	1 toft	2s
44 ROGER MILLER*	1 toft	2s
45 ALICE WASHERWOMAN*	1 toft	2s

TOTAL 7 tofts, of which the rents from 44 and 45 were allocated to the Tayllard revenue.

Table 2 *cont.*

THE MANOR AND DEMESNE

Receipts from the manor and orchard, 16s, less 1s 4d due to Walter de
  Evesham, the Steward of Agnes de Harcourt (*MM 6381*).
From the mill 42s, less 4s 8½d due to Walter de Evesham.
£9 12s 0d from 8 virgates of demesne.
TOTAL £12 10s 0d less 6s 5¼d to Walter de Evesham.
(Receipts from court fines varied from 25s 7d to 35s 3d and are not included in
  the rental or extent.)

---

† See appendixes 2 and 3.

thirteenth-century rentals (MM 6371) has been set out in full, but
incorporated into it is some of the information derived from subsidiary documents.[5] The names in capital letters are those of occupiers in
MM 6371, those in italics are those of subtenants in around 1315, the
number of the roll in each case being given in brackets. Each
landholder has been given a number in order to diminish the danger
of double counting where the same tenant held more than one
tenement, and the names of those tenants who were also listed in the
1280 tithing list have been followed by an asterisk. Taking the college
lands and the Apetoft lands together there were 77 landholders and
110 parcels of land, some of them very small indeed. It will be noted
that the demesne lands have not been listed on this roll, nor have the
Apetoft tenants been included, because these two categories will
have to be treated separately.

The extent of 1265 tells us that there was a messuage and nine
virgates of land in demesne valued at £7 12s (16s per virgate).* This by
itself does not tell us whether the demesne was in hand, farmed out
en bloc or was broken up into smaller parcels suitable for peasant
leases. It is probable that it was farmed out *en bloc*; if it was not then
we should have expected the college to have made a serious effort to
ascertain the distribution and value of demesne strips if the demesne
had been in hand when the college acquired it, or to have drawn up a
list of tenements and tenants if the demesne had been broken up into
small parcels. In fact, no extent or terrier of the demesne has been
discovered in the college archives and the earliest list of tenants does
not occur until about 1370 in the form of an addition to the rental
made *circa* 1316 (MM 6372). When the rental MM 6370 was drawn up
the eight virgates of the demesne were still divided into six shares,
but in 1286 the then Warden, Richard of St John (Werblysdon), leased
the demesne arable together with the *giardinium* and the mill to six of
the villagers for a total rent of £12 16s. The income from the courts
was reserved to the college and the custody of the manorial buildings
* In the extent nine virgates are noted, in all other documents only eight.

was granted to Rodulph prepositus, Radulf Carter, Robert ad Fontem, Robert Parson, Hugh Godwyne and Robert son of Robert Churt.[6] The six tenants who took the demesne land were not all the same as the custodians of the Hall, but all served as reeve at some point in their lives. The *custodes aulae* were Robert Sybile, Robert ad Fontem, Nicholas son of Robert and Robert his brother, Hugh Silvestre and Radulf Carter. By 1296–7 the mill, worth £2 per annum, had been let separately and the income from the demesne, as recorded in the reeve's account, and of the eight demesne acres at 24s each, yielded a total of £9 12s. The undated rental MM 6371 gives the revenue from the demesne as £12 10s which indicates that the rental was made between 1286 and 1296. By the time the undated rental MM 6372 was made, the demesne receipts stood at £9 12s, a figure which, according to the record of the account rolls, remained unchanged until the 1370s. However, by the 1370s the demesne had been divided into quarter-virgate parcels and was leased for 6s the quarter virgate to members of the Kibworth tenantry. A list of these tenants, written in a later hand, was added to the rental MM 6372, which had been made in 1315. From the 1320s onwards the transfer of quarter- and half-virgate parcels of demesne become fairly common in the court rolls, but still only in connection with a small number of the more prominent village families – Sybile, Heyne, Polle, Chorch and Carter – and it is not until after the plagues that the number of surnames connected with demesne parcels was significantly increased. When this happened, and when the list of tenants was drawn up, the demesne ceased to be treated as a separate category in the account rolls and demesne rents were lumped together with free and customary rents. We can therefore conclude with some degree of certainty that the demesne continued to be let to a small group of wealthier tenants, called 'custodians of the hall' in 1289,[7] until the period of the plagues, and was then broken up into separate quarter-virgate parcels let singly to any man who could afford the rent of 6s per quarter.

We have accounted for the Merton tenants and the demesne, but there still remains the messuage and ten virgates of the Apetoft estate. As described in chapter one, the college did not enter into possession of the estate until 1315. The earliest rental we have of it was that made in 1295 when Ingwardby transferred the estate to Fodringeye and Candevere (MM 2935). Another was incorporated into the rental numbered MM 6372. Comparison of the two lists shows them to be not quite a full generation apart: Robert Bron and William the son of Reginald held the same land in both lists, otherwise tenements had passed to tenants bearing the same sur-

Table 3. *Demesne tenants c. 1370**

Richard Champeden	*terra giardine manerii cum 7 toftis dicto giardino adiunctis.* 12s.	
+ Hugh Thorpe	$\frac{1}{4}$ virgate	6s
+ Henry Marram	$\frac{1}{2}$ virgate	12s
+ John Polle	$\frac{1}{4}$ virgate	6s
+ John Brown	$\frac{1}{4}$ virgate	6s
+ Robert Langton	$\frac{1}{4}$ virgate	6s
+ John Joye	$\frac{1}{4}$ virgate	6s
+ William Polle	$\frac{1}{4}$ virgate	6s
+ Nicholas Godyer	$\frac{1}{4}$ virgate	6s
Robert Godyer	$\frac{1}{2}$ virgate	12s
Robert Carter	$\frac{1}{2}$ virgate	6s
John Godyer	$\frac{1}{4}$ virgate	6s
+ John Man	$\frac{1}{4}$ virgate	6s
Nicholas Gilbert	$\frac{3}{4}$ virgate	18s
+ William Alot	$\frac{1}{4}$ virgate	6s
+ John Scholar	$\frac{1}{4}$ virgate	6s
+ John Carter	$\frac{1}{4}$ virgate	6s
William Godyer	$\frac{1}{4}$ virgate	6s
+ John Marnham	$\frac{1}{4}$ virgate	6s
Maybilla Godwyn	$\frac{1}{4}$ virgate	6s
+ John Hildefloy	$\frac{1}{4}$ virgate	6s
+ Robert Sandur	$\frac{1}{4}$ virgate	6s
William Chapman (Robert Crych)	$\frac{1}{4}$ virgate	6s
William Sybile	1 virgate	24s
+ John Nogge	$\frac{1}{4}$ virgate	6s
Nicholas Sandur	$\frac{1}{4}$ virgate	6s

Robert Man 1 cottage	*extracta de manerio*		Old rent 6s	New rent 2s
+ John Scolate 1 cottage	*extracta de manerio*		2s 6d	1s 6d
John Joye 1 cottage	*nuper erat pynfold dmo*		$4\frac{1}{2}$d	
(illegible) pasture			2s	

Total arable: 8 virgates for £9 12s 0d in rent.
Other parcels: demesne garden with 7 adjacent tofts, the pinfold, some pasture and 2 demesne cottages, rent 17s 10½d.

* This list, appended to MM 6372, was made after 1366 (William Alot entry) by the same scribe who had made the most recent inter-linear alterations to the earlier part of 6372. The names singled out with an + appear also in the 1381 Poll Tax list.

name as their predecessors in 1295. This would date MM 6372 to about 1315. In the following year, 1316–17, a memorandum in the account roll for that year (MM 6220) draws attention to the fact that the Steward, Thomas de Thurmaston, had in his possession one rental for Barkby and two rentals for Kibworth. One of these Kibworth rentals would almost certainly have been MM 6372 with its list of Apetoft tenants. MM 6372 also contains a list of tenants on land which had once belonged to Hugh Harcourt, Robert Holke, William de Reynes and Adam (Sybile) of Kibworth. Subsidiary lists, numbered MM 6374a–b, 6373a–c, 6373h, undated, but dealing with exactly the same persons and places, must likewise be dated to *circa* 1315.

Table 2 is based on MM 6371 and relates to the period 1280–90, and for the list of Apetoft tenants we could have used the Ingwardby list dated to 1295 (MM 2935). However, the subsidiary lists just referred to, which cast light on the important question of subtenancies, relate to the period around 1315. In order to display their contents meaningfully within the context of the tenemental framework, the later list of Apetoft tenements, MM 6372, dated to 1315, is the better choice. Table 4, therefore, is based on MM 6372 and relates to the period immediately before 1315. The names of the tenants in 1295 have been shown in brackets below the name of the 1315 tenant in order to facilitate direct comparison with table 2 and with the 1280 tithing list discussed later and set out in table 21. For the same purpose, the lists of so-called subtenants, which relate only to the period around 1315 and later, have been included in table 2, but in brackets.

Adam of Kibworth, William of Langton, Hugh Harcourt and Robert Holke were all alive and active in the late thirteenth century. At the turn of the century terriers were made of their four tenements and lists were drawn up of the various persons who now held land which had once belonged to these four men (see appendixes 2 and 3). These lists were incorporated into the rental for 1315 (MM 6372), and appear again thirty-three years later in the account roll of the reeve in 1348 (MM 6239, 6242). In the latter year the reeve was experiencing some difficulty in collecting the rents due from these parcels, and was directed by the auditors to draw up a precise list of who the tenants were, what land they held and what rent they owed. In one or two cases the land had passed to the succeeding generation, but for the most part the lists made in 1348 are identical with the lists made before 1315 yet, taken in isolation, the 1348 lists bear all the signs of current working lists. Against each name is a note as to whether the tenant has paid for half a year or a full year, the amounts received are minimal, ¼d to 3d, and the impression given is that these pieces of land have been leased for no more than a year or so and that there is an active market in short-term leases. The earlier lists allow us to correct this false impression. All four tenements were freeholdings, and the same group of tenants had a stake in their constituent acres and pastures which were distributed over three fields and lay, for the most part, next to Polle or Carter strips. What seems to have taken place at the turn of the century was the partition of these four free tenements and the rearrangement of strips with the object of producing consolidated blocks of free land. As can be seen in appendix 2, Robert Swan did particularly well out of the reorganisation, ending up with 2 messuages, 2 placea, 28 acres, 2½ rods and 1 twodolrod. Adam Sybile put 10 acres into the pool, half of which were 'let' to other members in the group, and he received as much back, some from each of the four tenements and all of it in his own hand. It is difficult to envisage how such an exchange of strips could be recorded, in the absence of maps, other than by listing the various tenants of the constituent strips of each traditional virgate. Just as on a modern Ordnance Survey map each block of land is given a number, and often there are several parcels of land within the block, each held by a different owner, so, in the oral tradition of medieval society, land was divided into units known variously as virgates, fees, full lands, tenements, bovates, oxgangs and so on, and the identification on the ground of each such unit was the common knowledge of all members of the community. Each unit was known by the name of its current holder, but if the ownership was so fragmented that no single name predominated, then the name of the last single owner was used as a permanent identification tag, often for several centuries. The causes of fragmentation were numerous: division among heirs, parcenage, alterations in land economy involving the reorganisation of the basic units themselves. Whatever the cause, the result in the records is the same: lists of names of persons holding land within the traditional basic unit which is said to be held, or to have at one time been held, by a named individual. From such a list alone it is extremely difficult for the historian to be able to identify the nature of the tenurial arrangement, the date or the cause of its emergence. Just at present the interest of historians centres upon the extent of the peasant market in land, and lists such as we have been describing are interpreted as lists of parcenors or subtenants. Many probably were, but the thirteenth century was also a period characterised by agricultural reorganisation, such as the shift from a two-field to a three-field system, changes which would have spawned vast numbers of such lists. The sad fact is that unless a list can be fully examined within the organisational context of the settlement, and the period to which it actually refers, it cannot be used as evidence either for a peasant land market or for tenurial reorganisation. This rules out a large proportion of the documentary material available (Jones 1972: 18–27 and 1979: 316–27).

Finally, although labour services had long since been commuted to money payments, it is interesting to know what these had been, and a list survives incorporated into MM 6370. The full virgater owed 2 days' ploughing without a food allowance and using his own

Table 4. *Apetoft tenants c. 1300–15*

TENEMENTS CHARGED WITH RENT ONLY:

46	HUGH HARCOURT (Hugh Harcourt) (*MM 6374b, 6292.*) *Subtenants* *c.* 1315†	1 mes. + 1 virgate rent 13s 4d 58 *Robert Swan* 5 *Nicholas Smith* 70 *Constance Sybile* 66 *Adam de Kibworth (Sybile)* 71 *John Chapman* 66 *William Atte Cross* 67 *Roger Polle* 62 *William Osborne* 72 *Robert Harcourt* 73 *John Smith* 66 *Roger de Hildesley* 75 *Juliana, wife of Hugh Harcourt*
47	WILLIAM POLLE capellanus (Nicholas Polle)	½ virgate rent 6s 8d
48	WILLIAM HEYNE (William son of Reginald Heyne)	1 mes. + 1 virgate rent 13s 4d
49	JOHN SMITH (Nicholas le Smith)	½ virgate rent 6s 8d
50	ROBERT HOLKE (Robert Holke I floruit 1289) (Robert Holke II floruit 1334) (*MM 6374b*) Subtenants *c.* 1315†	1 virgate rent 13s 4d 58 *Robert Swan* 59 *William Heyne* 60 *William Atte Cross* 67 *Roger Polle* 3 *Nicholas Polle* 62 *William Osborne* 9 *John Sybile* 76 *Nicholas Harcourt* 66 *Roger de Hildesley*

Total: 3 virgates, 2 bovates – elsewhere referred to as two half virgates – and 5 messuages. The rent charged was that normal for a customary tenement but by the fifteenth century these tenements were classified as free. Rent 53s 4d

CUSTOMARY TENEMENTS, services commuted:

9	JOHN son of SYBILE (Alex' son of Ive Sybile†)	½ virgate	rent 10s
51	HENRY WYAT (William Harcourt)	½ virgate + 1 acre	rent 11s
52	ROBERT BRON (Robert Bron)	1 virgate + 1 acre	rent 21s
53	THOMAS HARCOURT (Nicholas Harcourt)	1 virgate	rent 20s
54	WILLIAM MANN (John son of Hugh Mann)	½ virgate	rent 10s

Table 4 (*cont.*)

55 ROBERT ASTEL (Ive son of Asketil†)	½ virgate	rent 10s
56 JOHN ROBYN (William son of Robert)	1 virgate	rent 20s
57 HENRY WYTE (Henry Broun)	1 virgate	rent 20s
(MM 6372) Subtenants *c.* 1315	77 *Robert Wright* 3 *Nicholas Polle*	

Total: 8 messuages, 6 virgates, 2 acres. Rent £6. 2s 0d

† See appendixes 2 and 3.

plough; two days' harrowing and hoeing, the lord providing food; 2 days' mowing on the lord's meadow bringing one man to help him; an unspecified amount of time gathering and carrying hay using the lord's cart but without food; 3 days' reaping in autumn bringing two men and without food; on the fifth and sixth day of reaping he had to bring four men and all received a food allowance; for all other boon works he received food. He also had to carry the lord's corn to the market at Leicester using his own horse, but he was under no obligation to carry any further unless within the county; he had to gather straw for one day with one man and without food and to get straw together for roofing the buildings of the manor court whenever necessary; he also had other tasks but, unfortunately, at this point the roll is illegible; he might have had to carry coal on his own cart within the county.* It was also the custom for the men of the village to mow the lord's meadows and to receive beer worth 1s 6d whilst they performed this task. From each virgate a heriot was owed to the lord in the form of the second best beast, and a mortuary to the church in the form of the best beast. The remainder of the list is no longer legible.

The tenants on the Apetoft estate also owed labour services to the lord of the manor and these are described in a plea roll dated November 1287/8.[8] All who used to hold of Laurence Apetoft had to plough twice a year without food, but if a third turn of ploughing was necessary they were to receive food; they had to reap in autumn with food, and if the labour of the cottagers was not needed by the lord they were to pay him 1d in lieu of reaping service.

---

* The bridge over Burton Brook at the western extremity of the parish was known as *colebrigge* in the thirteenth century. The limitation of coal-carrying services to within the county would indicate that the coal was being brought from the Leicestershire pits rather than the Bedworth pits in Warwickshire.

We are now in a position to be able to look round the estate as the Warden saw it at the opening of the fourteenth century. The college owned the whole manor, which was comprised of the village and lands of Kibworth Harcourt, part of Gumley Wood,[9] the View of Frankpledge for Kibworth Harcourt and the court baron for Harcourt to which certain tenants in Gumley also owed suit,[10] and the advowson of the free chapel at Harcourt[11] (see below pp. 138–9). This amounted to one knight's fee.[12]

3

Administration

In general terms Kibworth was in no way singular with respect to its administrative framework. Some of its tenants held freely, others for rents, others for services. It was served by its own manor court and its tithing men answered twice yearly to the Sheriff's View'. On occasion it paid a royal tax, indirectly it was liable for the payment of scutage and aids. Its landholders paid tithe to the Rector and entry fines to the college, together with heriot, mortuary and, in some cases, marriage fines. But in the particulars of interpretation the village retained its own practices, as indeed did most other manors, and the degree of nonconformity in practice is an essential aspect of any study of the documents upon which our analysis of a society rests. The tendency of clerks to stick rigidly to the layout and formulae of those model court and account rolls which had been used in their training or which had been provided by their employer presents us with a problem which it is easy to underestimate. Local variations tended to be forced into a common mould or, if too refractory, were simply omitted, and although the number of literate men around, even in Kibworth, is impressive (see below pp. 37–9), it must be remembered that from literacy alone there is no automatic progression to intelligent analysis or to the interpretation of events and situations not yet reduced to verbal forms. Similarly, clerks were in command of a limited number of legal terms – not always fully understood – which they were inclined to use rather more freely than a trained lawyer would have done. To take but two examples of clerical idiosyncrasy: the commissioners for the survey now known as the 1279 Hundred Rolls were instructed to ascertain the bounds of each vill. When they came to the fen areas of East Cambridgeshire their clerks discovered that no records of the bounds were available, since no bounds had been determined across the watery wastes between settlements. Therefore, under the heading 'Bounds of the vill' the clerks entered the bounds of the marshes. Not only was this piece of gratuitous information quite irrelevant in the context, it was misleading, since they did not alter the heading to read 'Bounds of the marshes'.[1] Our second example, this time of the loose use of technical terms, is drawn from the same survey. The commissioner's clerks copied the rental of each major landholder in each vill and this allows us to compare the terminology used by these landlord's clerks to describe closely similar holdings within the same vill. We find a typical tenant holding customary land for rents, not services, described by one local clerk as a molman, by the neighbouring clerk as free, by another as a *censuarius*, by another as a villein. Similarly, on some manors cottagers were called crofters, on others thofters, on others *facini*.[2] It was no small matter whether a man was free or unfree, but his fate could be decided by the stroke of a pen! The moral surely is, trust not a medieval clerk any more than a modern one to mean what he says. Given this tendency to force all within a common model, medieval society as portrayed in the written records often appears monotonously uniform. This cannot in fact have been the case, since it had evolved out of an intensely regional, de-centralised and, until very recently, non-literate economic and political framework. Our task, therefore, is not only to reconstruct a village society as seen through the eyes of the Kibworth clerks, but if at all possible to query that clerk's reporting. This is no easy task, since it requires not only checking court rolls against account rolls but also a constant attention to what is written between the lines both literally and metaphorically. The fact remains that we are looking at a community through the eyes of the bailiff's clerk, and that bailiff had to justify his actions before the college auditors and the Steward. The influence of the college upon village affairs must therefore seem disproportionately great. The first duty of the bailiff's clerk was to write up the account roll and either he or the Steward's clerk wrote up the court roll, usually the former. The rolls themselves are described elsewhere (P. D. A. Harvey 1965, 1976); here we are concerned with their content, in particular with those aspects of community administration dealt with in the rolls of the manor court.

When Walter of Merton acquired the manor he also acquired the right and duty to hold the View of Frankpledge.[3] Accordingly, the View was held twice a year, in spring (April–May) and in the autumn (October–November), and was presided over by a Steward who was occasionally a Fellow of the college but more usually a professional man (see pp. 37–9). It dealt with infringements of the Assize of Bread and Ale – which were inconsiderable in this area – with debts, theft and battery, with treasure trove, as when Christopher Hychecock found 2s 4d, and Joan, wife of John Saunder, discovered 3s 0d,[4] and it collected a common fine at the spring court and 'head money' at the autumn court. In theory the *parva curia* or court baron was meant to sit every three weeks, for so it is recorded in the list of services due from the tenants,[5] but in practice it was held in conjunction with the View twice a year. For a short period in the second decade of the fourteenth century when Thomas of Thurmarston was Steward, the little court was held at monthly intervals; whether this was because he personally was in favour of reviving the practice, or because the economic and political upsets of the decade together with the integration of the Apetoft estate into the college rent roll necessitated reorganisation and a regime of 'thorough', we shall never know. Occasionally, as in 1277–8,[6] the Steward spent as many as nine days in the year on court business, but usually he spent no more than a couple of nights on each visit, so that the volume of litigation was restricted to what could be accomplished in so short a time. It is not surprising, therefore, that the transactions of the Kibworth court are less circumstantial and wide ranging than those of manors where the three-week rule still obtained.* Nor was the distinction between the two courts very closely observed; debts for example were sometimes entered under the proceedings of the little court, entry fines under the View. But the little court was used principally as a register of land transfers and associated incidents such as reliefs and heriots, with entry fines in the case of *post mortem* transfers, and with licences in the case of lettings or alienations *inter vivos*. It also dealt with estate matters, such as the repair of buildings, gates, roads and banks, damage to crops in the field and to hedgerow trees, non-enrolment into tithing and the occasional marriage licence. The reeve, whose principal duty it was to collect rents and other dues, used the court heavily as a register of uncollected debts for which he sought allowance from the auditors. The series is strong therefore on tenures and administration, weak on village gossip and scandal (cf. Britton 1977; DeWindt 1971). However, the court was a public forum by no means controlled by the reeve. In fact, the ratio of court and other officers to landholders was remarkably high: four chief pledgers, two affeerors, two ale tasters, six supervisors of buildings and twelve jurors for the court alone, in addition to the reeve, the bedel, the messor, the constable, the six custodians of the Hall,[7] the *custos campi* and the four *custodes vaccarum*[8] – these last could be more precisely classed as employees but for a duty which bestowed a very real power to favour or harass – and lastly the three *capellani*.[9]

* Cf. Research Project for Medieval Demographic, Economic and Social History from Manorial Court Rolls, University of Birmingham, for a computer analysis of the court rolls of Lakenheath (1310–1400) and Alrewas (1270–1400).

Table 5. *Composition of the tithings in 1290*

Tithing	Head	Heads of household	Sons	Brothers	Total
A	Robert le Bonde	21	19	–	40
B	Robert Sibile	16	10	–	26
C	Robert Churt	24	16	5	45
D	William son of Reginald	9	9	9	27
(E)	Unattached	4	10	–	14

At Kibworth the Frankpledge was made up of four tithings, each with its own head.* On the back of a court roll written in 1280 (MM 6376 8 Ed I dorse) is a list headed *Nomina Franciplegii de Kebworth* from which we can learn something of the composition of these tithings. We shall have occasion to examine the list exhaustively in chapter nine, but table 5 summarises briefly the figures relevant to the study of the Frankpledge as a whole.

At the foot of the three columns of names on the court roll is a list of names (E) which could be a continuation of tithings A, C or D or could be a list of persons who had not yet been assigned to a tithing. Of the four heads of household in this group (E) two had already been included in a tithing and the other two bore toponymic surnames and may have been strangers. The remainder in this group were sons, two of whom had already been listed. Several other men were also listed in more than one tithing, so that the total number of males has to be adjusted downwards to 146 names, comprising 71 heads of household, 63 sons and 14 brothers. As might be expected, heads of households were in a minority.

At this date the Apetoft estate had not yet been reincorporated into the main manor and was the subject of much negotiation. A note in the roll for 1289[10] states that the 'tenants of Laurence de Apetoft swear that they have always been distrained and amerced in the court of Saer de Harcourt and that the heads of tithing and ale tasters of Laurence de Apetoft owe suit to the court of Saer de Harcourt every three weeks'. This is perhaps an overstatement, since the court of Saer de Harcourt did not meet every three weeks and the only surviving list of the Apetoft tithing, dated 1282 (MM 6376 10 Ed I), names only ten pledgers, five of whom were Apetoft tenants and the other five were Merton tenants. No Apetoft tenant was head of a

* For a detailed discussion of the institution, see W. A. Morris, *The Frankpledge System* (Harvard Historical Studies, no. 14, New York 1910); for regional comparisons see J. A. Raftis, *Tenure and Mobility* (Toronto 1964), pp. 98–104, and D. A. Crowley, 'The later history of Frankpledge', *BIHR*, XLVII (May 1975), 1–15.

tithing in that year, but Apetoft tenants were not debarred from holding the office of chief pledger; in 1290, for example, Nicholas Harcourt – an Apetoft man – was elected to replace William, son of Reginald. In other words, for all practical purposes the Apetoft tenants enjoyed no separate identity in the court leet.

Freemen were not exempt from membership of the Frankpledge and were regularly sworn in at the age of twelve along with the customary tenants. The four chief pledgers acted collectively to present offences for which the culprits were subsequently fined, the amount of the fine being assessed by the affeerors. (The chief pledgers also acted as pinders: see below pp. 104, 133.) In terms of ranking, the office of chief pledger was at the lower end of the scale, a first step towards holding office as supervisor, juror or reeve. In the period 1361–1400 the normal term of office, and period between holding office, was one to three consecutive years. Some men held office more than once, totalling up to eight years, and in two instances up to twenty years. John Marnham senior, for example, held for a total of fifteen years between 1368–91 and John Couper held for twenty years between 1371–93. The same surnames tended to recur again and again as chief pledgers: Boton, Saunders, Marnham, Couper, Sybile, Heyme. Robert Saunders, for example, held from 1361–76, John Saunders from 1379–96 and John Saunders junior from 1397–9. After 1400 the pattern altered slightly. It became more common to hold office for one year only, with one-year intervals, while at the same time officials were elected with increasing frequency for periods of five to eight consecutive years or even longer, and by the end of the fifteenth century it was not unusual for men to hold for twenty or more years. Richard Wynlufe, for example, acted as chief pledger from 1415–45, a period of thirty years, and John Brown held for thirty-one years (1417–48). These two families established a virtual monopoly of two of the four tithings for much of the fifteenth century. The Browns held from 1410–22; 1417–48; and 1425–48, while the Wynlufes held from 1415–45; 1448–65; and 1473–84. Both were successful families in economic terms but neither were 'ancient' families such as the Harcourts, Polles, Sybiles, Joyes and Heyns, which families tended to provide reeves and jurors rather than pledgers.

As the fifteenth century wore on the role of the chief pledgers declined. After 1473 their names, which had hitherto always headed the court roll, were preceded by the names of the twelve jurors, and by the 1490s their names were placed at the foot of the roll. In 1489 their number was reduced from four to three, but there the decline was halted. In 1686[11] there were still three chief pledgers, George Eyre (gentleman farmer), Joseph Hubbard (cottager and shepherd) and William Grant (with 25 acres). By this date, however, the inhabitants were no longer divided into tithings; instead a simple list was kept 'of all the inhabitants' or, as they were still sometimes called, the *Decimar'*. Presentments by this date were made by the jurors or homage and it is to them we should now turn.

Until William Brerale's stewardship in the early 1390s, the homage was made up of six sworn men. These were men of standing in the village, who served for long periods, possibly for life, and who were called upon to give testimony in cases relating to land transfers, encroachments and dilapidations. In the 1390s this body of men was given the title *supervizores terrae et tenementorum* and at the same time a new institution made its first appearance; the twelve jurors, known variously as inquisitors, jurors or the homage. There were often thirteen of these men, sometimes eleven, but usually twelve. The office of supervisor was terminated in 1450 with the reorganisation which took place at that time, but the twelve-man jury continued into the sixteenth century, its numbers being increased to fifteen in 1500. The survival of court rolls in the sixteenth century is intermittent, but in 1594[12] the homage numbered twelve, in 1600[13] it numbered sixteen and in 1693[14] a list of fifteen names was still being enrolled.

A regular and valuable component of the income from the View of Frankpledge was the common fine of 9s 1d paid annually at the spring View. Occasionally, as in 1292–3 and 1327–9, the amount was increased to 20s and may include the sums collected in taxation and purveyance staggered over two or three years. The fine was recorded usually in the court rolls and sometimes in the account rolls, but ceased to be collected after 1448, except briefly in Henry VIII's reign, when an unsuccessful attempt was made to revive it. In addition to the common fine a head-penny fine (*denar' capitibus*) was collected from the tithing men at the autumn View until 1450. It was not taken every year and the amounts varied from around 7s to little more than 12d, but after the plagues collection became more frequent, until by 1410 it was taken more than twice a year; the amounts however dwindled from 4s 4d in the 1380s to 13d in 1450. The fine was raised by the heads of tithing from members absent from the manor at the rate of 2d per head[15] (cf. Raftis 1964: 100). Before the plagues, in the 1290s, the fine was not taken for absence in the sense of migration, but was simply the total collected in essoins, that is, failure to attend the court, and was paid not by itinerant wage labourers but by local freemen of some standing, such as Sir John Gryffen representing the suitors from Gumley, and the chaplain, the clerk, the doctor and the broker.[16] As such, it was not resented, but by 1380 it was, and it became one of the points at issue in the troubles of the 1400s (see below pp. 50–1). No new names were added to the list of emigrants after 1407 and the fine was dropped in the 1439 settlement and again in 1450 after a brief attempt to revive it.

Against the income from the common fine and chevage must be set the expenses of running the court and the forinsec expenses. Among the latter were included not only local and national levies, but also annual payments of 6d in palfreysilver paid to the Sheriff of Leicester[17] and 6s 8d paid annually to the Harcourt family at their Bosworth manor. This fine covered scutage and aids due to the Earls of Warwick which were paid directly by Harcourt.[18] Only incidentally do we hear of national levies. In 1314–15 the land of Nicholas Sybile was administered by the college during the minority of Sybile's son and a bedel was appointed who accounted for 1d in expenses for sending a knight to parliament, and for 3d levied on the crops for the twentieth.[19] On another occasion, in 1322–3 the reeve claimed expenses incurred by himself when summoned to Leicester to answer for the vill in matters concerning taxation and the raising of an army for the Scottish campaign.[20] In 1342–3 the reeve was put to expense in arranging a *dies amoris* between the tenants of Merton and of Warwick.[21] While it is true that Kibworth lay in a region less troubled than most by the king's purveyancers and by forced conscription to the army (cf. Maddicott 1975) the village was certainly not immune from taxation. In 1327 and 1334, 41 shillings and 48 shillings respectively was raised but no record of these sums was entered under forinsec expenses or the reeve's allowances.[22] We are therefore left to guess the heading under which these sums have been subsumed and, as mentioned above, the common fine, which was sharply increased in the relevant years, is the most probable candidate.

Similarly, the payment of tithes great and small went unrecorded. The collection of the small tithes was the subject of dispute in the 1290s and involved the reeve in visits to London and Leicester, but was settled in favour of the Rector of St Wilfrid's church, who also took the great tithes.[23] The chaplain of Merton's free chapel at Kibworth Harcourt thus had no regular source of income, which may help to explain why the position was so often vacant. The college, however, was responsible for repairs to this chapel.[24]

Income derived from amercements was negligible and the totals noted in the court rolls tally with totals in the account rolls, which would indicate that if the little court was occasionally convened in the absence of the Steward and his clerk no amercements were collected (May 1973: 389–401). Provision of the court would have been a costly business for the college were it not for the income from entry fines. In the medieval period such fines were regularly taken upon *post mortem* transfers when the widow or heir took up the deceased's land. A fine was also taken when a man took up demesne land by indenture or customary land in the lord's hand, and during the brief period when *ad opus* transfers were common. Apart from these cases no fine was taken upon transfers *inter vivos*. Thus between 1280–98 thirty-six land transfers were recorded in the manorial court and only fourteen entry fines were taken, and between 1320–47 only fifteen fines were taken from thirty-seven land transfers.* The value of these fines seems to have been arrived at by individual negotiation, taking into account status, perks, family circumstances and rent arrears, since the sums bear little relation to the size of the tenement. Most fines were in the region of 12d or 18d though 6s 8d, representing a year's rent, was sometimes taken from a half virgate, with the occasional leap to 26s 8d for demesne or free land and, in one instance, 66s 8d was taken in the late thirteenth century. Immediately after the plagues the level of entry fines fell to zero and remained so for long enough for the custom to lapse *de facto* if not *de jure*. The Warden had to remain satisfied with fixed rents until the inflationary pressures of the sixteenth century forced the college to seek some way of bringing rents up to an economic level. It did this by negotiating a system of seven-year fines, each fine being two and a half times the annual rent (see below, pp. 53, 62–4).

A heriot in kind was taken upon the death of a male tenant on free, customary and cottage land, and in cash from demesne tenants. It was paid by the widow or heir of the deceased, but if there was no heir, as was frequently the case in the late fourteenth century, and a new tenant had to be found by the lord, no heriot was charged. The animal taken was usually a *iumenta* (draught animal) in the pre-plague period, valued at between 2s and 4s, or a cow (cf. Harvey 1976, who notes that at Cuxham villeins seldom surrendered oxen). After the plagues it was commonly a cow worth between 6s and 9s, but occasionally a ewe was taken, or a pig or a colt and, in one case, a russet cloth worth 8d. It was not until the late fifteenth century that the money heriot became normal (Postan and Titow 1958–9: 392–417).

Leyrwite was rarely, if ever, taken at Kibworth, or merchet as such. However, various persons were fined on a number of pretexts in connection with marriage. Most marriage fines were noted in the account rolls only but, taking the account and court rolls together, in

---

* In the account rolls references are made to fines and heriots which cannot easily be matched – because retrospective – with the court roll entries. These instances there-fore have not been included. It should also be noted that in cases where the deceased had already divested himself of his interest in land, where he had retired, for example, no record was kept of his death, and the collection of the heriot due may have been overlooked by the steward.

the period before the plagues (1283–1348 in the account rolls) fifteen cases are recorded. Of these, eight fines were taken from men for their own marriage. Where the sum is given it lies between 6s 8d and 13s 4d. Three fines of 2s each were taken from women for their own marriage and four fines ranging from 12d to 6s 8d were taken from mothers for their daughter's marriage. In addition the Polle family had to pay 20s a year during the minority of the heir for his wardship and marriage.[25] All the persons concerned came from the leading families in the village and thought of themselves as free. The disruption caused by the plagues is reflected in the unusual number of widow remarriages. Normally widows at Kibworth had no cause to remarry, since they had more than enough unemployed male relatives to work the land and stood to lose the holding if they married again. However, widespread labour shortages after the plagues drew off surplus labour from the villages and the abundance of land on the market made it less necessary to safeguard the interests of heirs.* Thus in the short period from 1352–63 as many as five widows remarried, taking with them as much as $1\frac{1}{2}$ virgates each in land, for the term of their lives. In these cases the groom paid the fine for entry into the land for the lifetime of the widow, and such fines should really be treated as entry fines rather than marriage licences. The proportion of men paying for licence to marry remained high after the plagues; of the seventeen marriages recorded between 1352–1404, twelve fines were paid by grooms. This was predictable in a community where land usually went to the nearest male heir rather than to daughters in direct descent. The death or migration of male heirs left more land in the hands of women (cf. Searle 1979: 3–43). The supply of heirs in Kibworth did not begin to fail until the 1370s and licence fines continued to be collected infrequently until 1379, but after that date the custom lapsed. Post-plague fines varied from 6d to 24d and brought in a total revenue of 8s 6d in twenty-seven years, a sum hardly worth collecting. This is not the place to enter into the legal or theoretical justifications for levying merchet, neither is this the place to engage in a comparative survey of merchet forms. Suffice it to say that the forms were many and varied, but that whoever paid and for whatever reason, the lord benefited from a small fee.

In the same category can be placed the necessary purchase of a licence for permission to have a son tonsured for a career in the church. Several Kibworth boys took minor orders: John, son of Richard Godwyn, later known as Dominus John Godwyn;[26] the clerk

---

* When John Chorch claimed his deceased wife's land to hold 'by courtesy of England' his claim was disallowed because he was of villein status and his wife was a freewoman, but he was allowed to hold it '*ad voluntatem domini*' (MM 3405 31 Ed III).

Robert Heyne's son;[27] the sons of Nicholas and of Hugh Harcourt; and the sons of Reginald Sybile, William Saunders, Nicholas Saunders and Robert Carter; all, it should be noted, from what might be called the 'managerial' families in the village. Fines varied from 12d to 6s 8d and continued to be taken after the plagues until 1371. In the earlier period a fine was also sometimes paid by a man *ut erit liber* or *pro libertate habenda*,[28] and in the same period strangers had to pay for a licence to remain on the manor; this included villagers who had been away for some time. Robert Holke, for example, had to pay for re-entry in 1334.[29] Naturally enough this concern with immigration vanished after the plagues.

Mention of the tests of villeinage leads us to the broader question of legal status. In this area Kibworth does not conform very closely to the classical model, due possibly to the fact that assarting had not been possible, and therefore there were virtually no poor free tenants eking out an existence on minute holdings of assart land. Secondly, the demesne was farmed by a group of villagers who had no need of the customary services or of the full-time labour of the demesne cottagers. Consequently, both yardlands and cottage lands were held for a money rent. The distinction between customary and free tenants was thus easily lost sight of. The small group of free tenants were not of knightly status; they held customary land in addition to their free holdings and they frequently married into customary families. It was these free families who tended to dominate village life; they acted as witnesses to college agreements, they provided the manor with its bailiffs, clerks and chaplains, they served as jurors, ale tasters and affeerors, they bought and sold odd acres of free land from each other, they jointly leased the demesne from the college. The college was inclined to question their free status, the customary tenants found it hard to see in what the distinction lay and tended to arrogate to themselves the privileges of their kinsmen. There was, however, a difference: customary tenants paid a much higher rent, acre for acre, than the free tenants. A certain sensitivity to the question of free status is evident throughout the pre-plague period, and this was heightened perhaps by the keeping of written records of the court as well as of the manorial proceedings. In the court the interests and actions of lord, bailiff and tenantry were exposed to public scrutiny. The reeve called upon the collective witness of the tenantry to support his claims vis-à-vis the college, the tenantry sought redress from the Warden for unjust actions taken by the bailiff, and on at least two occasions the bailiff was dismissed from office at their request.[30] As an institution the court thus served a real need and was welcomed. However, as the generator of written records it was less acceptable. The rolls could be searched retrospectively for evidence of villein status and, as we have seen, it was the freeholders who paid for marriage licences, and at Kibworth they also owed heriots. Moreover, it was the freeholders who usually supplied the reeve, and the college continued to hold reeves responsible for uncollected rents and dues years after they had left office, for which purpose the college certainly used the rolls. A search was also made of the rolls for evidence of the villein status of the Polle and Mann families, and all entries relating to the payment of a marriage fine were sedulously copied out,[31] but no note was made of those entries which supported their claim to free status: the payment of relief instead of heriot, the payment of 20s a year for the wardship and marriage of a Polle heir who was a minor, the fact that on a list of all college tenants on all college manors[32] the Polles are clearly listed as free tenants. The Polles and the Manns were not the only families on whom a 'file' was kept; against many another name a tag of string has been attached in the margin or the words *nota* or *nota bene*. The tenantry was thus brought to appreciate the disadvantages as well as the advantages of written records. By the mid fifteenth century all this was in the past. Villein status had been abolished, fines were no longer imposed for licence to marry, to enter or leave the manor or to enter the church, and the court confined its activities to recording land transfers and by-laws. As such it was a wholly acceptable instrument of administration from the peasant point of view. This happy state of affairs was short-lived. By the end of the sixteenth century the court met only once in seven years and land transfers were negotiated privately with the Warden and were merely copied onto the rolls at seven-year intervals. In a society composed of gentry, medium farmers, artisans and a handful of landless labourers, the bailiff was always a gentleman, and dealt with the Warden as a social equal. He needed no support from the tenantry, neither could they bring about his dismissal. He ran the village as its squire. If the court had a function it was not self-evident in the modern world of the seventeenth century. Individualism is only a matter of degree but it undoubtedly characterised the seventeenth century to a level undreamed of in the early fourteenth century or, to put it another way, the degree of community self-help and enterprise which had characterised the early fourteenth century seems almost to have disappeared by the seventeenth. With no community organisation behind him, deference was a man's best course, and we no longer witness through the accounts and courts those frequent visits by the tenants to the Warden at Merton to complain about the reeve, about each other and about the college, neither do we get letters like that written *circa* 1448 by 'yowre owne manne John Pychard', butcher, who, in recommending to the college a promising young scholar, the son of Agnes Palmer, wrote

> and truly syr the manne desyryd to have conynge over allthynge nowgthe wytstandynge he mygthe have maysters in þe kynggis howse and in dyverse places but he wolde evermore have conynge and truly syr we prey youe alle yowre tenandis everyche one þt ye wolde cheryshe hym for truly syr he shull be at you in haste and forsothe ye wyll lyke hys condysshons have ye asayde hym a wyle bothe for governanse and person. Nomore at þs tyme but almygthe godde have you in hys kepynge. Wrytton at Kybworthe in þe feste of syent Huge mart.[33]   (See appendix 10)

There is a sense of partnership between the college and 'alle yowre tenandis' in this letter which by the seventeenth century had dissolved into paternalism (cf. Macfarlane 1979).

Let us now turn more directly to the administrative system and personnel employed by the college with respect to Kibworth. The college provided the courts, as we have been discussing, and it collected the rents. It took time to evolve a smoothly working system; initially, both the court rolls and the account rolls were lengthy and detailed with much overlapping, and the format changed almost yearly. Eventually the accounting system was reduced to an unchanging formula and the court rolls were used to record the ongoing responses to situations as they developed. It is with the court rolls, therefore, that our interest primarily lies.

Since we have just been considering the functions of the court, let us remain with the courts a little longer and look at the personnel involved and the running costs. The total revenue from this source, including entry fines and the common fine, seldom amounted to as much as £2 10s, although in the 1360s it rose to an average of £4 3s 10d and in the decade 1410–19 to £5 19s 2d. Against this must be set the expenses incurred, chief among them being the fees for the steward and the clerk. Until 1450 the college employed a professional steward for an annual salary of 20s plus expenses; thereafter, the revenue from the courts having fallen to around 12s per annum, the services of a steward were dispensed with. The steward usually spent a night at Kibworth on each visit and the expenses, which included board (bread, ale, meat and butter), peas for his horse and 8d paid to the jurors, generally came to about 3s per court. Sometimes he brought his own clerk, but he also made use of the services of the reeve's clerk, who was paid 1s a year in the thirteenth century. This was increased to 2s during Robert de Gaddesby's stewardship, and in addition he was paid at piece rates for any extra clerical work or for carrying documents to Coventry, Leicester, Bosworth, Oxford and elsewhere. In 1283, for example, he was sent to the Merton estate at Gamlingay in Cambridgeshire on business to do with the dower land of Saer de Harcourt's widow, for which he received 2d, and in the same year the expenses of the reeve, the clerk and a *narrator* at Leicester amounted to 17½d.[34] Lastly, parchment cost 2d a year or occasionally 4d. The actual costs of running the court thus amounted to rather more than half the revenue derived from the same.

The stewards themselves were professional lawyers and administrators serving the Leicester region and a number of lordships. The earliest named steward for Kibworth and for Merton's other Leicestershire estate, a moiety of the manor of Barkby, was Robert de Gaddesby. Presumably he hailed from Gadsby, a village to the north-east of Barkby. He served the college from 1295 or earlier until the second decade of the fourteenth century and again from 1323 until about 1345. Between 1314 and 1320 Thomas of Thurmaston took the little court, but Master Richard Haburne took the View of Frankpledge. The village of Thurmaston lies only a few miles west of Barkby. For one year, 1326–7, Roger de Mortimer presided over both courts, but otherwise the continuity is remarkable and was surely beneficial in those troubled years. In 1346 Simon Pakeman took office and was still in office in 1371 when a new rental was made 'by order of Simon Pakeman'.[35] In 1348–9 Robert de Gaddesby was recalled to help Pakeman, and both received a 20s fee that year.[36]

About Simon Pakeman somewhat more is known than of his predecessors. He came from one of those 'recognised professional families which supplied the official land agent class of men both for the crown and its greater subjects' (Levi Fox 1940: 72). He was steward of the Honor of Leicester and also of Leicester Abbey; he represented the shire in the parliaments of 1333–4, 1346, 1347–8, 1364–5, 1366 and 1368; he was a Justice of the Peace and was frequently engaged on royal business although, unlike most of his type, he never became wholly absorbed in royal affairs (*ibid.*: 35).* His duties under the Earl of Leicester would have brought him annually to Carlton Curlieu, Shangton, the Langtons, Smeeton Westerby, Stonton Wyville, Glooston and Cranoe, so he would seem an obvious choice as steward of the Merton estates. These men did more than

---

* Gaddesby, Thurmaston and more particularly Pakeman were men of considerable local standing. In this respect they differ from the stewards appointed by the college to administer its courts in other counties; these were either Fellows with local connections or were freemen with little more than 30–60 acres. (Aston, *History of the University of Oxford*, vol. I, forthcoming.)

merely preside over the court, and the style of government changes with each steward. We have already seen how Thomas of Thurmaston reinstituted monthly courts; he also took away with him the two Kibworth rentals in 1317, presumably for closer scrutiny, and the reeve and clerk had to make many journeys to Thurmaston. Similarly, Simon Pakeman ordered the making of a new rental in 1352; this was for some reason abandoned but he ordered another in 1371, this time with success, since the 1316 rental[37] was no longer used after this date. It was under his presidency that *ad opus* transfers were introduced, and it was he who admitted outsiders to vacant customary holdings on the old terms of hereditary tenure. On many other estates such customary tenements were let by indenture or leasehold, with far-reaching consequences in the sixteenth century.

As with the steward, so too the clerk was a local man. As at Cuxham, he is better known to us by his handwriting than his name, and on this evidence alone we learn that there was more than one literate man in the village. The clerk was appointed by the reeve and with each new reeve we get a new clerk, a new, usually well-formed hand and a new presentation of the material. The reeve sent *garciones* to Oxford and elsewhere with cash liveries and messages, but on business matters he either travelled there himself or sent his clerk, who in 1289 was called Robert Clericus, in 1300 Roger Clericus and in 1312 we at least have a full name: Robert son of William Heyne, clerk. The Heynes were one of the leading free landholders in the village and usually witnessed Harcourt and later Merton charters and other deeds. In 1331 Robert Heyne was again acting as clerk and in 1328 he was amerced *pro filio suo facto clerico absque licenc' domini*. In 1319 the clerk was one Richard, and in 1321 he was Robert, possibly Robert Godyer. In 1314 Richard Godwyn was amerced for allowing his son John to be tonsured without licence; this son later returned to the village as Dominus John Godwyn. It is interesting that these clerks or their descendants did not progress more rapidly to the influential position of reeve. Not until 1356 did a Heyne become reeve, and then only for one year, though by the fifteenth century the Polles and the Clerkes held the reeveship alternately. The reeve, however, may sometimes have done his own clerical work; Roger Polle, for example, sent in masterly, brief, but quite unorthodox account rolls from 1338–43, which give the impression of being of his own composition.

The skills required of a reeve at Kibworth were those of a rent collector rather than a farmer and, indeed, a bedel was employed whenever husbandry had to be undertaken, such as when a bull had to be kept over winter[38] or when Nicholas Sybile's land had to be administered by the college until the heir was of age.[39] Before the plagues reeves served for quite short periods, sometimes only for one year, but undertook more than one spell of office, and sons followed in their father's footsteps. Nicholas Harcourt, for example, served from 1317–20, Nicholas Harcourt junior from 1323–6, and one of the Nicholas Harcourts from 1326–9. The Polles, by contrast, seldom served a short term. Roger Polle served from 1328–48, William from 1387–1406, Robert from 1406–43, William from 1450–1, John from 1520–35 and William from 1535–7. Their nearest competitors were the Clerkes. William Clerke served from 1451–80, Thomas from 1538–45 and William from 1546–50. After 1550 the reeveship was held by two gentry families, the Rayes and the Saviles, until 1682 and beyond. As rent collectors the reeves were only moderately successful: rents not collected in one financial year were carried over as arrears into the following year, and by the time a reeve surrendered the office the total sum of arrears could run to as much as £21 19s 2½d in the eight years from 1297–1305 and to £60 0s 6¾d in the nine years from 1308–17. In the last case the famine and murrain of the years 1315–17 were contributory factors (Kershaw 1973: 3–50). Arrears were not carried over from one reeve to his successor and had usually to be written off, although the auditors made efforts to have the sum collected for some years after a reeve had left office.[40] However, these reeves were more than rent collectors; they travelled extensively on the business of the college not only to and from Oxford but also to London, Winchester, Coventry and Leicester, as well as regularly to Bosworth with the annual Harcourt noble and to Evesham with the dower rents of Saer de Harcourt's widow. They represented the college before the sheriff and before the Earl of Leicester, also before the clerks of the Royal Exchequer at Hallaton and at Leicester. They negotiated with the rector over the question of tithes and in 1342–3 arranged a *dies amoris* between the Merton tenants and those of the Earl of Warwick at Kibworth Beauchamp.[41] Thus, although they called themselves reeves until the fifteenth century, or sometimes 'serviens', in practice they fulfilled the functions of bailiff. By the end of the fifteenth century they did indeed begin to style themselves bailiffs, but by this date they were no longer elected by the tenants, but had become farmers of the manor, which they held by indenture (see below, pp. 36–7, 59, 64, 67). For their labours they received an annual stipend of 40 shillings.

The Oxford to Kibworth route was a familiar one not only to the reeves but also to the Warden and Fellows, who between them made at least three trips a year. Responsibility for the administration of the college estates rested with the Warden alone, but he could, at his discretion, seek advice or assistance from other Fellows of the college, including the three domestic bursars (*depositarii*) who held office concurrently. Rents were either brought to the college by the reeve or were collected by one of the Fellows and were deposited with the bursars. In July each year the accounts were audited by a panel made up of the Warden, the Vice-Warden, the three bursars and three to five Fellows.[42] The audit was carried out with a fair degree of thoroughness: entries were queried, omissions noted, allowances added and finally, when satisfied, the auditors attached a small schedule to that effect to the foot of the account roll. The accounting system of the college has been examined and described by Dr Lowry (1936), by Professor P. D. A. Harvey (1976) and Mr T. H. Aston for the first volume of the *History of the University of Oxford* and, since the subject has little bearing upon the lives of the peasantry at Kibworth, this is not the place to explore it further.

The estate policy with regard to Kibworth is another matter and the fact that the landlord's policy at Kibworth was on the whole non-directive does not, of course, signify that the economic position or the social position of the tenants were wholly unaffected by their land-lord's powers. These powers preserved the legal limitations of bondage and it may have subjected bond-holders to payments higher than those of freemen. But against these negative effects of manorial lordship it must be noted that the rents at Kibworth, even at their highest, were low and constituted a small proportion of gross income from land. Above all, in assessing medieval estate policy we need to be reminded that some, perhaps many, small estates were run with no clearly defined policy and were as a rule at the mercy of purely local forces, such as the prevailing custom or the dictates of regional economy. The most critical policy decision the college ever took with regard to Kibworth was probably that taken in the 1280s to buy out the founder's heirs and to re-establish a single manor coterminous with the vill. This prevented the disintegration of the manor into several large farms each with its own labour relations and policy and all that that would have entailed for community solidarity and cohesion. Once the Apetoft estate had been reintegrated into the principal estate in the early fourteenth century, the college merely responded, somewhat tardily, to events as they occurred.* The story of its policy cannot, therefore, be treated except as an integral part of those events, the first of which was indeed a momentous one, the Black Death and the succession of high mortalities which followed it. To this we must now turn.

---

* Mr Aston tells me that it was college policy on the whole to retain the direct management of its estates even in the fourteenth century. In this respect Kibworth was no exception.

4

The plagues and their consequences, 1348–1450

In 1348 William Carter married Emma Cok and they took the cottage next to Alice Carter's. Roger Polle was accused of maladministration of a tenant's land during the period when he, as reeve, was responsible for it while an heir was found, and the matter was referred to the Warden at Merton. Robert, son of Nicholas Polle, died and his land was taken by Henry son of Robert Jowet. Robert had held the land for only one year and the reeve reported that he could take no heriot *quia nichil habuit*. If anything, the year was more eventful than most. The events of the next five months were all the more terrible by contrast.

By the end of April forty-two deaths had been registered and two more in August – after which no court was held until 1350. Similarly, in Kibworth Beauchamp only one death was recorded in October 1348, one caused by 'pestilence' in March 1349, and then fourteen in rapid succession by 15 May 1349.[1] The deaths recorded in the court rolls were those of landholders only, so that to this number we must add an unspecified number of women, children and landless men to reach an estimate of the total death toll.[2]

For the steward, Simon Pakeman, the immediate problem was that of discovering and enrolling new tenants for forty-four holdings – only $4\frac{1}{2}$ customary virgates and $2\frac{1}{2}$ demesne virgates remained unaffected. In spite of the nightmare conditions the court met in April and again in August and tenants were immediately found for all save four of the forty-four tenements. The names of four persons who died are illegible on the roll but, of the remaining forty landholders who died, twelve were women and of these four were succeeded by a son, only one of whom was a minor. Therefore, these women must have been at least in their late thirties or early forties. Of the remainder we have no indication of age since their land was taken by husbands or kinsmen. Of the twenty-eight men who died, five left land to sons, three of them minors; eight were succeeded by a brother or close kinsman; seven were succeeded by men bearing different though familiar surnames and who may or may not have been related by blood or by marriage; five left land to their wives; and the land of three reverted to the college. The high proportion of brothers and minors succeeding to male tenants suggests that mortality was greater among younger men than among older ones. However, the fact that so many tenants were neither sons nor brothers makes any firm conclusion on age-specific mortality impossible.

In other parts of England there is some evidence for a falling-off in the demand for land by the 1290s or following the years of high mortality in 1316–18.* With the exception of two demesne cottages and a messuage called Bartholomewestyard, which were held from time to time by outsiders but for the most part remained empty, there is no sign of a slackening in the land market at Kibworth before 1349 nor, indeed, immediately after the first pestilence. Agricultural land was taken up without delay. In those cases where no immediate member of the family survived the villagers elected the new tenant from among rival claimants: a novel procedure. Some men found themselves to be the eligible heirs to more than one holding and, like Robert Godyer, pleaded infirmity. Robert Maister, who was about to marry a well-endowed widow, evidently felt that he would be unable to cope with yet a further extension to his enterprise and paid a fine to be free of the obligation. He was not alone in so doing. However, there were many more men eager to acquire land, as is evident from the number of widow remarriages, which rose from one in the half century before the plagues to five in the decade after 1348. A widow's land could be enjoyed for the term of her life only and yet fierce bargaining preceded some of these remarriages. Domestic buildings were less sought after and many were converted into barns. But cottages for some reason attracted a certain amount of speculative buying. William de Marnham, for example, took two cottages in 1351 at a reduced rent of 3s, and in 1354 he took another three cottages for 3s 6d for the term of his life.

However, the demand for land was not what it had once been and the bargaining position of the tenantry vis-à-vis the college was sufficiently improved for the tenants, by a sufficient show of reluctance, to succeed in persuading the college to waive entry fines. As the century wore on a genuine shortage of tenants made itself felt. In the second half of 1361 at least ten landholders died (probably more: the last fifteen lines of the court roll are illegible), involving 10 messuages and 6½ virgates. Five tenements in Hog Lane were permanently

* There are no surviving court rolls for Kibworth for 1316–18, but the reeve's arrears in 1317 stood at £73 19s 7½d, indicating a high level of mortality.

abandoned after this outbreak. In 1375–6 'pestilence' is alluded to in the court rolls and four deaths were recorded. In 1378–9 mortality was high in the country generally, and Kibworth was no exception, with three recorded deaths. Between 1389–93 nine landholders died, and between 1396–8 another five. Finally in 1412 eight landholders died. The average death rate in the 1390s, at 2.25 per year, may at first sight appear unexceptional. But expressed as a proportion of the total population of some fifty landholders, the figure represents 5 per cent. At that rate half the landholding population died out in the course of twenty years. This is a much higher turnover through death than in pre-plague years. Alongside the generally high level of mortality among landholders must also be set the deaths of dependant adults and of children, and the high emigration rate among males, and possibly among women as well. The net result of this combination of high mortality and increased migration was in the first place a steep decline in population but also, and equally significant from the tenurial point of view, the extinction of a very high proportion of traditional village families who had hitherto exercised a monopoly over the customary land in the village. This subject will be treated more fully in chapter ten, while its effect upon the size and age structure of the family will be considered in chapter nine. Smaller households and larger holdings made it both difficult and unnecessary to maintain pre-1349 levels of arable cultivation, and the evolution of new and more appropriate uses of the land resources will be discussed in chapter six.

In quantitative terms some idea of the extent of migration can be gained from a comparison of the number of adult dependants in households given in the 1280 tithing list with the numbers given in the 1377/8 Poll Tax returns (see p. 230). For a description of the process we can turn to the court rolls. The first men noted as leaving the manor in 1356 were Roger and John Man, who went to the nearby village of Shangton; John, son of Robert Godyer, who went to Wistow; John Couper who went to Carlton; and William Wylmot, who ventured further afield and took up residence with John Pocking at Leicester. John Man held half a virgate of bondland, and various other members of the Man family also held land including free tenements. Robert Godyer held half a virgate of bondland and he took another half virgate in 1357. Other members of his family also held land. Likewise Couper and Wylmot left land in Kibworth. The trickle of departures continued and the names were duly noted in the court rolls, together with their whereabouts, until 1407 when the four chief pledgers refused to present *nativi* living away from the manor. Thereafter, no list was kept until in 1440 it was briefly resurrected, for one year only, in which year the rolls were also searched to prove the villein status of the Man, Polle and Saundur families.

Where did they go and why? The Mans moved from village to village within a short radius of Kibworth Harcourt. In 1356 they were in Shangton, in 1359 in Kibworth Beauchamp, in 1363 in Sadington, in 1365 in Stonton (Wyville), in 1366 back in Shangton, in 1374 in Shenesby and Sadington, in 1379 in Shenesby, in 1380 John Man 'operarius' was taxed at Fleckney,[3] in 1388 they were in Nosely or Mosely, in 1391 in Kibworth Beauchamp, in 1408 in Kibworth Beauchamp and Gildmorton, in 1440 in Coventry and by 1524 three Mans were worth £18 in goods in a village in Gartree Hundred whose name is unfortunately illegible.[4] Many went to Coventry; Robert Godyer and John Heyne in 1363, Roger Sherman, the son of Robert Godyer, in 1365. The latter lived with Arthur the Wiredrawer. William Chapman went, in 1408, to Melbourne Grange near Coventry. Others merely went to Nether Kibworth, as Kibworth Beauchamp was commonly called. A branch of the Mans lived there, also some of the Godyers and the Carters. John Harry, one-time reeve of Harcourt, went there for a time before moving to John Harrington's house at Grantham. A branch of the Polles lived at Westerby. William Bond went to Fleckney in 1363, Robert Atte Cross to Shinston in 1375, Robert Heyne to Wistow in 1388, Hugh Godwyn to Waltham on the Wold in 1391 and to Ilston in 1408 and William Herry to Turlangton in 1430.

As can be seen at a glance, most migrants went to neighbouring small villages. Unless one were to make a careful survey of the conditions and particularly the estate policy of these villages it is useless to speculate upon the motives which induced men to give up land in their own village and venture upon the uncertainties of life as a 'stranger' in some other community.

However, some went to towns and we are fortunate in being able to follow the career of one family in particular. The Browns were an old family in the village holding parcels of free and customary land. In 1381 Adam Brown is described in the tax returns as a draper. In 1397–8 he granted a freehold tenement to four men of Market Harborough and in 1404–5 these men granted it back to Adam Brown with remainder to his son, William, and William's wife Agnes, the daughter of Richard Dykenhall of Coventry. In 1434 William Brown's son, another Adam, granted the land to William Wymondeswold of Coventry and Thomas Brown of Kibworth, in which deed he described his father as 'William Brown of Coventry and Kibworth'. The witnesses to this grant were John Michell, Mayor of Coventry (1434–5), mercer, Robert Southern and William Donnington, bailiffs

(W. Donnington was Recorder for Coventry from 1434–48 and held land in 1407 in Cossington and Willoughby Waterless in Leicestershire), Richard Wymondeswold and Roger Okburn (of Smithfield St, Coventry), together with four men of Kibworth. In 1437 Wymondeswold and Brown returned the land to Adam Brown, chaplain, and in 1437 Adam granted the land to Master John Arundel, Rector of Kibworth.[5] This last transfer may have followed on an action taken by William Repington, parson of the parish church of Kibworth, against Thomas Brown of Kibworth Beauchamp for 100s in 1432 (Farnham V: 252). According to Emden, John Arundel was Rector of Kibworth in 1436 and was readmitted in 1447 (Emden 1957: 49–50). In 1459 he became Bishop of Chichester and physician to Henry Beauchamp, Earl of Warwick. He died, a large-scale pluralist, in October 1477. It seems probable that he left this insignificant piece of land in Kibworth Harcourt to his old college. At any rate, from 1477 onwards Browns Place became part of a block of leasehold land held by the college and leased by indenture rather than by copyhold. This followed naturally enough, since this had been freehold not customary land.

No more is heard of the Browns in Kibworth Harcourt after 1484, but their activities in Coventry can be followed. There, William and John Brown were both prominent men; both were councillors in 1424 and John was also a collector. In 1435 William Brown, draper, contributed as much as 6s 8d towards the loan of 500 marks to the king; in 1437 he was bailiff, probably of Erle St; in 1439 he and John Brown were Electors of the city officials; in 1444 William was a member of the mayor's council and one of the 'wurthy men' who lent the Earl of Warwick 100 marks. In 1449–50, Thomas Brown, weaver, could 'contribute cloth towards the needs of the army' and in 1451 Thomas Brown, 'lynen' draper, was one of the eighty-nine worthy men called upon to consider the fortifications of the town, to consult upon a new charter and to raise 100 marks for Queen Margaret. In the late 1470s it is Nicholas Brown who comes to the fore as Warden of the City in 1478 and member of the Council. In 1481 he agreed to provide an extra forty soldiers for the king. He was Elector in 1483 and 1484. In 1485 the Recorder's Office became vacant and was offered to John Brown if Thomas Kebell did not accept it. In an extant letter, John Brown of London wrote to say that he knew nobody in Coventry save Robert Oulay the Mayor and Mr Symonds who had been Mayor in 1477 (Dormer-Harris: E.E.T.S., vols 134–5, 138, 146). Thomas Kebell was also a Londoner, he was a sergeant at law and his family held land in the Kibworth area. Nothing more is heard of the Browns in Coventry after 1497 and the scene changes to London.

There, William Brown, mercer, merchant of the Staple of Calais and son of John Brown, knight, Alderman of the City of London, married a wealthy heiress, Katherine, daughter of Edmund and Juliana Shaa, knight.[6] We need not follow the Brown fortunes further except to note that they had business connections with the Brudenells and the Verneys and an interest in an estate at Rufford in Oxfordshire and elsewhere.[7]

It is unfortunate that Brown is such a common name, but the fact that they remained in the cloth trade and that we know with certainty that the Kibworth Browns moved to Coventry, there to move in the upper echelons of the town's oligarchy, and that the Coventry Browns moved to London at the same time as a Brown appears on the London merchant scene, makes the continuity more than a possibility. The family seem to have had a knack of knowing when to abandon a sinking ship; they left Kibworth in the lean and chequered days of the early fifteenth century for Coventry in its heyday, and they left Coventry in the lean days of the 1480s. It was not clogs to clogs in three generations for this merchant family.

To balance the loss of its native families, Kibworth Harcourt received a flow of outsiders into the manor. In 1358 came William de Wistow and William de Clipston. Others came from Langton, Sadington, Burton, Nosely, Fleckney and Turlangton, and also from further afield: Leicester, Wigston, Walton and Medbourne in Leicestershire, and Rothwell, Daventry and Maydenwell (Maidwell) in Northamptonshire. Most of them were amerced for one reason or another and so entered into the purview of the written records, but few took land or remained for any length of time. Those who settled tended not to be known by a locative surname. The offer of reduced rents for two years and exemption from an entry fine tempted some to take up land, but many departed at the end of the two years; only a handful stayed on to lay the foundations of a new and stable community.

This constant movement of tenants into and out of the manor affected not only the revenue but also the administrative system of the college. Before the plagues, if one tenant wished to sublet land to another there was no need to record the arrangement unless it was for more than two or three years. The name of the first tenant was a sufficient label to identify the land in question, and one rental could run for as many as fifty years. But after the plagues, when every transfer was quite literally a surrender to the lord and not just a legal fiction, and when previous tenants were no longer even in the village, it became necessary not only to record every transfer, but also to keep a record of what might be called the tenurial descent of each holding. Thus A will be recorded as taking a holding held previously by B and before that by C, a system which rapidly led to confusion when short cuts were attempted such as A takes this land previously held by C – was this the same holding as that taken by A and previously held by B? Between 1280–98 the recorded turnover of tenants had been only thirty-six, by 1352–72 it had risen to a total of ninety-eight land transfers and in the first quarter of the fifteenth century the rate of turnover was so rapid that it becomes impossible to trace the descent of all but a handful of holdings. The 1315 rental[8] was abandoned in 1372 and its replacement, if there was one, has not survived. In 1439 a new rental was made, which was updated in 1452 and again in 1484 and 1500, so that it is once again possible to record the descent of each holding from 1439 onwards. In figure 16, showing the survival of individual families over the period 1280–1700, it will be noted that the period 1412–40 has not been included for this reason.

This rapid turnover of tenants and the difficulties encountered in recording transfers made rent collection an unenviable task. The court rolls become cluttered with lengthy lists of rents and small sums of money owed by various persons which the reeve had been unable to collect. In view of this it is perhaps surprising that arrears did not accumulate more rapidly after the plagues than before. But, as the list (table 6) of reeves and the accumulated arrears at the end of each period of office shows, 1349 was no turning-point in the history of rent collection. John, son of Ive's reeveship spanned the years of murrain and famine, 1316–18, the 1320s were years of military manoeuvring in the district and of additional local levies, and generally speaking tenants were poorer, their holdings being smaller and their households larger than in the post-plague period. The difficulties of rent collection before the plagues were therefore caused, in all probability, by the inability of tenants to find the money, and after the plagues by the difficulty of finding and distraining upon tenants.

It will be noted that the reeve did not simply hand over the duty of collecting bad debts to his successor when he left office. The college held each reeve to be personally responsible for arrears accumulated during his term, which was obviously sound policy from the college point of view. As can be seen, some of the smaller sums were eventually collected, but the larger sums had in the end to be written off. In 1381 they were all written off, no doubt a wise conciliatory gesture, although there is no actual evidence of disturbance in Kibworth in this year of the peasants' revolt. After 1387 the college adopted a more realistic policy in making allowances for small debts

Table 6. *Reeve's arrears, 1290–1448*

Reeve	Period of office	Years	Final arrears	Collection/remission
Robert ad Fontem *alias* Sybile	?–1294/5	?	£11 5s 2¾d	not known
Nicholas Chorche	1295–8	3	£ 6 7s 8d	
Roger Wade	1298–1307	9	£28 7s 8d	1326/7 allowed 9s 7d
John fil' Ive	1308–17	9	£73 19s 7½d	1326/7, £62 19s 6¾d outstanding
Nicholas Harcourt	1317–20	3	£ 6 9s 2¾d	
Henry Carter	1320–2	2	roll damaged	
Richard Nicholas	1322–3	1	£ 3 18s 11¾d	
Nicholas Harcourt jun.	1323–9	6	£10 17s 7½d	
Roger Polle	1329–48	19	not given	
Nicholas Chorch } brothers	1348–9	½	£ 1 13s 3d	1381 remitted
John Chorch	1348–9	½	£ 8 3s 7¾d	1370 remitted
Robert Brun	1349–56	7	£ 0 13s 4d	1369 remitted
John Heyne	1356–7	1	£ 1 13s 10¾d	1365 remitted
Robert Carter	1357–61	4	£ 1 12s 7¾d	{1367 reduced to £14 4s 8d
John Joye	1361–4	3	£23 11s 1d	{1381 remitted
Robert Carter	1364–8	4	£ 3 11s 3½d	1381 remitted
Robert Langton	1368–70	2	£ 3 2s 4½d	{1380 reduced to £1 2s 10d
Nicholas Gilbert	1370–4	4	£11 7s 5d	{1381 remitted
Robert Carter	1375–87	17	£14 16s 8d	
William Polle	1387–1406	19	–	
Robert Polle	1406–43	37	–	
John Caunden	1446–8	2	–	

at the end of each accounting year. Accumulated arrears at this date stood at £36 13s 2d, which sum was repeated at the head of each annual account roll until 1421, when the entire administrative machinery was thrown into disarray by a rent strike on the part of the tenants and arrears rose steeply to £76 13s 9¾d by 1430. A new accounting system was introduced in 1450 and thereafter arrears seldom accumulated except in the years 1502, 1532/4, 1558/9 and 1625.

We come now to the years 1400–39 in the administrative history of the manor. As has been mentioned in passing, the college agreed to remit most entry fines during the immediate post-plague years, but would not consent to a permanent reduction in rents. The year 1381 had passed uneventfully, but by the 1390s there were instances of rebellious behaviour in court on the part of some individuals, and a dangerous level of confrontation was reached in 1401. In that year the college threatened twelve tenants with steep fines if they failed to repair their houses. Now most of these tenants had two or more houses so this was not a reasonable demand. At the same time thirteen *other* tenants surrendered their holdings as a joint protest. Ten messuages, one cottage, seven bond and four demesne virgates were involved. As things turned out this was no more than a token action; the thirteen tenants continued to hold their tenements and Merton to collect the rents, but it was a dress-rehearsal. In 1407 eight tenants refused to present the names of persons who had left the manor, and after 1409 the list of absentees was abandoned.[9] In 1414 a dozen peasants from Kibworth Harcourt, Beauchamp, Smeeton Westerby, Shangton and Sadington declared themselves for the Lollard, Oldcastle, and the ringleaders, Walter Gilbert, a chaplain who was said to have induced the labourers to join him by bribing them with 20s, and his kinsman, Nicholas Gilbert, were among those hanged a week later in St Giles' Fields (McFarlane 1952: 174). In 1421 six tenants surrendered their lands (3½ virgates), this time in earnest. In 1422/3 the village had to find £16 13s 11¼d, this being the Harcourt contribution towards an aid for the Earl of Warwick, and by 1423, 16 tenements were in the reeve's hand, amounting to 11 bond virgates, all 8 demesne virgates and 2 cottages. One-third of the manor was without tenants, representing a loss in revenue of about £10 annually. The reeve managed to let some of the pasture appurtenant to this land for a small sum: 2s for the pasture appurtenant to one-quarter virgate of demesne land and 1s 8d for customary land, but by 1433 the college had lost some £95 in rents, against which could be set a mere £13 derived from the sale of pasture.

Eventually, in 1427 the college agreed that henceforth all 18 customary virgates were to be held 'at the will of the lord' and no longer '*in bondagio*'. It also consented to reduce the rent by 3s 4d per virgate.[10] It had been a long and expensive confrontation and the tenantry had emerged victorious. However, the land was not taken up immediately. In 1427 a list of the new tenements to be held 'at will' was made out, together with the names of the nominal tenants. These tenants then came forward in the following months and registered their entry into their tenement. Not all of them did so, and some tenements remained on the vacant list until 1439. In the following years a process of exchange seems to have been going on between tenants, and the college brought out a new list in 1429, and again in 1431, on which these alterations were noted. Meanwhile the 8 virgates of the demesne still remained with the reeve. In 1434, 3 bond virgates and three-quarters of a virgate of demesne were leased *en bloc* for a rent reduced from 72s to 54s, representing a reduction of 6s per virgate of demesne land. This left 7 virgates of demesne still in hand together with a few ex-customary virgates until 1439.

In October 1439 a special court was held to finalise and record the mutual consent of both parties, the college and the tenants, to the new tenurial arrangements.[11] The old classification of land into free, customary, Apetoft and demesne was reduced to two categories, free and held at the will of the lord. The settlement covered the customary, Apetoft and free land, leaving the demesne land still to be negotiated (see below, pp. 59, 63–4). By the time the 1484 rental was drawn up, the Apetoft land had been designated land held at will and the reduction in rents agreed to earlier was restated: 3s 4d for ex-customary land, 6s per virgate for demesne.[12] The Poll Tax lists for the Kibworth region show that the majority of villages in the area had adopted the practice of tenure *ad voluntatem domini* in place of tenure *in bondagio* by 1377–81.[13] Kibworth at that date still adhered to the old tenure, but change was in the air. The earliest reference to holding at will occurs in 1331, but the movement did not gather momentum until the 1360s. In 1358 Richard Malt, a newcomer, took up land 'at the will of the lord' which his predecessor, Henry son of Nicholas, scion of an 'old' family, had held 'in bondage'. In 1360 John Joye took at will a tenement which his father had held in bondage and there are half a dozen or so equally explicit examples of change. Unfortunately, we know nothing of the negotiations or motivation which lay behind these changes in tenure, neither do any differences emerge from the study of the court rolls. As table 7 shows, the tide of change was running strongly in the last decade of the fourteenth century. Finally, tenure *in bondagio* was ended in 1427.

It is clear that the change signified something to those concerned,

Table 7. *The shift from tenure* 'in bondagio' *to tenure* 'ad voluntatem domini'

Decades	Refs to land held *in bondagio*	Refs to land held *ad voluntatem domini*
1359–69	34	7
1370–9	4	3
1380–9	6	4
1390–9	7	20
1400–9	–	8
1410–19	4	16
1420–9	5	37
1430–9	–	44
1440–9	–	17
1450–9	–	–
1460–9	–	7

but it is not easy to discern in what precisely the advantage lay. Most of what we know of copyhold tenure is based upon the commentaries of lawyers and surveyors upon practice as it had become established by the sixteenth century. Most agree that copyhold tenure was derived from customary tenure in villeinage, but none venture to describe how it differed from the same (Calthorpe 1635: 89). According to Holdsworth, there were in the fifteenth century no generally accepted formularies or categories of copyhold (Holdsworth: vol. iii). Rodney Hilton has argued that the widespread adoption of rents *ad placitum* on the Leicester Abbey estates in the period 1340–77 is evidence of a peasant market at a competitive rate. 'The tenure *ad placitum* unprotected by custom, was essentially a tenure whose terms were dependent on market conditions, on the balance between the demand for land and the needs of the lord for rent or for the land itself' (Hilton 1947: 95–104; Harvey 1977: 246–7, 255). Given the low value of land at the time, this would operate in favour of the peasant, which may explain why the initiative came from the landholders at Kibworth Harcourt and why Merton was eventually prevailed upon to concede to their demands. But this explanation is not entirely satisfactory. Rents thereafter, far from reflecting market trends, became frozen: the rent fixed in 1427 still obtained in 1700. Moreover, land transfers ceased to be recorded in the court rolls and, if the manor accounts are to be believed, no fines were taken until 1594. The hereditary principle remained firmly entrenched, and every transaction 'at the will of the lord' was also made 'according to the custom of the manor', the latter being the operative phrase. The change in 1439 seems to have been no more than an acknowledgement by the lord of an agreed drop in rents and an agreement to cease using the term *nativus*. Possibly the misleading phrase 'at the will of the lord' was inserted by lawyers to preserve the distinction between the jurisdiction of the lord's court and that of the king – it had to be made clear that the tenant was subject to the lord in matters tenurial, even when the tenant owed no more in rent than 14s for 24 acres, a derisory sum in 1700!

The terminology was again altered by the Elizabethan statute (13 Eliz. c. 10) by which deans and chapters, parsons and vicars, colleges and hospitals were forbidden to lease their lands for longer than twenty-one years or three lives. Thereafter the tenants of Merton College duly took out twenty-one-year leases at seven-year intervals 'according to the custom of the manor' but continued to be called copyholders not leaseholders – only tenants of demesne land were called leaseholders!* The custom of the manor had nothing to do with leasehold and the like but with hereditary right and, predictably, tenements continued to pass from father to son in the same manner as before. At a much later date legally minded persons have fused the two strands into a category known as 'copyhold by inheritance but without fixed fines', a necessary if cumbersome phrase which restores custom to its historic position as the key to non-free tenures (Kerridge 1969: 37f; Postan 1966: 615; Bean 1968: 20, 22–5).

Many questions must remain unanswered concerning the period 1422–39. For example, how did the reeve cope with 19½ virgates (468 acres) on his hands? A passing reference was made to a *Custod' campi* in October 1419;[14] Simon Carter was elected to act as sub-bailiff or bedel in 1425, and the salary of the reeve Robert Polle was increased from 6s 8d to 40s in 1417.[15] Reeveship had virtually become a profession since 1375, since which date two reeves had held office for seventeen and nineteen years respectively. They were trusted with far greater responsibility but they were not *firmarii*, although Polle was once described as such in 1440–2.[16] It would seem that the land was simply allowed to lie fallow, grazed by the village flocks. But if this was the case, it is difficult to understand why some tenants were prepared to lease the grazing from some of these virgates for one-third of the rent of the virgate: in 1430, for example, the pasture appurtenant to 5½ virgates was leased for a total of 16s. Although no attempt was made by the reeve or his bedel to cultivate the arable, they did arrange the letting of a number of acres. In 1421, for example, 2 acres were let from William Dawe's land for 7d an acre to

---

* Cf. *VCH Gloucestershire*, VIII, p. 232. At Tredington, leaseholds for lives replaced copyholds, but the manor court continued to treat these new leaseholds as copy-holds.

John Polle. Five acres were similarly let at 7d an acre to John
Chapman from the holding of Nicholas atte Cross. From William
Parker's land were let 4 acres at 7d each to Simon Carter, and from
Simon Carter's land were let 2 acres at 14d the acre (this was barley
land) to John Bron and 3 rods at 11d per rod to John Russell. Finally,
he let 2 acres for 7d each to John Brown from the land of John Man
junior. The reeve had thus managed to let 15¾ acres of the 468 acres in
hand. This must surely indicate a remarkably effective boycott on the
part of the tenantry. After the settlement in 1439 the demesne land
was let without delay, with the exception of 3 cottages and 3¾
virgates.

The years 1400–39 were also characterised by clandestine departures. In 1422 a newcomer, John Burbage by name, *recessit extra hoc
dominio*, abandoning a messuage and two half virgates worth 22s in
rent. In 1425 Thomas Smyth, from a longstanding village family,
abandoned his messuage and garden worth 4s. In 1427 Johne Warde
abandoned 2 messuages, a cottage, 2 half virgates of bondland and 1
half virgate of demesne land worth 41s 11½d. In 1432 Philip Barre
abandoned a messuage and a half virgate and John Aunger abandoned a cottage worth 3s 6d (see chap. 7, Ten. 15). What caused men
to abandon their land and to depart secretly in the night is not
entirely clear. True, labour and rents were expensive and agricultural
prices low, but this was universal unless, perchance, they had heard of
land available for even lower rents elsewhere.

From 1400 onwards references recur at frequent intervals to land
left 'uncultivated' and 'fallow'. To one accustomed to a fully extended
system of arable, open field husbandry, the sight of so much land
frysca et inculta must have presented a depressing sight, and the
college bursars on their annual visits certainly found it so. However,
the local peasantry were quick to adapt to the changed economic
circumstances. They put the arable down to grass and expanded their
herds. Since the land has remained under grass ever since, we still
see today what the Warden saw on his visits: high-backed ridge and
furrow, grouped into furlongs, separated by headlands, continuing
in an unending succession of crests up hill and down dale, clothed,
however, not in barley, but in grass. The seventeenth- and
eighteenth-century hedges rise and fall as they traverse the ridges
and beneath the fox coverts the fossilised pattern of the medieval
plough can be found. These ridges were a perpetual reminder of past
land use, and even in the seventeenth century the surveyor William
Allen described this land as arable. The altered land use engendered
new by-laws, and as the college regulations regarding the upkeep of
buildings, roads, bridges, the common oven and so on came to be

copied into the court rolls, so too did the new by-laws concerning the land (see appendix 3). It is interesting that in spite of the acute shortage of wood both for building and for fuel, none of this surplus land was planted as woodland. Between 1422–32, no less than seven persons were prosecuted for felling ash, two for felling elms and fines were taken for felling apple trees and willows, but there is no record of systematic tree planting until the seventeenth century.

The sense of instability caused by the constant coming and going of faces new and old and the changed aspect of the open fields received further confirmation in the village street, where many of the houses stood uninhabited, *ruinosa, totaliter in decasu* or fallen to the ground. Though dilapidations were real enough, the dismal scene has been perhaps exaggerated by the college insistence upon a return to the status quo in 1348. The tenants took the more pragmatic approach of converting derelict houses into cattle sheds and barns, but the college vigorously resisted such conversions which permanently deprived it of rent from such properties – the notion of charging a rent upon a barn being unacceptable. Since the college had always provided the heavy timbers for buildings, the timber of collapsed houses was college property and permission had to be obtained from the reeve for its re-use in other buildings. The rolls therefore abound in applications for such timber, thereby providing us with a record of building activity in the century following the plagues. In the period between the first great mortality in 1349 and the second in 1361 the villagers were active in tearing down derelict houses to improve others, an activity encouraged by the college through the provision of beneficial rents, timber and the imposition of fines on tenants who allowed buildings to deteriorate. After 1361 tenants showed themselves less willing to take land, let alone maintain redundant buildings. In 1391[17] the college set up a commission called the *Supervizores terrae et tenementorum* to make an annual presentment of decayed land or buildings. The supervisors duly presented offenders but there was little the college could do to enforce compliance. In 1429 the supervisors' powers were extended to include an assessment of the cost of repairs, which sum was then charged against the tenant – but seldom collected. In 1421, for example, Simon Carter's house was in need of repair to its timbers and roof and he was given permission to fell two ash trees in his orchard for the purpose of carrying out the necessary work. In 1423 his *grangia* of four bays was still in need of attention, as it was in 1425 and 1428. In 1429 he pleaded lack of strength and lack of cash, his chattels having been distrained by the supervisors. His tenement was therefore seized. However, as is usually the case with such forfeitures, this was no more than an empty gesture. In 1430

Simon pleaded that he could not find a carpenter, but finally in 1432 the ash trees were felled and, since we hear no more of the case, the repairs were presumably carried out. Persistence was really the only weapon the college had – unless it undertook the work itself.

The college had occasionally repaired or rebuilt a cottage before 1349 and a detailed break-down of the costs of labour and materials was duly noted in the account rolls. After the plagues such activity was more frequently undertaken – the costs being by this time recorded in the court rolls. A representative example of such a building account is that drawn up for the repair of two demesne cottages next to the dovecote in 1348/9:[18]

for taking down and removing the old cottages	2½d
for the carriage of timber and thatching straw	2s 0d
thatching straw	4s 2d
lathes	1s 3d
lathenails	8½d
carpenter's fee	4s 6d
thatcher's fee	2s 4d
for building the walls	4s 4d
Total cost	19s 6d

In the third decade of the fifteenth century the college prosecuted its policy of rebuilding with particular vigour. In 1429 Margaret Smith was charged 13s 4d for dilapidations. In 1434 William Bron Smith was ordered to build himself a house of two bays at his own expense, using the crucks and beams of the old building. In 1437 Nicholas Hopkinson was charged 3s 4d for dilapidations and in 1440 his cottage was rethatched by the college for 11s. In 1439 Thomas Bysshop was charged 16s and in 1442 the college paid out 45s 11½d on repairs to his 'insethouse', of which sum Bysshop paid a third, namely 16s.* In 1437 Thomas Saunders was granted a house *on condition* that he rebuild the four-bay house – work had not commenced by 1443. Similarly, Robert Bron undertook to build a three-bay house, of which two bays had been built by 1439, and in 1429 Robert Polle undertook to build a three-bay house *de novo* in return for a twelve-year lease on it. These are only a few examples, but they serve to illustrate the attitude of the college and the villagers towards the problem of redundant housing.

The building accounts also tell us something about the quality of

---

* This was a house of five bays for which one new pair of crucks had to be bought from John Smarte of Kibworth Beauchamp for 3s. The carpenter was paid 8s, John and Thomas Carter were paid 13s 4d for pargeting. John Carter was paid a further 20s for providing the straw and for thatching, and Thomas received an additional 1s 8d for pugging the walls. Three hundred lathes were brought from Leicester for 10½d, together with 1000 brodds for 13d. MM. 6424.16; 6321.

house construction and the costs of materials and labour. Buildings were of cruck construction on a stone footing. The walls were of mud, strengthened with small timbers where necessary, and plastered. Roofs were thatched with barley straw or were tiled. Three bays were common, the largest house recorded being that of Roger Dexter with eight bays. Stones were re-used again and again, as were the crucks and major timbers. Some stone was collected off the fields but most came from nearby Medbourn; lathes and nails usually came from Leicester. Unfortunately, it is not possible to compare costs over time, except with regard to lathes and nails, because the amounts, distances and number of days is seldom specific. For example, in the account for the repairs to the mill house in 1497/8, five loads of stone were brought for 6s 8d, seven loads for 1s 1d and one load for 4d; the carriage cost was 8d. Similarly, when repairs to the chapel were being carried out in 1299, the carpenter's mate was paid 1d a day for eight days, while the carpenter himself was paid a lump sum of 2s 2d for we know not how many days. In fact, carpenters were always paid for the contract rather than by the day.

A particularly interesting set of accounts is that for the building of a hall, chamber and stables *circa* 1448.[19] Unlike the other buildings for which fifteenth-century accounts survive, this building can be identified with a messuage site and a building which still stands today. The content of these accounts is therefore discussed in chapter seven in relation to Tenement 9.

What emerges clearly from the Kibworth experience is that the full effect of the late fourteenth-century plagues were not felt until the 1420s. The immediate effect of the 1349 mortality was to put new life into the old system, but successive high mortalities so eroded the traditional stability of the population that the land market collapsed. In order to find tenants the college was reluctantly compelled to concede not only a drop in rents but also the abandonment of labour services and bond tenure. That Kibworth was not alone in this situation is witnessed by the unusual abundance of rentals freshly drawn up in the 1420s for manors across southern England generally.* The effect of the plagues cannot be assessed by the state of the economy in the 1350s or even the 1370s; it is essential to carry the story through to its conclusion in the 1420s.

---

* See the collection made by Dr R. Faith in her unpublished Ph.D. thesis (Leicester 1962); also the bunching in the 1420s is immediately apparent as one looks at the collections of rentals in any Local Record Office.

5

Kibworth in the early modern period, 1450–1700

The court of recognitions in 1439 effectively marked the end of the post-plague transitional period. By this date even the college had ceased to look back and, if not exactly looking forward, had come to accept the changed social and economic structure. However, the documentary sources covering the second half of the fifteenth century, though much impoverished in quality and character, remain medieval in inspiration, and our discussion of the early modern period must therefore begin with a prelude, 1440–1520, in which we must view a modern society through the perhaps distorting medium of medieval archival practice.

The court leet and the court baron continued to be held twice yearly until 1458 and thereafter only at irregular intervals. In fact, in the forty-two years between 1458–1500 it met in only fourteen of those years. A professional steward was no longer employed; the college seems to have sent one of its own men from Oxford when necessary for a fee of 6s 8d with expenses, and the reeve collected such small sums as were due each year, which seldom exceeded 10s. The use of the courts as a forum in which everyday disputes could be settled therefore lapsed, and the courts became no more than a channel of communication for the college. No longer did the court leet deal with brawling, petty theft, debt, stray dogs and rubbish in the streets, it merely recorded licences to brew ale and occasionally took a fine for harbouring vagabonds. In the court baron land transfers were rarely recorded unless a heriot was in dispute, but increasing space was given to recording the ever-lengthening list of by-laws, to which the college added its own repeated injunctions to mend roads, bridges, hedges and communal buildings, such as the bakehouse, while the description of strays and the details of the steward's expenses takes up more space than the subject would seem to warrant. The court rolls, therefore, are no longer our most important single source of data, but in compensation the rentals for this period are more numerous and informative.

Four rentals survive: one for 1484 which has been interlined and kept up to date;[1] one dated by internal evidence to 1500 which shows little sign of having been used as a working document;[2] one for 1527 which actually describes each tenement and has been much interlined, but which is written in an almost illegible hand and has been badly damaged;[3] and the fourth, in book form like the third, which has had the top torn off and is therefore incomplete but can be dated to the mid sixteenth century.[4] Something can be learned from these about estate policy and tenures, about engrossing and about the increasing role played by the mortgage.

In the first place, as already observed in the previous chapter, the number of free virgates was increased by 5 virgates in 1439, and the distinctions between the old forms of non-free tenures were dropped in favour of a single category: land held at the will of the lord. Of a third category, leasehold, there is no sign at Kibworth at this date, but its precursor had emerged in the form of the $3\frac{1}{2}$ virgates held by the reeve by *indenture*. This indentured holding was made up of 3 bond virgates and $\frac{3}{4}$ virgate of demesne land which had remained in the lord's hand in 1439. In that year William Peek, who held the Hall Close for 12s, added the $3\frac{3}{4}$ virgates, together with 4 messuages, to his holding for an annual rent of 30s. In 1441/2 he built himself a barn on the site of one of the derelict cottages for 64s.[5] In 1451 John Clerke replaced Peek as reeve and in 1477 Clerke took a thirty-year indenture on the Hallyard and other tenements amounting to 4 messuages, 3 virgates and Browns Place for 54s 4d.[6]* This became a very valuable tenancy which, when joined to a reeve's own lands, made him the single largest landholder in the village. By the late seventeenth century the reeve, by then styled bailiff, was in effect the squire of the village, so that it was through these 3 ex-bond virgates that the college retained effective control of the village in years to come.

Of copyhold there is only one small indication. In the 1527 rental those who did not hold freely were classified as holding *ad voluntatem domini per copiam*. However, since no record was kept in the courts of that date of any man's landed estate the phrase must have been used inadvertently. The earliest actual copy is that for Robert Standon, dated 4/5 Philip and Mary.[7]

Secondly, we see the engrossment of holdings being pushed to its logical conclusion. Hitherto the standard tenurial unit had been a messuage and half a virgate. By 1450 many landholders occupied one or more virgates with redundant messuages. As the level of population began to pick up again by the end of the century so the market

* The barn built in 1441 was not in fact Browns Place. (See chap. 7 Ten. 9.)

for house sites recovered and we find an increasing number of houses and tofts being detached from their arable lands and sold as separate units. Thus on the one hand the arable of two or more half virgates was transformed into a single and permanent agricultural unit and on the other the number of landless cottage units increased. The occupants of these cottages may have been merely the overspill from the households of larger agricultural enterprises, but it is more probable that they were members of the artisan sector which was expanding rapidly by the sixteenth century. In other words, a polarisation between relatively large farms on the one hand and cottage-based artisans on the other was taking place – which is not to suggest a polarisation between rich and poor, for artisans were not necessarily poor (cf. Spufford 1974). Acceptance of this process is reflected in the rentals. In 1484, for example, William Polle was registered as holding half a virgate for 6s 8d and another half a virgate for 6s 8d, but by 1527 he is said to hold one virgate. This abandonment of the old half-virgate unit is general at the beginning of the sixteenth century, although the virgate as a unit was still in use in 1700 and beyond.

Thirdly, although pleas for small debts were no longer recorded in the court rolls we have a hint in the rentals of larger-scale indebtedness in the form of mortgages. The turnover of surnames on the rentals from 1439 to 1484 and from 1484 to 1550 and beyond is very high, and yet many of the names which appear on the 1484 rental and are not present on the 1500 rental reappear on that for 1527. For example, Moor held land in 1484; by 1500 the same piece of land was held by Parsons and Goode, but by 1527 it was held by Moor again. Similarly, land passed from Parker to Swan and Saunder and back to Parker; from Marshall to Fysh and Jay and back to Marshall. One of these intermediary surnames from the 1500 rental was William Hackett. His name appears nowhere else among the Kibworth records, but one Thomas Hacket was worth £8 in goods in Saddington in 1524, Robert Hacket was worth £20 at Turlangton and John Hacket was worth £5 at Galby.[8] Now in 1505 Thomas Hacket took over three virgates from Saunder in Kibworth Harcourt, and the presence of a member of a wealthy family such as the Hackets on the 1500 rental followed by occupation of three virgates in 1505 suggests a lease which was in effect a mortgage. A rental was after all no more than a list of occupiers from whom rent was to be collected, it was not a list of owners – their names could be found in the court rolls. Thus if Parker arranged to raise a loan on the security of his land from Swan and Saunder he went through the motions of leasing the land to them and their names were entered on the rental. This may seem very cumbersome, but the use of mortgages at the peasant level was a new departure in the late fifteenth century. The evidence is, however, inconclusive and some other explanation may lie behind these short-term transfers in 1500. The whole question of debt in a village community is an immensely important one, but it is a subject about which it is singularly difficult to form a coherent picture (Goubert 1960). The early court rolls contain many references to small sums claimed by one villager from another, which references I have not attempted to analyse. The seventeenth-century family papers contain copies of mortgage bonds, and the probate inventories list credits and debts and occasionally refer to the laying-out of money at interest. From these sources one gains the impression that lending and borrowing formed an important element in village life at all levels, but further than this one cannot go.

From the landlord's point of view the period 1450–1520 was one of comparative stability. Along with other estate owners Merton showed a new interest in the machinery of administration. The layout of the account rolls was altered slightly, and in 1450 the Warden himself visited the manor for the first time in over a century. The question of rents and their collection was thoroughly investigated, and much had to be committed to paper for which no formulary lay to hand. This included the detailed break-down of the figures for the building of the new hall and stables. The reeve, John Caunden, made three separate attempts to organise his material into some sort of logical and presentable form but found it impossible to avoid doubling counting.[9] The resultant pages of jottings are therefore of greater interest to us than they were of use to the Warden, one Elias Holcote.* After the Warden's visit in 1450 the names of the bursars who visited the manor were always recorded in the account rolls, as also was the name of any manorial official who had the handling of money and, after 1558, at the foot of the account roll the name of the Vice-Warden or his representative was always given.

Prices began to climb after 1490, and before 1520 many great establishments were seeking to close the gap between rising expenditure and fixed incomes by raising entry fines. The Percies asked for

---

* In 1446 Henry Sever was presented by the college to the free chapel at Kibworth. He soon afterwards resigned the living but accepted it again in 1459 after he had been elected Warden of the college in 1455 (Brodrick 1885: 160). It is doubtful if he had much time to spare for the cure of souls at Kibworth Harcourt, neither it seems had his predecessor, Thomas Robert, Fellow of the college and President of the chapel at Kibworth who, in the words of Anthony Wood, 'did out of a zeal and love he had to the college, cull all the Bursar's Accompts out of the Treasury' with the intention of compiling an alphabetical catalogue of Fellows from Edward I to Henry IV. Small wonder that the village leaned towards Lollardy.

1 year's rent on leasehold and 1½ years' rent on copyhold, and they asked for it rather frequently. Other lords demanded steeper fines at longer intervals (Bean 1958: 43f; Stone 1973). Merton seldom exacted a fine and when it did it was at the fifteenth-century level. At a time when 'certain landlords were seizing any opportunity to abolish customary terms of tenure and to let out lands on short or terminable leases . . .' Merton was not even recording land transfers. Evidently, like the Crown and the monasteries, Merton was an 'unenterprising rentier' and a 'conservative influence' (*VCH Leics.* II: 195). The tenants at Kibworth were fortunate indeed, for agricultural prices were soaring.

The period 1520–1700

In 1516 the series of wills and inventories for probate begins for Kibworth and in 1574 the parish register commences. For the first time we have documents emanating from the inhabitants themselves and not from the college or central government, and these will be the sources from which most can be learnt in the sixteenth and seventeenth centuries, and which will be subjected to close scrutiny in the following chapters. However, the college continued to exercise a certain degree of remote control and influence and its estate documents continue to be of interest. In the remainder of this chapter therefore we will examine three aspects of village life which form the background to those changes in the pattern of living to which the second half of this book is devoted. None of these three aspects, estate policy, the emergence of the gentry and the rate of population growth, are susceptible of close analysis, save perhaps the last, because the documentary base is insufficient.

The college estate documents alter slightly in character during the sixteenth and seventeenth centuries. While the account rolls continue with uninterrupted and uninformative regularity throughout the period, the court rolls in their medieval form cease altogether in 1611, and between 1500–1611 courts were held in only twenty-seven years. In 1679 the series of courts at seven-year intervals begins with MM 6448–50. The decline of the court as an administrative instrument necessitated the production of a number of *ad hoc* documents. In 1609, for example, we have a memorandum on encroachments;[10] in 1619 one on Gumley rents;[11] in about 1578 the Book of Leases was inaugurated; in 1609 and again in 1635 the estate was surveyed and mapped; the rental was renewed in the 1550s as mentioned earlier,[12] and again at the close of the sixteenth century.[13] In addition to the Merton archives we also have the private estate papers of several local families, notably the Haymes, Parker and Humphrey families, which papers have now been deposited in the Leicestershire County Record Office, where a copy of the 1779 Enclosure Award is also to be found (the working map for which survives in the Merton muniment room). Sadly, the Public Record Office houses little information on Kibworth, since the Lay Subsidy Returns are wholly unrepresentative of the size and wealth of the community and, similarly, comparison of the Hearth Tax returns with the facts on the ground might tell us something about methods of tax assessment but little of value about Kibworth Harcourt.

Towards the end of the century a major innovation was introduced, designed to increase the revenue from the estate. The Statute of 1571 had made it obligatory for colleges to lease for three lives only and by 1594 the college had converted all its tenements at will in Kibworth to twenty-one-year leases (*Statutes of the Realm*, 13 Eliz. c. x, xi). The conversion did not affect the hereditary nature of what continued to be called copyhold held 'according to the custom of the manor', but it made possible the introduction of a fine payable every seven years. In spite of inflation, rents had remained at the 1440 level for over a century so that adjustment was long overdue. The new fines amounted to about £14–15 per virgate, and £4–£10 a half virgate. Relative to the early sixteenth century these fines were of course very high, but seen against the country as a whole they were well below average. Two to three years' annual improved value was generally regarded as reasonable for copyhold with arbitrary fines. Common law courts allowed only one and a half years' value, Chancery allowed one to two years' value, or one year's value plus heriot, or two and a half years' rent. Merton adopted the last option: two and a half years' rent per year on a valuation of 8d an acre at a time when the current value was nearer 6s an acre. The college also took heriots, but again at pre-inflation levels: when cows were fetching 20s it was asking 2s 4d or 6s. The copyholders at Kibworth could indeed consider themselves fortunate in having such a landlord! Relative to their size and value, smaller holdings were charged more than larger holdings, but this was usually the case everywhere, and on occasion rents and fines were reduced or excused in cases of hardship. In 1679, for example, West's fine was reduced 'by reason of his great charge of children'.[14]

During the Wardenship of Thomas Reynolds (1545–59) the old demesne land was leased by indenture. Explicit references to the demesne cease after 1440, and to trace what had happened to it we have to work backwards from 1607, in which year three holdings consisting of 2½ virgates, 2½ virgates and 2 virgates were united to form a single block of leasehold land. It is possible to trace these three holdings back to the 1484 rental alongside the reeve's indentured holding of 3 virgates ex-bond land and a three-quarter virgate of demesne land. Significantly, none of these four holdings appear in the 1439 list made for the court of recognitions, in which only free, customary and Apetoft virgates were included. It would seem that the demesne had been divided into three holdings after 1440, which holdings had been treated as copyhold in the sixteenth century, until the doctrine that demesne could not legally become copyhold was invoked and they were transformed into leasehold.* On this occasion the opportunity was also taken to impose a grain rent of 4 quarters of wheat and 4½ quarters of barley malt. The monetary value of this grain rent together with the fixed rent of £4 13s 10d a year brought in for the college between £13 13s 5d and £22 9s 4d a year and had the effect of raising the annual rent receipts from around £27 a year to about £40.[15] Together with this single block of 7 virgates went the office of bailiff, which was filled by the Ray family throughout the seventeenth century and then passed through marriage to the Fox family and later to the Foxtons.

Other oddments of ancient demesne or pieces of waste to which the college had a claim were also converted into leasehold. In 1578 Warden Thomas Bickley (1569–86) instituted the Book of Leases for all the college estates and in 1583 the account rolls record the first of such leases at Kibworth.[16] In that year the 3¾ virgates which had been held by indenture since 1477 (see above p. 59) were leased to John Barnard for an annual money rent of 22s 1d and an annual corn rent of 6 bushels of wheat and 9 bushels of barley malt.[17] This move was perhaps in response to the recent Elizabethan statute which required colleges to take some at least of their rent in grain.† It raised the income from this holding from 54s 4d to 70s. Barnard held the lease for thirty-three years, until 1616. His successor, Cooper, held it for only three years (1617–20), Bryan for six (1621–7), Standon for fourteen (1628–42) and Guy was still holding it in 1655. By 1755 Robert Hames held it, and when the manor was enclosed Thackney Leys was allocated to Hames in lieu of this leasehold.

In 1593 a similar lease was negotiated for 2 acres arable and 2 acres meadow in the open fields called the Swathes. Parker and Eliot were

---

* 2½ virgates: (Ten. 3) Held by Iliffe 1484–1599; by Bingley 1599–1601; Escheated.
  2½ virgates: Held by Parker 1484; by Saunder and Swan in 1500; by Kynde in 1538; not mentioned thereafter until 1607.
  2 virgates: (Ten. 21) Held by Clerke/Carter in 1484; by Polle in 1527; by Coxon in 1593; not mentioned thereafter until 1607.

† 18 Eliz. c. vi: in all new college leases the lessees should pay one-third of the rent in corn or malt and at a fixed price.

to hold this for a fixed money rent of 5s 4d together with 2 bushels 2 pecks of 'good and sweet wheat' and 1 bushel of barley malt. If transport proved difficult a money equivalent could be paid according to prices in the Oxford market held next before Michaelmas.[18] Sacheverell held the lease in 1616,[19] Burdett took it in 1627 and still held it in 1655.

The Hall lands and Balks were leased for 12s 10d.[20] The collection of yards and small pieces of land which had previously been attached to the indentured bond land was separately leased for 18s 10d to Mr William Gage who had married Nicholas Ray's widow. He did not retain them for long, and in 1611 he leased the bakehouse, a cottage, a meare and a rod in West Field as copyhold to Isabel Hubbard, and the remainder was equally divided between Nicholas Porter and Margaret Goodman to be held by copy. This is an interesting example of leasehold being sublet as copyhold.

The seventeenth century saw the making of two surveys, one in 1609–10, the other in 1635–6. In 1609 a 'plat' or map had been prepared showing the parish bounds and each house within the town ditch together with its owner's name. No attempt was made at this date to map the furlongs in the three main fields or to indicate individual strips. The court roll for 1611 ends with the following instruction to the jury:

> to meete together at the mannor house upon Munday being the thudd and twenteth daye of this monethe [September] by orther of the clerk in the mourninge of the same daye and they shall make he perfecke survey of all the lands of this mannor . . . as faire as they knowe and believe and they shall subscribe the same with their lands and deliver the same to Robert Raye before the 27th day of this moneth upon payne of everie one makinge defaults to forfeit 20s. And if any of them shawe obstinat in not agreeinge to the rest of his fellows he shall forfeit 40s.[21]

Unfortunately, the written schedule which should have resulted has not survived, if indeed it was ever made: we have only the 1609 map.

Plague in the year 1605 had taken its toll of village landholders and this may have created the need for a new survey and rental (see fig. 2). However, it may be more than a coincidence that in 1607 John Norden published his *Surveyor's Dialogue*, thereby putting within the reach of the Fellows at Merton some of his experience in estate management. The publication of Fitzherbert's *Boke of Surveying* in 1523 was followed by a more-than-usually detailed rental for Kibworth made in 1527.[22] Barlee's *Concordance* appeared in the same year as the college Book of Leases. Charles Calthorpe's *The Relation betweene the lord of a mannor and the coppy-holder his tenant* came out in 1635, and in that year Abraham Allen was commissioned to prepare a map and written survey of Kibworth for the Warden, Sir Nathaniel Brent.[23] Merton was not alone in its interest in map-making in Leicestershire. In 1636 Henry Paxton prepared a survey with maps for the neighbouring Brudenell manors of Slawston, Glooston, Cranoe and Stonton Wyville,[24] and in 1638 a map was made of the manor of Wistow (Eden 1975). Allen's map of Kibworth is beautifully produced, the survey is elegantly bound, but neither seems to have been used for practical purposes in the estate office. In the survey, land was apportioned between arable, meadow and pasture following pre-plague ratios and valued at 8s, 5s and 4s respectively. Since most of the arable was under grass by 1636, and the entry fines at the end of the century were still based on a land value below 4s the acre, Allen's survey bore no very close relation to the realities of estate management in 1636.

Finally, in 1679 a new series of court rolls was instituted.[25] The court met every seven years, presided over by the Warden, Sir Thomas Clayton, and the steward, Thomas Baker, gent. Copies were presented and all transfers which had taken place during the intervening years were formally enrolled. The by-laws were then examined and reviewed and these also were formally engrossed. These elaborately presented parchment rolls are accompanied by bundles of working-papers which had formed part of the preparatory work: lists of all the inhabitants, lists of land transfers, of heriots received, of by-laws, of trees planted, of disputes over wells and so forth, together with the tenants' copies. These working-papers for the courts held in 1679, 1686 and 1693 are of considerable interest, but the story they tell belongs to the social and economic world of the late seventeenth century and so carries us beyond the scope of this present study. Belonging to the eighteenth century, but more relevant to the earlier period, is the map made in 1779 preparatory to the enclosure of the parish. This map shows the furlongs in the three open fields and the strips within the furlongs, which are numbered, together with a detailed plan of the village.[26] The accompanying survey has not survived but a copy was made of it in 1818 by T. Eagle and this gives the total amount of freehold and copyhold land held by each tenant after enclosure without, however, indicating the position of land in the fields.[27] No copy survives of the post-enclosure map. The aerial photographs of the parish, made by the Royal Air Force in 1947,[28] clearly show the ridge and furrow as depicted on the pre-enclosure map, and they also show that the ridges were shorter and the headlands and sikes broader than was indicated on the map (see chap. 6).

In the medieval period the only 'estate policy' which affected the village was that of Merton College, but by the seventeenth century a number of private individuals had large enough 'estates' in the village for their policy to influence the lives of their neighbours. Of these new gentry the Parkers were the first to arrive in both senses of the term. They made their first appearance in the village in the late fourteenth century. By the mid fifteenth century they held several freehold and copyhold tenements including Tenement 6, which remained their main dwelling house until 1678 when they moved to the very fine Renaissance mansion on the village square, which is today known as the Old House. Tenement 6 was thereafter inhabited by a series of bailiffs: John Lamplugh, attorney, Captain Corrance and George Eyre, all themselves younger sons of gentlemen families. By 1737 Joshua Reynolds, who had married Rebecca Parker in 1616, ran it as the Crown Inn. Just how the Parker family made its fortune remains a mystery, but there is no doubt that they added 'tone' to the village in the seventeenth century.

The Parkers were joined in 1558 by Sir Thomas Ray, Yeoman of the Wardrobe of the Beds to Queen Mary. In consideration of his service, the Queen granted him the leases of the Tynemouth Priory lands in Preston, Eschirton, Whitley, Monkseyton, Morton, Enesdon and Backeworthe, worth £105 7s 0d in grain and rents.[29] He was also made collector and bailiff of Burton Lazars, Burton Lisle and Kibworth Beauchamp.[30] The family continued to remain based upon the parish of St Martin-in-the-Fields and to be connected with the Inns of Court throughout the seventeenth century. It is not clear how they had first come to be associated with Merton College, but Thomas's grandson Robert was a scholar at St Alban's Hall, Oxford, and was named co-attorney for Kibworth Harcourt with William Savile in 1605.[31] The Saviles of Orton, Northamptonshire, were bailiffs of the manor from 1560–77 and from 1598–1606.

The Foxes, the Foxtons and the Haymes were of yeomen origin. The Foxes held freely in the village before the plagues and so did the Haymes – if they were the descendants of the Heyns. Both families built up lands by careful husbandry and equally careful marriage alliances. Thus the Bryan, Lount and Watts inheritances were joined in the hand of William Haymes in the late seventeenth century and his daughter's son, Lebbeus Humphrey, settled in the village and bought up the Sheffield and Parker estates together with other tenements. The Foxes allied with the Foxtons and eventually took over the Ray leaseholds. These yeomen gentry proved more enduring than the Rays and the Parkers and by Enclosure in 1779, Haymes, Humphrey and Foxton between them owned two-thirds of the village in freehold, leasehold and copyhold.[32] Of other fourteenth-century peasant families, only the Carters survived in 1779, holding a few acres of freehold. The family papers of the Parker, Haymes and Humphrey families speak of a steady policy of buying up small sites. Lebbeus Humphrey bought up the whole of the south side of Hogate, tenement by tenement, as the cold wind of agricultural depression forced the occupants into debt, foreclosure and sale.[33]

In addition a number of non-resident gentry held land in Kibworth, notably Sir Tobias Hawes of Stoke Albany, Northamptonshire, Mr Joseph Sacheverall and one Buswell, probably the same man as George Buswell, gent., who bought 30 acres of land in Wigston in 1623; he was related to the Sir Euseby Buswel Pelsant Bart., of Cadeby, who was a feoffee for the school in 1722 (Nichols 1790: 640; Hoskins 1957: 203).* These gentlemen, Hawes and Buswell in particular, made a point of buying up small cottages and odds and ends of grazing, the sort of property hitherto occupied by widows and the poor. Hawes, for example, acquired the lease of 'le Pale' near the town cross for 4d a year,[34] he held it from 1611–16, after which it was held by two tenants each paying 4d.[35] Coleman's share passed to William Sheffield of Great Bowden in 1648 and in 1646 he bought the rest of the Coleman land. (Sheffield had been ejected by the Puritans from the rectory at Ibstock and resided in Kibworth so that his children might enjoy the benefits of the school. He died in 1673 – *ibid.*). Harold's share went to Buswell in 1621. Hawes and Buswell also held tenements 23a–b, 30, 33, 34, 35, 36, 37. Similarly, a property called 'le Mure', worth 6d a year in rent, was held by a succession of gentlemen: Parker 1610–21; Rylye 1624–34; Mr Joseph Sacheverall 1634–6; Wilkinson from 1636–42; and finally by Parsons. The hedges and ditches were leased for 6d by Bale, 1605–21, and Mr William Gage, as we have just seen, leased the bakehouse, a cottage, a meere and a rod in the West Field in 1611. Since these men were not resident, except Sheffield, they had no household to cater for the board and accommodation of their herdsmen and other paid labourers. It would therefore have been necessary for them to provide some other form of accommodation in the form of tied cottages, for which it was also necessary to acquire some grazing, since no stint in the common fields was appurtenant to such properties built on the waste. Hence their interest in such small properties. Both Smeeton Westerby and Kibworth Beauchamp de-

---

* In 1798 John Buswell of Islington, broker, was handling the financial affairs of the Rev. Thomas Thomas, husband of the Foxton heiress, Elizabeth (Bodleian: MS Northants. b.1, f.64).

veloped as weaving-centres, but there is no evidence that Kibworth followed suit, and there is little reason to suppose that these were weavers' cottages.

Thus it was that by the close of the seventeenth century Kibworth had been transformed into the typical 'closed' village, with a small circle of gentlemen and yeomen farmers, a growing number of craftsmen and tradesmen, a few husbandmen or small farmers and a group of landless labourers for whom housing was provided by their employers. The old and the retired tended to live under the same roof as the younger generation, but there was still a need for housing for the poorer members of the community – those whose names one comes to know through the alms clause in men's wills – and, for these, new houses were built on the few remaining patches of waste land at the crossroads and along the verges of roads. These were not migrants, they were the indigenous poor.

Population

Domesday statistics show south-east Leicestershire to have been relatively densely populated, with 10–15 persons per square mile as against 2.5–10 persons over most of the rest of the west Midlands (Darby and Terrett 1954: fig. 149, 150). Kibworth followed the general pattern with twenty-two householders and three serfs on 1203 acres. The standard holding had already been reduced to 24 acres, but we have little idea of the size of household such a holding was considered capable of supporting.

The level of population rose steadily during the twelfth and thirteenth centuries, and at the point when the Merton muniments take up the story most of the 24 virgates had been subdivided into 12-acre tenements, each supporting a household of five to seven persons over five years of age (see chap. 9). The extension of arable at the expense of pasture in the fields and the encroachment of housing onto the village roads and green bear witness to this phenomenon. A Malthusian crisis seemed to be approaching, but there are indications that the members of the village community were not unaware of the fact and took their own precautions. Land was not subdivided any further and, generally speaking, adults without land or an established trade remained celibate. The number of reproductive units was thus limited to the number of tenements and the rate of population growth held in check. Nevertheless, holdings were small, households large and the standard of living dangerously low, thus leaving the population particularly vulnerable to famine, cold and epidemics. In the light of seventeenth-century experience, we can assume with a fair degree of confidence that the mortality rate in thirteenth-century England was high, though not high enough effectively to reduce the size of households (Wrigley 1969: 77–8; *VCH Leics.* III: 132).

The plagues of the late fourteenth century, however, broke this particular equipoise: the total number of adults was substantially reduced, which made possible a return to larger holdings. Moreover, the size of households was reduced as celibate members were able to gain a livelihood, to marry and to set up separate establishments. Low agricultural prices and the constant shift of tenants from one village to another betokens a continuing low population level throughout the fifteenth century. Households remained small, tenements remained relatively large, the standard of living improved. It is generally accepted that the level of population began to rise again towards the end of the fifteenth century – certainly by the early sixteenth century – and Kibworth does not appear to have been an exception to the general trend (Hatcher 1977). At the same time agricultural prices improved – from the growers' point of view – so that on the larger holdings, producing a marketable surplus, income and nutritional standards were not affected by the increased size in households. But on the smaller holdings – of which there were not many at Kibworth – and in the households of the poorer craftsmen, a fall in living standards may have taken place.

Unfortunately, for the period 1450–1574 we have no *good* documentary evidence for Kibworth, only the late medieval court rolls and the probate material. We shall therefore have to content ourselves with a summary of demographic events at the national level. In the words of John Hatcher:

> The mid 1460s, the early and late 1470s, and the years at the turn of the century saw severe outbreaks of plague in many parts of the country, and in the autumn of 1485 there occurred the first, and by far the most lethal outbreak of the strange disease known as the English Sweat, which according to chroniclers spread over much of England killing 'young and old and all manner of ages' in great numbers.
>
> (Hatcher 1977)

The new rental made for Kibworth in 1484 may have followed such high mortality in the 1470s.

In 1516 the series of probate records for Kibworth begins. The tradition of making a last will and testament was strong in Kibworth, among rich and poor, men and women, and one or two wills survive for most years, rising to seven in 1538 (five deaths were noted in a court held in January 1539 – MM 6442.1), six in 1543–4, six in the notorious influenza year of 1558–9 and nine in 1592, in which year there were forty-one deaths in the summer months alone, and a total of 111 in the course of the epidemic which lasted from the winter of 1591/2 to the winter of 1593/4. As can be seen the wills provide only a very crude indication of disruptions to the demographic balance (Hollingsworth 1969: 237), but they are of some use in the absence of other documentary evidence. In 1640–1, for example, no entries were made in the parish register, but the number of wills rises to six for the two years concerned. According to Shrewsbury, plague was widespread in 1640 and was reported at nearby Oakham and Stamford (Shrewsbury 1970: 399). The parish register for Husbands Bosworth records exceptionally high mortality in that year, and in 1641 the death toll was high in Market Harborough and Great Bowden.* There is therefore good reason to believe that 1640 and 1641 were also years of high mortality in Kibworth.

The earliest surviving register for the ecclesiastical parish of Kibworth begins in 1574, and the demographic history of Kibworth can be resumed, but since the inhabitants of Kibworth Beauchamp and Smeeton Westerby are also included in the register these two vills will henceforth have to be included in the story.

The annual totals for baptisms and burials have been set out in the graph (fig. 1), and the years of exceptional mortality have been

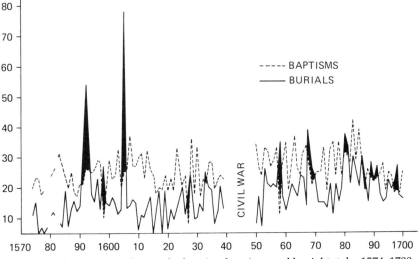

Fig. 1   Kibworth parish: graph showing baptism and burial totals, 1574–1700

* Dr R. Schofield has very kindly allowed me to use his date distribution lists of parishes with epidemics (RSS 112) and the annual mortality totals for the parishes of Medbourne and Holt, Great and Little Bowden, Slawston, Market Harborough, Saddington, Wigston Magna and Husbands Bosworth.

shaded in. The total number of births in the period 1580–1678 was 2758 as against a total of 1996 deaths, giving us an excess of 762 births over deaths. However, the pattern before and after the Civil War is noticeably different, and if we compare the birth totals for the fifty years immediately before the War (1591–1639) with the fifty years after it (1649–98) we find ourselves comparing the figures 1181 with 1355, giving us an excess of 174 births in the later seventeenth century. The corresponding mortality figures for the same fifty-year periods were 867 and 1017, giving an increase of 250 deaths in the later period. In other words, births exceeded deaths before the Civil War, but in the second half of the seventeenth century this favourable balance was reversed and deaths exceeded births.

In order to be able to assess the significance of this reversal and to explore its causes we need to know more about the total size of the three communities, the migration rate, the nuptiality rate, the age and sex of those who died and the causes of death. In 1603 there were 444 communicants, in 1670 there were 197 households (66 in Beauchamp, 63 in Harcourt and 69 in Smeeton Westerby), in 1676 there were 551 communicants and in the early eighteenth century about 150 families (*VCH Leics.* I: 267). In total numbers, therefore, the parish was expanding, though not greatly. We have no figures for migration, but in Kibworth Harcourt the tendency was for younger sons to leave the village (see chap. 9). The marriage data is summarised in table 8. Since the marriage ceremony was solemnised in the parish church of the bride we have figures for Kibworth women but not for men, and this is not in fact very useful, since these women for the most part lived the rest of their lives in other villages. If they had acquired an immunity to plague, typhoid, typhus, measles and other diseases, they took it with them and the women marrying into the village may not all have acquired a similar immunity. However, we can note that the number of Kibworth girls marrying before the War was 240, and after it 230, although the number of girls born remained constant, and in the years immediately following high mortality the number of marriages increased, possibly implying a higher rate of widow remarriage.

We turn now to the age and sex of those who died, and the causes of death. On the matter of age the register does not allow of any great subtlety. Before 1625 no more than the name of the person buried was given, after that date the name of the father was also given in the case of children, but unless the burial followed very shortly after the baptism we have no way of knowing the age of the children who died without going through the additional procedures of family reconstitution. Since only the Harcourt families have been reconstituted no

Table 8. Kibworth parish: decennial tables of births, deaths and marriages

| Decade | Births | | | Deaths | | | | | | | | | Marriages |
| | Girls | Boys | Total | Summer 26 March – 30 September | | | | Winter 1 October – 25 March | | | | Total per decade | |
				Men	Women	Children	Total S	Total W	Men	Women	Children		
1580*–90	91	131	222	31	20	4	55	52	27	25	0	107	58
1591–1600	110	131	241	63	68	7	138	125	64	54	7	263	85
1601–10	138	122	260	58	60	6	124	74	31	36	7	198	46
1611–20	111	123	234	21	29	7	57	61	23	28	10	118	26
1621–30	117	123	240	42	17	5	64	80	39	39	2	144	42
1631–9	102	104	206	32	34	2	68	76	40	34	2	144	41
Subtotals	669	734	1403	247	228	31	506	468	224	216	28	974	298
1640–8 Civil War													
1649–58	137	130	267	25	25	27	77	100	34	37	29	177	36
1659–68	143	144	287	19	33	40	92	101	24	36	41	193	13
1669–78	119	159	278	26	31	41	98	77	30	19	28	175	67
1679–88	152	144	296	32	36	54	122	130	37	34	59	252	79
1689–98	117	108	225	35	47	39	121	99	35	40	24	220	35
Subtotals	668	685	1353	137	172	201	510	507	160	166	181	1017	230
TOTALS	1337	1419	2756	384	400	232	1016	975	384	382	209	1991	528

* No entries for 1582
S = Summer
W = Winter

distinction between neo-natal mortality, child mortality and adolescent mortality has been attempted. The fact that not all child deaths have been identified before 1625 affects not only the adult mortality figures but also exaggerates the increase in child mortality figures after the Civil War, and this in turn affects the following discussion on the medical causes of death.

When we come to observe sex selective mortality we find that between 1591 and 1639 male deaths exceeded female deaths by 114, whereas in the 1649–98 period female deaths were in excess of male deaths by 14. Therefore, not only in aggregate figures was the number of deaths higher in the late seventeenth century but a greater proportion of that figure were women and children. Was this due to a change in the pattern of disease, to diet, to altered work and living arrangements, or to a decline in the standards of midwifery? We know that standards of food and housing, which had improved very markedly in the sixteenth century, continued to do so until the end of the seventeenth century (see chaps. seven and nine). We know next to nothing about standards of midwifery at that date and will have to leave that an open question. However, we can explore the pattern of disease further.

As figure 1 shows so clearly, the early seventeenth century was characterised by a relatively low level of mortality interrupted by two very serious crises years, 1592 and 1605. The later half of the century saw nothing so dramatic in the way of crisis mortality, but was dogged by more frequent and prolonged periods of fairly serious epidemics and a higher general level of mortality, even when allowance is made for an increase in the total size of the population at risk. Figure 2 anatomises three of these crisis periods in order to distinguish winter from summer mortality, and table 9 shows the respective mortality rates of men, women and children in these three epidemics.

The histogram for 1590–3 shows a steadily rising mortality level through the winter of 1590/1, the summer of 1591 and the winter of 1591/2 followed by a very abrupt increase between April and September 1592. Winter brought some respite, but the level rose again until March 1593. The profile is indicative of a vector-borne epidemic, that is, an infection transmitted by ticks, lice or fleas. There is a slow build-up, an abrupt climax and a gradual decline. In this case it could have been plague or typhus. At the national level this was not a serious plague year, although outbreaks were reported in Devon, in Northumberland and at Norwich and, more significantly, at Leicester (Shrewsbury 1970: 247). Mortality was also high at Saddington and Wigston Magna in 1590, at Husbands Bosworth in 1591, at Great

Table 9. *Sex selective mortality*

Dates	Season	Men	Women	Children	Subtotal	Totals
	Winter 1591/2	12	7	3	22	
1592	Summer 1592	20	18	2	40	
	Totals	32	25	5	62	62
1605	Summer 1605	33	34	2	69	
	Winter 1605/6	5	5	0	10	
	Totals	38	39	2	79	79
	Winter 1657/8	3	10	2	15	
1657/9	Summer 1658	7	4	6	17	
	Winter 1658/9	6	4	6	16	
	Summer 1659	3	4	2	9	
	Totals	19	22	16	57	57
	TOTAL	89	86	23	198	198

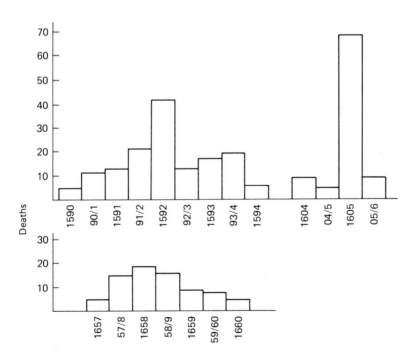

Fig. 2   Three crisis mortalities at Kibworth Harcourt

Bowden, Wigston and Husbands Bosworth in 1592 and at Medbourne and Holt in 1593 (Wilshere 1968–9: 45–71; Griffin 1967–8: 24–34). Moreover, the Thames and the Trent were very low in 1592 and draught, while it did not affect the harvest at Kibworth, may well have affected the quality of the water supply and so facilitated the spread of typhoid or dysentery. Whether plague, typhus or typhoid, men were more susceptible than women.

Kibworth escaped the terrible plague outbreak of 1603 but in 1605 the parish suffered a serious summer outbreak. The profile is so abrupt that this cannot have been a vector-borne epidemic, it must have been water- or droplet-carried and since it is unlikely to have been pneumonic plague it was probably typhoid or dysentery. Once again, bubonic plague was not general in the country in this year although Leicester had been affected in 1603 and was to suffer again in 1607 and 1609, and Northampton was infected in 1605. On this occasion men and women were equally susceptible and it could be argued that the older, indigenous males in the community had acquired immunity, while the younger generation and the women who had married into the parish were facing the contagion for the first time and were thus at greater risk.

The epidemic of 1657–8 typifies the crises of the second half of the century. It developed during the winter of 1657/8, peaked in the summer of 1658 and continued into the following winter. Several members of the same household tended to succumb. Mortality was high in 51 of the 399 parishes studied by Schofield for 1657 and in 62 parishes the following year. It was also high in the neighbouring parishes of Slawston and Market Harborough and it had been high in Great Bowden in 1653–4 and again in 1658. It would seem likely that this epidemic was typhus or possibly malignant influenza. In two years, 19 men died, 22 women and 16 children. It does seem that the older generation, having survived previous encounters, had acquired immunity, leaving the women and children at risk, but one cannot prove this without case studies based on family reconstitution, and even then one would not know if survivors had actually contracted the disease and recovered.

Apart from disease, the higher death rates of the second half of the seventeenth century could be attributed to famine. Death by starvation was still all too common on the Continent at this date and also, it has been argued, in the remoter parts of England such as Cumbria (cf. Appleby 1973: 403–531; Goubert 1960). Although it is certainly possible that one or two of the very poor may have died of starvation or hypothermia as they do in our cities today, there is no evidence of widespread starvation, nor was famine likely in this rather affluent corner of Leicestershire, with relatively easy access to the East Anglian grainlands. Of the years associated with high mortality in Kibworth, only 1698 coincided with bad harvests. Similarly, years associated with bad harvests, such as 1612 or 1639, were not followed by high mortality.

6

The open fields and husbandry

Three pre-enclosure maps survive for the manor of Kibworth Harcourt. One, made in 1609, gives details of the messuages in the village and the manor boundaries. The second, made in 1635, fills in to some extent the boundaries of the three open fields and names the Ways, the Cowcommon and other internal features, while the third, made in about 1780, gives all the furlongs and the strips within the furlongs. After enclosure, the greater part of the land went down to pasture, so that the old ridge and furrow remains plainly visible in most furlongs. Comparison of the 1780 map with aerial photographs made in 1947 shows that the ridges on the ground and the tenurial strips marked on the map coincide (Beresford M. 1948: 34–45; 1949: 472; 1950: 34–55; Kerridge 1959: 14–35; Mead 1954: 34–42). Therefore, we have an almost complete picture of the open fields as they existed in 1780. What is lacking is the name of the owner of each strip, but this lacuna can to some extent be filled in by deduction.

There were three fields: the East, the North, and the West. The East Field or Howe Field (map 4) is halved by the Cole Pit Way, made up of Haagate and Whistle Gate. These run through the centre of the field following the valley floor in an east–west direction and lead into the lordship of Turlangton. South of the Cole Pit Way lie 243 acres, which in turn can be subdivided into an arable area of high land rising steeply to 400 feet around the sixteenth-century windmill, and falling away southwards to a low-lying pasture area abutting on the small stream which forms the boundary between Kibworth Harcourt and Kibworth Beauchamp. In the fifteenth century this stream was liable to flood its banks and needed constant attention for which the whole village was responsible. When Market Harborough was founded, between 1160–70, a new track was easily formed across the common pasture of Kibworth, called Harberg Gate (Hoskins 1965: 53–67). In 1726 this became a turnpike road and in the days of the mail coach was named the London Road. In 1300 it crossed the stream at Church

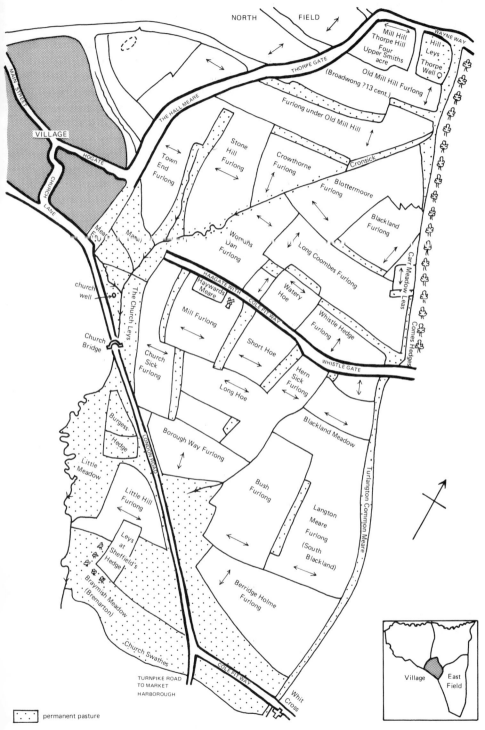

Map 4   The East Field or Howe Field

Ford but by 1443 we know from the court rolls that there was a bridge.[1] Branching east from this road runs another branch of the Cole Pit Way to West Langton, and at the point where this track reached the boundary there stood in 1609 a cross, called Whit Cross. From this point north to Whistle Gate stretched Langton Meare Furlong, sometimes known as South Blackland. Berridge Holme Furlong is not referred to before the seventeenth century and its name suggests low-lying pasture land. West of the Langton Meare ran the Hern Sike abutting on Short Hoe and Long Hoe, which give their names to the entire field. These two and Mill Furlong are probably among the oldest arable furlongs in this field. Church Sike is first mentioned in association with untended gutters in the fifteenth century,[2] but its high ridges could suggest earlier cultivation.

North of the Cole Pit Way lie 171.9.14 acres. The land slopes steeply up to the site of the fifteenth-century mill. Once again the area can be subdivided according to its natural features. A spring bordered by rough pasture runs diagonally across it from north-east to south-west and to the south of this the furlong names indicate relatively late cultivation: Whistling Valley, Long Coomb, Blottermoore and Blackland Meadow. Moreover, the furlongs are not approached by regular herringbone pattern ways as are the older furlongs. Just north of Cronsike we find Crowthorne Furlong, a triangular piece of land, probably an old spinney as its name implies. With the possible exception of Stone Hill Furlong, the remaining furlongs are among the oldest in the township. The reasons for this statement will be discussed later.

The North Field (map 5) covered about 415.0.03 acres in 1635 and unlike the other two fields was not bisected by a road or way. This was because its arable was concentrated in the southern and eastern parts of the field and approached by the Thorpe Gate and its branching ways, while the western half was comprised of leys, moors and common pasture. The London Road formed the western boundary of the North Field. It began at the cross by the north-eastern corner of the village, where the Cole Pit Way from Wistow entered the village, and ran northwards following the line of the valley to Burton Bridge and thence to Leicester via Glen Magna. In 1421 the village was ordered to mend the '*regiam viam versus pontem vocat Burton Brigg*'[3] and the 1609 map depicts a sturdy single-arched bridge.

The most arresting feature of the North Field is Banwell Furlong. This measures 1000 yards from east to west. The length of its furrows, which run from north to south, varies from 166 yards at the west end to 113 yards at the centre and 153 at the east end. J. E. Sutton found that ridges on Oxfordshire clay lands were seldom more than 500

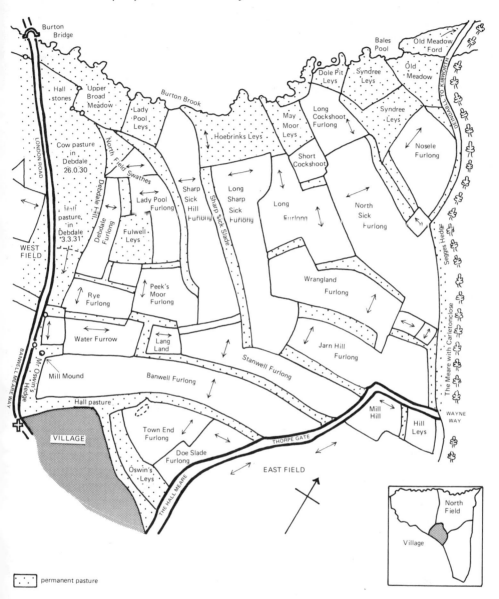

Map 5   The North Field

yards long or less than 100 yards, and varied in width from 4–24
yards, though most were between 7–13 yards in width (Sutton 1964:
99–115). E. A. Pocock found that the ridges at Clanfield in Oxfordshire were between 176–220 yards in length (Pocock 1968: 85–100). So

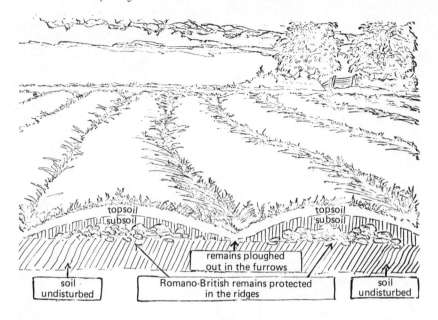

Map 6   Archaeological section through the ridges of Banwell Furlong

by Oxfordshire standards the Banwell ridges are short, but it must be remembered that the land in the Oxfordshire villages cited is flat while the gradient at Kibworth is fairly steep. The shape of the Banwell Furlong is similar to the furlongs at Clanfield, Chalgrove (Gray 1969: 20) and Water Eaton, but more of this later. A cross-section of the ridges at the west end of Banwell Furlong exposed an undisturbed layer of Roman remains under the ridges and nothing under the furrows (see map 6). Therefore, we can be certain that the ridges have not wandered or been altered in direction. We can also be certain that the furlong was cleared in Roman times and as at Withington in Gloucestershire (Finberg 1964: 21–65) there seems no reason to believe that the site went out of habitation between *c.* 360 when a Julian coin was dropped in the village and the early sixth century when Saxon immigrants made their presence felt (Hoskins 1934: 110–47). We can, therefore, take Banwell Furlong as a model of a Romano–Celtic or early Saxon field at Kibworth. What are its characteristics? Accessibility: it is reached by a way at both ends and provided with headlands 45 feet wide; short ridges, on average about 150 yards long and 7–8 yards wide; great length – there are 117 ridges in Banwell. These characteristics are repeated in several other furlongs in the three fields. Reference has already been made to Old Mill Hill Furlong, Furlong under Old Mill Hill and Town End Furlong in

East Field; in addition we should note the Ridgeway and Cold Acre Furlongs in West Field, and also Low Ash and Town End. And in the North Field there are Stanwell, Langland and Water Furrows which together equal Banwell in ridges. Long Furlong is not long in shape but its ridges are unusually long; Wrangland is, as its name implies, crooked; Jarn Hill or Eagle Hill was probably without its eastern extension when originally laid out. It should be noted that all these are readily accessible from Thorpe Gate or from the open pasture of Debdale.

With the exception of Syndree Leys, all the remaining furlongs and meadows are mentioned in the literary sources which begin *c.* 1275. One may hazard the guess that Syndree Leys, which derives its name from the old English *syndrig*, meaning 'not joined to others', was assarted by a free tenant. This and other meadows bordering Burton Brook lie on an outcrop of micaceous, silty lower lias and were prized as meadowland, being divided into doles or twodelrods (two-dole-rods) and were reached either by the deindabll to Kibworth or by the Sharp Sike, which retained wide grassy sidelands even when under the plough, or from the Cow Pasture, which at no time came under the plough according to the evidence of maps and aerial photography. Alan of Portsmouth[4] held arable on Sharp Sike as early as 1300, which gives us an interesting hint of communal action by the villagers that does not reappear again until the sixteenth century. The ploughing-up of Sharp Sike and other sikes which provided access to arable furlongs as well as grazing can only have been permitted or tolerated by common consent of the landholding community (Homans 1941: 85). The expansion of arable at the expense of pasture was widely practised in thirteenth-century England (Postan 1973: 214–48) and almost certainly at Kibworth where the population per square mile was relatively dense. The small furlongs lying at a distance from the roads in the North and West Fields probably belong to this period rather than to the pre-Conquest epoch.

The West Field or Carrs Field (map 7) is the largest and most varied of the three fields. The Cole Pit Way or Carrs Gate enters the lordship from Wistow at the Cole Bridge Ford and runs in a south-easterly direction along the valley to meet the London Road and the Main Street of the village at the cross already described. To the north of it lie 294.3.06 acres and to the south 173.3.10 acres. Possibly the most interesting feature in this field is the Upper Ridgeway Furlong. As has been pointed out in chapter one, the Jurassic Way may have run through Kibworth, in which case it would have followed the course of the Ridgeway through the West and North Fields. It ran along the southern boundary of the four Ridgeway Furlongs and Shower Gate,

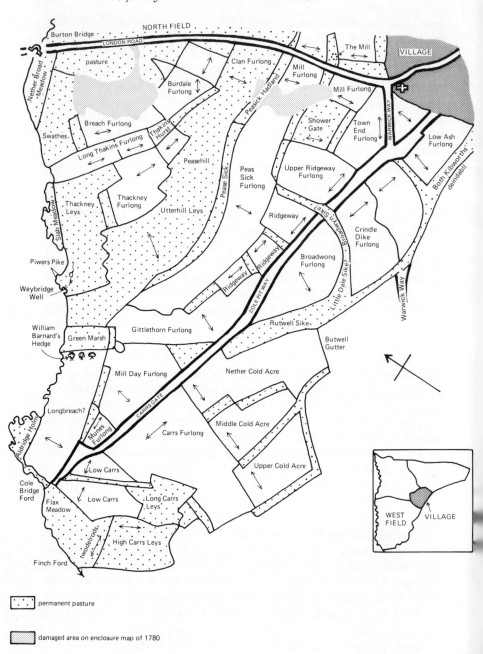

Map 7   The West Field or Carrs Field

and along the southern headland of Banwell Furlong to Thorpe Gate where it turned north-east to Tilton. The Ridgeway Furlongs seem to belong to the same period of clearance as Banwell and Stanwell Furlongs; their ridges are the same in length and total half the number in Stanwell. To this group we can perhaps add Upper, Middle and Nether Cold Acre. The position of Town End Furlong and Low Ash Furlong together with their high ridges would indicate for them also early cultivation. The practice at Kibworth seems to have been open fields from a date well before the Conquest.

South of the Ridgeway lie two furlongs of arable surrounded by sikes. The name of one of them, Crindle Dike, and the circle on the ground which shows up on the aerial photograph, suggests an ancient enclosure or barrow. Beyond the Cold Acres lies an extensive area of meadow called Carrs which has at some date been cultivated, either in the thirteenth or the nineteenth century but not at an earlier date. To the east of Carrs lies a perfectly flat stretch of meadow known as Flax Meadow, the only indication we have of flax cultivation in the township.

North of Carrs Gate lies an irregular patchwork of fields traversed by spring waters and gutters which drain into Burton Brook. Further eastward the ground rises to take two furlongs both of relatively late and impermanent cultivation, Peas Sike and Utterhill Leys. Eastwards again lies an area known as Thackneys, which perhaps bordered an old reed bed which supplied the villagers with thatching reeds. The area became broken up into small rectangular fields which, as already suggested, may have been the result of thirteenth-century conversion of pasture and waste. Beyond Thackney lies pasture and Swathes. There were Swathes in each of the three fields: these were meadowlands (apart from 2 acres arable in the North Field) and were held by lease in the seventeenth century, which would imply that they had once formed part of the demesne.

This preliminary survey of the open fields can be usefully concluded by a few general observations. First, some of the road system was almost certainly older than the field system. Cultivation began at the roadsides and worked outwards. The result was a coherent system of fields abutting on the roads and separated from each other by broad headlands or ways. Beyond the early fields lay a belt of pasture which was later brought under the plough by communal agreement, resulting in long common furlongs where the terrain permitted, or in small rectangular furlongs where less suitable land was pressed into service.

Second, there seems to be no trace whatsoever of a reorientation of ridges in the fifteenth or sixteenth century, such as has been envisaged by S. R. Eyre (Eyre 1955: 80–94). Post-enclosure cross-ploughing has resulted in a chequer pattern which shows up clearly on the aerial photographs on the few fields where this has been attempted – mostly within living memory. The cross-section on Banwell Furlong already referred to showed clearly that no reorientation had been carried out of the ridges on this furlong. Nevertheless its headland describes a reversed S sweep. The ridges on Banwell and on all the furlongs are straight, splaying out slightly at the upper end with a very slight bias leftwards, but hardly enough for one to be able to say that the ridges follow the line of a reversed S. All the ridges are more or less standard in length, about 150 yards. From this it seems clear that straight ridges in combination with a reversed S *headland* can be associated with very early cultivation, and that there is no need to posit a drastic reorientation of ridges in the early modern period. Moreover, the Kibworth layout is not peculiar to south-east Leicestershire but is to be found in Oxfordshire, and a hunt through other pre-enclosure maps would probably reveal examples in many other areas.

The acre: its size, distribution and use

In 1300, where this study begins, the majority of peasant proprietors were half virgaters, all growing the same crops, under the same conditions, each for his own home consumption. The difference in prosperity between one peasant and the next depended largely on the size of his family and the size of his holding. This chapter will, therefore, be devoted to determining the size of his holding in acres, the distribution of these acres over the three open fields of the town and the degree of manœuvre permitted to him within the limits of communal farming, regulated by village by-laws, in the use to which he put his land.

The standard acre is a relatively modern unit of land measurement and had not been universally adopted in Leicestershire as late as 1700. This is understandable, since ridge and furrow does not readily lend itself to standardisation; each ridge or selion has its own length and its own width, it must be ploughed as a single unit – one cannot plough with an ox-team one side of a ridge or one end of it only; between each ridge runs a drainage furrow which is not cultivated. However, people of that time had a disconcerting way of talking about 'acres' when they meant a ridge or a group of ridges. Therefore, each piece of evidence needs to be sifted with care and every opportunity taken to cross-check conclusions (Maitland 1907: 383–5).

For this reason I have chosen to make an initial approach by comparing two sources which ignore the ridges altogether: Domesday (*VCH Leics.* I: 323), which estimates in ploughlands, and the Survey made in 1635, which measures in standard acres and no doubt for this reason was never a working document.[5] The manor and township of Kibworth Harcourt were coterminous, so that the estimates of total area made in the two documents cover the land of both customary and free tenants and can be directly compared with each other.

Domesday provides our starting-point. It runs:

> The same Robert (de Vesci) holds twelve carucates of land in Cliborne. In King Edward's time ten ploughs were there. In demesne there are three ploughs and three slaves; and ten villeins and six sokemen and five bordars and one frenchman have five ploughs. There are 16 acres of meadow. It was worth 40s 0d; now 60s 0d. (*VCH Leics.* I: 323)

Before using the information so provided, a point of interpretation needs first to be cleared up. There were ten ploughs in 1066, there were only eight in 1086, yet the value by that date had risen from 40 to 60 shillings. In his introduction to the Domesday entries for Leicestershire, Professor Stenton noted that this discrepancy is very common in the county, especially for the south and south-east. He set himself to elucidate these entries and established in the first place that the formula 'TRE there were x ploughs' did indeed mean that there were actually x ploughs there at that date; it was a more precise way of saying 'There is land for x ploughs.' Secondly, he suggests that the 'valuit' entry does not refer to the value of the manor in 1066, but to its value after it had been devastated by the Conqueror in the latter part of 1068, when he marched from Warwick to Nottingham to suppress the first revolt of Edwin and Morcar. The swathe of devastation extended from High Cross to the Soar at Loughborough and along the Welland valley as far as Slawston and Medbourne, as can be clearly seen when the 'valuit' entries are plotted on a map (*VCH Leics.* I: 277–305). Ten ploughs at Kibworth certainly fit the later evidence where eight ploughs do not, so I am prepared to accept Professor Stenton's conclusions and to work on the TRE figure of ten ploughs.

The total acreage in 1635, including meadow and pasture, was estimated to be about 1440 acres by the surveyor Abraham Allen. This same area was estimated to be 10 ploughlands in 1066, not all of it arable. From 1300 onwards the virgate was consistently taken as 24 acres and, since the population was less rather than more in 1066, we can take the virgate of that date to be not less than 24 acres. In 1086 there were ten villeins, six sokemen and one frenchman occupying five ploughlands. At Kibworth, villeins and sokemen alike held virgate holdings but the frenchman held more, probably three. In all, one can say that there were approximately 20 villein virgates occupying five ploughlands. This would give them 480 acres arable and 240 acres pasture. There were three ploughlands of demesne cultivated by serfs and a further two ploughlands which had gone out of cultivation between 1066 and 1086, possibly as a result of the devastation caused by the Conqueror in 1068. In all, then, there were five non-villein ploughlands, which were possibly divided between arable and pasture along the same lines as the villein land, that is 480 acres arable and 240 acres pasture.

By 1300 the demesne had been halved in size and the Apetoft estate had come into being. The latter was in fact 240 acres arable and could conceivably have been formed out of the demesne waste. By the same date the number of villein virgates had increased from 20 to $26\frac{1}{2}$, thereby reducing the 240 acres of villein pasture to 84 acres. In 1635 the cowcommons and balks were still reckoned to be about 89.2.1 acres, though by this date of course much of the arable had also been returned to impermanent pasture or leys.

However approximate such a line of deduction may be, it illustrates with a sufficiently tolerable degree of accuracy the general point that, between 1086 and 1300, the expanding population had been accommodated not only by halving villein virgates but by greatly reducing the area of pasture. With 240 acres of villein pasture, it would hardly have been necessary to graze the stubble except to manure the land and, consequently, there would have been no need for common husbandry on the open fields (Thirsk 1964: 3–25). With only 84 acres of pasture and some 47 villein households, each with one or more beasts, pigs, geese and sheep, stinting of both pasture and stubble would have become a matter of necessity, and with it, common husbandry.

It is not always easy to discover the number of acres to the virgate in a particular region and, moreover, virgates have a way of shrinking in size, especially during the period 1086–1300. Since I have just stated authoritatively that the virgate at Harcourt contained 24 acres, and will later use this figure in the more exact context of peasant budgets, it would be as well to set forth the evidence at this juncture, showing how this figure was arrived at.*

* Chibnall found that at Sherington the Domesday virgate was reckoned at 30 acres but that arable did not amount to more than 20–5 acres including the fallow (Chibnall 1965: 106).

Table 10. *Number of acres per yardland of arable and meadow in 1635*

Copyholders	Yardlands	Total acreage arable and meadow	Acreage per yardland
Mr Raye	7	171.25	24.46
W. Watts	3	73.5	24.5
W. Burgess	3	82.5	27.5
T. Coleman	3½	89.5	29.5
J. Bryan	2½	62.5	25
H. Allwood	1	28.5	28.5
R. Standon	3	68	22.6
T. Carter	2½	56.25	22.5
N. Oswin	1½	40.25	26.8
R. Burdett	½	17.75	(27)
		(less 4.25 for the swathes)	
W. Goode	½	18	(36)
R. Bryan	½	12.25	24.5
H. Bryan	½	12.25	24.5
R. Chapman	½	11.25	22.5
R. West	½	12.5	25
W. Carter	½	13.75	27.5
N. Lount	½	11.75	23.5
Freeholders			
W. Parker	3¼	87.75	27
W. Graunt	1	24	24
Mr Buswell	3¾	99.5	26.5
Mr Sacheverell	4	118.75	29.68
G. Fox	2¼	57	25.3
N. Kinde	1	26.5	26.5
Widow Foxton	¼	5.25	(21)
R. Carter	½	12.25	24.5
J. Smith	½	10.75	21.5
Widow Hames	½	5.5	(11)
Glebe	–	7.5	–

Thus, 7   yardlands contained 22.5 acres each
    12.5 yardlands contained 24.5 acres each
    8.75 yardlands contained 25.0 acres each
    6.25 yardlands contained 26.5 acres each
   11.75 yardlands contained 27–8 acres each
    1.75 yardlands are anomalous and are bracketed thus: ( )

The 1635 schedule gives the total acreage of arable and of meadow held by each tenant in each field together with the size of each tenement in virgates. Table 10 sets out this information in tabular form and from it one can see that the largest single group of virgates was that containing 24.5 acres. The remainder were for the most part between 26–8 acres and a few were just under the standard level and contained only 22.5 acres. So 24 acres of arable and meadow in 1635 was considered to be a virgate, and with each customary virgate went a share in the common pasture known as the 'cowcommon', which included a stint of four cows and twenty-four sheep. The dispersal of land which had constituted three virgates in the early fourteenth century allows one a glimpse of the assemblage of arable strips and shares of meadowland known as 'two-dol-rods' which made up a virgate at this earlier date. The terriers of these virgates are set out in appendixes 2 and 3. From these we learn that a virgate consisted of some 20 acres arable with additional meadow and rights to common pasture. We do not know how many twodelrods there were to an acre but there could be as many as ten to the virgate and Adam de Kibworth held 5½ acres pasture with his half virgate, and one can assume that with each virgate went about 4 acres meadow and pasture. Thus the thirteenth-century virgate consisted of some 20 acres arable and 4 acres pasture and meadow.

However, one cannot be content with these fourteenth-century land measurements unless one has some way of demonstrating that the acres referred to in the terriers are standard acres and not field acres. Fortunately, it is possible to do this. The physical lay-out of the open fields and the furlongs in them has already been described and the point made that the ridges on the ground, which can be seen and counted without difficulty on the 1947 aerial photographs, correspond with the tenurial strips marked in by the surveyor on the 1780 map. Further, it has already been noted that the length of the furrows on Banwell Furlong is roughly the standard length for all the early furlongs. To measure the length of the Banwell ridges was not an impossible undertaking.

Banwell Furlong measures 31 standard acres and contains 117 strips, the last 17 of which on the eastern end are less than full length on the ground. Interference is caused at the centre of the furlong by a rectangular pit on its southern boundary (possibly the original 'Ban-well'?) which causes the furrows in this area to be some 120 feet short of the norm. If we leave these shortened furrows out of our calculations, we are left with an average furrow length of 480 feet. The ridges are 24 feet wide which gives us an aerial measurement of 24 by 480 feet or 11,520 square feet. The Banwell ridge measured just over a quarter of an acre.* This is very convenient, since we can take one ridge to equal approximately one rood. For all practical purposes the villagers would have reckoned in ridges, but when asked to

---

* I am glad of the opportunity offered here to record my gratitude to Mr Aggas of Kibworth Beauchamp who measured these ridges for me on a cold January day.

provide information in terms of roods and acres the bailiff would have substituted rood for ridge and by this form of ready reckoning his four-ridge acre would have been slightly larger than a standard acre in surface area, but about the same as a standard acre in ploughed area if allowance is made for wastage in the furrows.

There remains one more interpretative hurdle to be overcome, however. In the sixteenth century the appraisors of corn in the field for purposes of probate were usually careful to value the sown land by the acre but occasionally slipped back into using what was for them the more familiar unit, the 'land'. These lands were not in fact acres but ridges and, if the ordinary man behind the plough had not yet grasped the difference between an acre and a rood in the sixteenth century, how often did he get it right in the thirteenth century? The simple answer probably is that the ordinary man was not usually asked to engage in such arithmetical exercises in the thirteenth century; these were left to trained men. It was a fashionable doctrine among estate managers in the thirteenth century to standardise the measurement of the acre wherever possible, the standard unit being the king's perch of sixteen and a half feet (Oschinsky 1971: 314–15). As is so often the case when bureaucratic logic flies in the face of common sense little progress was made on this front until the eighteenth century and enclosure, but Merton College was not untouched by the spirit of enthusiasm and in 1318 the Fellows had a measured survey made of the demesne land at Cuxham (Harvey 1965: 42), and it is possible that they had a similar survey made for Kibworth at the time when they took over the manor. Certainly the terriers made at that time use roods and acres; that is, all except one, that made for Alan of Portsmouth's land,[6] one and a half virgates of which remained unmeasured and we get the typical terms used for unmeasured lands as they lay in the furlongs: he had 109 selions (i.e. ridges), 3 roods, 2 *culturae* (unusually large or small or odd-shaped ridges) and 2 bovates (i.e. 1 virgate). The moral would be that although for the sixteenth century one must treat land measurements, especially those given in the inventories, with due caution, for the thirteenth century one can accept the distinction between acres and roods as accurate but must allow that both are only approximations to the standard units.

On these grounds it would be safe to assume that the average ridge approximated to a standard rood in area, thus giving a customary acre which was only marginally larger than a standard acre. In the early medieval period the acre was made up of about twenty acres arable and four acres of meadow or pasture, although in practice the arable had encroached heavily on the pasture, as is evident from the ridging up of sikes and scrub areas in the thirteenth century. The 1635 Survey assigned twenty-four acres of arable to the average virgate together with carefully regulated rights to grazing on the cowcommon. The survey was of antiquarian interest only, since by the seventeenth century most of the so-called arable was under grass, but it serves our present purpose well, since it confers the belated blessing of tradition upon what was in the late medieval period the unorthodox use of pasture for arable: in 1300 it probably was the case that all twenty-four acres were under the plough, or very nearly all. Thus for the period 1300–1700 we can assume a twenty-four-acre virgate, of which between twenty and twenty-four acres were arable.

Now, in comparison with many other areas, twenty-four acres is rather small for a virgate, so it is worth noting that in 1066 the virgate, or land for one household, may have been nearer thirty-six acres. If, as discussed above, 1440 acres were judged sufficient for ten ploughs in 1066, then the assessors must have been reckoning on 144 acres to the ploughland, and if on four virgates to the ploughland then with thirty-six acres to the virgate, a much more normal size for this type of soil than twenty-four acres.* This does not mean that thirty-six acres were ploughed each year, but that thirty-six acres could support the average tax-paying household with one plough. It is instructive to note that in the seventeenth century thirty acres was considered a safe size for a small tenant farm in this area: the tenant would never fall behind with his rent on a farm this size.[7] The reduction of the size of virgates from thirty-six to twenty-four acres represents the first phase in the process of accommodation to rapidly increasing population growth in the thirteenth century. The second phase was characterised by the subdivision of virgates into thirds or halves held first jointly by two families and later as two separate tenements. Across England both processes can be seen taking place and the point at which we pick up the story at Kibworth is at phase three: if each family had only twelve acres and the number of mouths to be fed continued to increase, could subdivision be carried any further?

The distribution of strips in the open fields

Each of the three open fields at Kibworth is so self-contained that one is tempted to wonder if, at any time, they had in fact been self-sufficient units. If they had, it was before 1300 since, from that date,

---

* The *average* size of the virgate is 30 acres, but in Cambridgeshire for example 36 was more common except on the fens, and in Gloucestershire 48, though here virgates of 60 and 80 acres were not unusual. The most frequent equation for virgates to the hide or carucate is 4, but again 3, 5 or 6 is not uncommon.

three types of evidence all point to the same conclusion, namely, that each tenant held strips in each of the three fields.

The first is a terrier drawn up in about 1300 for Alan de Portsmouth's land. Alan had received from his uncle, William de Merton, a share in the manor of Kibworth Harcourt which amounted to about five virgates.[8] Of these, one and a half were without a customary tenant and, as we have just seen, a terrier was made in which the strips involved were described in terms of selions and *culturae*. The term *cultura* normally means a furlong, but, as is so often the case with medieval surveys, where a rich variety of local terms have to be squeezed into the very limited Latin vocabulary of a local clerk, *cultura* could not here mean a whole furlong, and what the clerk seems to have been searching for is a term to describe a piece of land held in severalty, smaller or larger than a normal rood.* At any rate, Alan held a *cultura* in the East Field at Thorpe's Well and in the West Field *tota cultura super* Seladewong, which may refer to Slab Meadow. In the North Field he held three parts of four selions in Darlicrest and three parts in Norshul, and half a selion next to Maymoor and *in Debdale unum selionem in uno loco et in alio loco unum selionem*. From this we learn that there were three great open fields each made up of several furlongs and a few *culturae*. We also learn that Alan's selions in the furlongs normally lay side by side, since if they did not, as in Debdale, the clerk was at pains to say so. Lastly we learn that Alan's share of land was fairly evenly distributed over the three fields. Thus he has 37 selions (i.e. ridges), 5 roods and 1 *cultura* in the East Field whose total acreage was 414.4.34; 42 selions in the North Field out of the 415 acres in that field and 30 selions, and 1 *cultura* in the West Field out of a total acreage of 467.6.16 acres.

Our second piece of evidence is the Survey of the whole manor, made three hundred years later, in 1635.[9] In the case of fifteen of the copyholders, the Survey sets out clearly how much land each tenant held in each field, from which it is evident that their land was evenly distributed over the three fields. For the remaining customary tenants and the free tenants the Survey simply gives the total arable 'in the fields'. The reason for the abrupt change on the part of the surveyor is not known, but we are fortunate in being able to compare the 1635 Survey with the Terrier of School Land made in 1675.[10] This Terrier names the tenants whose land abutted on each strip of school land and among these neighbours are many whose lands were lumped together by the 1635 surveyor as lying 'in the fields'. The School Terrier shows that their land also was distributed across three fields

---

* The term is used on one other occasion in the Kibworth records, in the court rolls for December 1422 (MM 6421) where it is used to mean a bundle of 3 roods.

Table 11. *Number of strips mentioned in the 1675 School Terrier*

	East Field	North Field	West Field
Ray	5	6	6
Watts	2	3	2
Burgess	1	2	1
Sheffield (Coleman)	2	0	3
Carter[a]	6	2	8
West	0	1	0
Lount[a]	3	2	2
Parker[a]	15	13	13
Graunt[a]	3	0	2
Fox[a]	2	1	3
Smith[a]	0	1	1
Cave	2	1	2
Guy (Allwood)	3	6	4
Cox	4	4	8
Parsons	0	2	3
Clarke	0	1	3

[a] No details of distribution are given in the 1635 schedule

and, moreover, was not consolidated within those fields but lay in scattered strips. Evidently, enclosure such as had been achieved by that date had not seriously undermined the open field system with its communal grazing rights over the stubble.

The third approach is a more general one: the probate inventories for village after village in Leicestershire show that during the sixteenth and seventeenth centuries farmers were planting exactly equal acreages of peas and spring barley. If communal grazing was still practised, and judging by the constant alteration to by-laws it was, then these farmers must have had an equal number of acres in each of the three fields. As against the hundreds of examples for the early modern period, we have only one for the medieval, but it tells the same story. In 1314/15 an enquiry was made into the state of Nicholas Sybile's land.[11] It was reported that of his 15 acres under plough, he had 7½ acres in the peas field and 7½ acres in the barley field, 2½ acres of which were sown with wheat.* Interestingly, in the following year Nicholas's heir, John Sybile, sowed 7d worth of oats as well as 18d worth of wheat, 4s worth of peas and 4s 6d worth of barley.

* It was a not uncommon practice among the larger holders to sow a few acres of wheat or rye, because if the consumer wished to bake bread he needed to add either wheat or rye to get the dough to rise. One furlong in the north field was therefore allocated to these cereals.

Land use

The characteristic feature of the Kibworth region before the four-teenth-century plagues was the self-sufficient family farm. Each farming unit could normally be expected to support a family and its livestock in corn and fodder, and to yield very little in the way of surplus to sell and, consequently, little cash with which to buy in supplies. As we have already seen, the most common size of holding was twelve acres and the average family size in the region was five persons (see chap. 9). Intensive farming within the limits of medieval technology would have been just sufficient to match the output of holdings of this size with the family needs, including the payment of rent. What made the match imperfect was that an average household could be expected to lay out cash for the purchase of essential commodities which the holding did not produce, such as salt, iron, the occasional purchase of stock or payment of tax or amercement, in addition to the regular payment of rent and tithe (see chap. 8). How then was this cash generated? One possible source could of course have been ancillary occupations such as carting, occasional wage work or village crafts. However, in a society as overwhelmingly rural as Kibworth, these ancillary sources would probably have been insufficient to provide an average household with the cash needed. We must therefore assume that some produce was sold to yield cash, thus leaving the family with food and fodder below what would now be considered an adequate level or subsistence. This is, in fact, what happened and may still happen in peasant communities cultivating holdings theoretically capable of maintaining families on the margin of subsistence (see table 15).

Had the region been more favourably situated with regard to market outlets a very different pattern might have emerged, with smallholders specialising in the production of cash crops, such as wheat or wool, and buying in barley for home consumption. In such a situation high land values and an active market would almost certainly have seriously eroded family attitudes to land and given rise to a greater variety in the size of holdings. In fact there were many farming regions of England structured along these lines, but south-east Leicestershire was not one of them (Kosminsky 1956; Goody *et al*. 1976; Wrigley and Smith forthcoming; Dyer 1980; Raftis 1957; De-Windt 1971).

An agricultural system is a complex organism and we can seldom hope to reconstruct the total picture for any one region. At Kibworth the account rolls are not as informative as one would have wished, since the demesne had been broken up into quarter-yard land units and leased as such to villagers since at least the mid thirteenth century. Therefore, we have little direct evidence for sowing rates and yields and have to borrow figures from neighbouring estates (see chap. 8), but for other aspects the court rolls more than compensate for the lack of detail contained in the accounts. Of first importance to our present investigation are the by-laws, which begin to be written down in the fifteenth century and become steadily more detailed, until by the seventeenth century we are in a position to be able to reconstruct the farming calendar with some precision (appendix 4). The Orwins and Professor Ault have already made us familiar with the broad outlines of farming practice in pre-industrial England (Orwin 1967; Ault 1972). The Kibworth by-laws allow us to observe how these practices had been modified to meet particular local needs, and how they were altered over time as there grew up alongside the traditional communal system a vigorous and commercially orientated system of capitalist farming, albeit on a small scale.

The staple crops at Kibworth throughout the period were peas and spring barley. Since bread-flour made from barley alone will not rise without the addition of some wheat or rye flour, a small portion of the barley field at Kibworth was allocated to rye, and later to wheat. The only other crop was flax, grown in Flax Meadow beside Burton Brook south of Cole Bridge Ford in the West Field. Barley likes a well-prepared tilth but it grows too rank and tall if that seed-bed is too rich, so its place in modern rotations follows roots on a light soil and wheat on heavy, cold soils of the Kibworth type (Watson and More 1962; 234–5). Today, at Kibworth, it follows peas,[12] and the indications are that this rotation was also followed in the early modern and medieval periods, thus letting the peas have the full advantage of the fallow and the barley the advantage of a better tilth on better-broken land. We learn from the by-laws for example that the field to be laid down to fallow was divided into sheepwalks, and a 1611 by-law adds: 'No inhabitant shall keep his sheep on the separate doles until six days after the grain called whitcorne has been carried away.' The term 'whitcorne' in the Leicestershire inventories was used to describe both wheat and barley, but since both straw crops occupied the same field the distinction is not of importance in this context; what matters is that fallow followed a straw crop not a peas crop. The rotation was probably fallow, peas, barley, fallow. The barley sown was spring barley, probably six-row barley or possibly four-row, since neither were good for malting and the region was characterised by a lack of emphasis on brewing before the late fifteenth century when possibly two-row barley was introduced from East Anglia.

The heavy clay soil and equally heavy plough used in these parts of

Leicestershire made necessary a plough team of up to eight beasts, most of them milch kine but including some mares.[13] The land was ploughed once before December for barley and once before February for both barley and peas, after which sowing could commence as soon as weather conditions permitted. By the seventeenth century, if some wheat was to be sown on the larger farms, the land was ploughed on 11 November and sown by 30 November. Barley has a shorter growing period than other crops and could be harvested in early September, or earlier if the quality of the straw was to be preserved, but the grain often had to be kiln-dried.* Peas ripened later, but they too were probably cut before reaching full maturity in order to retain the food value of the haulm, and were left stacked in the field for some time to dry out slowly. Broadly speaking, two of the three fields were available for pasture for three to four months at the end of the year, while the fallow could be grazed for seventeen to eighteen months. In addition there was the common hay meadow, called, perhaps misleadingly, the Cowcommon, together with a number of meadow closes called Swathes bordering the two brooks, the rough pasture verging the drove ways and watercourses and lastly, the headlands. These sidelands, sikes and headlands were suitable for tethering beasts and their total area was really quite extensive, as can be seen on the aerial photographs which show so clearly the internal boundaries where cultivation gave way to verges (see frontispiece).

The quality of these pastures varied considerably and they were exploited accordingly. The Cowcommon was allocated to cows (including oxen). It provided the early spring bite, followed by a hay crop and aftermath and could be rested in autumn. In 1679 some of the fallow field was added to the cow pasture and was 'doled out'. This suggests the permanent grassing over of arable land and a decrease in the number of sheep in favour of cattle. The fallow field had time to sward over tolerably well and therefore provided the staple pasture for the sheep. The stubble provided autumn pasture for all forms of livestock, thus relieving the fallow and Cowcommon. The sikes, sidelands and headlands provided tethering grounds for cattle and horses; the latter, it will be noted, had no especially designated area. These different categories of pasture made necessary the constant moving of stock from one area to another and consequently engendered a formidable number of by-laws, and although the by-laws tell us little about numbers and profits, they tell us a lot about attitudes and management. So let us spend a little time on animal husbandry, beginning with cattle.

* According to the by-laws, the harvest took place as early as 1–12 August.

There was a persistent tradition among Kibworth clerks to note the colour of any beast mentioned; we therefore know the colour of all the strays and of most of the animals taken as heriot. The cows were commonly red and could have been of the same stock as Lincolnshire Reds or Devons; a few were black, possibly of Welsh origin; and one was described as *ahakeford* and may have been a Hereford (red with a white head). They would have been much smaller than the modern cow, seldom weighing as much as 1000 pounds and rarely yielding as much as two gallons a day when in milk. Therefore, they would not have needed more than 15–20 lb of hay a day during winter or 20 lb of barley straw and peas haulm. One acre of barley today yields about 21 cwt (2352 lb) of straw if cut before fully ripe, and this amount, at the rate of 20 lb a day, would feed a cow for four months. One acre of peas would yield 3340 lb of haulm or feed for 112 days. Now the cow did not need 40 lb of fodder per day, neither did the medieval crop yield as much straw or haulm, so taking one with the other we can take as the rough guideline that the straw and haulm off 2 acres of arable would feed a cow for six to eight months.* In addition there was a small amount of hay available; one cannot say precisely how much, because we do not know the size of each yardlander's share of the hay crop off the Cowcommon, but there was at least 1 acre per yardland in the Debdale Cow Pasture and his total share may have been as much as 3 acres. Now an acre of good meadow today can yield as much as 5 tons, but one would still not expect to get more than one ton off old meadow, so let us take one ton per acre in medieval Kibworth. At 20 lb a day the produce of one acre (2240 lb) would last a cow four months. So a man with a full yardland of 7 acres barley, 7 acres peas, 7 acres fallow and 3 acres meadow could in theory overwinter six cows. However, he also had horses and sheep to feed – his stint was twenty-four sheep – and young stock to bring forward, so we shall have to reduce the number of cows. But before turning to the winter keep of sheep let us complete this study on cattle by examining their summer pasture. The wetness of the land made stall-feeding over winter inevitable, roughly from October to May, but for the first week in May the cattle were allowed to take the first bite off the Cowcommon; they were followed for a brief period by the horses. The Cowcommon was then fenced off for hay and the cows returned to their stall regime until 24 June, when they could be tethered on the headlands until 1 August. Stretches of sideland could also be leased for the summer months by

* William Marshall, reporting on Cheshire in 1809 observed 'a cow in the course of a year will consume the produce of three statute acres of land' [namely, hay and straw thereof] (York 1818), vol. 2, p. 40.

those who could afford them, provided the reeve was paid in advance, but there were other stretches open to all, the only rule being that no man could tether his animals on the same spot twice. After the hay had been carried from the Cowcommon, sheep were put on it from 18 July until 1 August, then one cow and calf per yardland could graze on the aftermath. There they remained until September when the harvest had been carried and the gleaners finished, then those who held arable land were allowed to turn their horses and cattle onto the stubble, until the land became too wet.

Cows were thus primarily stall-fed beasts. Sheep on the other hand were kept out on the pasture for the better part of the year. The total area of arable at Kibworth was 1296 acres, all of which were available for grazing from harvest to late November, and one-third of which, as bare fallow, was available for eighteen months, namely, 432 acres. These 432 acres were doled out as sheepwalks and were occupied by sheep more or less continuously, being joined by pigs and geese in autumn. According to Grosseteste (*Rules*, c. 9) 'each acre of fallow land can support at least two sheep for one year', but this was probably an over-optimistic estimate, since the stocking rate on good pasture even today is two ewes with their lambs. Professor Hoskins's estimate of $1\frac{1}{2}$ ewes per acre is more realistic and according to this rate the Kibworth fallow could support 648 sheep (Hoskins 1965: 151). In the early fourteenth century there were at Kibworth 24 yardlands and 8 one-quarter yardlands and if we divide the estimated number of sheep by the total number of yardlands we reach a figure of twenty-four and a half sheep. The actual stint was in fact twenty-four sheep,* which would seem to confirm our estimate of both the stocking rate and the acreage of fallow. Except in unusually bad weather the sheep spent the winter and spring months on the fallow, but were allowed to take the first bite of the aftermath after the hay had been carried from the Cowcommon, from 18 July to 1 August, when they were joined by other beasts. After the harvest, horses and cattle were the first on the stubble: sheep were debarred until six days after the harvest (1678) and by 1686 were not allowed onto the barley field until two days after the grain had been carried and not onto the peas field until twelve days after the harvest. They remained on the stubble until it was ploughed, 11 November in the case of wheatland, December for the first ploughing of the barley field, February for the first ploughing of the peas field.† On 25 March the sheepwalks were

---

* A memo dated 1609 (MM 2784) states that thirty sheep per yardland was 'unreasonable'.

† If the ground became too wet they were kept in movable folds of wooden hurdles, thatched at the sides and tops, and fed on straw and haulm. The repair of the common fold was a constant injunction in the court rolls.

officially closed, and it was in March and April if not earlier that dry feed would have become necessary at the rate of 2–3 lb hay a day, or 1 lb peas with $\frac{1}{2}$ lb hay. Twenty-four sheep, each consuming 2$\frac{1}{2}$ lb hay a day, would demolish a ton of hay in only thirty-seven days. At most a yardlander would have 3 tons of hay, some of which he would wish to reserve for his horses and for his cows immediately before calving, so let us work on the lines that he had two months' feed. Our yardlander needed at least 2, preferably 3 acres of straw and haulm together with some hay per cow and 2 tons of hay with some haulm and straw for his sheep. He had in fact about 14 acres of straw and haulm and some 3 tons of hay, which would allow a good 3 acres arable each for his cattle with 1 ton of hay, leaving 2 acres and 2 tons of hay for the sheep. By being less generous to his cows he could, on this showing, keep an additional heifer or a horse.

Neither cows nor sheep were often found straying; cows because they were in stall, sheep because few places were out of bounds. Pigs were sometimes found foraging in the village street at night, together with the occasional duck, but the most frequent occupiers of the pound were horses and mares (see below pp. 102, 104). This may have been partly due to the fact that horses, though numerous in the fourteenth century and increasingly so in the fifteenth, were relatively late arrivals on the agricultural scene. From time immemorial the Cow-common had been assigned to cattle, and the fallow had been assigned to sheep, leaving only the verges and stubble for horses in competition with other stock. No type of pasture has been assigned exclusively to horses, and it was left to the ingenuity of horse owners to find sufficient pasture for them in early spring and between 24 June and 1 August along the sikes and headlands, but they were not allowed on the sidelands, and had to be led not driven to the tying grounds (1434, 1595). After 1 August all horses had to be confined to their owner's land until 12 August or after the grain had been carried. This rule was necessary because the mares were in work during the harvest season drawing the hay carts, and foals and yearlings tethered on the headlands near where their dams were working, or tied to the traces as was sometimes the custom, or even allowed to follow the carts freely, were an immense nuisance and could also cause damage to the still-standing crops. After the harvest had been carried horses were allowed onto the stubble, together with the cattle, sheep, pigs and geese, there to remain until taken into stall for the winter. One small concession made to the horse owner was the right to put horses on the Cowcommon from 8 May until the meadow was put into defence.

For the early twentieth-century farmer the season of heavy work was the winter, and it was during this season that he had to find something in the order of 16 lb old oats and 16 lb clean, hard hay each day per horse. During the off-season in summer he had to find only bean straw and some 5–6 lb concentrates per half day's work. The medieval horse was not only a much smaller animal than ours, requiring less food, but was used more for harrowing and carting than for ploughing on the heavy Leicestershire soils, and its work season ran, therefore, from late spring to autumn, thus coinciding, for the most part, with the season of outdoor grazing. The dry-food requirements of the medieval horse were therefore relatively modest: according to Walter of Henley (c. 39) a *working* horse needed a daily ration of one-sixth of a bushel of oats and 12d worth of grass in summer, while the author of the *Anonymous Husbandry* (c. 49) advises that mares should be given oats from 29 September until 3 May, at the rate of one peck every three nights (Oschinsky 1971). No oats were cultivated at Kibworth, but horsebread was baked in the common oven, a mixture of barley chaff and peas with possibly a little barley. However, for the most part horses subsisted on barley straw and haulm in much the same manner as the cows, with a wisp of hay from time to time. As we have seen, a full yardlander could have managed to feed a horse in addition to his stint; he could also of course have kept more than one horse at the expense of a cow or some sheep. In the course of 1348–9, the plague year,[14] a total of twenty-five animal heriots were taken, of which ten were cows, ten were horses and five were ewes. Clearly, in this matter of 'the best' beast, horses were considered 'better' than cows, and a horse was taken rather than a cow. It is perhaps surprising how many smallholders had opted to keep a horse. Those who did usually had an extra quarter yardland of demesne which would have yielded a few extra acres of straw, but may not have entitled the holder to a larger share of the Cowcommon – although *demesne* meadow may have been appurtenant to demesne arable. Presumably the owner of the horse-mill kept a horse or two (though the miller from the windmill had only a ewe in 1349), while the reeve, the carter, the clerk, the leech, the brokers, the draper and the wheelwright may well have preferred horses to oxen for transport. Nevertheless, several other Kibworth smallholders with an extra quarter or half virgate surrendered a cow in heriot, and we may conclude that the horse, still given the lowly title *iumenta* in the fourteenth century, was not indispensable.

In the light of this fourteenth-century evidence, Leicestershire's later fame as a centre for rearing large black carriage horses was less of a novelty than the eighteenth-century commentators supposed. However, the size and colour may have been a recent development

(Edwards 1979: 90–100). Kibworth lay only a few miles from Hallaton and Market Harborough with their regional horse fairs, and very near to the great national horse fair at Northampton, but throughout the period under study only three black horses found their way to the pound. Kibworth horses were greys and its mares were bays or sorrels. In spite of their presence in force, their fame and their value, horses remained an optional extra as far as open field farmers were concerned, but it must be remembered that, parallel to the traditional system, commercial farming was developing apace, and many far-mers had their own separate closes in which they could run horses freely along with beef stores or sheep. The by-laws tell us about the traditional system; we must look to the inventories to tell us about innovations.

By the seventeenth century Leicestershire was also famous for her beans and pigs. While it is not true that Kibworth wholly abandoned peas in favour of beans it is true that the pig population had increased by this date. Their appearance was the natural corollary of the emergence of small herds of privately managed dairy cattle, since butter was made from the cream, cheese from the skim milk and the residue, the whey, could be fed directly to the pigs – it was common, and still is, to run a channel direct from the dairy to the pig trough. Brewing also was far more common by this date and brewers' grains were thus to be had on a more regular basis. The pig, therefore, flourished on the by-products of other commercial enterprises. Thus, Thomas Raye, who in 1559 kept two bulls, fourteen milch kine and seventeen followers, also kept a boar, two fat hogs, three sows and seven shotts. Likewise, Thomas Reynolds, in 1538, kept three pigs alongside his herd of seventeen cattle and one bull. But pig-keeping was also the prerogative of the poor. The by-laws of 1545 confirmed the right of every cottar to keep a sow and six piglets on the open fields until 9 October. In 1611 every cottar was entitled to keep two sows on the open fields after 18 October, in other words over winter, but by 1679 the stint had been reduced to only one hog per cottar. All pigs had to be ringed by 9 October and had always to be in the charge of a swineherd. Complaints were sometimes made about pigs straying in the streets by day and by night but only two pigs, white ones, were ever impounded as strays according to the official record in the court rolls. The medieval pig was a very much smaller, more hairy and more nimble animal than the modern specimen, but fulfilled much the same function – it served as the principal supply of quickly produced and easily cured *meat* for a population which still valued cows, sheep and poultry for their products rather than for their flesh. The sows did well on plenty of green matter throughout the summer and were overwintered on tail corn, millers' offals, peas and barley. The young were slaughtered and cured in autumn, the hams possibly being hung in the kiln.

Geese seldom got a mention in the by-laws or as strays; all we know is that they were allowed to remain on the stubble until 1 February, when, presumably, they were moved onto the fallow or Cowcommon. Unless they are to be fattened for market in the winter months geese require no extra feed, and are thus the poor man's best friend. Neither geese nor chickens were often mentioned in the inventories. In 1559 Thomas Raye had poultry worth 20s and Robert Coleman kept poultry worth 103s 4d, a few others kept 3s 4d worth, but most appraisors passed over the poultry yard in silence. Not only poultry were overlooked; bees seldom got a mention, and dogs and cats never – though we know that dogs were around in sufficient numbers to cause complaints between neighbours.[15]

Lastly, we come to bulls, rams and stallions. A bull for the town herd was provided by the manor together with pasture for its keep, worth 3s 4d when leased. But there were also other bulls; one, for example, was impounded in 1397 and another in 1418. The court roll of 1434 refers to both young and mature bulls owned by villagers, and a by-law of the sixteenth century defined a private herd as anything more than twelve cows, and such a herd was not entitled to the services of the common bull. We have already noted the bulls and dairy herds of Thomas Raye and Thomas Reynolds. Raye also kept a stallion, and a white ram was impounded in 1533, but even if unrecorded there must always have been a stallion and ten or more rams at any given date in the village.

The by-laws have virtually nothing to say about harvesting except with respect to gleaners, who were not allowed to enter a furlong whilst there were still stooks standing (1679), and in 1686 it was ordained that 'he that hath two cows shall gather no clots [dung] nor gleane, nor rake any corne or beans or straw upon other men's lands'. This is surely an interesting comment on how relative is men's notion of poverty. In 1340 a man was expected to raise a family and support one or two adult relatives on a two-cow holding (half a yardland) and as such was no poorer than the majority of villagers; at the end of our period a man with *only* two cows was in a minority and could be numbered among the 'poor' in the community. Gleaners were given six days before the cattle were turned on to the stubble. Winter, reckoned to begin in October, saw the threshing of grain, mending of hurdles and carting of dung. The jurors made their rounds checking the mere stones (the position of some of which can be seen on map 5), the hanging of gates and mending of roads. All the ways and ditches had to be cleaned by 30 November (1611), and when ploughing commenced each landholder had to fence his share of the field or furlong, and the clods of earth, left up on the headlands by the turning ploughs, had to be shovelled back onto the ridges. While on their rounds the jurors also took note of any encroachments and these would be dealt with at the next meeting of the court.[16] Livestock on the commons were rounded up once or twice a year and unclaimed – because unauthorised – animals remained with one or other of the frankpledgemen until claimed and redeemed for a small fine commensurate with the value of the animal.* If unclaimed for a year and a day they became the property of the college. Only two or three animals a year were impounded; of those that were, many were old and sick and ended their days there, being not worth the 6d or 12d fine – and dogs were apt to devour the carcass before it could be properly disposed of – but a few, such as the black bull in 1397 already mentioned, were of considerable value in nuisance as well as in cash terms.

So far we have looked at lists of by-laws, of heriots and of strays, all of which are found in the court rolls. These are obvious sources and cover a long time-span, but something can also be learned from the record of one-off disputes and short periods of friction. In 1421, for example, a considerable amount of land lay in the lord's hand following the rent strike and the reeve, Robert Polle, leased out certain acres annually at the standard rate of 7d per acre for peas land and 14d for barley land.[17] These entries give us an insight into the practice of subletting at Kibworth. In some other parts of England the buying and selling of small pieces of land was a common feature of the peasant land market even before the Black Death, but at Kibworth such sales were very rare indeed. However, the leasing – or mortgaging – of constituent portions of a half virgate was a possible, or perhaps even a common, strategy for raising extra cash. In the first two decades of the fifteenth century a number of tenants were engaged in a rent strike and, technically, their land was forfeit to the college.[18] While their land was thus in his custody the reeve let, or continued to let, a few acres from some of the forfeit holdings to other men in the village, most of whom were vigorous speculators in land at this period; namely, Brown, Russell, Carter, Polle and the miller. He also let the herbage from these holdings annually together with the herbage from other virgates in his custody and the demesne herbage.[19] Table 12 shows the number of arable acres let from each virgate or half virgate and the difference in value between peas and barley land.

* Strays were first entered on the rolls in 1394 and the last such entry was made in 1552.

Table 12. *Value of peas and barley land in 1421. (Also illustrates the subletting of up to five acres in the virgate.)*

Late owner	Tenement	Lessee	Acreage let	Pence per acre	Crop
N. Atte Cross	1 virgate	J. Chapmen	5	7d	peas
W. Dawe	1 virgate	J. Brown	2	7d	peas
J. Man	1 virgate	J. Brown	2	7d	peas
W. Parker	1 virgate	S. Carter	4	7d	peas
P. Barr	¼ virgate	R. Milner	1	7d	peas
S. Carter	1 virgate	J. Brown	2	14d	barley
J. Couper	½ virgate	J. Russell	1	14d	barley

The plagues and general dislocation which characterised the early fifteenth century occasioned the setting-up of a body of *supervisors*, whose duty it was to assess the damage caused to college property by tenants who had abandoned the land and left the manor secretly. The supervisors' reports offer a fleeting glimpse of farming practice in that century. In 1422, for example, John Burbage abandoned a messuage with half a virgate held for 10s rent and half a virgate of demesne held for 12s rent, to the lord.[20] The supervisors assessed the damage at half a mark (3s 4d) and went on to report that five acres had yet to be ploughed and another seven needed a second ploughing, the cost of which, at 8d the acre, would come to 8s 0d. Evidently they did not think the five acres would need a second ploughing, so it must have been destined for a peas crop, while the twice-ploughed seven acres were destined for barley. Few managers of demesne estates would have considered paying 8d an acre for ploughing, but in this situation the plough and plough team had to be hired in addition to the labour of a ploughman and his boy.

At the same December court William of Leycester surrendered a quarter of a virgate on the grounds of old age. The assessors found that the land had been once ploughed and his pledgers undertook to give it a second ploughing before 1 February. Later it was found that 3½ roods had not yet received a first ploughing and 7 roods needed a second ploughing, which would cost 3d per rood for each sort of ploughing (*per quale cultura*), total cost 2s 8d. At 12d an acre this was even more expensive than on John Burbage's land. Next William Norman surrendered a quarter of a virgate of demesne which had been once ploughed and his pledgers undertook to give it a second ploughing before 1 February. Finally Adam Polle surrendered half a virgate of demesne land which was found to be twice ploughed to the supervisor's satisfaction. Evidently ploughing was expected to be finished by the end of January when the peas were sown. Taken together, these entries tell us that two ploughings were considered quite sufficient for the cultivation of the two spring-sown crops, barley and peas, the land being ploughed once before December and once before 1 February. We also gain some idea of the cost of ploughing, which goes far to explain why this area went down to grass in the fifteenth century – it will be noticed that John Burbage had only twelve of his twenty-four acres under crop. The cost of ploughing would also account for the determined effort on the part of the tenants to obtain a reduction in rents and why Merton was so reluctant to accede. Eventually the college agreed to abandon the collection of that portion of the rent which represented commuted labour services, and in doing so relinquished a source of revenue which was increasing annually in value.

Our third source, the probate inventories, throws abundant light on the sixteenth and seventeenth centuries.[21] The inventories reveal the increasing independence of farming practice within the open field system, while at the same time serving to remind us how closely this independence was tied to the size of a man's holding, which offers a retrospective clue to the secret of the stability of the older economy based on the virgate for so many centuries, and points once again to the importance of inheritance customs.

No great change took place in the cropping of arable during the early modern period. Some of the more substantial farmers grew a little wheat for home consumption, and beans tended to replace peas towards the end of the seventeenth century, but the staple crops remained barley and peas. Where the change came was in the conversion of arable to pasture within the framework of the medieval open field system. In this respect Kibworth Harcourt may stand as a type for the villages to the north of Market Harborough which built up a reputation for producing some of the best grazing in the land, while remaining 'unenclosed'.

For the purposes of this enquiry, I have taken as the standard pattern of land use the form for which the common field system was ideally suited, the tenement of Thomas Deykyn. Deykyn died in 1544 leaving 6 acres under barley, $3\frac{1}{4}$ under wheat, and $8\frac{1}{2}$ under peas. If we allow for a further 8 acres fallow we arrive at a total of 25 acres or one yardland. He also left nine cows, and two bullocks; he was, in fact, entitled to a stint of four cows and twenty-four sheep, and this together with his fallow and pasture would be sufficient for his eleven 'great beasts'. So we learn that Deykyn had been cultivating the maximum acreage of land and kept enough livestock only to work his plough and supply his dairy. He kept no sheep. In 1568, John Iliffe with 88 acres was similarly making the maximum use of arable; also William Marshall in 1607 with 15 acres; Samuel Clarke in 1692 with 12 acres; and William Carter in 1709 with 38 acres.

At one remove from this norm were those who divided their lands equally between arable and pasture, notably the Carter family with their 60 acres and 2½ stints supporting ten cows and sixty sheep. When he died in November 1603, William Carter's seventeen cows, two colts, sixty-nine old sheep and twenty-four lambs required some 25 acres in addition to the stint. His crops in store were worth £46. Barley in the latter part of 1603 was worth 15s 0d a quarter, and peas 13s 0d in Leicestershire; and if he had planted the conventional 20 acres barley and 20 acres peas his yields would have been of the order of 40.8 quarters barley and 23.6 quarters peas worth £46 (see chap. 8). Since he had 30–40 acres available for arable the strong probability is that the crops in store were in fact the produce of his land. In other words, some 25 acres were devoted to pasture and 35 to arable. The inventory for Thomas Carter in October 1641 tells the same story of 25 acres pasture and 35 arable, as does the inventory for William Carter in 1670, but there is the note that a mortgage of £150 had been raised on the land. By 1709 the holding had been reduced to 30 acres and 2½ cowcommons, and William Carter had given up his horses and mares, cut down the number of cows and sheep to the number his cowcommons alone could support, and concentrated upon cultivating 25 acres of arable.

At two removes from the norm were Thomas Raye in 1559 and Robert Standley in 1639 who cultivated little more than one-third of their arable and kept the remainder under grass. Raye held 206 acres leasehold of old demesne and no cowcommon. His two bulls, fourteen cows, six heifers, eleven yearling calves, one stud, seven geldings, four mares, two foals and 180 hoggerels required 137 acres. His wheat in store in October was worth £6 13s 4d which would be about 15 quarters at current prices and would represent the produce of 8 acres. His barley was worth £18, that is 40 quarters or the produce of 20 acres. His peas were worth £13 6s 8d, that is 33 quarters, or the produce of 33 acres or less. Thus there was a fairly even distribution between peas field and cornfield. This gives an approximate total of 60 acres and he had two ploughs. This approximation fits comfortably into the 69 acres of land Raye did not need for his livestock. It is reasonable to conclude that of his 206 acres, 137 or more were under grass and 60 under crop. There is no way of telling whether *all* his pasture came under the plough at regular intervals, but one can claim that, if he so wished, he was in a position to practise up and down husbandry. Robert Standley's main holding was near Loughborough, but he had 73 acres leasehold in Kibworth Harcourt, including cowcommon. Of this, he was ploughing about 20 acres and kept nine cows and four horses on his stint and fallow. Of the remaining 40–50 acres nothing is stated in the inventory save that George Fox, Robert Bryan and the village shepherd Christopher Hubbard owed him £13 1s 8d. In the light of the following paragraph, it would seem that this money was the rent due from pasture leased to these three men, pastures which amounted to two-thirds of his land in Kibworth.

In 1605 Robert Bryan and in 1672 George Fox were concentrating on sheep and dairy farming. According to the 1635 Survey George Fox held 52.2.6 acres of tillage, 4.1.39 acres of meadow, 1.3.35 acres of meres and two cowcommons; a total of 59 acres. In February 1672, when his inventory was drawn up, his livestock occupied 47 acres over and above the stint. He had only 12 quarters of wheat, barley and peas in store and he had no plough. If he had land under the plough, then he must have been leasing additional grazing either from somebody like Robert Standley or from his relatives in Fleckney, where the Kibworth branch of the Fox family had enjoyed the use of a virgate in the sixteenth century. Concentration upon sheep farming alone cannot have been lucrative; even if we allow him 3 lb of wool per sheep at 20s 0d a tod, his annual wool revenue would not have exceeded £15. The description of his house and furniture supports this impression of a relatively modest income, which must have been supplemented from the proceeds of an inn, since strangers occasionally died at Fox's house.[22] What is of particular significance about Fox's inventory is that it shows us that the 52 acres described as tillage in the 1635 Survey were in fact pasture. The 1675 Terrier of School Land also describes most of Fox's strips as leys, headlands or doles.[23] In 1605 Robert Bryan had more sheep than his 36 acres could support. He needed 81 acres pasture and he had some crops in the ground. He too must have been leasing pasture either from Standley, with whom his name is associated, or from other members of his family who held another 2½ yardlands of copyhold in Kibworth Harcourt and half a yardland in Smeeton Westerby. His annual revenue from 180 sheep cannot have amounted to more than £19 from wool sales, and if his fifteen cows yielded a gallon of milk a day, which the contemporary writer Gervase Markham reckons was 'good', then they would have been bringing in about £37 a year (Markham 1623: 175). Like Fox he enjoyed other sources of income; he was a butcher and he ran an inn, the Rose and Crown. In this case also, the Bryan land in 1635 is described as predominantly arable, whereas in practice if was pasture.

There remains a fifth category: those who sublet their copyholds.

Robert Oswyn was subletting 30 acres in 1573, which practice was still continued by his descendant, William Osywn, in 1674. By 1673 Robert Watts was subletting the 88 acres John Iliffe had been farming in 1568. Thomasine Coalman lived in Great Bowden and sublet 96 acres in Harcourt to William Smyth in 1646.[24] In 1635 Nicholas Lount had only four cows on a cow pasture and 11 acres arable, so may have been subletting. After 1618 Raye was licensed to sublet his leasehold lands;[25] and by 1679 William Burgis was licensed to sublet 91 acres; Joanna Woolman to sublet one-eighth of a yardland reserving to herself 1 cow pasture; and Edward Avery to sublet the western half of that messuage which had once belonged to John Bryan.[26] Correspondingly, lessees were taking up these leases, mostly outsiders. Mr George Buswell, gent., of Cadeby held 105 acres and many small tenements in the village. He also bought some 30 acres of land in Wigston Magna in 1623, where he is described by Professor Hoskins as 'an outsider who was buying other small properties in the village' (Hoskins 1957: 203). Another such was Mr Sacheverall who in 1635 held the 129 acres once farmed by the Polle family.

Several observations may be made upon these findings. In the first place the distinction between arable and pasture which is made by the 1635 Survey is theoretical rather than descriptive. 'Tillage' meant more than land which *could* be ploughed, it meant land which was subject to common grazing in winter and when fallow. So whether it was actually ploughed or not it remained subject to communal by-laws, and its possession entitled the owner to grazing rights in the cow pasture and fallow and a share in the meadow commensurate with the acreage of his arable. Secondly, men with under 30 acres tended to exploit their arable to the full or to sublet it. Men with over 30 acres often altered the traditional proportions between arable and pasture in favour of pasture, putting down to grass 50–70 per cent.

With barley and peas prices doing so well and wool prices more or less static, the question arises, why did the larger farmers prefer to extend their pasture? The answer may lie in some quite simple factor such as rising meat prices or the desire to reduce labour costs. But it may lie in more sophisticated considerations. If, as Dr Kerridge suggests, the up and down system was fairly widely known and appreciated by the seventeenth century, then the expansion of pasture may reflect the adoption of up and down husbandry and a consequent increase in the crop yield per acre.

Dr Kerridge sets out the case for up and down husbandry as follows (Kerridge 1967). The open field system could accommodate two forms of pasturing. There was land over which the township had the right to pasture the common flock and herd when it was fallow, but which could be hedged around or fenced off for meadow before Lammas: this was known as tenantry land. Then there was land, usually demesne land, over which the township enjoyed no such rights, and this was known as severalty land. Thomas Raye's land at Kibworth is a good example of the latter type; it did not *look* like enclosed land, since it lay in scattered strips among the open fields with one or two compact blocks, but he enjoyed no rights of pasture on tenantry land nor the villagers on his.

If the holder of tenantry land wished to decrease his arable and keep more livestock, he could grass over some of his arable strips but he could not withdraw them from the use of the common herd when the field lay fallow or under stubble. Instead he was in many villages allowed to keep more beasts in the herd, usually two sheep per acre put down to grass (Chibnall 1965: 235–6). The village could reach a common decision to increase the pasture at the expense of the arable, in which case every landholder was required to grass over a number of strips in the same furlong, which then became part of the cow pasture. Individuals could not then plough up these strips without common consent.

According to Kerridge, one of the underlying principles of open field husbandry was that land was either permanently arable or permanently pasture, and the rotation was one which did not allow a quick conversion from arable to pasture. This was because wheat generally came first in the rotation, and the ground for wheat was prepared by four or five ploughings in summer, which thoroughly exposed and destroyed the grass roots as it was intended it should. This meant that when the land was returned to fallow it did not readily sward over, but produced a crop of weeds, and then came under the plough again.

Certainly at Kibworth the permanent pasture was never ploughed, but Kerridge's point about the difficulty of swarding over did not apply. This was because the area under winter corn was negligible and the ploughing for the spring crops was done from November to February. Moreover if, as has been suggested, peas preceded barley in the rotation then the usual five ploughings for barley would not have been necessary. The grass roots, therefore, stood a good chance of surviving the period of cultivation and the land would sward over quickly when left to rest.

Up and down husbandry did away not only with the system of permanent pasture and permanent arable, but it also reduced the arable to about a quarter of the total acreage of the holding. However, the reduced acreage produced a higher yield per acre, so there was no great loss in grain output while there was a gain in revenue from livestock, since the system improved the soil structure and its fertility while the increased number of livestock carried on the land made available more manure. Production costs were lowered, since fewer ploughs, plough beasts and ploughmen were required. It was generally accepted that all grassland whatsoever needed to be ploughed up at least once in twenty years, so graziers were prepared to set aside a portion of their pasture for arable each year, which they either cultivated themselves or leased to nearby corngrowers or to local smallholders in return for their grazing. At Kibworth George Fox, as we have seen, concentrated on livestock husbandry and kept no ploughs. Standley on the other hand cultivated only his arable and let his grassland to graziers. Raye cultivated only one-third of his land; unfortunately we do not know what the other three large farmers in mid seventeenth-century Kibworth were doing, namely Parker, Buswell and Sacheverell, but like Raye they were gentry and may well have been as sophisticated in their use of land.

The introduction of up and down husbandry stimulated developments in the area of livestock husbandry. Speaking of an area within a ten-mile radius north of Market Harborough, the management of pasture had become a fine art by the nineteenth century; how often to plough it, which crops would improve it, how to get a better sward, what proportion of animals to put upon it in a given month under prevailing weather conditions. As has already been said, barley was put at the end of the rotation in order to preserve the grass, the land was also heavily manured – not so much for the sake of the crop as for the betterment of the turf coming up underneath it. Lime was brought in from Neville Holt and in later years grass seed was selected and sown: two parts perennial rye grass to one part wild white or red clover. As soon as the sown grass could bear it, that is, after a year or eighteen months, cattle were put on it, but not sheep until the third year. This was considered the best year of the ley. After midsummer the pastures were scythed of weeds and broken grass and pricked of thistles. The rate of stocking was usually one beast and two sheep on two acres of temporary ley as against four acres of permanent grass. Graziers kept a permanent stock of riding and cart horses and a few milk cows; overwinter their pastures carried sheep that were fattening for sale in spring and early summer, while in late spring they carried beef stores for summer sale. The number bought depended on the state of the grass, which was not allowed to grow too high or to be cropped too short. 'The skill of grazing resided in meticulous grassland management, in acute judgement of stock, and in watching the market' (Auty in Stamp 1937: 254–7; Kerridge 1967: 110).

The improvement in pasture did not lead to an improvement in cattle weights during the seventeenth century, due to the Leicestershire farmers' habit of weaning calves as young as possible (Fussell 1949: 160), but it did lead to the introduction of a new breed of sheep; a heavier, polled, long-woolled beast which throve on rich pasture. Ultimately these Lustre Longwools usurped the position of the short-woolled fallow sheep in the county and swung the Leicestershire wool trade away from the cloth markets of the west midlands to the worsted centres of the north and east, and also made its mark on the London meat market (Bowden 1962).

The Kibworth inventories record very few beef stores, the emphasis being on dairy cattle, horse rearing and sheep fattening. Livestock prices soared during the period 1550–1630. In 1550 a good cow fetched 20s 0d, in 1600 40s 0d, and by 1630 50s 0d, after which prices levelled off to a steady plateau at 50s 0d. The price of mares rose even more dramatically; in 1550 the average price stood at 15s 0d, by 1600 it had risen to just over 30s 0d and by 1630 a good mare fetched 70s 0d. This sudden increase in the value of saddle horses as well as of carriage horses calls for some explanation; Defoe comments on their numbers in the area and their fine quality but offers no explanation for the shift in market values (Defoe 1971: 409; Edwards 1979: 90–100). The evidence of dairying is less impressive; every household had its cheese press but there are seldom examples of cheeses stored for sale in the cheese chambers of yeomen farmers.

By May 1779 the village lands supported 960 sheep, 96 horses and 48 cows.[27] The control of so much livestock on open fields could present certain problems, but these were evidently not insuperable, since no movement was made to abolish the open field system at Kibworth or in the surrounding villages. Presumably, preference was given to cows and mares because they could be tethered, whereas steers are more difficult to control. Sheepwalks were set aside for the sheep flocks and usually the fallow was reserved for them.[28] When enclosure came to Kibworth, it was not at the instigation of the bailiff or any influential man in the village, but followed on the suggestion of the agent employed by the college to supervise the enclosure of its other Leicestershire manor, at Barkby.[29] He remarked that it would be a good moment to enclose Kibworth as well, and so it was done, causing the minimum of stir either at Kibworth or at Merton. Map 14 shows that most of the other parishes in Gartree Hundred which became famous for their pasture were not enclosed until the late eighteenth century and some not until the nineteenth.

If some farmers were prepared to adopt innovations such as up and down husbandry it comes as no surprise to find permanent quick-set hedges marked on the 1635 map. This was a practice very much in vogue in the sixteenth century, not only in the interests of good husbandry, but also as a means of providing timber. Among the seventeenth-century court rolls for Kibworth survive lists of persons who are to plant specified numbers of trees, usually in the form of a hedge. One such hedge was planted along the boundary with Turlangton from Whistle Gate to Burton Brooke. Others bear the names of seventeenth-century landholders: Sheffield, Oswyn, Burgis and William Barnard. Only Burgis's hedge completely surrounds a small field; all the others run along one side only, separating permanent pasture from arable. None of them imply permanent enclosure; they were simply planted along permanent boundaries between common pasture and common arable.

When we bring together these aspects of land utilisation illuminated by the probate inventories, what emerges for the seventeenth century is an open field village with three great fields each containing an area of permanent pasture in addition to the arable. The arable was ridged up into lands which were coterminous with tenurial strips and were subject to communal rules controlling grazing rights over pasture and arable. A man's strips were more or less equally distributed over the three fields, were not grouped together within one or two furlongs, but lay intermingled with the strips of other villagers over many furlongs. The system had been evolved to meet the needs of smallholders, each one desirous to make the maximum use of his arable, while at the same time supporting a sufficient number of plough beasts and, when conditions were favourable, such as in the fifteenth century, some sheep as well. By the seventeenth century the smallholders were in the minority and their interests no longer governed the management of the fields. Nevertheless, the old system was continued because it lent itself to adaptation. Large farmers, with a surplus of land over and above what was needed for subsistence, could exploit this surplus land in accordance with market trends. Some concentrated on livestock, others on arable, others leased it piecemeal to graziers. Meanwhile, the common lands continued to support the livestock of the cottagers, many of whom had lost their land but held on the grazing rights appurtenant to these lands. Enclosure, when it came, tidied up appearances, but did not fundamentally alter the direction of specialisation; this had already been set towards grassland husbandry as early as the fifteenth century.

7

Village morphology and buildings

The village of Kibworth Harcourt is of peculiar interest in that the morphology of the village can be fairly reliably dated, and the majority of the present house sites together with their owners can be traced back to 1484 (and some to 1440). The construction of most of the houses standing today, post-war buildings excepted, is of eighteenth-century brick but, in many cases, behind the brick can still be found the stone footings and cruck framework of the late medieval houses described in the fifteenth-century repair bills. From the sixteenth century onwards the wills and inventories of occupiers tell us something of the interior furnishings of some of these houses. Unlike many villages, the site of this village has not been changed since 1086, nor have messuage sites altered much, and the axis of houses has altered not at all since the late fifteenth century (Hurst and Hurst 1969: 167–203; 1957–71; Beresford 1975). Yet in spite of this fundamental continuity, the appearance of the village altered considerably between 1086 and 1484.

Investigation into the morphology of the village necessarily begins with the modern maps and works backwards to the maps of 1780, 1635 and 1609 (Roberts 1977; Aston and Rowley 1974). Using the written evidence of court rolls, rentals and wills, the process of map making can be carried back with confidence to 1484. Beyond this date we enter into an area of speculation. We are much helped at this point by a rental of 1527 which describes many of the village messuages as being 'assart', in other words, built on waste land.[1] When these assart lands are plotted on a map and compared with the map of freeholdings the two are seen to coincide. For freeholds in 1527 one can, therefore, substitute wide grass verges, droveways and pasture before 1484. Seen against such a background the manorial buildings and customary tenements stand out clearly, both the older group of customary holdings and the younger group of sokeman's holdings. The infilling of the droveways and central pasture and the encroach-

114

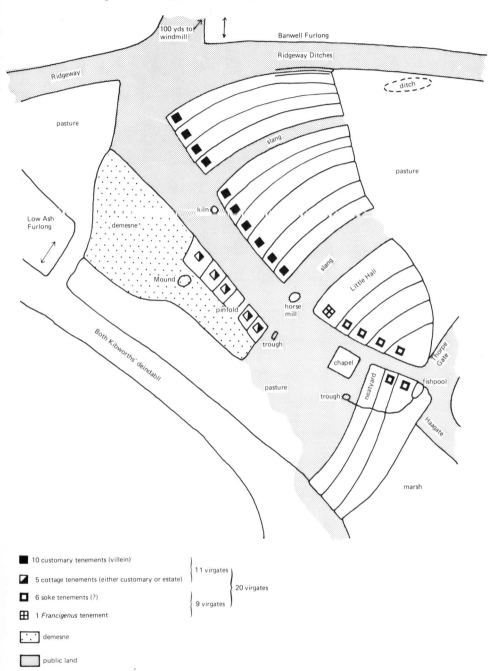

Map 8   Kibworth Harcourt, 1086

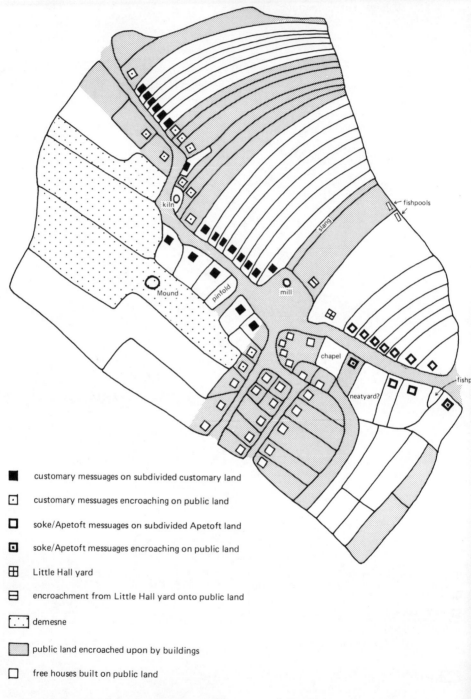

kiln

fishpools

slang

Mound

pinfold

mill

chapel

neatyard?

fishpo

■   customary messuages on subdivided customary land

▣   customary messuages encroaching on public land

◻   soke/Apetoft messuages on subdivided Apetoft land

◻   soke/Apetoft messuages encroaching on public land

⊞   Little Hall yard

⊟   encroachment from Little Hall yard onto public land

⬚   demesne

▨   public land encroached upon by buildings

◻   free houses built on public land

Map 9   Kibworth Harcourt, 1340

ment onto the main street had already taken place at the time the 1340 rental was drawn up. It had not taken place when the Domesday description of the manor was made. Map 8 shows a conjectural plan of the village with the 'slangs' or droveways still open, the village street still spacious and grass verged as is typical of the surrounding villages to this day, and enough messuages to accommodate the ten

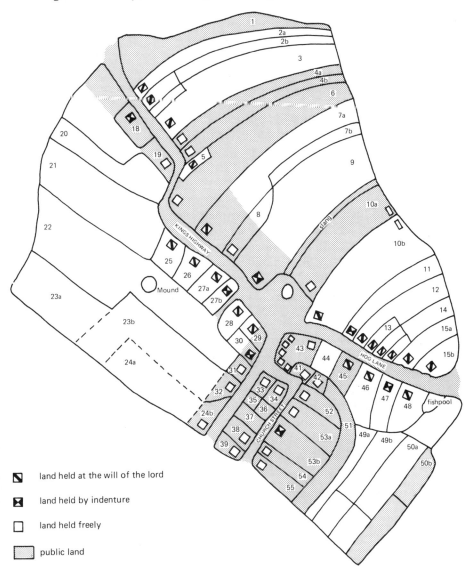

land held at the will of the lord

land held by indenture

land held freely

public land

Map 10   Kibworth Harcourt, 1484

customary tenants, five *bordarii* and six sokemen, together with one larger tenement for the *Francigenus*. Map 9 shows the process by which these same customary tenants found room for their expanding families. Holdings in the open fields were halved, and housing found for the owners of the second half by building, not on the orchards and curtilages of the old messuages, but upon the public ways and the pasture next to the Beauchamp boundary. Map 10 illustrates the process by which this subdivision was reversed. Half virgates once more became full virgates and the houses on the waste became superfluous. Many of them were demolished, but the land they had occupied was not returned to public use, it remained in the hands of the families who had utilised it and became free pasture closes. The seventeenth-century maps 11 and 12 show how, as the population slowly expanded again, the process of subdivision was not repeated. Arable holdings remained large, and indeed continued to grow, so that extra-familial labour was required to cultivate them. Their owners, therefore, systematically acquired the freehold sites on the old waste land and erected labourers' cottages on these. This gave rise to a shortage of cottages for old people and for artisans, and so we find in the eighteenth century (map 13) a return to the practice of building cottages on public ways for the 'poor' who were, according to the Poor Law definition, people with claims on the village, that is, people related to village families. Formerly, they would have been accommodated in the cottages now occupied by farm servants.

The somewhat bold and generalised claims of the last few paragraphs require a fairly detailed exposition of the evidence which lies behind them. At the risk of tedium, I have, therefore, set out the evidence for each of the fifty-five tenements which, read in conjunction with the maps, should read as clearly as is possible given the variety of documents used. References are not given to the maps of 1609, 1635 and 1780, or to the rentals unless this is not clear from the text, or to the parish register for dates of marriages and death. Not every reference to the court rolls is given, but only the first, in order to indicate that the references following are drawn from the court rolls under the date quoted.

The customary tenements north of the King's Road

Tenement 1 known as Townsend Close is described as 'assart' on the 1527 rental and so does not form part of the customary land. The northern end of it is traversed longitudinally by an unexplained series of mounds and ditches. There has been no building on the site since the sixteenth century. During the seventeenth and eighteenth centur-

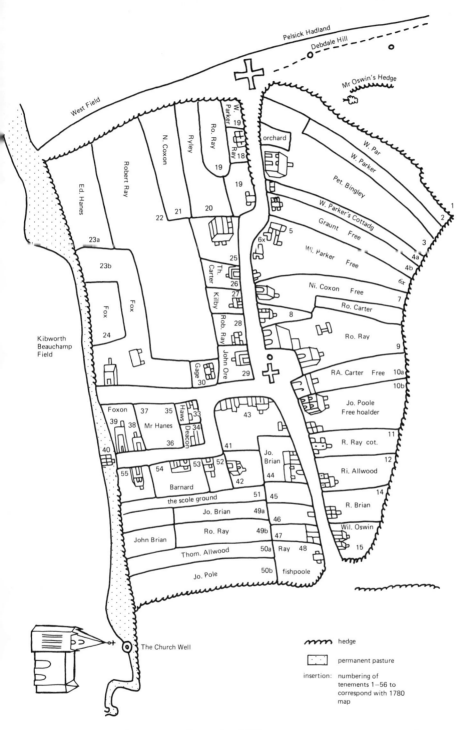

Map 11   Kibworth Harcourt from the 1609 map

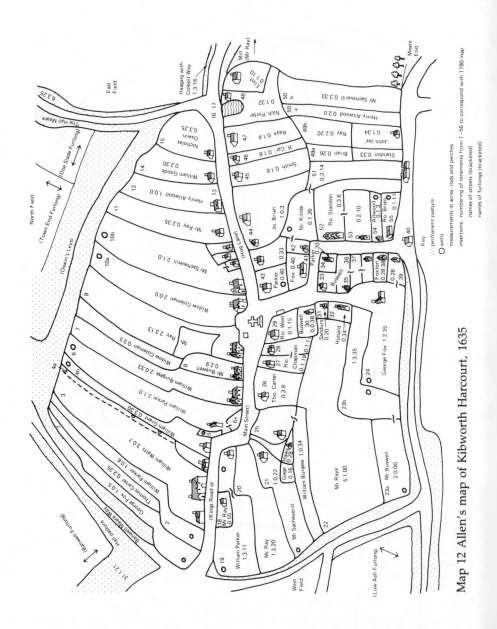

Map 12 Allen's map of Kibworth Harcourt, 1635

permanent pasture

damaged area on enclosure map of 1780

2   meeting house   free
5   John Weston   free
11   pre-enclosure   G. Foxton   free
     post-enclosure   L. Humfrey   free
13   Edward Cooper   copy
16   Perkin's widow   free
17   Perkin's widow   copy
21   John Turney   part free part copy
27   Pen Orchard   lease
     post-enclosure   Geo. Foxton
29   Mrs Wright   copy
30   Lebbeus Humfrey   free
31   Will Throne   free?
32   Lebbeus Humfrey   copy
33   Thornton   free
34   Will Mitchell   free
35   Will Swingler   free
36   R. Haymes
37   R. Haymes   free
38   pre-enclosure   school
38   post-enclosure   R. Haymes—by exchange with school
39   Wyatt   free
40   post-enclosure   R. Haymes—by exchange with school
41   Gabriel King   free
42   John Garrett   free
45   Francis Fletcher   free
46   Wm. Hayes   copy
47   Geo. Foxton   bruchyard   lease
51 ⎫
52 ⎬ post-enclosure   Rob. Haymes—by
53 ⎭ exchange with school   free
56   Will. Haymes   allotment

Map 13   Kibworth Harcourt, 1780

ies it was held as one among many tenements by the Fox and later the Foxton families about whom more will be said later.

Tenement 2 consists of two messuages thrown together to form one tenement held by the Parker family from the fifteenth century until 1743. With these two messuages went two virgates in the open fields. In 1768 the most westerly of the two house sites was separated from its garden and close and became the site of the Methodist chapel which can still be seen today.[2]

Tenement 3 consists of four half-virgate messuages which were thrown together in the fifteenth century to form a single holding known today as Paddocks Farm. The process of amalgamation can be traced in the court rolls thus:

(*a*)   1 mes. + ½ v. @ 8s 4d annual rent:
        1411–12 John Milner surrendered this to Ric. Wynluf @ 10s 1d[3]
(*b*)   1 mes. + ½ v. @ 8s 4d annual rent:
        1415 Margaret Saunder surrendered this *ad opus* Ric. Wynluf @ 10s 0d[4]
(*c*)   1 mes. + ½ v. @ 9s 6d annual rent:
        1427 William Leycester surrendered this to John Caunden (pledge Ric. Wynluf) @ 9s 6d[5]
(*d*)   1 mes. + ½ v. @ 8s 10½d annual rent:
        1428 John Smith surrendered this to Richard Wynluf @ 8s 10½d[6]

By 1439 Richard Wynluf held two virgates and four 'cottages' for 32s 2½d a year.[7] He did not need all the houses and by 1432 the one which had belonged to Nicholas and Margaret Saunder was reported to be in a ruinous condition.[8]

By 1484 Richard de Gretham held the tenement and in 1491 it passed into the family of John Iliffe of Gumley, and remained with them until 1599.[9] Henry Beaumont then took it for one year only and passed it to Peter Bingley, also from Gumley.[10] By 1635 William Watts held it, possibly in the name of his wife, Margaret Ray, since it passed to his daughter Dorothy rather than to his two sons, Henry and William. Dorothy married Robert Lount of Kibworth Harcourt[11] and their daughter Anne married William Haymes.[12] By 1780 the various branches of the Haymes family held more than 523 acres and had enlarged Tenement 3 to include Tenement 2 and Tenement 4a.[13] The Stops family from Slawston have farmed it for the last two generations and it is still leasehold.

Tenement 4a is characterised by three wells and by the spring at its northern end, which supplies the small stream that runs along the northern boundary ditch of the village, through the two fishponds on

Tenement 10, to lose itself in the fishpool and marsh at the eastern end of the village. The tenement was held freely by the Parkers from 1428–1743 and had passed to William Haymes by 1780. It was probably in origin part of a drove road to the pasture between Banwell Furlong and the village upon which a cottage was built in the twelfth or thirteenth century to accommodate the owner of a subdivided virgate, the other half virgate remaining with the older house.

Tenement 4b likewise was held freely by the Parker family. No land was attached to it and it too was probably part of an old drove road enclosed in the twelfth century. The Parkers made a habit of subletting it, to the Grants in the seventeenth century and to the Perkins in the eighteenth. The Perkins held grazing rights on the Segges at the boundary with Turlangton.

Tenement 5 was called the Westyard,[14] presumably because it lay immediately to the west of the main Parker holding, Tenement 6. The Parkers held it by copyhold from 1484–1743 and on it were three cottages sublet to the Grant and West families in the seventeenth century.[15] After enclosure it became freehold, and three modernised cottages occupy the site today.

Tenement 6, like Tenement 4b, enjoyed no arable in the open fields; it consists simply of a two-acre freehold close. It would seem that it was part of the same droveway as Tenements 4a and 4b and that houses were built on it in the twelfth century to accommodate the extra households which had resulted from the division of a whole virgate holding in the open fields. The Parkers held it from 1484–1743.[16]

Tenement 6x. Some explanation is needed for the abrupt southward swing of the road opposite Tenement 6. It seems that in the T-junction where the droveway entered the main street stood the common kiln where grain could be dried off and barley malted. The kiln belonged to the manor and was leased out, together with eight acres, for 3d a year. The Parkers held it from 1484–1743. By 1600 a malt kiln was a common feature in Leicestershire villages; according to the inventories there was at least one in each village, run by a wealthy yeoman. Gervase Markham regarded them as too common to be worth describing and limited his observations to the more unusual type of kiln, such as the new French kiln and the traditional Celtic kiln (Markham 1620: 199–202; Stocks, H. 1923: 364). A common kiln would not only economise in labour but also in that more rare commodity, fuel. The site today is occupied by a recently restored early eighteenth-century house known as The White House. Until they moved to the Old House in 1678 this was the mansion house of the Parker family. After the move it became the house of successive bailiffs who were also sons-in-law; for example, John Lamplugh, Captain Corrance and George Ayre. By 1737 it was held by Joshua Reynolds, who had married Rebecca Parker in 1716. He ran it as an inn, to which period of its history the spacious cellars bear witness today. It was sold, together with the rest of the Parker estate, to Mr Thomas Peach, attorney-at-law in Market Harborough, in 1743.[17]

Tenement 7. In the 1340s Tenement 7 was three half-virgate copyhold tenements. These were amalgamated in the course of the fifteenth century and in 1484 Robert Symson held one virgate, four half virgates, three messuages and a toft for 36s 8d. This group included Tenements 21 and 25. By 1500 Symson's land was held by William Marriott for 33s 4d. Marriott was still holding this land in 1527 for 43s 2d, but it passed to Humphrey Miller in 1540.[18] According to the 1609 map, Nicholas Coxon held Tenement 7, which is described as $3\frac{1}{2}$ virgates, a messuage, a toft (Ten. 25) and a close (Ten. 21) for 43s 2d. But the backyard of one of the three half virgates had been detached and was held by Robert Carter. By 1635 this detached portion had passed to Widow Coleman and eventually was incorporated into Tenement 9. William Burgess held Tenement 7 in the seventeenth century and Robert Haymes in the eighteenth in conjunction with The Paddocks.[19] Tenements 3 and 7 are still leased jointly from Merton today.

Tenement 8. Priory Farm would appear to be the southern end of a customary tenement whose orchard and curtilage have been incorporated into Tenement 9. On it stands a well-built timber-frame house on a stone base. The earliest reference to its ownership is not earlier than 1609, for which year the map tells us that a certain Hawes held it. This was Tobias Hawes of Stoke Albany, Northamptonshire, who also held Tenement 23, a corner of 21, and 33, 35, 36 and 37. The earliest reference to Tobias Hawes is in 1588,[20] and in 1596 Robert Hawes married Cicely Gage, a connection presumably of the Mr Gage who married into the Ray family and acted as bailiff of the manor. By 1635 all these holdings had passed to Mr Buswell who held 110 acres in the open fields, together with 17 odd acres. There is no indication of either the Hawes or the Buswells having lived in the village – no baptisms or burials are recorded for either family – so one must presume that they put in a bailiff who occupied Tenement 8, while their employees occupied the four cottages, 33, 35, 36 and 37. By 1780 the whole group of tenements had come into the hands of the Haymes family, and is today held in conjunction with Tenement 24, number 8 being the house of a shepherd to Mr Briggs, owner of the Spinneys.

Tenement 9 is an H-shaped, timber-frame building called the Manor House. The north wing, with its deep stone footing, stone fireplace and massive roof timbers, is exactly aligned with Tenement 8, Priory Farm, and both buildings may at one time have stood flush with the road. In which case, the cross wing and south range stand on what had once been the road. The cross wing is timber framed with unusually heavy tie beams. The diagonal 'dragon' beam of the westernmost room of the south range indicates a timber-framed upper storey, jettied on two sides (Brunskill 1971: 55, fig. k). This, together with the cruck construction of this wing, indicates an earlier date than the 1702 set in the chequered brick face of the south wall (Farnham V). Therefore, the encroachment onto the road must have taken place not later than the late medieval period; it is called 'assart' in 1527. Further enclosure of the square took place in 1886 when the then bailiff, John Phillip, extended the garden eastwards as far as the slang and southwards to the line of the south wall of the house, thus enclosing a not inconsiderable area of common land and creating much resentment in the village.[21]

The association of Tenement 9 with the bailiff began in 1439 when William Peek is noted as holding the Hall Close, 3 messuages, and 3 half virgates for 42s 6d. In 1477, the next bailiff, John Clerke, took out a 30-year indenture on the Hall-land, four messuages, three virgates and Browns Place at 54s 4d.[22] From 1507–75 the Polle family held the indentured tenement together with the office of bailiff.[23] The Rays held it from 1575–1706,[24] when the last of that family, Thomas Ray Dand, whose initials T. R. D. appear as a plaque on the outer wall of the south wing, sold to the Foxtons, who held it until 1797. When the last of that family died the office and property passed to the son-in-law, the Reverend Thomas Thomas of East Farndon, Northamptonshire.[25] The property remained college leasehold, but both the Reverend Thomas and, later, John Phillip made considerable alterations. By the early twentieth century it had been adapted to provide two labourers' cottages but was rescued and restored by Mr J. E. Bartlett, of Brackley, Northamptonshire. In 1972 it was sold by the college to Mr P. G. Thurnham and a new chapter in its long history has begun.

Although called the Manor House today there is no reason to

believe that Tenement 9 was the site of the medieval manor house. This, one would expect, would have been situated in the Hall Close within the curial complex south of the pound, kiln and horse mill, and it is doubtful if it would ever have been of any size or significance, since there is no evidence to suggest that any member of the Harcourt family ever lived in Kibworth, not even Saer de Harcourt. Occasional reference is made in the pre-plague court rolls to an *aula* held by Matilda Parsons (at other times referred to as a *parva placea*) and to a demesne garden and dovecote, but that is all.[26] The present tenement was probably created out of the three half-virgate customary messuages for which no tenants could be found in 1439. In 1448 the college erected a building called Browns Place, for which the building accounts survive.[27] The real Browns Place was almost certainly Tenement 53, which had in fact belonged to the college as non-customary land (see below Tenement 53). It may be that all the pieces of old demesne land held of the college by indenture in the fifteenth century were collectively known as Browns Place, since the name is ascribed to three different units within it – the 1448 building, Tenement 53 and, on the 1780 map, Tenement 20. The present building on Tenement 53 bears no resemblance to the hall, chamber and stables built by the college in 1448, whereas Tenement 9 does, especially now that the timber framework has been exposed by the new owners: timbers which the surveyor for the *Victoria County History* could only guess at (*VCH Leics.* V: 178). At any rate the Manor House serves as a visual expression of the 1448 accounts and as such will be described later in this chapter, when we shall be considering building materials (see below pp. 143–4).

Tenement 10a: a two-acre close lying 'between the Great Halleyard and the horse mill with a garden and close called Lytilhalleyard',[28] was bounded on the north by one of a pair of fishponds and on the south by the horse mill which was enclosed within a mud wall and roofed over with thatch.[29] The presence of the horse mill prevented further encroachment upon the road, hence the sudden widening of the road at this point. A 'slang' or cart-way still runs along its western boundary, crosses the town ditch and opens out onto the pasture south of Banwell Furlong. No arable was attached to this close and, although it is labelled copyhold on the 1635 map, it was usually referred to as freehold. Its free status and lack of arable suggests that the slang once included Tenement 10a, but was encroached upon from the Little Hall yard to the east. Such a broad slang would have acted also as a boundary between the old settlement to the west and the later settlement to the east called the Apetoft sub-manor.

By 1527 Christopher Carter held one messuage and close *'iuxta Hallplace'* together with 3½ virgates for 42s 0d. The Carters continued to hold this land throughout the sixteenth century, but in 1611 Robert Carter surrendered the whole group of tenements to William Coleman for the remainder of the 21-year lease.[30] In 1628 William Coleman renewed the lease[31] and in 1646 his widow, Thomasine, sold it to William Sheffield of Great Bowden who obtained a licence to sublet it.* In 1764 William and Nathaniel Sheffield sold the lease to Lebbeus Humfrey who united it to Tenement 10b.[32] On the 1780 map the united holding is labelled 'freehold'. Humfrey, who also owned the Old House and the Spinneys and used the former as a hunting lodge, built stabling for fifteen or so horses on Tenement 10, and the foundations of these can still be seen as humps in the grass of the present paddock.

Tenement 10b was known as the 'Lytilhalleyard'. This could be understood to mean that it was simply the smaller of two hall yards, but it could also have been the name given to the curial buildings of the small sub-manor known as the Apetoft estate. To it were attached two virgates of land in the open fields. In 1432 Thomas FitzEustace (a name not otherwise connected with Kibworth) granted to John Russell of Kibworth Harcourt, the son of Simon Russell, 'a house in Kibworth between the great halleyard and the horse mill, with the garden and close adjoining called "Lytilhalleyard" to himself and his heirs freely and for ever'. The Russells were a leading villein family in Kibworth Beauchamp in the mid fourteenth century; in 1351 Richard Russell held one messuage and one virgate there freely for 9s 9d; Simon paid poll tax there in 1377 and representatives of the family were still there in the sixteenth century.[33] In the 1480s John Polle purchased one messuage and two virgates at 2s rent annually from John Russell.[34] This was Tenement 10b only: 10a was taken by the bailiff, Thomas Clerke, and was subsequently held by the Carter family as has been described. The Polles still held Lytilhalleyard in 1609,[35] but by 1635 Mr Henry Sacheverell of Ratcliffe upon Soar held it, together with the lease of the Swathes and some 133 acres freehold. A row of small houses can be seen along the southern boundary of this tenement on the seventeenth-century maps, but these had been replaced by a fine barn and stables by 1780, by which time the property had come into the hands of Lebbeus Humfrey.

---

* 1672–1759, William Sheffield's house (Ten. 10a) was the licensed meeting-house for Presbyterian worship. (*VCH Leics.* V: 182; LRO DE 526/126. Indenture dated 1646.)

Tenement 11 consisted of a leasehold close of 2 roods and 35 perches and with it went one virgate in the open fields. Little is known of its early history, but evidently no tenant could be found for it in the 1430s, since it became part of the bailiff's land held by lease or indenture. The Rays held it throughout the seventeenth century and it passed with the rest of the Ray lands to the Fox and then to the Foxton families. In 1772 Lebbeus Humfrey bought it for £140 and added it to Tenement 10b.[36]

Tenement 12 consisted of a copyhold close of one acre and one virgate of arable in the open fields. The Saunders family held it from 1358 or earlier until 1500, by which date they held two messuages, two tofts and one virgate for 22s 4½ reduced to 15s 8½d. By 1527 Christopher Woode (the earlier form of the Alwood surname) held one messuage, two tofts and 1½ virgates for 22s 4½d reduced to 15s 8½d. The Alwoods continued to hold the tenement until 1670 when the heiress, Margaret, married John Cave.[37] At some point in the eighteenth century the Cave lands passed to the Coopers, a family which had been leasing land in the village since 1617.[38] At the time of enclosure William Cooper was allotted 10 acres 16 perches copyhold and William and Mary Cooper received 10 acres 19 perches copyhold lying next to each other in the North and East Fields.[39] Today four small cottages occupy the road frontage of Tenements 12 and 13.

Tenement 13 does not appear as a tenement separate from 12 until 1780, when it is noted on the pre-enclosure map as held by Edward Cooper, while the land behind it still belonged to Tenement 12.

Tenement 14 consists of a messuage of 2 roods 30 perches copyhold, to which two half virgates in the open fields were attached. In 1371 Dominus John Godwyn and Nicholas le Tayllour held half a virgate each on what was probably this tenement. By 1400 Richard Godwyn held both half virgates.[40] The Godwyn family died out and the land was held by John Caunden from 1427–39.[41] By 1484 this tenement was definitely held by John Moore, while the two houses were held by Edmund Tayllour. In 1500 William Parsons held both houses and one half virgate, the other half virgate was held by John Gude. By 1527 Richard Gude held both the land and the houses. Hugh Rowerth, 'shoomaker', held one of the houses in 1594 and Robert Bryan, butcher, held it in 1599.[42] The other half virgate was still in the hands of the Gude family in 1635, but by 1700 it had passed to the Carters. In 1716 Elizabeth Carter married a bricklayer, Nathaniel Johnson, and the tenement was still in the hands of the Johnson descendants in

1780. In that year the lease was sold by Mr John Moore Johnson to Mr Woodeforde for eleven years. The property, which went for £15 15s 0d, then comprised one virgate, a barn, an orchard with home close adjoining and 9 acres 2 roods of 'oddland', which had lately been in the occupation of Richard Carter.[43] Today a small farm occupies the site, with a paddock behind. The incorporation of the previous owner's name into the Johnson surname casts an interesting light on the strength of family association with land. Another such instance occurs in the Haymes family. In 1894 Robert Bryan Haymes sold the land which his family had inherited through the Lount connection from the Bryans in the seventeenth century.

Tenement 15 is a triangular messuage of 3 roods 25 perches copyhold, bounded along the north-east by the village ditch. To it were attached two half virgates in the open fields. In the early fifteenth century, one half virgate was held by the Saunders family for a short time, while the other was held by Richard Fleckney who had received it *ad opus* from William Norman in 1421.[44] In 1433 he passed his half to William Aunger who by 1484 had acquired the other half and reduced the building to a toft. He held one messuage, one toft and one virgate for 13s. This tenement was held by Nicholas Mugyr in 1527 but passed afterwards to Robert Oswin. The Oswins were still holding it in 1679 and the arable just north of the tenement is still called Oswin's Leys,[45] but by 1780 William Haymes held it as part of his two virgates copyhold. Three modern houses occupy the road frontage today.

Tenements 16 and 17 provide a straightforward example of the Harcourt practice of building small landless cottages on pieces of waste ground.[46] These two and the Poor's Houses to the north are eighteenth-century examples; Tenement 40 belongs to the seventeenth, Tenements 30–42 and 52–6 belong to the twelfth and thirteenth centuries. Tenements 16 and 17 stand on the triangle of waste between the road to Carlton, the road to Turlangton and the Town End Furlong. One was copyhold, the other freehold; both belonged to the Perkins family, who also held half a virgate in the open fields, that is, Tenement 4. One was used as a dower cottage in 1780 by widow Perkins. North of this pair of cottages stood a huddle of dwellings on the Hall Meare just outside the town ditch. These are labelled Poor's Houses on the 1780 map but were locally known as the 'City'. One is a relatively large and attractive house, another is of cruck construction and until recently the last of the mud cottages stood in this area (*VCH Leics*. V: 178, pl. facing p. 320). The remainder are small, nondescript labourers' cottages.

Tenement 18 consisted of 55 perches of leasehold ground surrounded by freehold. It formed part of the bailiff's collection of leasehold sites in the seventeenth and eighteenth centuries and by 1780 was known as a Poor's House. Its leasehold tenure indicates that it once belonged to the demesne. Possibly a curial building stood here, jutting out into the roadway and encouraging the northward encroachment of other tenements on either side of it.

Tenement 19 occupied just over two acres of free pasture surrounding Tenement 18 on three sides. It represents a strip of ground taken from the roadway along the northern boundary of the demesne and corresponds to the southward encroachments made by Tenements 6–9. The Parkers probably came into possession of it in 1484 or earlier, though Robert Ray held a portion of it in 1609. They certainly held it in 1635 and sold it in 1743 to Mrs Wright, who also held 12½ acres copyhold and 5½ acres freehold. It was sometimes called Townsend Close and is therefore easily confused with Tenement 1.[47]

The demesne and freehold closes to the south-west of the village

Tenement 20 was an L-shaped leasehold close of just under an acre. It was held by the bailiff from 1484–1780 as part of a group of tenements which included Browns Place. Browns Place itself, however, was Tenement 53b, not Tenement 20 as shown on the 1780 map.

Tenement 21 was another rectangular close of just over an acre, but held by copyhold. A small building stood on its western boundary with a frontage on the main road. This was held successively by Mr Coxon and Mr Sacheverell in the seventeenth century, and by John Turner in the eighteenth. Two small pieces of freehold were carved óut of the southern part of this tenement in the seventeenth century; one of 16 perches was held by Mr Gage, the other, of 28 perches, by Mr Hawes. These had belonged to Mr Riley who sold them to Thomas Dent, woollen draper of Hallaton in 1588. The Riley tenement consisted of one messuage, a croft, nine acres of arable and one selion for 10s a year in rent.[48]

Tenement 22 known as the Hall Close consisted of 5¼ acres of land, including the Mound, and has always been administered by the bailiff until its sale by the college in 1973. If there was ever a manor house it must have stood somewhere on this site. Since the Harcourts never subinfeudated Kibworth Harcourt, no man of rank would have inhabited the manorial buildings and indeed the only reference we have to its early occupants is the bundle of four documents in which Adam Sybile of Kibworth Harcourt and Richard Sybile, Rector of South Kenelingworthe, released to Merton College their interest in one-ninth of the chief messuage called the Halleyard in Kibworth, the ninth presentation to the chapel, a ninth share in the windmill, the right to free bull and free boar and to common pasture and to land in the common fields together with court baron, View of Frankpledge, and the right to strays, homage, wards, reliefs, escheats, heriots, scutage and the services due from his tenants save suit at court. They reserved to themselves the southern part of the Halleyard and the demesne touching it.[49] The Sybile connection with the village went back to the thirteenth century and they are found attesting grants, acting as jurors and leasing small amounts of land; they also held customary land and acted as reeves from time to time. There was certainly no great gulf between them and other men of the village. Adam's son John inherited as a minor and Merton appointed the reeve as the boy's ward.[50] The goods he was responsible for comprised a chair, two tables, a cart, some planks, a hayfork, three wooden buckets, a ploughshare and plough beam, an iron shovel, a salting trough and one or two unidentified objects.[51] John's son William inherited in 1361 and alienated the holding without licence to William Polle in 1368. For this action the tenement was forfeited to the college and was found to be in poor condition.

Meanwhile, the Halleyard was being leased out for its pasture and garden. William Heyne was leasing the pasture in 1358,[52] Richard Chapman from 1368–89,* William Peeke from 1389–94.[53] When next mentioned, in 1438, a William Peeke was still holding it. It passed to John Clerke in 1477 who took out a thirty-year indenture in that year for the Halleyard and certain other tenements.[54] It had probably become part of the reeve's land while in Peeke's tenure. Subsequently it was held by the manor bailiff until 1973 when it was sold by the college.

Thus the early village lay-out would appear to have been a group of customary holdings to the north of the main east–west roadway, a group of manorial buildings to the south and the various utility buildings, such as the horse mill and fold, lying between the two.

---

* MM 6407.16, 6408.7. In 1282 Radulf prepositus, Radulf Carter, Robert ad Fontem, Robert Parsons, Hugh Godwine and Robert son of Robert Churt were granted the custody of the *domus de manerio* (MM 6376) and they renewed the lease in 1286 (MM 6377), in which year the Dovecote was taken by John de Chenesby (MM 6379) in whose name it was still held in 1397 (MM 6408.16). In 1334 the bailiff was amerced *per aula discoperta et alius dampnis* (MM 6401).

Tenement 23a consisted of a rectangular freehold close containing two acres which formed the south-west corner of the village. There were never buildings on this land and since it was freehold its records are scanty. However, it was held by Tobias Hawes in 1609 and passed, together with his other freehold properties, 35, 36 and 37, to Mr Buswell by 1635 and was held by Lebbeus Humfrey in 1780.

Tenement 23b consisted of an L-shaped freehold close containing just under two acres. It was held by Fox in 1609, but by 1635 had been transferred to the Buswell estate, and in 1780 belonged to Lebbeus Humfrey. Today it forms part of the grounds of the Spinneys, the home of Mr Briggs.

Tenement 24 consisted of another L-shaped freehold close of 1¾ acres. By 1609 a house had been built at its western end across the *'venella'* which used to divide this land from the island of freehold sites in the centre of the present village.[55] This house, known as the Spinneys is interesting for its many wings and eighteenth-century additions.

The customary cottage tenements with quarter-virgate holdings in the open fields

A row of cottage tenements standing in quarter-acre messuages lines the south side of the *via regis*. With the exception of the pinfold, they commanded quarter virgate holdings in the open fields and were held by copyhold tenure. On the thirteenth- and fourteenth-century rentals they form a separate category by themselves; they follow immediately after the customary tenements under the heading *cottagia*, and are held separate also from the demesne cottages (see table 2 'Cottages'). It is tempting to see these five cottage tenements, each with 5–6 acres arable, as the five *bordarius* holdings mentioned in the Domesday entry. If this was in fact the case, then presumably their holders did not hold by hereditary title but at the pleasure of the lord; they were estate tenants. However, by the thirteenth century they, as also the soke tenants, were holding by hereditary right and were classed as copyhold by the sixteenth century. In this they were fortunate.

Tenement 25 often held in conjunction with the pasture close, 21, was held by John Pyfford in 1484. The Marriotts held it in the 1530s and Humfrey Miller in 1540, together with Tenement 7.[56] By 1609 Nicholas Coxon held it and by 1635 it had passed, together with the rest of the Coxon properties, to William Burgess. Robert Haymes held it in 1780.

Tenement 26 occupies two messuages, making a total of 3 roods 8 perches. The Carters held it throughout the seventeenth century. It was bought by Randolf Lea from William Clerke in the early eighteenth century and sold to Thomas Varnham in 1733.[57] Neither the Leas nor the Varnhams lived in the village – Varnham was a blacksmith from Foxton – and the house was sublet first to the Perkins, later to John Heaps and to Pywell in the eighteenth century.

Tenement 27 occupied 1 rood 19 perches leasehold and is described in the transcript of the 1780 Survey as Pen Orchard. It seems there was a house on the pinfold from an early date. In 1372 John Joye held a *placea vocat le hallepynfold* for 4d rent.[58] John Skolas rebuilt the house on *una placea terre vocat le hallepynfold* in 1370.[59] John Cooper sublet it to Adam Brown from 1393–1402. When he died in 1402 the rent was raised to 2s. The pinfold is not specifically mentioned again until 1511 when the villagers were ordered to 'construct' the pinfold.[60] Again in 1540 John Kynde and the smith, William Clerke, were amerced for not mending their share of the 'pynfoldgate'.[61] The pinfold was probably not a pound for stray beasts, since there was apparently no official pinder. Strays were definitely kept by the bailiffs or the frankpledgemen in their own yards, so that there was no need for a pound. However, there was a need for a common sheepfold, since the clay soil was often too wet to allow sheep on the open fields throughout the winter (see above pp. 100, 140).[62] Consequently, manure had to be collected in the fold and to be carted out to the fields. There is in fact one reference to a ewe-yard.[63] The 1609 map gives Tenement 27 as held by Kilby and Tenement 28 as held by Ray. The map-maker has almost certainly got the names the wrong way round, since the Ray land was leasehold, and Tenement 27 was leasehold in 1780, not 28. Richard Chapman held the pinfold in 1635 together with 28. By the eighteenth century the Varnhams were leasing it. John Varnham of Kibworth Harcourt, blacksmith, sold the lease to John Foxton in 1752, who gave it to the Reverend Thomas Ray Dand of Sheepy.[64] It is today the site of the Three Horseshoes public house.

Tenement 28 occupies 1 rood 17 perches of copyhold together with half a virgate in the open fields. It is separated from the pinfold by an access lane to the Hall Close. In 1527 William Kilby held it but, since there were six half-virgate holdings for 7s 4d in 1500 and 1484, it is not possible to deduce which of the six was Tenement 28 in the late fifteenth century. The Kilbys continued to hold the land until 1610, when Francis Kilby died leaving a messuage, a toft and half a virgate to his wife Margery and son Robert. By 1635 the land had passed to Richard Chapman and by the late seventeenth century to John and Judith Brigstock. In 1686 a jury of eighteen villagers swore that the spring in the Brigstock's backyard had always supplied the manor house by a channel which ran across the street from the Brigstocks' spring to the well of the manor house.[65] This well was filled in during the 1960s. By 1780 Thomas Varnham held the land.[66]

Tenement 29 occupies 1 rood 15 perches copyhold to which was attached half a virgate in the open fields. Its sixteenth-century tenants cannot be traced, but by 1609 John Ore held it, and there had been Ortons in the village throughout the previous century. By 1635 it was held by Richard West and it later passed to the Smith family. Mathew Fox purchased the lease 'two several' times from William Smith and, in his will dated 1721, he left the tenement with its half virgate to his two grandsons, Thomas Wright and George Foxton. The two were to give 5s each to the poor annually out of the rent from this tenement.[67] According to the 1780 map Mrs Wright held the property, she being presumably the widow of Thomas Wright. A small Georgian house stands on the site today with a stable yard on the eastern side.

The freehold cottages without land in the open fields

As we move southwards the character of the village alters abruptly. We enter an area of freeholdings typified by very small yards and the absence of land in the open fields and the accompanying farm buildings. As freehold properties of little value, they were poorly documented, and were it not for the seventeenth-century maps we would have had to guess at their existence from the surplus of known families over known tenements in the seventeenth century. Although the definite evidence for their existence does not date back beyond the 1609 map, it is probable that these freeholds first made their appearance in the twelfth and thirteenth centuries when population pressure in the village was at its greatest. It is unlikely that outsiders were allowed to settle in the village and these encroachments on the village pasture were probably an agreed arrangement whereby the overspill from the households of customary tenements was accommodated. The expedient of sacrificing grass verges to house space was adopted again in the seventeenth century, to which Tenements 40, 56, 49 and George Fox's house on Tenement 24 stand witness, and in the eighteenth century when the Poor's Houses on the Carlton Road and the houses on both sides of the Beauchamp Road were erected.

The island of properties in the centre of Church Street was thus the 'city' of the pre-plague era. During the fifteenth century many of the cottages may have been abandoned, since even cottages with land attached in Hog Lane were left empty.[68] In the seventeenth century they were bought up by members of the new class of large land-holders as cottages for their farm labourers. Thus Tobias Hawes held a close and four cottages in 1609. We do not know how much arable he held but his successor, Mr John Buswell, held 110 acres.[69] Buswell held Tenement 8, probably for his bailiff, the same four cottages, 33, 35, 36 and 37, also Tenement 30, and a close, Tenement 23. The close may have been acquired to provide pasture for his men's cattle, since they would not have enjoyed pasture rights in the common fields. By 1780 the Buswell lands had been taken over by Robert Hames, who kept 36 and 37 and rented 38 and 40 from the feoffees of the village school. He farmed 384½ acres in 1780 and, in addition to his own house and the Rose and Crown Inn, held eight cottages in all (8, 25, 36, 37, 38, 40, 52, 53) and a close, 51.[70]

This was the area of estate cottages then, the only exceptions being the manor cottages, 30–2, and 34 which was possibly the old bakehouse.

Tenement 30, known as Le Pale, was college land leased at 4d a year to farmers in need of cottages for their labourers.[71] It occupied 38 perches but had been much reduced by 1780, when its yard had been incorporated into Lebbeus Humfrey's freehold 23.

Tenement 31 was another such, possibly the tenement constantly referred to in the leases and accounts as 'Le Muro'.[72] It too was leased for a nominal sum by large farmers, presumably for their labourers.

Tenement 32 was copyhold and occupied in the seventeenth century by the town shepherd, traditionally members of the Hubbert family.[73] Their house faced onto the Hall Close rather than on to the street.*

Tenement 34. In addition to their cottage the Hubberts also held a '*domus pistor; Anglie* a bakehouse', and a piece of ground called a 'meere' held by copy of court roll, in the late seventeenth century.[74] This could have been on Tenement 32, or it could have been on Tenement 34 which was certainly the bakehouse in the nineteenth

---

* 1661. William Hubbert's will. John Hubbert was to live in the bay next to the Hall Close and Isabel was to have the two *nether* bays.

century (Woodford 1868: 68). Tenement 34 was freehold and was held by Deacon in the early seventeenth century, by Parsons in 1635[75] and by William Mitchell in 1780. Little else is known of it, but a bakehouse, wherever it was, was essential to the village since fuel was so costly and scarce. (A fine bakehouse was demolished in Smeeton Westerby in 1972.)

Tenements 52–5 and 41–3 are likewise examples of pre-plague encroachment onto public land. Tenements 52–5 originally formed an island on the waste bounded to west and to south by a road leading to the church (at one end lay the parish church of Kibworth Beauchamp, at the other the chapel of Kibworth Harcourt) and to the north and east by a branch of the same road linking the two churches. When the eastern road was blocked by Tenements 41 and 42, its southern half became a long strip of pasture known as the 'school land' in the seventeenth century, and called Tenement 51 on the 1780 map.* Tenements 52–5 ceased to be a visible island but they remained landless, freehold properties, all except Browns Place, which was either 52 or 53, and which survived more complicated history.

In 1386 Richard Chapman granted to Adam Brown, draper, a tenement which had formerly belonged to Dominus William Polle and which stood between the tenements of Hugh Man and Nicholas Harcourt.[76] This was Tenement 53. In 1438 Adam Brown, *capellanus*, grandson of the aforementioned Adam Brown, granted the land to John Arundell, the rector of Kibworth Beauchamp.[77] According to Emden, this John Arundell later became Bishop of Chichester and chaplain and physician to Henry Beauchamp, Earl of Warwick. He died, a large-scale pluralist, in 1477 (Emden 1957: 49). It seems that John Arundell gave Brown's land to Merton College, for in 1448 some £26 was spent by the college on building a new hall and chamber together with stables at Browns Place.[78] When in 1477 the various parcels of college land still untenanted were united with 3 virgates of vacant customary land to form a single holding by indenture, Browns Place was included.[79] This explains how a humble freehold became a substantial college leasehold property with 3 virgates of arable land. Little is heard of it during the sixteenth century but from 1583–1616 it was held by William Barnard, who in 1600 renewed the lease for a rent of 21s 0d, 6 bushels of wheat and 10 bushels of barley malt.[80] Cooper held Browns Place from 1617–20,[81] Brian from 1621–7,[82] Standon from 1628–42† and Guy from 1642–79.[83] Thornton held it

* 1501. Nicholas Thorp's messuage lay 'in le chyrche Lane' (MM 6439.1).

† MM 6362.1628–42. Also LRO 1639. Standon's will: house, parlour, little parlour, chamber over house, chamber over parlour, one chimney.

after Guy, then Haymes took it in 1679–1755[84] but seems to have lost it later, for in 1758 another Robert Haymes bought the lease off John Rogers of Costock for £370.[85] The Haymes still held it in 1780, by which time it had been divided into three labourer's cottages.

Tenement 54, to the south of Browns Place, occupied a quarter of an acre, and was held by the Alwoods in the second half of the seventeenth century. The Alwoods also held a half-acre close nearby, Tenement 50a, and a virgate in the open fields attached to Tenement 12. By 1780 this little group of holdings had been broken up and the house and part of the yard of 54 was held by Thomas Carter, the eastern end of the yard having been lost to Robert Haymes.

Tenement 55 was, and still is, called the Rose and Crown Inn. It was held by the Bryan family in the seventeenth century as one of their many properties and by the Haymes family in the eighteenth and nineteenth. It was sold by Mr Robert *Bryan Haymes* in 1894.[86] Next to it, Tenement 56 was held by a cadet branch of the Haymes family. A group of seventeenth-century wills and deeds referring to the Cross Building in which the Bryan, Freeman and Hodge families had an interest may be referring to the present Rose and Crown building.[87]

The Old House, the Chapel and the Copyhold Messuages South of Hog Lane

If we retrace our steps to the junction of Church Street with the King's Road and Hog Lane we find on the corner of Church Street and Hog Lane a fine brick building with stone dressings dating from 1678. This is the Old House, standing on Tenement 43. The house is remarkable for its period, both because the use of brick is early for this district, and as an example of the fully developed Renaissance house (*VCH Leics.* V: 178). A scrolled pediment on the front of the house bears the date 1678 and the arms of William Parker, who moved to this house from the White House (Ten. 6) at about this time. The site was already held freely by Parker in 1635, together with a second cottage to the east, but in 1609 the site was occupied by a row of small cottages facing west and a small house facing onto Hog Lane. Tenement 41 to the south was likewise occupied by a row of cottages which had disappeared by 1635 and been replaced by a single large house belonging to Fox. A memorandum made in 1609 provides the clue: it runs, 'William Parker hath a house built on Foxunes Green which is thought to belonge of right to the colledge because built on waste.'[88] Foxune's Green was Tenement 41 and on it there were five cottages in

1599, when Thomas Fox died. He also held Tenements 24 and 39, both freehold. Evidently a row of cottages built on common land had been bought up by Parker and Fox in the early seventeenth century and demolished. They divided the land equally, each took one rood. Parker built his fine new house on his share, and Lebbeus Humfrey, when he acquired it, continued the policy of creating a gentleman's country seat at the expense of village tenements. He absorbed the Fox share and bought up Tenements 44 and 45 to provide the house with the garden which such a house deserved, and acquired the tenements opposite, 10a, 10b, and 11, for the stables. The lay-out of these gardens in a series of distinct rectangles reflects the boundaries of the messuage sites they overlie. The site of the horse mill in the square was incorporated into Tenement 10a, the town cross was removed from the square and an attempt was made to remove the trough also, but this the Warden refused to allow.[89]

From the square the ground slopes away eastwards towards the marsh. A road, known today as Albert Street but in earlier times as Hog Lane or Howgate (the gate to How Hill), provided access to the East Field and to Turlangton beyond. Its southern side was bounded by a row of copyhold tenements each standing in a quarter-acre curtilage and bounded to the south by a ditch, which drained into the pond on Tenement 48 known as the Fishpool.

Tenement 44 is the most westerly of the copyhold tenements on Hog Lane, and covers a full acre of ground. The Bryans held it in the sixteenth and seventeenth centuries, but nothing is definitely known of its earlier history. Two theories can be put forward: first, that it is the site of the four cottages in Hog Lane for which no tenants could be found in the late fourteenth century, hence its present size:[90] four roods, and the two virgates attached to it in the open fields. Against this must be set the absence of any reference to this new holding in the rentals of 1439, 1484, 1500 and 1527. The second theory is that it is the site of the free chapel of Kibworth Harcourt, for which so many documents survive for the early period, but which disappears without trace in the sixteenth century (Brodrick 1885: vii, 160, 224, 243, 247).[91] The site of Tenement 44 was one well suited for a church or chapel. It stood at the end of the village street, between manor and village, dominating all that went on but not obstructing the movement of carts and cattle around the kiln, the mill and the drinking troughs. The site is similar to that of Slawston church and indeed of many others all over England. The chapel seems to have been served by a chantry priest. Thus in 1296 Robert son of Reginald was amerced *quia non contruxit capellam sicut perceptum fuit ei per capitulum* (MM 6391;

6220), and in the late fourteenth century reference was made to Dominus John Godwyn[92] and Dominus William Polle.[93] In 1446 William Polle acted as proxy for the Warden in receiving the chapel,[94] in 1484 John Chapman was chantor,[95] and was succeeded in that office by a member of the Smith family,[96] who also held one virgate for 5s 0d a year freely. (By 1651 it had become the 'school land' but was still held for 5s 0d a year.) In the early sixteenth century Dominus William Polle fulfilled the duties of a curate,[97] but there is no further mention of either chapel or priest after the Reformation. Thereafter the village was served by St Wilfred's church, which stands half way between Harcourt and Beauchamp and was reported to be in a ruinous condition in 1526 (Bowker 1968: 132). The Bryan family moved into Kibworth Harcourt from Smeeton in 1541 and took a messuage and two virgates freely next to Parker's land.[98] The virgates were not true virgates, but were made up of the Hall grounds and Balkes, and later rentals regarded both messuage and arable as leasehold.[99] The coincidence of the dating cannot be ignored. We know there was a chapel, which disappeared completely in the late 1530s. The Bryans took up a newly created tenement in 1541 on a site which would have suited a church very well. If the priest's house had been attached to the chapel, as was a fairly common practice,* when the chapel was suppressed it could have been converted into a domestic building with very little trouble, and when the building was demolished in the eighteenth century even the memory of its exact site was lost. By the eighteenth century Woodford was speculating as to where the chapel may have stood (Woodford 1868: 22), and the village bristles with theories today.

Tenement 45 was regarded as freehold in 1780. Topographically it forms a prolongation of Tenement 51 and it may indeed have been a public way running behind the chapel.† No house stood upon it in 1609, but by 1635 the quarter-acre messuage boasted a house and was occupied by the Smith family. The Smiths had held land in Harcourt since the thirteenth century at least. They continued to hold land throughout the sixteenth and seventeenth centuries, but in the early eighteenth century they were in difficulties. When William Smith died in 1716 aged 65, he held only a quarter of a virgate which he instructed his executors to sell, dividing the proceeds among his four children.[100] Francis Fletcher purchased the quarter virgate and added to it half a virgate which Mary his wife had inherited from William

* For example, the Chapel of St John in Jerusalem at East Hendred, Berks.

† MM 2945. In 1336 Elias Taylour paid Adam Sybile 2d for a cottage 'in the kyrheland'.

and Alice Clerke.[101] In 1757 William Fletcher sold the close to Theophilus Henshaw of Loughborough, who conveyed it to John Fox for £43.[102] In 1772 the grandson of Francis Fletcher sold the same close to Lebbeus Humfrey for £43.[103] Possibly the first sale was a form of mortgage subsequently redeemed. The close 'now in Mr Humfrey's bottom garden' is described as bounded on the south and east by William Haye's close, on the west by Lebbeus Humfrey's and on the north by the yard and dwelling-house of Francis Fletcher. Today even the dwelling-house has been absorbed into the grounds of the Old House.

Tenement 46 was a one-rood messuage of copyhold land with one virgate in the open fields. Its history is very similar to that of Tenement 45. From the fourteenth to the early eighteenth century it was held by the Carter family, but they too fell into financial difficulties and sold the lease to William Hayes. Today, it has disappeared beneath the orchard of the Old House.

Tenement 47 occupied one rood 32 perches of leasehold without arable in the open fields. It formed part of the indentured lands held by the bailiff and is called the 'Bruchyard' on the 1780 map. The meaning of this word and of the names of the other yards held by indenture is not clear. They appear on a variety of documents and on none of them are they legible or intelligible, and one suspects that successive scribes simply copied the hieroglyphics without themselves knowing what they meant. The clearest is the entry on the 1527 rental which describes John Polle's lands as including the 'Bathyard, Foalyard, yowe and kylne yard'. If the yoweyard was the pinfold and the kylne yard Tenement 6x, Tenement 47 could have been a brute or neatyard and Tenement 30 the foalyard. Alternatively, 'Bathyard' could be understood as referring to the 'Bakeyard' (Ten. 30) in which case the 'foalyard' would have been Tenement 47. Tradition lingers in the village today that there was a pound near the fishpool off Hog Lane.

Tenement 48 occupied nearly an acre of copyhold in 1635. In 1316 the Warden of Merton granted Roger Caumpe, Rector of the Church of Kibworth, one close called the 'Fyspolyard' with a *vivarium* for life at an annual rent of 6s 8d.[104] According to the account rolls the rent from the pasture and fishpond had dropped to 12d by 1360.[105] John Alot held it from the 1360s to 1391.[106] In 1430 the *'fossat procedans a stagno ad finem villae'* was repaired and the tenants were permitted to water their beasts in the *'Stagno ad finem villae'* otherwise known as 'Pynder's Pit'.[107] In 1434 and in 1443 all the villagers were called upon to repair the *fossat vocat ffyshepulende*.[108] The Saunders took the Alot land in 1432 and were still holding it in 1500. By 1599 William Gage held Fishpondclose for 5s 0d a year, and it was still in the bailiff's hands in 1609.[109] However, by 1635 it had been divided into two. Nicholas Porter held the western portion for 2s 6d, and Eliot held the eastern half. With these two portions went, similarly divided, Hayward's Meare, the gravel pits, Church Hadland, Coombes Meare and Howgate, amounting to nine acres, one rood and fifteen perches.[110] After 1693 no more is heard of the eastern share which had passed to the Goodmans,[111] and it is possible that the two halves were reunited in the eighteenth century. Between 1700–11 Fishpool Close was held successively by Geoffrey Parker, Thomas Perkins and Randal Lea.[112] In 1740 Thomas Flotcher bequeathed Fishpooldike to his niece, Mary Holyock, wife of William Holyock of Beauchamp, labourer, while Tenement 45 passed to his nephew, William Fletcher.[113] By 1780 William Hayes held the Fishpoolyard in addition to the two closes, 49 and 50, and to 56.9 acres arable.

The small copyhold closes in the South-East

The south-eastern corner of the village was occupied by 1–3 rood closes of copyhold land attached to the tenements in the western end of the village. For example, in 1609 John Polle held Tenement 10b north of Hog Lane and Tenement 50b to the south of the lane; Richard Alwood held Tenement 12 to the north and Thomas Alwood held the close 50a; Robert Bryan held Tenement 14 to the north and the close 49a together with Tenement 44. Unlike the larger closes on the western side of the village, these eastern closes tended to be regular in shape and to be subdivided both lengthwise and across and to be reunited again according to family convenience. Encroachment began in the eighteenth century, when a number of cottages were erected along the southern boundary facing the road to Kibworth Beauchamp. In the 1950s the remainder of the closes were built over by a private housing estate.

Closes and buildings

Up to this point we have been considering tenements simply as ground space within the village. It is possible to be a little more precise.

A customary tenement or messuage consisted of a house, garden, orchard and close. If we take as typical the messuages to the north of the King's Road a clear distinction can be seen between the house and garden area and the close behind. The closes have been ridged up, but it is not possible to say at what date.[114] Either the closes represent a furlong which, during the reorganisation of the fifteenth century, was enclosed and turned into separate closes attached to the messuages north of the King's Road, or, they were ploughed up after the amalgamation of holdings had thrown together groups of closes large enough to be ploughed. I am inclined to favour the latter explanation, since beyond the town ditch lies an area of permanent pasture and a triangle of land which only came under cultivation relatively late, probably in the thirteenth century. It is unlikely that an area of permanent pasture would have lain sandwiched between two arable furlongs. Closes are mentioned in the court rolls from 1380 onwards,[115] usually in connection with the repair of party fences and of ditches, and it would seem strange if, in the early days when the village was first laid out, houses were not each provided with a generous private close where young or sick animals could be cared for and an orchard planted, in addition to a vegetable plot or 'garden'. It must remain, however, an open question.

The messuages were divided from one another by *sepes* or hedges; these were presumably dead fences or mud walls, since the court order that all householders should repair their fences was a routine one in the fifteenth century, and many offenders were amerced.[116] Brushwood was prized and even more so trees. The felling of elm[117] and ash[118] trees are noted in the court rolls and the offenders fined, except in those cases where the college had failed to provide timber for the construction or repair of a cottage and the aggrieved tenant had taken matters into his own hands. Occasionally the bailiff was authorised to fell a tree for building purposes.[119] By the seventeenth century, college tenants were expected to plant a certain quota of trees on their lands,[120] and the whole village had been surrounded by a live hedge.[121]

The buildings on these messuages were characteristically placed on the boundary of the site, facing directly onto the street, with the yard and close behind, aptly called the 'backside'. Throughout the period the dwelling-houses were built on the long house plan, one room deep, though whether or not one 'room' was a byre or barn it is impossible to say. A series of building accounts for the fifteenth century throws considerable light on the type of construction and cost of labour and materials in this period.[122]

The normal model was that of the cruck frame on a stone base with mud walls, timber ridge-pole and wall-plates, and a straw-thatched roof. The standard bay was sixteen feet by sixteen and the recorded houses are all of three or more bays. One pair of cottages *insemel iacentis*[123] made up eight bays. Granges or barns were built to the same specifications. The last of the mud cottages built on these principles was demolished in the 1960s. By the sixteenth century chimneys were considered desirable and by the eighteenth century brick was replacing mud. In some cases the mud walls were taken down, an extra few courses of stone were added to the base, in order to raise the height of the crucks to allow for a second storey, and the walls rebuilt in brick. In other cases a brick face was simply built up against the mud face. A good example of the latter method can be seen in Mrs Swannock's cottage in Turlangton where the gap between the brick and the plaster is wide enough to allow a camera to be inserted and a photograph taken of the old outer face of the original mud wall. Tile capped mud walls are still common in the region as party walls between backyards, although the art of puddling mud for this purpose is, today, a dying one.

From the inventories we learn that the addition of a second storey was already common by the sixteenth century. A typical house, such as Robert Standley's on site 52, in 1639 comprised four ground-floor rooms; the house, parlour, little parlour and kitchen, and two first-floor rooms; one over the house, the other over the parlour.[124] Less typical were the Manor House and the Paddocks. Completely untypical was the Old House which falls outside the scope of this present study. A series of building accounts for a hall, chamber and stables survives.[125] They refer to a building erected in 1448 and called Browns Place. The present building on Browns Place, Tenement 53, bears no resemblance to the 1448 building, but there is a certain similarity between the building described in the accounts and the present Manor House, which in 1448 belonged to the same group of indentured holdings known as Browns Place. At any rate the Manor House serves as a visual expression of the 1448 accounts. These depict a timber-framed building on a deep stone base, with lime-plastered walls, a slate roof and tiled floors. The north wing of the Manor House consists of a stone base several courses deep and a stone chimney on the north side. Brickwork has replaced the plaster above the stone, but the tie-beams are of massive proportions though they support today nothing more than a roof of machine-cut slate. The stone base continues round the central and south wings and the tie-beams of the central wing are as massive as those of the north wing, quite out of proportion with the size of the building and the weight of the roof. The south wing is of cruck construction, but the interior is well fitted with closely studded partitions on the ground floor. The stone for the 1448 building was carted from Medbourne, eight miles away; the great timbers came from Rothley Temple, an estate in which the Harcourts had always had a close interest (Clarke 1882: 89–93); the lesser timbers and lathes were brought from Lutterworth; the spars, ridge-tiles and probably the nails came from Leicester, the lime for the plaster from Barrow, while the slate was brought from Kirby. The carriage costs were therefore very considerable, in addition to the cost of the materials themselves and of the skilled labour of carpenters, stonemasons and plasterers. The grand total came to £26; some idea of how large a sum this was can be gained by comparison with other building costs; for example, almshouses built in Stratford-upon-Avon between 1411 and 1417 cost £5 9s 9½d; the schoolhouse built in 1427 cost £10 5s 6½d and a six-bay barn built in 1488 cost £22 2s 5½d (Lloyds 1961: 23–4). It is far from clear for whom this hall and chamber was intended; by the mid sixteenth century it had become the bailiff's house and was occupied by the Rays until they built themselves a more sophisticated dwelling in the eighteenth century. It then became the house of the Reverend Thomas Thomas who made considerable alterations and additions. It next became two labourers' cottages until rescued and restored by Mr J. E. Bartlett of Brackley, Northants. In 1972 it was sold by the college to Mr Thurnham who has done much to restore its fifteenth-century features.

If the Manor House was the expression of wealth in the fifteenth century, the Paddocks and the White House typify seventeenth-century affluence. From 1491 until 1599 the Paddocks was occupied by the Iliffe family (Ten. 3). In 1568 John Iliffe's house was described in his inventory as comprising a 'haule' in which the cooking was done, a parlour where the family slept at night and a chamber in which eight stones of wool were stored.[126] It is possible that this could be a description of the relatively small but well-constructed 'house' partially embedded in the present eighteenth-century structure; its south wall forms part of the north wall of the eighteenth-century building, but later northward extensions have caused it to look like an inner partition wall (see figs. 3 and 4). By the mid seventeenth century the property had come into the hands of the Watts family. Robert Watts, when he died in 1673, was possessed of a house consisting of a hall and parlour, a chamber with a beer cellar under it, a chamber over the parlour, another chamber, a milk cellar, a chamber over the house and another over the entry, a kitchen with a chamber over it, a malt house and a malt chamber, a coalhouse and a stable for three horses; in other words eight living-rooms, two cellars and three outhouses in addition to the stable.[127] We know that Robert Watts occupied the Paddocks,[128] but it would seem that at this date the house, though extended to cover the present ground-plan, was of

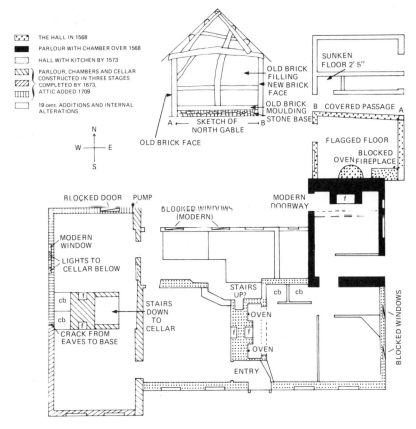

Fig. 3   Ground floor of Paddocks Farm (1568–1673)

two storeys only. Bridgett Watt's inventory, made in 1683,[129] describes a similar eight-roomed house with two cellars (probably not below ground level at this date) and various outhouses, to which description John Hames's inventory, made in 1686, has nothing to add.[130] (How the house came to be in the possession of John Hames is not clear, since his son William did not marry Anne Lount, the granddaughter and heiress of William Watts, until about 1694.) The next known landmark is 1704, by which date the height of the house had been raised to provide a third storey, and it is at this point that the present brick structure replaced the plaster walls above the level of the stone footing, for in the east gable is inserted the date, 1704, in burnt brick. The stone footing does not appear to have been disturbed and the basic measurements of the house are still the traditional sixteen feet by sixteen. At a date shortly after this a cellar was

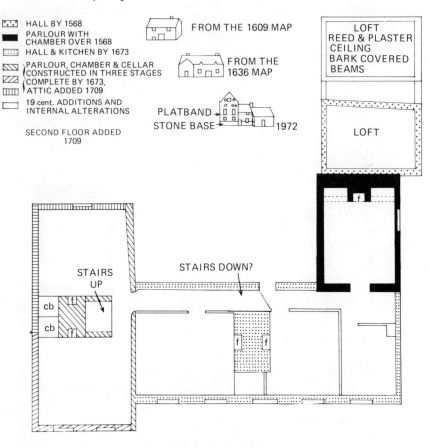

Fig. 4   First floor of Paddocks Farm (1568–1673)

excavated below the northern half of the west wing. This operation may have caused some subsidence of the western wall and some necessary reconstruction, since the brick moulding below the eaves continues northwards as far as the crack which traverses the entire wall from top to bottom at the point where the cellar begins, and there the moulding abruptly stops.

Thus on site 3 can be traced, not only the amalgamation of four half-virgate tenements to form one large messuage, but the subsequent transformation of the house on that messuage from a humble three-roomed cruck dwelling, to a three-storeyed, fourteen-roomed brick building, panelled within, well proportioned without, the fit dwelling for an eighteenth-century squire (see above p. 122).

8

The economy of the small landholder

Give me neither riches nor poverty, but enough for my sustenance.
Proverbs 30.v.8

A very common unit of landholding, the virgate, together with its poor relation the half virgate, slowly died out in the period 1400–1700. The axe was laid to the root in the fifteenth century, during which the number of half virgates at Kibworth Harcourt was reduced from thirty-eight to eight. However, of the eight survivors, the last did not succumb until 1700, by which date the virgate as a unit had also disappeared. Their protracted struggle for survival provides the material for the following analysis.

It is the object of this chapter to try to recapture the economics of what had been a tenacious and stable way of life and to study the causes of its decay. The subject has been approached from two angles, one tabular, the other descriptive. An attempt has been made to reconstruct the income and expenses of the virgater and the half virgater over a period of 330 years in order to relate and compare the four main factors in the Leicestershire smallholder's economy: namely, grain prices, wool prices, wages and rents. Of course, such a task is not easily fulfilled and it has been necessary in the pages immediately following to describe at some length how each set of figures has been arrived at. The compilation of tables 14 and 15 has, I think, been justified for two reasons. First in that it has achieved that which it was intended it should achieve: it points the direction and causes of trends during the process of decay. Secondly, it has reiterated the need for more regional studies; for *local* price series, *local* wage rates, *local* sowing rates and yields, since these differ so widely from one county to another. It likewise throws into relief the need to differentiate between rural and urban economies; for example, between growers' prices and retail prices, between shopping lists and employment opportunities in the town and in the country.

The inventories of the early modern period allow one to describe in some detail the amenities or lack of them normal to households of the virgate and half virgate income brackets, and to compare these with those of the more wealthy – and even with those of the less wealthy in terms of landed property, namely, those servants in husbandry whose inventories were seldom taken, but whose accommodation is described in the inventories of the rich and whose wages are recorded in private accounts and in official schedules.

Land use

In 1370 the most common size of holding at Kibworth Harcourt was the virgate of 21 acres arable and 3 acres pasture held for 20s rent per annum, and the half virgate of 9 acres arable and 3 acres pasture held for 10s per annum. Throughout the period the arable of the smallholder was cultivated on the three-course system, with one field under peas, the other under barley with some wheat and the third fallow. So on his 21 acres arable the virgater would have roughly 7 acres under peas, 7 under barley and 7 fallow. This even division can still be seen in the inventories of countless Leicestershire husbandmen in the sixteenth and seventeenth centuries, as well in Kibworth as elsewhere in the county. With the virgate went, as we have seen, a stint of four cows and twenty-four sheep.

The price series

Price series based on urban retail prices introduce a wide margin of error to calculations concerning sums received by growers in small rural markets.* They must, therefore, be discarded in favour of more appropriate sources, the best of which are the sales accounts of farmers such as Robert Loder, Henry Best and Sir Thomas Pelham (Fussell, *Camden Soc.* liii; Best Robinson, *Surtees Soc.* xxxiii).[1] Unfortunately, this type of source material does not survive in sufficient quantity to provide the base for a continuous price series, but it can be used to cross-check another source, namely, the values placed on crops and wool in the probate inventories for the archdeaconry of Leicester.[2]

Unfortunately, we have no explicit statement in any of our records of the criteria used when making these evaluations. It was usual at this period to sell corn in the field well in advance of the harvest, so

---

* J. T. Rogers, *A History of Agriculture and Prices in England,* vols. ii and iv (Oxford 1866, 1882). Nevertheless, for want of a better source, the average price for the decades 1290–1300, 1371–80, 1411–20 have been based on Rogers's averages in tables 14 and 15. See also E. H. Phelps Brown and S. V. Hopkins, 'Seven centuries of the prices of consumables compared with builder's wage rates', *Economica,* NS, xxiii (1957), 296–314; and Findings of the Beveridge Committee, Box I, Institute of Historical Research.

that the art of assessing the probable yield of a crop and its market value was well developed. This would be a common-sense approach, but we should check it. Examination of inventories from widely separated villages in the county revealed a pronounced tendency to place the same value on the quarter of barley, malt, peas or wheat, give or take a few pence, and a continuous graph showing the rise and fall in prices in any given year could be drawn; in other words there was no haphazard and meaningless scatter of prices. Moreover, the pattern of the graph was repeated year after year, betraying a regular seasonal tide of price levels. Therefore, the appraisors were referring to a common yardstick in their valuations. That this yardstick was the current market level is borne out by comparison with farming accounts, such as those referred to above, and with the weekly bulletin published by Houghton in the late seventeenth century, which reported the current price for the best wheat, barley, malt and peas in the markets of Leicester, Melton Mowbray, Oakham and Northampton.* Lastly, when these local market prices are compared with urban retail prices, they are found to be lower, as one would expect, but otherwise to follow the same general trends, with occasional marked deviations reflecting local harvest conditions.

The inventory data can, therefore, be accepted as a reliable record of Leicestershire market prices. The number of surviving inventories is considerable, but relatively few record grain, peas or wool in store, and when they do, they do not always give a separate value for each product; thus the number of relevant entries is in the end quite small. For the sixteenth century, therefore, it was necessary to take a ten-year period, from 1551–60, in order to get a sufficiently large number of entries, and a six-year period, from 1570–5, later in the century. The number of surviving inventories is greater for the seventeenth century so that the time factor made it necessary to take only five-year periods, which yielded about the same number of entries as for the sixteenth century. Unfortunately, for the late seventeenth century the inventories tend to become perfunctory and less informative, though the levelling off of seasonal fluctuations is an interesting phenomenon and would repay further investigation.

Dating remains a problem. The archdeaconry began its year on 25 March. The accounts with which one would wish to compare the inventories began their year on 29 July. Since we are interested not only in the prices of grain stored but also in the value of crops in the

---

* Unpublished material gathered by Mr Giles Harrison, the Central London Polytechnic, to whose generous assistance I am much indebted. John Houghton's *Collection of Letters for the improvement of Husbandry and Trade* was published in 4 volumes in 1727 by Richard Bradley, FRS.

field, the dates of both inventories and accounts have been adjusted throughout to conform with the calendar year running from 1 January to 31 December.

In fact, not many entries relate to the winter months; they tend to be bunched within the period from February–July. Prices tended to rise after February to reach a peak in May–June and to fall abruptly in July, presumably because by July shortage of money and the relative abundance of fresh food and pasture made it both necessary and possible for men and beasts to do without barley and peas.

The histograms in appendix 7 give a reasonably accurate impression of the range in prices a small farmer had to contend with over a five-year period. For example, between 1601–14, which spanned a plague year in 1605, his peas might be worth 4s a quarter in one year and 40s a quarter in the next. As has been noted, prices were usually at their highest a couple of months before the harvest, at a time when few farmers had much remaining in store to sell, if indeed they had not already sold the bulk of their crop before or just after the previous harvest in order to settle debts, pay wages and buy seed corn. So it is towards the lower end of the spectrum that one must look; a small farmer can be said to have received from 4s to 13s 4d for his peas crop, not for him such dazzling sums as 40s. I have taken the arithmetic mean as the basis for my calculations for the peasant budget but it should be borne in mind that even this figure is probably on the generous side.

It is worth noting in passing that peas and barley were about equal in value, and that in spite of the labour and fuel costs involved, malt was not very much dearer than barley, except in years of scarcity when its manufacture was forbidden and its value could soar to as much as 70s the quarter, but in such circumstances customers were presumably equally scarce.

Prices for the period from 1290–1490 have been taken from Thorold Rogers' classic work on agricultural prices. His data, as also that used by Lord Beveridge and D. L. Farmer (1957–8: 207–20), is largely derived from institutional sources and refers to retail prices for wheat and barley and, unfortunately, yields no price series for peas.

Since peas were given much the same value as barley in the sixteenth-century inventories, it has been assumed that the same was the case in the earlier period. However, both peas and barley almost certainly fetched lower prices in local markets than in retail centres such as Oxford, Cambridge and Farnham. Therefore, the receipts and the cost of cereals and legumes given in tables 14 and 15 are higher than was in fact the case.

Sowing rates and the yield per acre

We have no firm evidence for the customary sowing rate in Leicester-shire during the period from 1300–1700. Fitzherbert was an advocate of thick sowing and in his native Derbyshire barley was indeed sown more thickly than elsewhere, at 4 bushels to the acre (Fitzherbert 1534; Bodl. Douce xx 3(2) fo. 10). The modern practice is to sow thinly at Kibworth Harcourt at 2 bushels to the acre which yields 6, 8.5 and 10 quarters in bad, average and good years, an increase per grain of 16, 22.8 and 26.2. The theory behind thin sowing at Kibworth is that the land is too rich for barley and would produce an overtall, 'rank' crop if thickly sown. Thin sowing ensures the maximum number of tillers and therefore many ears per plant, and short stems which can better withstand wind and heavy rain.* The table in appendix 6 shows that on clay soils the most common sowing rate at an earlier date was about 3 bushels and, since the Leicestershire yields were not high, I have taken 3 rather than Fitzherbert's 4 bushels as the sowing rate at Kibworth for barley, and 2 for peas. In fact we do have one piece of direct evidence for Kibworth Harcourt. In 1314–15 the 15 acres belonging to the late Nicholas Sybile were administered by the reeve (MM 6219), and we are told that 7½ acres were sown with 16 bushels of peas, giving a sowing rate of just over 2 bushels per acre, and 5 acres were sown with 10 bushels of barley, giving a sowing rate of 2 bushels per acre. This supports our estimate for peas and indicates that our estimate of 3 bushels per acre for barley may be too high. However, since 1314–15 was a notoriously bad year for crops, and seed corn may have been scarce, it would be wiser to place our trust in estimates rather than in this single scrap of direct evidence.

Yields per acre in England generally were extremely variable both from year to year and from district to district. For a small farmer with limited reserves a succession of poor harvests or of low prices could prove disastrous, so that it is important to discover not only the average yield and the spectrum of yields but also the year-to-year sequence of good and bad harvests. Once again farmers' accounts are the best source of information concerning yields, but are too few in number to provide the basis for a quantitative study. Consequently, historians have preferred to rely on contemporary estimates such as those of the Georgical Committee in 1664–5 (Lennard 1932–4: 23–45) and of Gregory King in 1697 (in Thirsk and Cooper 1972: 196). These

---

* Information supplied by Mr M. Stops, Paddocks Farm, Kibworth Harcourt. This is the largest farm in the parish and is leased from Merton College. Watson and More (1962) recommend a sowing rate of 2–3 bushels in modern conditions and the average *national* yield per grain today is from 14–21.

estimates agree well enough with the account rolls, and in general terms the barley yield per acre in the period from 1200–1400 was in the region of 13–23 bushels, increasing to up to 30 bushels by the seventeenth century. Gregory King's average of 16 bushels of barley per acre errs if anything on the generous side, but is broadly correct as averages go.

A third source of information can be found in the probate inventories, which have the advantage of providing a year-to-year record of harvest yields. Their use involves several interpretative difficulties, which are discussed in appendix 5.

Figures 5, 6, 7 and 8, based on the data supplied by the inventories, give some idea of the range of yields, their sequence and the general impression that on the whole the yield per acre had increased somewhat in the 130 years between 1570–1700; an impression shared by M. K. Bennett who believed that yields improved generally during the sixteenth and seventeenth centuries from an average wheat yield of 9 bushels per acre in 1500 to 12.75 bushels in 1650 (Bennett 1935: 12–29). I use the word 'impression' advisedly, having in mind the yields shown below for 1639, and for 1698, which year was also marked by high mortality (see fig. 1).

Unfortunately, peas ground was nearly always reckoned in customary rather than in statute acres, so that it is not possible to obtain similar figures for peas yields. Had this been possible, the peasant budget could have been calculated separately for each year of the four groups of years selected, thereby throwing into high relief the crests and troughs of the smallholder's annual income. As it is, the arithmetic mean has been taken for each of the groups of years and the calculations for the table have been based on these. Thus 7 acres of barley in the period from 1570–5 yielded 7 × 8.8 bushels,* that is 61.6 bushels or 7.7 quarters, a yield of 1.1 quarters per acre.

The modern rate of sowing for peas is higher than for barley but the yield per acre is less; thus 16 stone of peas will yield 23 cwt in an average year, giving a yield per grain of 11, whereas 10 stone of barley will yield 34 cwt. However, the old practice was to sow peas more thinly than barley, and the yield then as now was roughly half that of barley, as is confirmed by the appraisers who, for the same holding, would put only half the value on peas land as on barley land, in spite of the fact that the value of peas per quarter was the same as for barley. Peas are more susceptible to weather conditions, especially

---

* See appendix 5 where the average yield between 1570–1700 is seen to be 1.92 quarters. Nevertheless, a steady yield of 2 quarters from 1290–1700 gives an unduly optimistic picture of the returns of the half virgater, while minimising those of the full virgater who could better withstand a series of poor harvests.

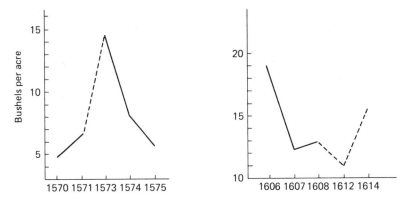

Fig. 5   Expected barley yields in June, 1570–5
Fig. 6   Expected barley yields in June, 1606–14

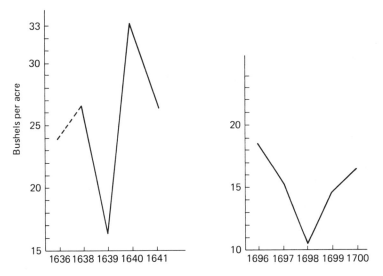

Fig. 7   Expected barley yields in June, 1636–41
Fig. 8   Expected barley yields in June, 1696–1700

during the harvest, but on the whole good weather for barley is good weather for peas, so we can estimate the peas yield in any given year to have been half that of barley. Thus, 7 acres of peas in the period 1570–5 would have yielded 7 × 4.4 bushels, that is, 30.8 bushels or 3.85 quarters, a yield of 0.55 quarters per acre.

Table 13. *Sowing rates, grain yields and prices at Kibworth Harcourt* (sowing rate: barley 3 bushels per acre; peas 2 bushels per acre)

		Yield per acre in quarters[a]	Price per quarter[b] in shillings
Barley	1290–1500	2	As given by J. T. Rogers[c]
	1371–1560	2	As given by J. T. Rogers
	1570–5	1.1	7.49
	1606–14	1.7	15.06
	1636–41	3.12	14.57
	1696–1700	1.75	23.14
Peas	1290–1300	1	As given by J. T. Rogers
	1371–1560	1	As given by J. T. Rogers
	1570–5	0.55	8.65
	1606–14	0.85	13.3
	1636–41	1.56	16.8
	1696–1700	0.88	21.5

[a] See p. 152 fn.
[b] See appendices 5 and 7.
[c] For Rogers's prices per quarter see p. 148 fn; pp. 160–3, and table 14 and 15.

Wool prices and wool yields

In the course of the sixteenth century the quality and the output of wool changed in Leicestershire. The large, long-stapled 'Leicester' breed gradually replaced the medieval short-stapled breed (Bowden 1962: 25–31). As the county produced less fine-quality wool it eventually ceased to supply the western woollen industry and came instead to supply the worsted industry in the north and east (ibid: 58, 64, 72). Thus in both production and marketing the sixteenth century witnessed a period of transition. Nevertheless, the price of wool steadily rose until 1603, after which date prices began to fall off as competition was encountered from Spanish and Irish wool imports (ibid: table 3). Richard Coleman's inventory for 1580 refers to 'small sheep' which would imply the presence of other 'large' sheep in the town flock. Allowance must, therefore, be made for an increase in the weight of fleeces during the sixteenth century. The average yield per sheep in the mid fourteenth century was 1.4 lb, by the mid sixteenth century it had risen to 1.9 lb and by the eighteenth century or earlier it had risen to 3.14 lb (ibid: 96; Thirsk 1967: 666; Grosseteste, *Rules* c. 10). Henry Best's better-quality sheep in 1641 yielded 3 lb and these were not the large, long-stapled breed (Best Robinson, 1857: 24). For the same period, poor-quality sheep in the chalk country of Wiltshire were yielding 2½ lb (Kerridge 1951: 141). So it seems reasonable to take 3 lb per sheep for the mid seventeenth century at Kibworth, while adopting the national averages for the earlier centuries, namely, 1.4 and 1.9 lb.

The marketing opportunities for growers in the Kibworth area were good. In 1600 Leicester city erected a 'very fit woolhall with convenient storehouses' and held a free market every Wednesday, Friday and Saturday (Bateson 1905: 281, 416). In 1618 the city was granted a Charter of Staple of Wool whither woolbroggers carried their wool for sale to 'divers northern clothiers [who] have usuallie bought their woolls in Leicester'. By the end of the seventeenth century the stockingmakers of Leicester claimed that they bought 200 tods of wool annually and employed 2000 poor people of Leicester and the adjacent villages (Stocks 1923: 178, 536). By this date, Kibworth Beauchamp and Smeeton Westerby both supported a relatively large framework knitting population. So the 'petty breeders' of Kibworth Harcourt could sell their wool to small clothworkers or spinsters at Kibworth Beauchamp, or could sell to the middlemen who supplied the Leicester market. Husbandmen usually sold their wool at or near shearing time for cash, undertaking either to supply a specified weight or the entire crop, and accepting the price current at the time of the contract or at the time of delivery. After shearing, the fleeces, whether sorted or not, were packed in canvas bags and stored in the grower's house on wooden boards free from damp until collected by the buyer (Bowden 1962: 13, 85–91).

From the point of view of the virgater or half virgater it was the grower's price which mattered, not that received by the middleman and the clothier, these being some 10 per cent and 20 per cent higher respectively (Bowden 1952). The inventories give the value of the wool to the grower, and it is upon figures drawn from the Leicester archdeaconry inventories that the decennial averages quoted in the table have been calculated. Checked against the price quoted in Houghton's Newsheet for Melton Mowbray in 1699–1700, the appraisor's figure is about 4s below Houghton's figure, but tallies exactly with the figures mentioned in the accounts for William Heyrick's estate at Beaumanor.* For the earlier period from 1290–1490, wool prices have been based on Thorold Rogers' retail prices. Lloyd's prices were found not to differ significantly from those of Thorold Rogers, and since neither dealt with the East Midlands, there seemed little to choose between them (Lloyd 1973). Bowden's figures relate to growers' prices in the Durham region from 1551–1614 and, predictably, tend to be a shilling or so below Leicestershire prices as

---

* Giles Harrison. Prices collected for Leics. and Northants. 1640–1700; see also appendix 7.

given in the inventories. According to Oxfordshire inventories, Oxfordshire wool prices dropped behind Leicestershire prices in the seventeenth century.

Family size

No demographer or economic historian can avoid the difficult question of family size, but until very recently little attempt was made to see the problem in regional as well as national terms. Since most of the national figures for the medieval period have been based on highly specific local studies the cart may seem to have been set before the horse (Titow 1969; Hatcher 1977). However, the serious examination of local differences in family structure is now underway and, in addition, the Cambridge Group for the History of Population and Social Structure has recently begun to push its researches back into the medieval period and to bring together and interpret work carried out in isolation elsewhere.[3] The Kibworth source material is sufficiently comprehensive for us to be able to reconstruct a relatively precise picture for the village and the locality without the need to extrapolate from other studies, therefore no more need be said at this point, though a full study of the Kibworth material will be undertaken in the following chapter.

Diet

Although the sumptuous and often bizarre menus of the medieval banquets provided upon occasion in the households of the great have received their due share of publicity, the daily ration of everyman has had fewer exponents. No medieval chronicler was moved to expatiate at length upon the diet of the peasantry, and it was not until the eighteenth century that the matter became the subject of social comment – and even then, attention was focused upon the plight of the urban poor rather than on the normal rations of the countryman. Latterly, an increasing number of social historians have turned their attention to the history of diet, but the emphasis still remains on the shopping basket – or begging bowl – of the urban poor (Ashley 1928; Baker 1966; Burnett 1966; Oddy and Miller 1976; Stouff 1970). One of the pioneers of the scientific study of the history of diet was the Professor of Biochemistry at University College London, Sir Jack Drummond, who, with the collaboration of Anne Wilbraham, brought out *The Englishman's Food* in 1939. Further historical material has since been brought to light, but on the whole the biochemical interpretation and comment remains valid and retains its usefulness. Since the book is easily accessible it serves as a useful point of reference in an as yet little-studied subject.

According to Drummond,

> the basic diet was made up of brown or wholemeal bread, milk, cheese, a considerable amount of butter largely used for cooking purposes, eggs, honey, occasionally bacon or poultry, salt, pulses, onions, leeks, parsnips, garden turnips and cabbage, supplemented in season by such fruits as apples, cherries, wild berries and nuts. Except at marriages, harvest festivals and boon works, the peasant did not drink ale but rather whey, buttermilk or simply water.
>
> (Drummond and Wilbraham 1958: 75)

In terms of food value such a diet was more wholesome than that of the upper classes of society and compares favourably with that of the average Englishman today. There is little evidence of endemic rickets or of scurvy and night blindness in the rural population before the eighteenth century, and the average height of men and women was about the same as it was in 1939, diminutive suits of armour notwithstanding. However, famine was not unknown in the more remote corners of England, though it was very much less widespread and frequent than on the continent (Appleby 1978). As a sample of a peasant diet in the fifteenth century, Drummond took 1 pint of milk, 1 pint of whey, 2 oz cheeze, 1 oz bacon, 2 lb brown bread and 2 oz peas. This he analysed into its nutritive components which reads as follows: calorific value 3200, protein 100 grams, fat 60 grams, calcium 1.6 milligrams, phosphorus 2.8 grams, iron 17 milligrams, vitamin A 1450 international units, vitamin D 9 international units, vitamin B 1.9 milligrams, riboflavin 2.8 milligrams, nicotinic acid 22 milligrams, vitamin C 20 milligrams (Drummond 1958: appendix A). Today the normal daily calorific intake lies between 2000–3000 calories, though in practice it is often less, much less in certain under-developed countries. The fifteenth-century peasant did not fare too badly provided, of course, that he did in fact receive the full ration.

For the amounts of barley and peas consumed historians have three main sources of evidence, none of them conclusive. These are corrodies, liveries and maintenance agreements. Corrodies were free dining-rights or food allowances granted to favoured tenants or household officials in recognition of past services. Ageing freeholders without heirs also found it convenient to surrender their land to an institution or secular lord in return for board for the remainder of their days. The quality of food at a rich man's table or even a monastic table was of a rather different order to that common in the average peasant household, therefore corrodies are of little use in the present context (Stuckert 1923; Hamilton Thompson 1925: 113–34; Kershaw 1973; Morgan 1946: 130–1). On many large estates, over 80 per cent of the full-time labourer's remuneration was paid in the form of a grain livery and other perks. Unfortunately, we cannot accept these liveries as straightforward food rations, because too many hidden and variable factors affect the issue: for example, the ratio of livery to cash payment reflected changes in the price of grain and could alter from year to year; some liveries included provender for horses, others included an allowance for the wage-earner's family, others took into account the value of the other perks received. Thus the author of the *Anonymous Husbandry*, c. 13, recommends that the dairyman 'because of the benefits he has from milk he ought to take one quarter of corn every sixteen weeks where the other servants have one quarter for every twelve weeks'. This would give the dairyman half a bushel per day or three quarters two bushels a year, as against the other servants who received four quarters a year. At Bolton Priory, each man received 11½ quarters of oats; at Crowland Abbey 4½ quarters of rye and barley; on the Bishop of Winchester's estates 4–5 quarters of grain and, on the monastic estates of Ramsey, Ely and Bec, a similar livery was usual. By the standards of the time even 4½ quarters was generous (at Bolton and Beaulieu each lay brother consumed little more than an estimated 2½ quarters of corn a year), and one must assume that such a livery was intended to support the man's wife as well (Kershaw 1973: 55–9, 132).

The third source, maintenance agreements, are more useful. These were made between elderly peasants and their heirs or successors, or between joint heirs, whereby one party gave up his or her government of the land in return for maintenance, and the agreement was formally witnessed and recorded in the manorial court. Each case was *sui generis*; factors to be taken into consideration were the size of the holding, the total number of persons dependent on it, the number of persons to be maintained, the amount of work the retiring party would be able to contribute, contributions to be received from other sons or daughters, the degree of friction envisaged and so on. A number of these agreements from several estate collections have been printed and more recently a collection of thirty-seven cases from the unpublished court rolls of some of the manors of the Abbey of Bury St Edmunds in East Anglia, between the years from 1263–1408, has been brought together by Dr Richard Smith and provides us with a more localised sample.* Many agreements simply offer 'board and lodg-

---

* Very kindly made available by Dr Smith.

ing', others enter into considerable detail as to the place of residence, the quality and amount of food, the nature and cost of clothing. With regard to food, quantities vary from a few bushels to several quarters. One can, however, detect a slight preference for ½ bushel of grain per week together with pasture for stock (or, in lieu of pasture, 8 bushels of oats per year for stock). This would give a total of 3 quarters and 2 bushels of grain and pulses per annum, an amount sufficient to support two persons. Another fairly frequent allowance was 2 quarters and 2 bushels plus pasture for stock, an amount sufficient for one person. These amounts are reminiscent of the liveries recommended in the *Anonymous Husbandry*, as noted above. Four maintenance agreements were recorded in the Kibworth court rolls,[4] but only one mentions a food allowance: Nicholas Gilbert agreed, in 1360, to provide his mother and stepfather, John and Agnes Mayster, with a room of three crucks to the west of the messuage, *una placea in curtilagio ad cassas ponendis*, 2 silver solidii, and a quarter of peas and the same of wheat per year.[5] In this case an allowance of 1 quarter per person per year was agreed, an amount fairly common elsewhere.

A fourth approach is to draw up budget tables for the region under study, such as tables 14 and 15 for Kibworth, and see how much was in fact available per person. The Kibworth tables show that not until the mid sixteenth century could the half yardlander provide his household with more than one quarter of grain with pulses per person per annum. By contrast, even in 1290 the full yardlander could provide an annual allowance of 2 quarters per person. Since 71 per cent of the tenements in 1290 were of only half a yardland, the majority of the inhabitants must have subsisted on only 1 quarter of grain and pulses per year. This then is the basic ration allowed in the tables. For the purpose of the tables it was not necessary to specify the exact proportions between barley and peas, even if this could be ascertained, since the market price for both crops was approximately the same. How much bread 1 quarter would make is difficult to say, since the bushel, being a measure of volume, will vary in weight from grain to grain and from harvest to harvest. One has also to allow for the loss in weight in milling; roughly speaking, 10 bushels of grain will give 8 bushels of flour. However, in general terms, 2 quarters of barley and peas will provide a daily ration of 2 lb bread, the amount Drummond based his calculations on.

However, Drummond makes no mention of porridge. Most of our sources come from institutional archives and treat bread as a commodity to be stored and doled out, a use to which loaves of bread lend themselves more readily than porridge. Moreover, bread was normally eaten stale, dunked in pottage, so that stores of loaves could

Table 14. *Revenue and expenditure for one virgate, 1290–1700 (namely, 24 acres arable and pasture)*

CONSTANTS: *Family size* 5.0 persons (1280–1345): 3.96 (1371–1490); 3.34 (1550–1700)

Food 1 quarter barley per person per year

7 acres *barley* required 2.25 quarters seed. Therefore 7 times the yield less 2.25 gives the surplus for any given year
7 acres *peas* required 1.75 quarters seed. 7 × yield less 1.75 = surplus
7 acres *fallows* + 3 acres meadow and pasture supported 24 sheep

1290–1550 *yield per sheep* = 1.4 lb   *yield of flock* = 1.3 tods[a]
1550–1636 *yield per sheep* = 1.9 lb   *yield of flock* = 1.62 tods
1636–1700 *yield per sheep* = 3.0 lb   *yield of flock* = 2.57 tods

	1290–1300 1371–80	1411–20	1481–90	1551–60	1570–5	1606–14	1636–41	1696–1700
Surplus								
Barley in quarters	11.75 11.75	11.75	11.75	11.75	5.45	9.65	19.59	10.00
Peas in quarters	5.25 5.25	5.25	5.25	5.25	2.10	4.2	9.17	4.41
Wool in tods	1.00 1.00	1.00	1.00	1.36	1.36	1.36	2.14	2.14
Price								
Barley in shillings	4.00 4.00	3.66	4.18	9.00	7.49	15.07	14.57	23.14
Peas in shillings	4.00 4.00	3.66	4.42	8.17	8.65	13.30	16.80	21.50
Wool in shillings	10.00 11.00	7.46	6.80	10.46	12.41	18.86	19.15	20.00

160

Receipts									
Barley in shillings	47.00	47.00	43.00	49.12	105.75	40.82	145.33	285.43	231.4
Peas in shillings	21.00	21.00	19.21	23.21	42.84	18.17	55.44	154.06	94.82
Wool in shillings	13.00	14.30	9.70	8.84	16.95	20.10	30.55	49.23	51.40
TOTAL REVENUE	81.00	82.30	71.91	81.17	165.54	79.09	231.32	488.72	377.62
Expenses in shillings									
Tithe	8.1	8.23	7.19	8.12	16.55	7.91	23.1	48.87	37.76
Rent	20.00	20.00	20.00	12.00	12.00	12.00	30.00	30.00	30.00
Food for x persons(see family size)	20.00	15.84	14.49	16.55	30.06	23.81	50.30	48.66	77.29
TOTAL EXPENSES	48.10	44.07	41.68	36.67	58.61	43.72	103.43	127.53	145.05
SURPLUS CASH	32.90	38.23	30.23	44.50	106.93	35.37	127.89	361.19	232.57
Day wages in pence									
Common servant		2–4	1–2	1½–3½	2–5	2–5	2–9	3–8	4–8
Harvester		2–5	2–3	3–5	5–10	—	5–16	6–12	6–12

a 1 tod = 28lb

Table 15. *Revenue and expenditure for half a virgate, 1290–1700 (namely, 12 acres arable and pasture)*

CONSTANTS: *Family size* 5.0 persons (1280–1345); 3.96 (1371–1490); 3.34 (1550–1700)

Food 1 quarter barley per person per year

3 acres *barley* required 1.13 quarters seed. Therefore, 3 times the yield less 1.13 gives the surplus for any given year.
3 acres *peas* required 0.75 quarters seed. 3 × yield less 0.75 = surplus
3 acres *fallow* + 3 acres meadow and some pasture supported 12 sheep

1290–1550 *yield per sheep* = 1.14 lb	*yield of flock* = 0.6 tods
1550–1626 *yield per sheep* = 1.9 lb	*yield of flock* = 0.81 tods
1636–1700 *yield per sheep* = 3 lb	*yield of flock* = 1.28 tods

	1290–1300	1371–80	1411–20	1481–90	1551–60	1570–5	1606–14	1636–41	1696–1700
Surplus									
Barley in quarters	4.87	4.87	4.87	4.87	4.87	2.17	3.97	8.23	4.12
Peas in quarters	2.25	2.25	2.25	2.25	2.25	0.90	1.80	3.83	1.89
Wool in tods	0.6	0.6	0.6	0.6	0.81	0.81	0.81	1.28	1.28
Price in shillings									
Barley	4.0	4.0	3.66	4.18	9.00	7.48	15.07	14.57	23.14
Peas	4.0	4.0	3.66	4.42	8.17	8.65	13.30	16.80	21.50
Wool	10.00	11.00	7.46	6.80[a]	10.46	12.41	18.86	19.17	20.00

Receipts in shillings									
Barley	19.48	19.48	17.82	20.35	43.83	16.23	59.79	119.91	95.34
Peas	9.00	9.00	8.24	9.94	18.36	7.79	23.94	64.34	40.64
Wool	6.00	6.60	4.48	4.08	8.47	10.05	15.28	23.22	25.60
TOTAL REVENUE	34.48	35.08	30.54	34.37	70.66	34.07	99.01	207.47	161.58
Expenses in shillings									
Tithe	3.45	3.51	3.05	3.44	7.07	3.41	9.90	20.75	16.16
Rent	10.00	10.00	10.00	6.66	6.66	6.66	16.66	16.66	16.66
Food for x persons (see family size)	20.00	15.84	14.49	16.55	30.06	23.81	50.30	48.66	77.29
TOTAL EXPENSES	33.45	29.35	27.54	26.65	43.79	33.88	76.86	84.07	110.11
SURPLUS CASH	1.03	5.73	3.00	7.72	26.87	0.19	22.15	123.40	51.47
Day wages in pence									
Common servant		2–4	1–2	1½–3½	2–5	2–5	2–9	3–8	4–8
Harvester	2–5	2–5	2–3	3–5	5–10	–	5–16	6–12	6–12

a Lloyd 1973: 44

be kept for two to three weeks. It does not follow that in his own home the peasant used his meagre grain supply to bake bread. Our Kibworth peasants grew barley and peas, neither of which make good bread; barley rises hardly at all without the addition of wheat or rye, and beans or peas meal cannot be formed into loaves 'because it will crack and be brittle, therefore it is commonly made into cakes'. A sort of bread or cake was also made from barley mixed with peas meal; according to Gervase Markham, 'you shall take of barley two bushels, of peas two pecks, of wheat or rye a peck, a peck of malt; these you shall grind together and dress it through a meal sieve', leven it over night in a sour trough, then add boiling water 'for you must understand that the hotter your liquor is, the less will the smell or rankness of the peas be received' (Wilson 1976: 230–3). Peas bread was still much in use in the late eighteenth century, though bread made from the seeds of miscellaneous weeds such as fat hen, cockle drake and darnel was rarely to be found by this date – except in the Orkneys. As late as 1801, the vicar of Kegworth, not far from Kibworth, could write, 'the bread generally eaten in this parish is a mixture of wheat and barley, in proportions varying according to the respective means and inclinations of the several inhabitants'; a view in which the vicar of Sproxton concurred, 'more barley bread is used in this parish than any other sort' (Hoskins 1949: 127–53).

More attractive than coarse bread of this sort and far more economical was porridge; no tolls had to be paid for milling and no quantitive loss incurred through the same process. The barley grains were sprouted in a damp, warm atmosphere; a process which could take about a week in winter. The sprouted grains could then be thrown into the pot to thicken and flavour the stew, or they could be boiled separately until soft. The water was then drawn off, sweetened and drunk immediately as barley water, or allowed to ferment. Meanwhile, more water was added to the barley grains and they were boiled until they formed a soft jelly. This was then flavoured with liquorice or herbs and eaten with butter, or thinned with stock and sipped as barley broth. Once prepared the barley porridge could be kept for several days and eaten cold, and if treated carefully would ferment rather than grow mould, and in its fermented state was commonly called beer. Dried peas could be similarly treated, and flavoured with pieces of bacon, onions, or even honey, and thickened with meal, flour or breadcrumbs. In terms of food value, more protein is made available from barley if it is eaten together with peas, since the latter supply the extra essential amino-acids necessary for the better utilisation of those amino-acids derived from barley.

Seen in this light, the distinction between barley porridge in its various forms and beer is a fine one. Common sense would suggest that in barley regions very little if any of a man's meagre ration of grain went into brewing ale. Not only would it have been superfluous and an unbelievable waste of a vital and scarce resource, but the whole process of malting and then brewing ale requires *space*, fuel, equipment, time and much labour, as against barley water stood in a jar. Cases of licences to brew ale do not feature extensively in the Kibworth court rolls until the late fifteenth century (see below p. 189), though elsewhere long lists of offenders against the Assize of Ale are recorded in the thirteenth century – though what sort of ale these people brewed, in what quantities, how regularly and for whom has not yet been systematically studied. Even in the sixteenth century ale remained something of a luxury in Leicestershire: in 1564 the Assize of Ale fixed the price at between 3d–3½d the gallon, and between 4d–5d in 1595 (Bateson 1923: 110). Now for a man whose daily wage did not exceed 5d when he was lucky enough to find work, a halfpenny a pint was a lot to pay.

Porridge and pottage were thus probably the staple fare of the English peasant rather than bread and ale. In quality, content and consistency, pottage is almost infinitely adaptable and as such defies a general assessment, though it can be said with a fair measure of confidence that the habit of long, slow simmering effectively removed all traces of vitamin C. With the exception of plants or roots which were exceptionally bitter or actually poisonous, anything that grew went into the pot, even primrose and strawberry leaves! Meat was rarely added, since meat was a luxury in the medieval world. Draught animals and sheep at the end of their working lives were slaughtered, similarly bull calves and weakly lambs, but such cullings were not a regular occurrence. Only pigs were specifically reared for meat, and although perhaps not common in medieval Kibworth, by the six-teenth century a pig in the yard or a flitch of bacon in the kitchen was commonplace according to the testimony of the inventories (see above pp. 102–3). By the early seventeenth century a flitch of bacon was valued at 5s; by the 1630s the price had gone up to between 6s 8d and 15s in Leicestershire.

Dairy products, 'white meats' as they were called, provided the chief source of animal protein. Robert Loder expected a cow to yield about one gallon a day between Whitsun and Michaelmas and Gervase Markham agreed that 'one gallon is good, two is rare and extraordinarie' (Markham 1623: 175, 189). Certainly in the pre-plague period it cannot have been more and may well have been less, though with a proportionately higher butter-fat content. By the late eight-eenth century Arthur Young noted that a Leicestershire Longhorn, winter-fed on hay, could give 3 gallons a day or £5 worth in a season (Fussell 1949: 164). Allowance must therefore be made for a threefold increase in yields over the period we are considering. Butter was made from the cream, cheese from the skim milk and the buttermilk (liquid left after churning) was either drunk or made into curds, or it was used to fatten pigs. The curds were often eaten with wine or ale, and the whey (whig) from the cheese press was also drunk. As we have seen, with each medieval yardland went a stint for four cows, while in the early modern period the much larger holdings supported correspondingly larger numbers of livestock, of which a high propor-tion were cows (see above pp. 98–9). It is not surprising therefore that a cheese press was to be found in many houses by this date, together with cheeses in the cheese chamber. Since it takes the milk of several cows to make a large cheese worth storing, we do not find cheeses in the inventories of the two-cow establishments; on these, small flat cheeses would have been made on a daily or weekly basis. The households of both Robert Loder and Henry Best accounted for large quantities of cheese, and their servants consumed about 4 oz of butter each per day, mostly in the rancid, liquid form used for cooking (Fussell 1936: 45). According to the *Anonymous Husbandry*, c. 31, a cow could be expected to yield 77 lb of cheese between 1 May and 29 September, a figure which Walter of Henley, c. 87, increases to 99 lb for stubble-fed cows. If we take Walter's 72 oz of cheese per week and divide it among the average Kibworth family of five, in the early fourteenth century, we get a daily ration of 2 oz per person per cow and, assuming two cows, a daily ration in season of 4 oz at most, which is more than Drummond allowed for. Towards the end of our period improved milk yields and smaller households would have made the individual ration proportionately greater. Ewes milk was also used for cheese. Ewes will give milk from lambing until the end of August at the rate of 1–3 pints a day; let us say $1\frac{1}{2}$ pints. In the opinion of the author of *Husbandry*, c. 28, 1 gallon of ewe's milk is equal to $1\frac{1}{2}$ gallons of cow's milk for cheese and butter. So if we suppose that the whole of a half yardlander's sheep stint of twelve was comprised of ewes, the daily yield would have been in the region of 2 gallons, sufficient to add an extra ounce or so to the daily ration in season.

Lastly, every messuage included a 'backyard' (upwards of $\frac{1}{4}$ acre) and an orchard, in which it was common to keep pullen and bees. Of the orchard Gervase Markham wrote with some justification, 'no ground a man occupieth (no, not the cornfield) yieldeth more gaine to the purse, and housekeeping (not to speake of unspeakable pleasure) quantity for quantity than a good orchard' (Markham 1623: 8). In addition to cultivated fruits there were of course wild fruits, but these were probably not abundant at Kibworth, since only very small patches of marsh and thicket remained and the villagers had no access to Gumley wood in which the manor had an interest.

Outgoings

One of the essential elements of subsistence husbandry is the avoidance of outlay on stock or equipment which cannot be bred or manufactured on the holding. The chief items on the expense account were therefore rent, tithe and small cash levies taken from all households for 'headsilver' (see above p. 31), the occasional royal tax, wages for the town hordsmen, mill tolls and court amercements. Taken together these fees seldom amounted to more than a few pence per household, against which can be set the small amounts raised by the sale of surplus lambs or small artefacts in the market. We have no records concerning tithe except the note in the Enclosure Award that 0.13 of the total acreage was to be set aside for the rector in lieu of tithes both great and small.[6] The inhabitants of Kibworth Harcourt had at one time enjoyed a free chapel of their own, but paid tithe to the church of St Wilfrid, and one-tenth has been deducted as such from the sum of their receipts. As discussed above, rents and fines were fixed (see above pp. 52, 62).

In the matter of stock and equipment, the loss of breeding-stock could present itself as a major calamity. Perhaps one of the functions of parish guilds in the countryside was to provide collective assistance for restocking.* But fire, flood and murrain aside, replacement of stock was not a source of expense, nor were buildings and plough gear. Crucks and heavy timbers were provided by the college; straw, an expensive item, by the villagers. Most sixteenth-century inventories list timbers in the yard suitable for making or repairing ploughs and carts: ploughs increased in value from 5s to 10s between the early sixteenth and the late seventeenth centuries, carts were slightly more valuable, being valued at as much as 20s by the close of the seventeenth century. Iron was used and reused, but the blacksmith's fee can be considered an expense, though unfortunately we have no record of the scale of fees charged or return services requested.

Tables 14 and 15 speak for themselves. Rarely did the subsistence farmer, the half virgater, manage to do more than cover his costs from the produce of his holding alone. High wool receipts aided him in the

---

* For the loan or hire of cows in the medieval period, see Professor Sir Michael Postan's contribution to the introduction in *The Book of William Morton*, ed. P. I. King. Northamptonshire Record Society Publications, xvi (Oxford 1954), pp. xxxv–xxxvi.

fourteenth and sixteenth centuries, low rents in the fifteenth and sixteenth, but in the seventeenth the rise in rents was not offset by rising wool receipts, while the price of foodstuffs continued to rise so that it became more than ever necessary to supplement his income by finding part-time employment.

At all times, then, the subsistence farmer relied more or less heavily upon supplementary earnings. If we are to look below the small group of husbandmen and yeomen to the group of artisans, subsistence cultivators and servants, we must endeavour to discover something about the balance between supply and demand for full-time and part-time labour, both in the agricultural and the service sector, and also about the wages offered.

The movement of wages 1300–1700

The two principal sources for material on wage rates are estate accounts, which yield valuable information on the full-time wages actually paid to servants in husbandry and to pieceworkers in particular localities at specific dates, and the wage rates proclaimed annually by Justices of the Peace as enjoined by the Statute of Artificers.* These proclamations set out in great detail the wages appropriate for a wide spectrum of employments, taking into account the age, sex and experience of workers, the season of the year and the rate with or without food liveries. It was intended that justices should adjust wages to meet fluctuating food costs while, at the same time, protecting the small farmer from excessive wage costs in regions where labour shortages might tend to inflate wages – they were to 'protect one class of worker against another' as Tawney put it (Minchinton 1972: 65). Broadly speaking, Justices in the sixteenth and early seventeenth centuries made a serious attempt to hold the balance, but their successors following the interregnum tended to be less conscientious (Hindmarsh 1932). An insufficient number of Justices' assessments have so far been discovered to provide a complete coverage of the English counties, and none survive for Leicestershire, but fortunately Rutland and Northamptonshire are

---

* Indispensable monographs are those by Lord Beveridge 'Wages on the Winchester Manors', *EcHR*, 1st ser., VII (1936); and 'Westminster wages in the manorial era', *EcHR*, 2nd ser., VIII (1956–6), 18–35; Thorold Rogers, *The History of Agriculture and Prices in England*, vol. IV, 1401–1582 (Oxford 1882); W. E. Minchinton ed., *Wage Regulation in Pre-Industrial England* (London 1972) – being an introduction to and reprint of R. H. Tawney's 'The assessment of wages in England by the Justices of the Peace' (1914) and R. K. Kelsall's *Wage Regulation and the Statute of Artificers* (London 1938); E. H. Phelps Brown and Sheila V. Hopkins, 'Seven centuries of building wages' and 'Seven centuries of the prices of consumables compared with builder's wage rates' in E. M. Carus-Wilson ed., *Essays in Economic History*, 2 (London 1962).

relatively well represented. Tables 16 and 17 have been compiled from accounts and proclamations in print, which have been simplified in the case of day rates to show only the extremes, that is to say, the lowest rate – that for winter with livery – and the highest rate – that for summer without livery. The tables also serve to illustrate the differentials between male and female, town and country, county and county, winter and summer, with and without food and, in so doing, they contrast this form of source material with that found in farm accounts. In the case of full-time adult labourers, farm accounts are directly comparable with proclamations, but in the case of task workers the complexity of the scales as revealed in the proclamations is met, perhaps understandably, with stark simplicity: the total wage bill in cash and kind is noted with seldom even an estimate of the number of persons employed, let alone for how long or at what rate. There are ways round this difficulty, but the final figures are far from precise. Household accounts, for example, which were kept up to date on a daily or weekly basis, record the amounts paid out to gardeners, carpenters, carriers, laundrices and the like (Hudleston, *Surtees Soc.* 168); the notebooks of gentlemen farmers like Loder and Best contain memos on the proper wages for certain seasonal tasks such as shearing, mowing, thatching; medieval reeves when rendering their accounts often translated a day's work into money terms for the purpose of evaluating unwanted labour services, and the authors of treatises on estate management often provide estimates of the number of workers required to perform specific tasks, such as mowing an acre of hay, together with an estimate of the total cost per acre (Miller and Hatcher 1978: 49–53). The geographical distribution of estates with surviving accounts tends to be highly localised, and Leicestershire happens to be one of the least well-endowed counties in this respect (Hilton 1947; *VCH Leics.* II: 145–200). This may reflect the low level of demesne farming in the county: the home farms of the 'gentry' were small, requiring only a handful of permanent workers, drawing upon the local village only for harvesting, and possibly operating an accounting system based on tally sticks well into the fourteenth century. Kibworth Harcourt had lost its demesne farm, so the chances of picking up seasonal work were so remote that to have lifted a figure from Beveridge's tables and inserted 1½d in the wages column of tables 14 and 15 under the years 1290–1300 would have been misleading; the space has therefore been left blank. Tables 16 and 17 convey some idea of the most and the least that a man could earn in one day, but this does not, of course, imply that a man worked for any stretch of time at the same rate, or that he could find employment every day of the week, month or year.

Table 16. *Annual wages of 'servants in husbandry' in addition to board, lodging and sometimes clothing*

Date	12–15 years	16–20 years	Boy	Best woman	Common servant	Bailiff	Source
Realm 1351						–	25 Ed III 2.cc.1–7
Kibworth 1390						10s	MM 6276
Kibworth 1414						40s	MM 6300
Norfolk 1431						28s	EHR (1898) 299–302
Realm 1444		–	9s	14s	18s 4d	28s	Rogers IV p. 115
Northants. 1560		–	–	20s	20s	45s	EcHR I (1927–8) 131–4
York 1563		10s–13s 4d	–	20s–25s	20s–24s	30s–36s	H and L II[a] pp. 223–4
Kent 1563		–	20s	26s 8d	38s 4d	48s	EHR XII (1926) 260–73
Lincs. 1563		4s under 20	20s	33s 4d	26s 8d	33s 4d–41s 4d	H and L II pp. 221–3
Lincoln 1563	10s	20s	–	–	26s 8d–80s	40s–80s	H and L II pp. 225–7
Rutland 1563		–	20s	26s 8d	38s 4d	50s	Rogers IV pp. 120–3
Rutland 1610		–	20s	26s 8d	40s	52s	Archaeologia XI (1794) 200–7
Norfolk 1610		–	28s	33s 4d	40s	66s 8d	EHR XIII (1898) 522–7

Place							Reference
Lincs. 1621	16s	–	–	24s	33s 4d	46s 8d	HMC. Ruts. I pp. 460–2
Suffolk 1630	–	–	33s 4d	30s–40s	40s–55s	60s	EHR XII (1897) 307–11
St Albans 1631	–	–	–	–	–	–	VCH Herts. IV pp. 227–8
Gloucs. 1632	–	–	–	30s	40s	80s	Rogers VI p. 694
Heref. 1632	–	–	25s–30s	20s–24s	40s	53s 4d	EHR LVII (1942) 115–19
Shrewsbury 1640	–	–	30s	34s	46s 8d	60s	T. Salop. Arch. Soc. LVII (1956) 136–42
Worcs. 1663	–	–	–	40s	50s	80s	HMC Various I. p. 323
Heref. 1666	–	–	25s	30s–35s	40s	110s	EHR LVII (1942) 115–19
Somerset 1666	–	–	–	–	40s	80s	Somerset Quarter Sessions Rec. IV. p. 13
Northants 1667	–	35s	–	35s	60s	120s	EcHR I (1927–8) 133–4
E. Yorks 1669	–	–	–	36s	55s	80s	EHR LII (1937) 283–9
Warwick 1685	23s 4d	–	–	35s	50s	90s	Archaeologia XI (1794) 208–11

Table 16. (cont.)

2.cc.1-7

Date	12–15 years	16–20 years	Boy	Best woman	Common servant	Bailiff	Source
Somerset 1685	–	–	–	30s	90s	90s	HMC 7th Report (1879) Appd. 698–9
Wilts. 1685	–	50s	–	70s	100s–120s	120s	HMC Various I. p. 174–5
Bucks. 1687	20s–33s 4d	50s–60s	–	40s–50s	80s–90s	100s–120s	Bucks Sessions Rec I pp. 227–9
Oxon 1687	–	32s 6d	–	50s	–	120s	Oxford Rec. Soc. XVI (1934) pp. lxiii–lxiv

^a Hughes and Larkin *Tudor Royal Proclamations* 1969.

Table 17. *Day rates, showing the range from winter to summer, with and without food, in pence per day*

Date	Carter	Mason and carpenter	Thresher per quarter	Female mower	Male mower	Labourer	Source
Realm 1351	–	1½d–4d	1½d–2½d	–	2d–5d	–	25 Ed III 2.cc.1–7
Leics. Borough 1365	16d–24d	4d–12d	–	–	–	2d–4d	Leics. Borough Records II p. 140
Norfolk 1431	–	2d–3d	2d–4d	–	–	1d–2d	EHR (1898) 299–302
Realm 1444	–	3d–5½d	–	–	–	1½d–3½d	Rogers IV p. 115
Northants 1560	–	5d–8d	–	–	5d–10d	2d–5d	EcHR I (1927–8) 131–4
York 1563	2d–5d	5d–10d	3d–5d	–	4d–9d	–	H and L II pp. 223–4
Kent 1563	4d–8d	–	2½d–10d	3d–7d	5d–11d	3d–9d	EHR XLI (1926) 260–73
Lincs. 1563	2d–8d	4d–12d	8d–10d	2d–6d	4d–10d	–	H and L II pp. 221–3
Lincoln 1563	–	4d–10d	5d–12d	–	5d–10d	–	H and L II pp. 225–7
Rutland 1563	4d–8d	–	2½d–10d	3d–7d	5d–11d	3d–9d	Rogers IV pp. 120–3
Rutland 1610	4d–9d	4d–14d	4d–16d	3d–9d	5d–16d	2d–9d	Archaeologia XI (1794) 200–7
Norfolk 1610	4d–9d	4d–14d	4d–16d	2d–9d	5d–16d	2d–9d	EHR XIII (1898) 522–7
Lincs. 1621	3½d–8d	4d–10d	5d–8d	1½d–6d	3½d–9d	2½d–5d	HMC Ruts. I pp. 460–2
Suffolk 1630	–	8d–16d	8d–24d	4d–8d	6d–16c	4d–12d	EHR XII (1897) 307–11
St Albans 1631	–	–	–	–	10d–14d	4d–5d	VCH Herts. IV pp. 227–8
Gloucs. 1632	–	12d	16d	–	–	4d–8d	Rogers VI pp. 694

Table 17. (*cont.*)

Date	Carter	Mason and carpenter	Thresher per quarter	Female mower	Male mower	Labourer	Source
Heref. 1632	–	6d–12d	4d–6d	–	6d–12d	3d–8d	EHR LVII (1942) 115–19
Shrewsbury 1640	–	8d–14d	–	4d–8d	6d–16d	3d–8d	T. Salop. Arch. Soc. LVII (1956) 136–42
Worcs. 1663	–	6d–12d	–	4d–8d	6d–12d	–	HMC Various I. p. 323
Heref. 1666	6d–12d	5d–12d	8d–12d	–	6d–12d	4d–8d	EHR LVII (1942) 115–19
Somers. 1666	–	7d–16d	5d–12d	6d–16d	8d–16d	–	Somerset Quarter Sessions Rec. IV. p. 13
Northants 1667	–	12d–18d	8d–12d	4d–8d	6d–12d	3d–8d	EcHR I (1927–8) 133–4
E. Yorks. 1669	–	12d	5d–12d	3d–6d	6d–10d	–	EHR LII (1937) 283–9
Warws. 1685	–	6d–16d	4d–8d	2d–4d	6d–12d	4d–8d	Archaeologia XI (1974) 208–11
Somers. 1685	–	12d–14d	4d–12d	4d–7d	7d–14d	–	HMC 7th Report (1879) Appd. 698–9
Wilts. 1685	–	–	3d–10d	6d–12d	12d–18d	–	HMC Various I. pp. 174–5
Bucks. 1687	–	8d–14d	–	4d–8d	6d–16d	3d–8d	Bucks Sessions Rec. I pp. 227–9
Oxon. 1687	(£5.00 p.a.)	14d–16d	9d–10d	6d–10d	10d–16d	–	Oxford Rec. Soc. XVI (1934) pp. lxiii–lxiv

In the course of the period under consideration, from 1300–1700, a significant alteration took place in the balance between subsistence farming and supplementary employment among the group of married smallholders. As the number and size of smallholdings diminished, so the dependence of the smallholder upon alternative employment increased, and two factors assumed vital dimensions in their lives: namely, the number of days' work they could get in a year and the amount in real wages that could be earned in a day. Given little technological progress during the period, job opportunity and food costs mirrored faithfully the fluctuations in population levels. A low population level in the fifteenth century increased the amount of work a man could get and also the wage he could command, while at the same time food prices fell. The reduction in the number of smallholders and the increase in the number of landless cottage labourers which also took place during this period did not present serious side effects until the population level began to rise in the last decades of the century. By this time the agricultural economy had adjusted to conditions of labour shortage by converting arable to pasture, and later demands for higher wages did not encourage a return to labour-intensive forms of husbandry. Successive sixteenth-century governments were faced with the problem of encouraging arable cultivation in order to provide employment for the rising tide of vagrants, and for this they had to keep wages down, while at the same time they had to ensure that wages bore some relation to rising food costs: again, in order to reduce the number of destitute poor. In the seventeenth century population growth levelled off, prices steadied and as the labour pool shrank so wages and job opportunities improved, or at least did not deteriorate further.*

A few general remarks can be made about the figures in these tables before moving on to an examination of the Kibworth area in particular. The rise in the wages of both categories of servant in the mid sixteenth century is conspicuous, but while those of the servant living in, usually referred to as a 'servant in husbandry', continued to rise slowly during the seventeenth century, those of the part-time man did not, and those of the artisan made only slight increases. Servants in husbandry were hired by the year and were provided with bed, board and sometimes clothing by their employers. Their wage can therefore be looked upon as a year's savings. This was the way in which single men and women could accumulate a small

---

* Tawney argued the scarcity of wage labour in the sixteenth and seventeenth centuries, but later work has shown that, if anything, there was under-employment by the mid seventeenth century. See Minchinton 1972: 16, 65–8.

amount of capital. They were in fact mostly young people, they seldom stayed with the same employer for more than one year and it not infrequently required the intervention of a Justice of the Peace to hold them to their contract if conditions were not to their liking, or the prospect of better pay elsewhere presented itself (Kelsall 1938: 36ff; MacFarlane 1970: appendix B). The enlarged farms of the sixteenth and seventeenth centuries expanded the demand for full-time servants, but, in spite of the number of 'vagrants' on the roads, this demand does not seem to have been fully met. The full-time farm labourer, living in a tied cottage and serving the same farmer for a lifetime, was a way of life to be developed in the next century.

The wage of the skilled day-labourer, represented in the table by carpenters and masons, rose less steeply than that of the unskilled labourer in the period from 1445–1563. Nevertheless it nearly doubled. After this date the rate with food remained more or less static, though the rate without food increased by 4d–8d. It is noteworthy that builders' wages did not increase substantially during the period of the 'Great Rebuilding', from 1570–1640.

Wages of the unskilled labourer doubled between 1444–1560, and had doubled again by 1630, after which they remained static for the remainder of the century. Women's wages likewise rose between 1563–1630, after which they fell to below the 1560 level. A similar trend can be seen in the wages of threshers: between 1430–1560 the rate with livery remained static but the rate without more than doubled. In the period from 1560–1630 both rates doubled again, after which they fell. The rise after 1560 may well reflect the activities of the Justices in relating wages to food prices, since otherwise we should expect the rate of unemployment in this period to have given rise to a fall in wages.

Turning now to Kibworth and the rental as it stood in 1372 we find 14 full virgates held by twelve families, 38 half virgates held by twenty-two families, 27 quarter virgates carved out from the demesne and held by nineteen families, 12 cottages held by twelve families and 4 disintegrated virgates held by fifteen families, there being about fifty-five families in the village at this time, some with more than one branch.[7] Thus, already by 1372 the number of landholding families was contracting and holdings were becoming larger: roughly 18 acres per family. The size of households was also shrinking, thereby creating a demand for extra-familial labour in some households (see below pp. 230–6. The precise character of extra-familial labour raises problems of terminology and definition. A man, a woman and a boy was a sufficient labour complement for a 12–18 acres holding (of which 8–12 acres were arable) and, where a deficit existed, it could be made good by 'borrowing' surplus labour from other households. If only keep was offered and no wages the net result was to even out imbalances between the size of households and the size of the holdings which supported them without fostering the circulation of cash between households. But in an arable, labour-intensive region, holdings of more than 24 acres required more than a three-hand team to cultivate them, and the ratio of large to small tenements was an important factor in determining the overall balance between supply and demand for extra-familial labour. At Kibworth before the plagues (apart from one three-virgate tenement) there was only a handful of full-virgate tenements; therefore, the supply of labour far exceeded demand.

Those landless men who were fortunate enough to find work in return for keep would have been rash to have asked for wages as well. Therefore, from the point of view of the household budget, there is no need for us to distinguish between true sons and surrogate sons. But after the plagues the position was reversed: labour was in short supply and labourers could demand a wage. It is in this period that the term *servientes* appears for the first time in the Kibworth court rolls, the first such *serviens* to receive mention being Matilda the servant of Robert Palmer in 1358.[8] References to *servientes* appear in the court leet section of the rolls, where they appear as brawlers or trespassers or as being sworn into tithing: in the latter circumstance their age is sometimes noted and we learn that some at least were boys of only twelve years of age or thereabouts.[9] The surnames of these servants are not always given but, when they are, they are the names of strangers and none of them subsequently appear under the Court Baron section as taking up land. The Polle family, bailiffs from 1387–1443 and from 1510/20–1537, employed such a servant in 1373, 1389, 1391, 1393, 1397, 1406 and 1520. The Browns, a family of drapers, employed a servant in 1373,[10] 1393, 1410 and 1442. Other employers were William Wright who employed a woman servant in 1375, Richard Chapman (1376), Robert Smith (1385), the Tailour family (1389) (also recorded on the Poll Tax lists), John Couper (1412), one of the Hildesleys (1412), John Peek (1413 and 1440), John Parker (1474) and John Haford, who employed a wiredrawer in 1425–6. These servants seem to have been apprentices or full-time servants in husbandry.

The term *serviens* also appears on the tax returns for this period, but here it was applied to a much broader category of persons, including grandmothers, aunts and married children; in fact all adult dependants seem to have been included in this category, whether or not they worked for a wage.* The criterion was apparently that of landlessness, since minors with land or heirs to land were classified as servants until they entered their inheritance. The age at transition from son to servant is nowhere made explicit, but it was probably around eighteen, or earlier in the case of sons who had achieved financial independence (see also pp. 205–8, 227–9).[11]

As we move on into the sixteenth century the court rolls become less informative and the term servant in the tax returns is dropped in favour of the phrase 'assessed on wages'.[12] Of the twenty-four names on the 1524 subsidy roll, fifteen appear on the 1527 rental and, of the ten assessed on wages, three are recorded as landholders on the 1527 rental and another four were from landholding families. Those assessed on wages in the sixteenth century earned more in wages than they did from agricultural produce, but they were not for the most part landless men.[13] No direct comparison can therefore be made between the servants of the late fourteenth-century Poll Tax lists, and the wage-earners of the early sixteenth-century subsidy lists. Omitted altogether from the two subsidy lists of the 1520s were the genuinely landless men and women. However, the earliest surviving wills date from this decade, and the first inventories by the end of the century. Some servants were the recipients of bequests made to them in wills, others made wills themselves. Table 18, based on wills, gives some indication of the value and size of holding which could and did support one or more servants. Among the employers from Kibworth are included some from neighbouring villages who happen to have been related to Kibworth families. Clearly a complete list of all employers within the hundred would have been more satisfactory but the very abundance of probate material for the Leicester archdeaconry creates a prohibitive time problem. However, it is clear from the Kibworth example that men with quite large holdings often employed only *one* servant, and we have no instances of men with less than 24 acres employing extra-familial labour. Such an observation has a familiar ring to it. Gregory King estimated that not more than 150,000–200,000 persons earned over £3 a year in the entire kingdom, while some 350–400,000 earned under £3 and could be classed as common servants, women and boys (Thirsk and Cooper 1972: 769). Similarly, R. H. Tawney noted 'the small part which wage labour played in the agricultural economy of seventeenth-century Gloucestershire'. He found that the majority of yeomen and hus-

---

* R. H. Hilton, in his study of the Poll Tax returns for some West Midland parishes, makes the same observation, namely, 'persons described as servants could also be the offspring of the family'. *The English Peasantry of the Later Middle Ages* (Oxford 1975), p. 31.

Table 18. *Wealth and trade of men known to have employed servants in the Kibworth area*

Date	Employer	Village	Occupation	Sum of inventory	Size of holding	Servants
1520	Amicia Polle	Kibworth H.	Widow	£43 7s 0d	Extensive copyhold	1
1526	R. Smyth	Kibworth B.	–	£22 0s 0d	3 virgates, copy.	1
1538	W. Marriot	Kibworth H.	Husbandman	£21 6s 8d	2 virgates, free.	1
1538	R. Ryliff	Kibworth H.	Husbandman	£21 18s 4d	1 virgate, copy.	2
1544	T. Deacon	Kibworth H.	–	Legacies meagre	–	pl.
1545	T. Carter	Kibworth H.	–	£25 17s 8d	–	1
1552	R. Coleman	Foxton	–	£63 13s 4d	–	pl.
1554	T. Freeman	Gumley	Husbandman	Generous legacies	Extensive	2
1558	W. Jurdan	Foxton	Heir to have 'occupacion'			
1558	R. Rogers	Kibworth H.				
1559	J. Eleston	Gumley		£66 6s 8d	–	1
1559	T. Raye	Kibworth H.		£36 0s 0d	–	pl.
1560	W. Hull	Kibworth H.	Lawyer–courtier	£332 16s 6d	4–7 virgates	pl.
1564	W. Dorman	Fleckney		£44 0s 0d	–	2
1569	J. Coleman	Foxton		–	–	1
1572	T. Arsere	Smeeton	Herdsman	£13 14s 6d	–	1
1572	W. Bowden	Kibworth B.	Rector	£200+	3 farms, 2 mills	pl.
1572	T. Clerke	Kibworth H.	Husbandman	£111 4s 0d	–	1
1581	J. Eliot	Kibworth H.	Carpenter	–	–	1
1584	T. Freeman	Gumley	Husbandman	£79 5s 0d	–	pl.
1586	T. Bayley	Kibworth H.		£40 + £40 lease	2½ virgates, free.	5
1590	R. Fox	Smeeton		£66 2s 4d	–	1
1591	R. Brian	Smeeton		£103	3 virgates +	pl.
1598	M. Coxon	Kibworth H.	Bailiff to Raye		–	pl.
1604	M. Eastwood	Kibworth	Widow	–	3 virgates +	1
1605	R. Bryan	Kibworth	Yeoman	£380 0s 6d	1½ virgates, copy.	pl.
1605	T. Watts	Turlangton	–	£300+	–	pl.
1620	W. Coleman	Kibworth B.	Husbandman		3½ virgates	1
1636	T. Coleman	Kibworth B.		–	–	1
1640	J. Bingley	Gumley	Rector	–	–	pl.
1646	D. Coleman	Kibworth B.	Yeoman	–	–	2
1659	T. Brudenell	Stonton W.	Gent.	–	–	pl.

179

bandmen employed no servants but relied on the work of family and relatives (Tawney 1934–5: 52). As the table indicates, the same can be said of Kibworth Harcourt. In an area of relatively small farms, cultivating some barley and peas but concentrating increasingly on livestock, this corner of Leicestershire employed a very small proportion of the nation's full-time labour-force. Table 19 also indicates that at least some full-time labourers earned sufficient to marry, set up house and have children; they were not all living-in servants.

The general character and the long hours of the work performed by the servant in husbandry differed little from that of the husbandman, and it might be as well to consider their daily routine before moving on to examine other types of wage-labour, such as piecework, craftwork and small-town commerce.

Gervase Markham describes in detail the ploughman's day in late December when the peas ground was being broken (1620: 145–7). The ploughman would have to rise at about 4.0 a.m. in order to have his team in the furlong by 7.0 a.m. He kept his team in the field until 3.0 p.m., during which time he ploughed 1–1½ acres of stiff clay. The remaining daylight hours were spent in rubbing-down and feeding the plough beasts. When there was no ploughing to be done he would be set to carting hurdles, dung and fuel in spring, hay, barley and peas in summer.

One of the most detailed and interesting accounts of the shepherd's day has come down to us in Henry Best's farming notes. At times the pressure of work was great, but for relatively long stretches of the year the shepherd was valued for his skill in observation and judgement rather than for the hours of work he put into the job. It was a nice question whether to employ a full-time shepherd at £2 a year and livery worth £10 or to risk one's flock with the common herd. In some years Henry Best kept over 200 sheep, but he kept on his shepherd in 1641 when he had only 32 sheep and 13 lambs (Best, *Surtees Soc.* xxxiii: 94). There were at least four private flocks of this size in sixteenth-century Kibworth and more in the seventeenth. So there were perhaps four shepherds in the village in addition to the common shepherd. However, since only the common shepherd held a cottage, we must assume that the others, if others there were, lived in with their masters.

A number of the servants alluded to in the inventories were women. Of these some were undoubtedly 'chief women' who could 'cook, bake, brew, make malt, and oversee other servants', in the words of the Justices of the Peace for Rutland in 1610, who granted them a maximum wage of 26s 8d. Others were but 'simple servants' who could do 'but out-work and drudgery'; in other words, milk the

Table 19. *Personal estate of employees*

Date	Employee	Village	Occupation	Sum of inventory	Dependants
1569	W. Craxnell	Smeeton	Labourer	£13 4s 2d	Wife, no children
1572	T. Arsere	Smeeton	Herdsman	£13 14s 6d	Wife, no children
1575	N. Polle	Hallaton	Labourer	£3 0s 0d	Wife, 3 children
1580	R. Coleman	Kibworth H.	Cottar	£13 8s 4d	Wife, 2 children
1584	J. Burgess	Smeeton	Labourer?	£11 16s 0d	Single
1589	J. Meane	Fleckney	Cottar	£10 6s 4d	?
1590	H. Almey	Smeeton	Labourer	£18 18s 6d	?
1590	E. Bosden	Medbourne	Labourer	£23 7s 2d	?
1633	J. Varnam	Turlangton	Servant	£17+	Single
1636	T. Goodman	Kibworth B.	Labourer	£17 2s 4d	?
1652[a]	E. Porter	Kibworth B.	Labourer	–	'Old'
1654	J. Jeffery	Smeeton	Labourer	–	Married that year
1656[a]	N. Porter	Kibworth H.	Labourer	–	–
1661	A. Porter	Kibworth H.	Widow	–	–
1682	N. Porter	Kibworth H.	Labourer	– (messuage)	Wife, 1 son
1697	J. Carter	Kibworth H.	Labourer	£14 in legacies	Single

[a] Their deaths mentioned in the parish register, but no surviving will or inventory.

181

cows, look after the poultry and 'sweepe the house and wash the dishes' (Best, ibid: 133). Again, these were mostly single women and lived in. It seems that if the master of the house died, the contract ended, since the provision is frequently made in the wills, 'my servant x to have so much *if she stay*'.

These full-time servants shared in the economy of the village and they doubtless shared the same cultural outlook, but in many respects they were outsiders. They were unrelated to anyone in a community where everyone was related to everyone; they were birds of passage and one may well ask why outsiders held these jobs and not villagers. The families with large holdings needed all their members, but those with smallholdings did not. The question of livery may have been the deciding factor. Just as Robert Loder worked out that it cost him more to keep a man living in (Fussell 1936: 72), so the man in service must have reckoned that he could live better at his master's expense, and for this reason preferred to live in neighbouring villages where he could live in, rather than in his home town where he could be expected to live in the parental home. This would help to explain the scatter of familiar Kibworth names over the surrounding villages within a short radius; very few of this diaspora held land in other villages; many are specifically described as 'labourers'. Seen in this light, the Poor Law system of returning unemployed persons to their home town was both reasonable and practical.

The work-load of a servant in husbandry left little time for small-time farming on his own account though, as we have seen, some had a cottage of their own and a cow in the yard (see above p. 135). Strictly speaking, of course, such servants were not self-sufficient family farmers and so do not fall into the category of *peasants* (there is no place for them in tables 14 and 15), but their presence affected the structure of peasant households. By contrast, the true, landholding peasant had too much to do on his own land to be able to spare much time for work outside the holding. He was not looking for work as a full-time servant in husbandry, but welcomed occasional short contracts: weeding, harvesting, hedging and ditching or part-time tanning or wheel-making. Opportunity for seasonal employment at Kibworth depended heavily on the number of larger farms in the area which still practised extensive arable cultivation. The survey made for Merton College in 1635 lists the total acreage of each freeholder and copyholder, and also notes the proportion between pasture and arable on each tenant's land. Unfortunately this distinction is misleading, since much of the land listed as arable in the open fields was in practice under leys. There were twelve farms ranging from 40–206 acres, the rest were smaller (see above p. 89).

Of the 1117 acres covered by these twelve farms, 888 acres were officially designated as arable in 1635, but it is difficult to estimate the proportion actually under crop. The old system would have put as much as half under the plough, the rest being fallow or permanent pasture. The up and down system, for which there seems some evidence in the seventeenth century, would have put only one-third under the plough. So the arable would have been from one-third to one-half of the total acreage; that is, 359.5 to 539.27 acres.

To calculate the number of harvesters required we have two statements to go by. First, Henry Best's estimate that one man could mow 1½ acres in one day (*Surtees Soc.* xxxiii: 114).* Second, the 'roll of all inhabitants' at Kibworth Harcourt for 1686, which lists seventy-three men.[14] This list includes one or two yeomen–gentry and some old men, so let us take sixty men in the village both willing and able to work during the harvest. Sixty men could mow 360 acres in four days, or 540 acres in six days.

Best goes on to note that for his barley crop he employed one stooker, three binders and four to six rakers to every six mowers (ibid: 53–4). So with the sixty mowers would go ten stookers, thirty binders and fifty rakers. This gives us a total labour requirement of 150 men and women. In practice, of course, the barley and peas were not harvested concurrently, so the labour-force required can be halved. When harvesting his peas, Best liked to use units made up of three men, two women and a boy (ibid: 93). Women and boys were paid less than men so it is reasonable to suppose that they were employed in preference to men whenever the nature of the work permitted it. So out of the sixty or so available male harvesters, only about thirty would be needed for the peas harvest and rather more for the barley harvest, since 'bindinge and stookinge of wintercorne is a man's labour and requireth as much and rather [more] ability and toyle than the other' (ibid: 42), namely mowing and shearing. So thirty men and forty-five women and boys might hope to get from four to twelve days' work bringing in the barley and peas at the rate of 12d a day without food for the men and 8d a day without food for the women. There would be the chance for another 3–4 days' work getting in the hay crop at the same rate of pay. A man, woman and boy, working without food for sixteen days could earn 37s 0d between them.

The harvest home festival marked the end of the season for supplementary earnings. During the winter months there was only threshing at 8d a quarter until the seed corn was threshed, and

---

* Gervase Markham estimates 1½ acres grass on level ground, 2–2½ acres barley on level ground and 1 acre wheat on level ground (*Husbandry*, p. 141).

thereafter at a lower rate. Hedging and ditching was paid by the rod according to the breadth and depth of the ditch. The rate varied between 5d–12d the rod in mid sixteenth-century Kent and 3d–6d the rod in mid seventeenth-century Suffolk. Hedging cost 1½d the rod in both counties at both dates. The rate for day-labour in winter dropped to 4d with food and 8d without. In March it went up to 6d and 12d (see tables 16 and 17, notes). By this date women and children could earn a few pence for weeding in the fields, and by June there was the possibility of being hired to wash sheep: at 3d the score with food, at the rate of 120–130 sheep a day. A week or so later came shearing time, when a shearer could earn 4d per score at the rate of 60–70 sheep a day. For every shearer two winders would be needed, a man to help the shepherd and a couple of children to mind the tar-pot and to collect odd locks of wool (*Surtees Soc.* xxxiii: 18–22, 94, 96). Spread among sixty men, the opportunities for winter work did not go very far!

On the whole, it would seem that the demand for labour in Kibworth Harcourt did not quite meet the supply, though there does not seem to have been an acute shortage of work.* However, in many parts of England men lived in one village and worked in another, often quite some distance away. Map 14 will show that this cannot have been the practice in Gartree Hundred. The map shows the parishes of the Hundred, with the 1831 boundaries, the date of their enclosure when much of the arable was put down to pasture (*VCH Leics.* V), and the population of the parishes in 1603.† It will be seen that to the north-east of Kibworth Harcourt lay parishes enclosed in the sixteenth and seventeenth centuries, mostly under grass and with populations of less than 100 communicants. These offered little or no work for outsiders. North, west and south lay parishes enclosed in the eighteenth century, only six of which had a population of over 200; Great Glen, Burton Overy, Kibworth Bauchamp, Foxton and Great Bowden, which lie strung out along the Leicester–Market Harborough route, and Theddingworth which lies in association with the market town of Husbands Bosworth. The parishes with under 200 communicants would have enjoyed the same balance between supply and demand as Kibworth Harcourt; those with over 200 may well have found difficulty in supporting the additional numbers and have been sending labourers out rather than receiving them.

* In 1801, however, there were only 348 acres under the plough in the fields of Kibworth Harcourt, Beauchamp and Smeeton Westerby together; the outcry then about unemployment will be appreciated.

† *VCH Leics.* III pp. 168–9 based on the *Liber Cleri* of the Diocese of Lincoln, 1603 (Lincs. Rec. Soc. XIII) which lists communicants, i.e. persons over 16 years of age.

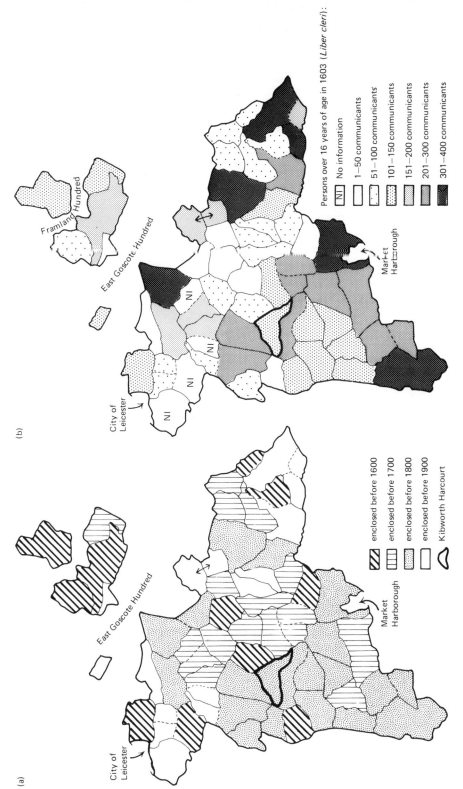

(a)

City of Leicester →

East Goscote Hundred

Market Harborough →

enclosed before 1600

enclosed before 1700

enclosed before 1800

enclosed before 1900

Kibworth Harcourt

(b)

Framland Hundred

East Goscote Hundred

City of Leicester →

NI

NI

NI

NI

NI

Market Harborough →

Persons over 16 years of age in 1603 (*Liber cleri*):

NI   No information

1—50 communicants

51—100 communicants

101—150 communicants

151—200 communicants

201—300 communicants

301—400 communicants

Map 14   Enclosure and population in Gartree Hundred

One can conclude that supplementary employment was restricted to the hay, barley and peas harvests, a total of two to three weeks' employment in the year.

There remains one last sector of employment which has not been discussed, the service sector. In the fourteenth century hereditary craftsmen, such as the smith and the carpenter, were also small landholders; by 1700 they were cottars. In the fourteenth century they formed a distinct group, secure in their monopoly of a small number of indispensable crafts which provided a regular income in addition to the produce of their land. Land was constantly being hired or let by them; they frequently held more than one half virgate; they stood surety for one another. Other half virgaters had to rely on seasonal work to raise money for their rent; the craftsmen were in occupation of the only regular part-time employments in the village. By 1700 the half virgate holding had disappeared, leaving, on the one hand, the landless wage-earner and on the other the landless village craftsman. The wage-earners left the village, but the craftsmen remained, preserving fifteenth-century surnames into the twentieth century. They were in not quite the same category as the simple half virgater: their links were with the surrounding market towns, Hallaton, Harborough, Glen Magna, Barrow on Soar, whereas the names of the simple half virgaters are not found in the towns but in the surrounding villages.

Kibworth Harcourt supported a carpenter, a miller who ran two mills (a horse mill and a windmill), a tailor, a butcher, one or more bakers or brewers, a smith, a carter, a growing number of innkeepers as traffic increased along the London road, a common neatherd, a shepherd and a swineherd. There was no large-scale employer in the village, so artisans relied not on annual wages with livery but upon the prosperity of the yeomen, husbandmen and cottagers among whom they lived, and who engaged their services for short-term contracts.

Carting was well paid in the medieval period. According to the Leicester Borough accounts, a carter could earn 1s 4d to 2s a day, a carpenter 1s 0d, a slater 9d (Bateson 1923: 140). But we are given an interesting insight into the economics of the business at the village level in 1448. In that year Merton College put up a new building in Kibworth Harcourt consisting of a hall, chamber and stables worth £26. The bailiff, John Caunden, made three incomplete attempts to draw up the accounts for this outlay, and from these we learn that nearly every man in the village took the opportunity to earn something by carting. They were not paid at the same rate as the Leicester carters of 1365–66; for example, William Heyne received only 3s for carting timber from Rothley Park, which lay some miles to the north of Leicester city.[15] It becomes clear that most men had their own cart and the beasts to draw it, so that there was no demand for a professional carter within the village itself or within the immediate vicinity; carting meant long distance enterprises, and it is significant to note the number of carters who head the lay subsidy lists as being more wealthy than their fellow townsmen.[16] In Kibworth, the Carter family played a vigorous part in the rapid series of land transactions which took place in the fifteenth century. By the sixteenth century Goodman Carter was known as Master Carter and was worth £226 in movables.[17]

Where there are carts and ploughs there must be a carpenter-cum-wheelwright. The thirteenth-century rentals mention a '*carpentarius*',[18] and in the sixteenth century there were two: Thomas Kilpeck, worth £36 3s 4d when he died, and John Eliot from Newbold Verdun, worth £46. During the intervening period no reference survives to a carpenter, but the family of Wrights is prominent, and if not they then some other family must have performed the vital functions of a wheelwright in this farming community.

A windmill and a horse mill belonging to Merton College were leased for varying lengths of time, usually to the same man. The circular horse mill, surrounded by a mud wall and roofed over with thatch stood in the village square to the north of the town cross.[19] The thirteenth-century windmill stood on the high ground to the north-west of the village.* In 1356 the timber of this mill was sold, except for the sailyards, and building expenses were incurred for the next year or so.[20] It was probably at this juncture that the mill was moved to a higher site: to the north-east of the village, on what is today called Old Mill Hill. In 1448 the mill received a new look and in 1515 it was entirely rebuilt '*de novo*' on which occasion it was probably again moved, this time to its present site on the third of Kibworth's hills, south of Whistle Gate.[21] A fine postmill is depicted on this site on the 1635 map.

The men who leased the mill were nearly always outsiders and none established permanent links with the village. The longest connection was formed by the Bryslante family, five of whose members successively ran the mills between 1412 and 1445. The last was dismissed from office for charging excessive tolls,[22] and he then took the mill at Kibworth Beauchamp: there he was killed with 'a bastard sword' in 1451 by John Attelok, his successor at Kibworth

---

* See maps 5 and 8. The site was excavated and positively identified by Mr Aggas and Mr Yates, of Kibworth Beauchamp.

Harcourt.[23] The millers' trade was a specialised one; most of the men who leased the Kibworth mills had held mills elsewhere and their sureties were millers from other villages. The fact that they did not stay long in Kibworth and that they were constantly accused of charging excessive fees would suggest that the amount of barley to be ground in the village did not meet their outgoings, chief of which was their rent of 26s 8d per annum.

In addition to the common mill there was the common oven, the upkeep and repair of which was the responsibility of the whole village in the fifteenth century.[24] In the seventeenth century the Hubbert family for years occupied a *parva officina* called the bakehouse[25] (see chap. 7, Ten. 34), and it was here that housewives, in an area short of fuel, brought their dough to be baked. In addition to the common bakehouse there were bakers licensed to sell horse bread and 'human bread'. In the fifteenth century, licensees were the wives of the more prosperous villagers, but by the sixteenth century licences were taken up by outsiders from Leicester, Market Harborough and Bowden Magna.[26] None of these later licensees settled in the village so it is possible that their premises were sublet to a local.

For many generations the Parker family leased the 'kiln' from Merton College[27] (see maps 8 and 9). This was probably an open kiln, used for drying grain in wet years and for malting barley. A good example of such a kiln was discovered at Barrow in Rutland (Bolton 1960: 128–31), and another at Great Casterton, also in Rutland (Corder 1951: 53–5).* Corn-drying kilns are common along the northern margin of corn cultivation, where the grain has to be harvested before it is ripe, and in Britain Sir Lindsay Scott has traced them as far south as Northamptonshire (Scott 1951: 196–208). To Gervase Markham they were such a familiar feature of rural life that he does not trouble to describe the normal seventeenth-century kiln, but concentrates upon the 'Ancient forme', the new French kiln and, what he found was the best, the west-country type which, however, suffered the drawback of being only capable of drying about 8 bushels at a time (1623: 190–299). It is curious that the kiln so seldom features in English manorial surveys, although it is conspicuous in Welsh surveys. It may be that the corn-drying kiln was so integral a part of the agrarian economy that, like the organisation of the open fields and the village flocks, it remained outside the cognisance of the

* Search of the wills and inventories for Leicestershire for the years 1570–5, 1606–14, 1636–41 and 1696–1700 revealed similar kilns at Burton Grange, Hootone, East Langton, Thorpe Arnold, Shilton, Saxalby, Melton Mowbray, Hungerstone, Turlangton, Blaby, Whetston, Barrow on Soar, Naseby, Disworth, Burstall, Foxton, Newbold and Ashby de la Zouche.

manorial lord. Be that as it may, the upkeep of a kiln was considerable, the skill required great. To brew the malted barley into ale or beer also required time and skill. From the mid fifteenth century onwards there were about four or five wives or widows of the more prosperous villagers paying an annual fee of 4d–8d for the licence to brew and sell ale. For example, Katherine Polle (1486–1511), the Mariots (1489–1531), the Parkers (1456–84), the Brewsters and Bradleys, whose connections extended to Leicester and Coventry (1521–39), the Pyffords (1452–89), the Wrights (1499–1511) and the Bryans, who were also butchers (1590s). Many of these wives were also bakers in the earlier period, and their husbands ran inns. The Parkers ran an inn in the seventeenth and eighteenth centuries and this building, the White House, still boasts two extensive subterranean cellars. The Bryans ran the Rose and Crown, which still flourishes today, George Fox ran an inn in the seventeenth century, and in 1778 there was an inn called the Red Lion next to George Foxton's house (Nichols 1790: 639).

Butchering was a sideline, carried on in conjunction with baking or with moderately prosperous farming.[28] As has been said, the demand for meat in the village was small and the big cattle markets at Harborough and Northampton too near for the graziers to require the services of a middleman. Only four men are known to have been butchers: John Pyfford (1443–81), renowned for 'drawing blood' in brawls, John Kynde (1532–52), Christopher Bryan (1594–1601) and Ambrose Deacon in 1610.

There was a skinner in the thirteenth and fourteenth centuries,[29] a sadler in the fifteenth,[30] a tanner in the sixteenth[31] and eighteenth (Nichols 1790: 637) and a glover[32] and shoemaker[33] in the seventeenth, all possibly referring to the same establishment. John Polle, glover in 1643, may have been related to the John Polle, shoemaker, who died in Harborough in 1639 worth £50 18s 0d.[34] Similarly, there was a draper in the thirteenth century, a tailor[35] in the fourteenth, a webster and a draper in the fifteenth[36] and a fuller in the sixteenth.[37] One or two women in the seventeenth century are referred to as spinsters, which implies spinning as a livelihood, but the stocking knitting industry which took root in Kibworth Beauchamp, Smeeton Westerby and Turlangton seems to have made no progress in Harcourt or, indeed, in any other village in the region except Little Stretton (*VCH Leics.* III: 4).

There was always a blacksmith and always herdsmen, but more will be said about these when we come to describe living conditions. The 1300 rental lists a leech, a washerwoman, a thresher and two 'brochurs' or broggers.[38]

Thus it cannot be said that the village supported a large number of artisans. With difficulty it supported a miller. It always needed a wheelwright, a smith and herdsmen. A tanner, tailor, butcher and carter maintained a precarious position within it. Comparatively wealthy bakers, brewers and innkeepers supplemented their income derived from other sources by providing these services. To repeat, in the fourteenth century, these village craftsmen held half virgates like most other villagers and enjoyed the advantage of a steady source of supplementary income. They retained their land longer than their fellows but lost it in mortgages in the seventeenth century and lasted on as cottagers until the twentieth. The half virgaters who did not enjoy these opportunities for supplementing their income took steps to increase their lands in the fifteenth century; those who did not, lost what they had during the inflationary years of the late sixteenth and the early seventeenth centuries and became landless labourers.

So far in this chapter we have been attempting to translate the resources and expenditure of the peasant household into monetary terms in order that we may be able to compare the prosperity of two clearly defined economic groups – the full and the half yardlanders – and to chart the fluctuations in that prosperity over time. However, not every aspect of economic life can be reduced to figures. Unlike industrial plant, land, if well managed, appreciates in value over time; similarly, the family household, in the course of successive generations, accumulates wealth in the form of housing, furniture, education, family tradition, seniority in the village hierarchy, none of which are susceptible of tabulation. The margin of surplus cash is a sufficiently sensitive indicator to enable us to discern trends which will not be manifest in the style and manners of a group until many years later; therefore, tabulation is a necessary foundation, but *how* a man spent his surplus is also of critical importance: conspicuous consumption, like over-generous legacies, could ruin a peasant as surely as a duke.

The evidence of archaeology reveals a marked improvement in peasant housing standards in the fifteenth century, while the evidence of wills and inventories in the sixteenth and early seventeenth centuries allows us to look inside these houses; to relate the size of the household to the number of rooms – and of beds – and to note the number and quality of household items added to the household store by successive generations. We will start at one end of the social spectrum, and work our way across the economic groupings from London lawyer to agricultural labourer, looking through the collections of inventories which have survived for several representative Kibworth families.

Thomas Ray, courtier, lawyer, yeoman of the Queen's Wardrobe of the Beds, brought the novelties of London to Kibworth in the mid sixteenth century.[39] He occupied what is today called the Manor House and acted as bailiff to Merton College (see chap. 7, Ten. 9 and pp. 102–3). His house stood in a class apart for size and comfort, though it was modest enough by national standards. He died in 1559, shortly after his arrival. In the hall stood a cupboard, a frame table with two carpets, a chair and seven busset stools with nine cushions and wall hangings. The new parlour contained a cupboard, a standing bed and a pallet bed, two coffers, a carpet and a hanging. In the old parlour was a standing bed, four chests, and a press with hangings. The chests contained a 'dyaper table cloth', 1½ dozen towels, 1 dozen topboard cloths, 26 pairs of fine sheets, 24 pairs of coarse sheets, 12 table cloths and 3 dozen napkins. In the closet over the parlour were 10 carpet cloths for tables, 5 pairs of fustian blankets, 7 pairs of woollen blankets, 4 feather beds, 3 flock beds, 6 bolsters and 16 pillows, 8 counterpanes, one of them scarlet, 2 quilts, one of them covered with sarsenet, 1 standing bed with 'test and corthens of sarsenytt', five little stools, two chairs and eight cushions, a chest, two cupboards, one coffer and a trundle bed. In addition there was a buttery containing porringers, candlesticks and similar utensils; a chamber over the buttery containing two bedsteads, a cupboard and a coffer; a chamber over the hall containing another bedstead and a store of 10 stones of wool; a storehouse containing pitchforks and other instruments of husbandry; a milkhouse, larder, kitchen, maid's place and men's chamber, in which there was a malt kiln. In all, his personal estate was worth £332 16s 6d.

More wealthy than Ray but less sophisticated was the *yeoman Robert Bryan* who died in 1605 worth £380. A widower, he lived with his son Robert and his butcher brother Christopher in a house comprised of a hall with a chamber above it, a kitchen, dairy, servant's chamber and cheese chamber. This may have been Tenement 44, the free chapel of former days. His silver spoons were worth 30s; the rest of his silver £13. A maid and servants looked after his needs. His fifteen kine had provided him with seventy cheeses and he ran 180 sheep on his 1½ virgates and leased land (see above chap. 7, Ten 44 and p. 108).

At the western end of the Main Street still stands *John Iliffe's* house (described in chap. 4). Opposite stood a similar seven-roomed house (Ten. 26) for which the inventories of the Carter family have survived for 1641, 1670, 1690 and 1709. The earliest inventory mentions a hall and parlour with chimney between them, a little parlour and kitchen, and a chamber over the parlour. By 1670 there was a chamber over the hall, by 1690 there was a chamber over the little parlour, by then called the buttery. Thomas Carter, husbandman, died in 1641 worth £222, but the inheritance was split between his sons William and John, and the family fortunes declined thereafter (see chap. 7, Ten. 26 and pp. 260–1, 262–4).

From husbandman we turn to *blacksmith*. This is a straight tale of declining fortunes. In February 1692 *Samuel Clerke* died possessed of goods worth £30 19s 0d. His debts amounted to £32. His brother and sister lived under the same roof and he left a wife and five young children. The house in which these nine people lived consisted of a hall, parlour and shop with a chamber over the parlour. The hall contained a table and three chairs, one 'loyndiron' (endiron, which implies a chimney), 2 pewter plates and 3 pans. The parlour contained a bedstead, a cupboard, a coffer, a trunk, two barrels and two tubs. The chamber over the parlour contained simply a bed. In his shop were his bellows, hammers and other instruments. Without the house he kept a horse, two cows and a hog. Twenty-five shillings worth of barley lay in his barn, 21s worth of peas and 11s worth of hay. Out in the field was sown wheat worth 21s. His debts included 42s for meat, 10s for coal, 3s 9d owed to John Hubbard for shepherd's wages, 20s to Miss Cox for house rent and, finally, 15s 4d for 'a dockter in the house'. The 20s must have been a loan from Miss Cox rather than rent, because the house was copyhold and leased in Clerke's name from Merton at 4s a year plus 6d for the shop and a £3 fine every seventh year. Clerke's widow and only son died before 1700 and the property was divided. The shop passed to his brother Daniel who died in 1729 worth only £13 5s. The hall then contained two tables, a grate, 1 crock, 3 small pans and some pewter. The parlour contained one bed, the chamber over it two bedsteads and some 'small bedding'. The shop was still there and he kept one cow, but business had evidently not been good. The land, meanwhile, had been divided between Samuel's two surviving daughters, Mary Fletcher and Alice Clerke. By 1772 Mary Fletcher's share had become part of Lebbeus Humfrey's 'bottom garden'[40] (see chap. 7, Ten. 45).

The inventories of two *shepherds* survive. In 1662 *William Hodge* left £7 15s 8d, a three-roomed house and a cow, pig and 2 ewes with lambs in the yard. In 1661 *John Hubbert* senior left to his shepherd son, John, 3 sheep and one bay of his house. His wife, Isabel, was to have the other two bays. It was a one-hearth house[41] (see chap. 7, Ten. 32) next to the Hall Close and was held from Merton College. Both the daughters were married.

In 1541 *John Smith, tanner*, left a three-roomed house and £38 12s 0d worth of goods. The hall contained a board, two forms, a cupboard and three chairs. In the parlour were three coffers, four mattresses and some bedding; in the kitchen three cupboards and the usual array of kitchen utensils including 2 saltcellars. In the yard was a horse, 2 kye, a heifer, 3 hogs, 3 loads of hay and some coal. In 1716 *William Smith* occupied a similar three-roomed dwelling with two hearths, and with the house went a quarter of a virgate. He was worth only £11 6s 0d, and he instructed his executor to sell the land in order to settle debts and pay off the mortgagee. The remainder was to go to his two sons and two daughters. This land also became part of Lebbeus Humfrey's 'bottom garden'[42] (see chap. 7, Ten. 45).

Richard Deacon, husbandman, was worth £52 13s 4d in 1570, but he and his five children occupied a two-roomed dwelling (see p. 106). His grandson, Nicholas, died in 1593 leaving five surviving children, the eldest of whom inherited the lease of the farm while the younger, Ambrose, set up business as a *butcher, baker* and *brewer.*

Richard Rowerth and his three children occupied a two-roomed house (Ten. 14). The lease of his half virgate was worth 20s a year and in 1584 he kept 27 sheep worth £6 5s and no cattle. This was double the stint to which he was entitled, so perhaps he had put his arable down to leys or else rented some additional grazing. His eldest son, Hugh, became a *shoemaker* and kept on the half virgate for an annual rent of 7s 4d, plus a fine of 70s 6d to be paid every seventh year.

The *cottar, Richard Coleman,* lived with his wife and two children in a single room containing a table, a form, two chairs, three stools, one old ambre, two coffers, two bedsteads, a board, shelves and various utensils. Outside in the yard were his pullen, 4 kye, 4 ewes and lambs, 6 other 'small sheep' and one small hog. His peas, barley and hay were worth 26s 8d in November 1580, and all his possessions were worth £13 8s 4d.

In the village there were always *the old* to be provided for by their children. Reference has already been made to Nicholas Gilbert's provision for his parents in 1360. In 1520 *John Polle's widow*, Amice occupied a complete house to herself comprising hall, parlour and kitchen. She had 6 kye, 3 calves, five score sheep, hogs, pullen, wheat, barley and peas in the barn, firewood and timber, and a precious coffer worth £10 standing in the parlour. However, most widows were less fortunate. In 1624 *Richard Rylye*, yeoman, left his wife, Alce, 1 acre arable in every one of the fields of Kibworth Harcourt, 2 loads of hay to keep her cow each year, 'a room for a board in the house she now dwells in and room about the barn to lay her corn and hay in', a bedstead, her furniture 'and the old pied cow'. In the same year *Henry Watts*, husbandman, left his wife half the household goods and two of his best kye, half a yardland which her son was to plough and dress for her, one load of coals a year and one load of wood every two years, the bay of the barn next the stable to lay her corn and hay in, part of a hovel to lay her peas in, 'the chamber over the parlour for her own use and room in the hall to make her a fire'. Her son was to do all her carting for her. The house was Tenement 3, by this time extended to its present size, but without the second-floor lofts (see chap. 7, Ten. 3, and figs. 3 and 4). In 1632 *Nicholas Porter*, labourer, instructed his son John to build his mother a chimney in the parlour where she dwelt (chap. 7, Ten. 48) or else to

> build her one sufficient bay in the yard and make her a
> chimney in it for her to live in, and she shall have leave to
> keep beans and one pig in the yard and have the third part of
> the hovel that is in the yard and one cow and all the
> household goods that she brought with her and 18s 0d a year,

in addition to diet, washing and lodging and a cow and a sheep kept with his own. Unfortunately no inventory was made, but John and his wife Alice renewed Nicholas's lease of the western half of Half Hayward's Meare, the eastern half of the gravell pits, a dole on the western side of Church Hadland, the northern part of Combes Meare, a piece to the east of Hogate and a close called Fishpooledike next to Marsh Field. For this collection he paid an annual rent of 6s 11d and a fine of 20s every seventh year, which was raised to 30s in 1693.[43] The house at Fishpooledike had been abolished by 1779. This was all grazing land, so he would have had to buy barley for three adults, as well as find 18s for his mother each year. Only if he worked full time for 50s to 80s a year could he hope to meet these expenses.

These inventories tend to confirm the impression gained from the budget tables, and from figures 18 and 19, showing the return to legacies in kind among the poorer landholders in the late seventeenth century, and of a decline in the fortunes of the smaller landholders towards the end of the period we have been studying. Some, like the Clerkes, still lived in houses which had been enlarged and improved in the previous century; they had retained their cupboards and chairs and their permanent bedsteads, which contrast so markedly with the trestles and boards of the late medieval period, but no new items of furniture had been added. Fortunately, they had also retained the custom of making a will and having an inventory taken of their goods, so that the halt, and in some cases the decline, in the standard of living is clearly set before us.

If we look back to tables 14 and 15, we see that a holding of 12 acres arable and pasture in heavy clay country producing mainly barley and peas could provide the average family with its food for the year, but could not produce enough surplus to pay the whole rent regularly, or to supply a ceremonial and replacement fund. Seasonal employment provided the necessary surplus. This balance between smallholding and seasonal employment can fairly be called subsistence level within the context of Kibworth Harcourt. Reduction in the opportunities for seasonal employment, for example, large scale conversion of arable to pasture, could upset this balance, as also could the increase in the number of smallholders and cottars competing for seasonal jobs such as harvesting.

Rural economy in the medieval period rested on the maintenance of this delicate balance. The smallholder held his land in return for works or rent. If it was rent he owed, then there had to be a demesne or one or more large agricultural units in his vicinity which could offer him employment for wages; he could not squeeze the rent out of his land. Ideally, there had to be a nice balance between large holdings and small holdings, and the number of very small holdings had to be very small indeed. In the thirteenth century the 8 or 9 virgates of demesne at Kibworth Harcourt were leased out in quarter-virgate pieces, and there was no longer a big employer in the village. It is not at all clear from what source the half virgaters derived their surplus for rent during this period; possibly from wool sales or from quarter-virgate shares of the demesne. In the fifteenth century many, in fact most, of the half virgaters became full virgaters, able to pay their rent out of the profits of their land and no longer dependent on occasional employment. Sixteenth-century inflation allowed the virgater to increase his profit margin and to set aside enough capital with which to buy or lease more land. The virgate, therefore, was a less stable unit than the half virgate; additions were constantly made to it, so that by 1635 there were only four single virgate tenements in Kibworth of 18, 20, 27 and 31 acres respectively: the rest were over $2\frac{1}{2}$ virgates, the largest 7. These multi-virgate holdings offered employment for a small number of semi-landless men. However, no return was made to the medieval system. There were by this date few half virgaters; that is, men who did not look for more than seasonal work. Therefore, either higher wages had to be paid to attract living-in servants or labour requirements had to be reduced. The latter was the obvious course in the excellent grazing region round Kibworth. So a new balance was arrived at: one of moderate-sized pasture farms on the one hand and landless, full-time craftsmen on the other. The way of life which depended upon both land and wages did not return.*

* 'Depuis la rupture de l'economie traditionnelle de type domanial, l'union metier auxiliaire – exploitation agricole a fait place a une complementarite artisanat-agriculture' (Ibarrola 1966: 13).

Medieval historians not infrequently talk about peasants being 'burdened' with labour services. From this discussion of the seventeenth-century situation it will be seen that while the virgater may have looked upon labour services as a burden and a nuisance, the half virgater may well have preferred a low rent and certain employment to a higher rent and the necessity to seek employment at low rates.

There seems little reason to believe that the thirteenth-century economy in Leicestershire supported a large labour-force. Poor transport facilities prevented the county from becoming a wheat-growing area; the crops grown were barley and peas, which require less intensive cultivation. The lay estates in the county did not comprise many manors, and on these manors the demesnes were small in extent; most were under 150 acres in arable. Labour services actually performed were not heavy; on none of the manors examined did Professor Hilton find week-works performed, at most seventeen days in the year were demanded (*VCH Leics.* II: 145–98). Fourteen to twenty-one days' work in the year was the most a seventeenth-century wage-labourer might hope to get. What is notable is that a large proportion of the thirteenth-century peasantry paid money rents and, correspondingly, manorial demesnes were cultivated by wage-labour. Now the number of thirteenth-century demesne farms was very much less than the number of seventeenth-century yeoman farms and the number of half virgaters very, very much greater, so that it is difficult to imagine how these half virgaters managed to raise the money for rent and why they consented to actually pay for the privilege of uncertain employment.

The problem can be more clearly seen in concrete terms at Kibworth Harcourt. Here, *c.* 1250, a demesne of some 190–220 acres had been cultivated with the help of relatively heavy labour services. A virgater owed two days' ploughing per year with his own plough and without food; two days' harrowing and hoeing with food; two days' mowing on the lord's meadow with one man, and an indefinite amount of gathering and carrying hay using the lord's cart; four days' autumn reaping with two men and without food; two more days' reaping with four men this time with food; various other carting services within the county.[44] There were at the time this list was drawn up sixteen virgaters and thirty-two half virgaters. So for six days' harvesting there would be 176 men to harvest about 144 acres of barley, peas and some wheat. We have already seen that sixty men could mow 360 acres in four days, and if one adds the stookers and rakers, then 150 men and women would be sufficient. Evidently the bailiff at Kibworth Harcourt could get in his entire harvest with the help of labour services alone. But the number of plough services were not sufficient; two or more full-time ploughmen would have been necessary.

So the supply of employment at Kibworth was much the same in the thirteenth century as in the seventeenth, but the demand was far greater. The rent too was greater: 10s in the thirteenth century as against 6s 8d from the late fifteenth onwards.

Yet these men somehow found the money and paid their rents. Their diet and their standard of living must have been of an entirely different order to that of the fifteenth century onwards, and it is scarcely surprising that the 'peasant house' does not appear in the rural landscape before the late fifteenth century.

The commutation of labour services to money payments introduced an imbalance to the economy which ended only in the plagues of the late fourteenth century.*

* 'Et cependant tous ces paysans qui theoriquement ne pouvaient vivre sur leurs terres, ont vecu . . . mais ils ont vecu en s'en dettant' (Goubert 1960: 182).

9

The size and composition of the peasant household

The inheritance pattern practised in a region will normally be that best suited to the local economy and serves to define the size and age structure of the domestic group. It also is true that the smaller the tenement the more restricted will that group have to be. In chapter five it was argued that a 24-acre holding could comfortably support a household of three to five persons, whereas a 12-acre holding could not. The reasons are summarised in tables 14 and 15. Other factors enter in, such as whether rent was paid in cash or in labour, but it is clearly important that the size of the household in relation to its landed resources should be carefully examined. This is the subject of the present chapter.

In the seventeenth century the term *household* was more familiar than the term *family*, and by household a man meant all those persons who sat at his 'board': children, grandchildren, other relatives, servants – the unit of domestic consumption – and it is in this sense that we shall be using the term. The adult members of the group contributed to the domestic economy either directly, by working on the family land, or indirectly, by working for wages outside the household, by operating small-scale craft production or by engaging in trade. At Kibworth, as in many parts of England, houses were relatively large and all members shared the same roof, but in other regions a single production and consumption group might be made up of two or more residential units. The mapping of residential customs has not yet been systematically undertaken, but it is an important element in any demographic or economic survey.

Because the size of a family tends to expand and contract in a regular develpmental cycle – unless held steady by the importation of servants during the periods of natural contraction – we must be able to determine the length of the cycle – the generation span – and the presence or not of servants as the first step towards establishing the average family size. In very general terms, where land is abundant and cheap, the size of the farming enterprise can be tailored to suit the changing size of the family, as Chayanov observed for parts of Russia (Chayanov 1925: 64). Where land is scarce and expensive it makes better sense to tailor the household to meet the requirements of the farm, which Berkner found to be the practice in eighteenth-century Austria (Berkner 1972: 398–418). There is a place for both models in medieval England, but at Kibworth the Berkner model is undoubtedly the more appropriate. Any inhabitant from Kibworth would have agreed wholeheartedly with the Dordogne peasant who, in response to the suggestion that his family might sell land to raise a dowry for a daughter, explained, 'Sell, land! One never sells land, one only buys it.' On the small medieval holdings, it was always a case of too many children and never enough land, in the early modern period servants were brought in to help cultivate the large new farms; there was no question of parting with so much as one acre.

In order to establish the average household size at Kibworth at various stages in its history, it is necessary to reconstruct the developmental cycle as set out in table 20. The model demands reasonably precise information on six basic points, and we shall examine the evidence for each of these points, first for the early modern period, because it is the better documented, and then for the medieval period. The six points and six sections are:

1 The average age of men at first marriage. This indicates the generation span.
2 The average length of life of landholding men. This indicates the generation overlap.
3 The average number of children in a completed family.
4 The infant mortality rate.
5 The birth interval.
6 The age at which children left home. If a child received a child portion to be paid in instalments, it is also necessary to know when the last instalment was paid and the child ceased to be economically dependent in any way upon the holding.

The early modern period, 1574–1700

Our sources for this period consist of the wills for probate, the court rolls and rentals and the parish register. The register was opened in 1574 and runs from that date to 1640, and from 1649 to 1700 and beyond. The occasional gaps of a year or so can be filled in by reference to the Archdeacon's transcripts and therefore do not present a problem, but, unfortunately, neither source provides full coverage for the interregnum. Ideally, therefore, the study should be

Table 20. *Developmental cycle of the seventeenth-century household, showing the number of consumer units on a 12- and 24-acre holding*

Year	1	2	3	4	5	6	7	8	9	10	11	12	13	14	15	16	17	18	19	20	21	22	23	24	25	26	27	28	29
Grandfather	X	X																											
Grandmother	X	X	X																										
Husband	X	X	X	X	X	X	X	X	X	X	X	X	X	X	X	X	X	X	X	X	X	X	X	X	X	X	X	X	X
Wife	X	X	X	X	X	X	X	X	X	X	X	X	X	X	X	X	X	X	X	X	X	X	X	X	X	X	X	X	X
Sister																													
Brother																													
Sister																													
Brother																													
Daughter	x	x	x	x	x	X	X	X	X	X	X	X	X	L															
Son			x	x	x	X	X	X	X	X	X	X	X	X	X	X	?	?	?	?	?	?	?	?	?	?	?	?	?
Daughter							x	x	X	X	X	X	X	X	X	X	?	?	L										
Son											x	x	D																
Daughter															x	x	x	X	X	X	X	X	X	L					

Consumption units:

	1	2	3	4	5	6	7	8	9	10	11	12	13	14	15	16	17	18	19	20	21	22	23	24	25	26	27	28	29
12 acres	4	4	4	3	2	3	3	4	4	4	5	5	5	4	4	3	4	4	3	3	3	3	3	2	2	2	2	2	2

Average = 3.34 persons per household

	1	2	3	4	5	6	7	8	9	10	11	12	13	14	15	16	17	18	19	20	21	22	23	24	25	26	27	28	29
24 acres	4	4	4	3	2	3	3	4	4	4	5	5	5	4	4	5	5	4	4	4	4	4	4	3	3	3	3	3	3

Average = 3.82 persons per household

Note: D = died   L = left home   ? = may have remained at home on 24-acre holding, but not 12-acre holding   x = under five years old

200

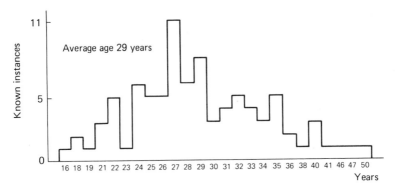

Fig. 9 Age at first marriage for men in the seventeenth century

broken into two parts; before, and after, the Civil War. However, since the number of families we are dealing with is rather small, and not all of them cover both periods, the exercise was found to be unjustified and the seventeenth century has been treated as an unbroken whole. General trends in fertility and mortality can be better appreciated in figure 1 which is based on aggregates for the entire parish, that is, Kibworth Beauchamp and Smeeton Westerby as well as Harcourt.

The generation span and the age at first marriage of men. To discover the average number of years from birth to first marriage of males the register was searched for vital statistics of birth, marriage and birth of first child. Since marriages were seldom solemnised and recorded in the parish of the groom, the birth of the first child was found to be better documented than marriage data. If we make the perhaps arbitrary assumption that the first child was born a year after marriage we can take the date of marriage as one year before the birth of the first child, and thereby increase the number of instances of known date of birth and marriage to eighty-seven. The age distribution at first marriage for men for these eighty-seven cases is given in figure 9, and the average age was in the region of 29 years. In only twenty-six cases do we know the age at marriage of women in Kibworth, with an average age of 23.6 years. At the national level women married only a year or so younger than men in the early modern period, so either the smallness of the sample has produced a distorted result for women's marriage at Kibworth, or Kibworth practice differed quite markedly from national averages. Twenty-nine years for age at first marriage for men conforms closely to national averages (Wrigley 1976).

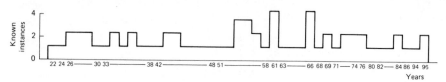

Fig. 10   Age at death of landholders at Kibworth Harcourt, 1536–1700

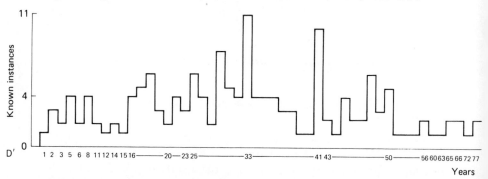

Fig. 11   Length of marriage of men at Kibworth Harcourt in the seventeenth century (date of marriage and death known)

The generation overlap. The length of overlap between grandparents and grandchildren can be established by two processes. In the first, the age at marriage, doubled, can be subtracted from the age at death. In the second, the probability of overlap can be deduced from two slightly different sets of data: the time elapsed between a man's marriage and the birth of his first grandchild, and the time that elapsed between a man's marriage and his death.

The first of these requires us to know the average life span of a married man. In sixty-nine cases the register gives us the date of birth and death of married men at Kibworth, and this, the most direct source, yields us an average of 55.8 years. In order to increase the sample, 173 cases were taken for which the dates of marriage and death only were known. The average length of marriage in the seventeenth century was found to be 32.13 years. If we add the average age at marriage to the average length of marriage we arrive at a total of 61.3 years. Alternatively, since men often postponed marriage until they had acquired land, we can add length of landholding to age at marriage in the seventeenth century and thereby arrive at an average lifespan among landholders of 60.65 years. These three approaches give us an average lifespan which varies between 55–60 years. Since this is somewhat unsatisfactory, a second approach to the problem of generation overlap can be made by means of the theory of probability.

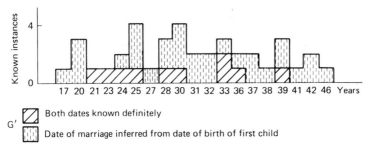

G' Both dates known definitely

Date of marriage inferred from date of birth of first child

Fig. 12 Time elapsed from the marriage of a man to the birth of his first grandchild in the seventeenth century

Two histograms (figs. 11 and 12) were prepared, one showing the time that elapsed from the marrriage of a man to the birth of his first grandchild (G¹); the second showing the time elapsed between a man's marriage and his death (D¹). In this way the two best-represented data sets were utilised. The data was punched onto computer cards, and using the equations

$$P = \sum_{t=0}^{\infty} \left[D(t) . \sum_{i=0}^{t=1} G(i) + \tfrac{1}{2}G(t) \right]$$

$$Q = \sum_{t=0}^{\infty} \left[G(t) . \sum_{i=t}^{t=\infty} (i-t) . D(i) \right]$$

and multiplying P by Q the following results were arrived at.* The

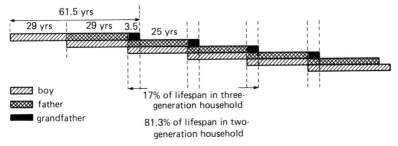

boy
father
grandfather

17% of lifespan in three-
generation household

81.3% of lifespan in two-
generation household

Fig. 13 Generation overlap in average Kibworth Harcourt household in the seventeenth century

* I should like to acknowledge here the assistance given by John Milton, now of Imperial College, London, and Paul Griffiths at the Oxford University Computing Laboratory.

probability of a man being alive when his first grandchild was born (P) was 0.5. The average overlap of grandfather and grandchild in those houses in which a grandchild was born (Q) was 7.27 years. Therefore, the average length of overlap of grandfather and grandchild over the whole community of Kibworth Harcourt was 3.74 years. In other words, grandparents and grandchildren shared the same board for an average of 3.74 years in every generation.

Number of children per completed family and infant mortality. Using the charts for reconstituted families for Kibworth, the necessary data can be extrapolated for the number of children born to each father, the birth interval and the number of deaths among children below and above the age of five. Comparison of the wills made by some of these fathers with the information given in the parish register reveals a slight tendency towards under-registration of baptisms. Where given the choice, the number of children referred to in the will has been preferred to that provided by the register.

A total of 956 children were born to 192 fathers, giving an average of 4.87 children.* Of these, 160, or 1 in 6, died before reaching their twenty-first birthday and the majority (70 per cent) did not live to see their fifth birthday (Schofield and Wrigley in Webster 1979). In the last century, Russian peasants did not include children under five among the 'mouths to be fed', and in present-day England the Department of Health and Social Security does not give a child its first increase in allowance for food and clothing until it has completed its fifth year. Since our primary interest is in the number of mouths to be fed in each household it seems reasonable to take a child's fifth birthday as the point from which to include it as a consumption unit at its father's table. If 70 per cent died before reaching the age of five, then four surviving children would seem a reasonable round number to use for the model. The sex differential for the period was negligible. Taking all baptisms in Harcourt, Beauchamp, Smeeton and Westerby, boy baptisms outnumbered girl baptisms by only seventy-seven. Therefore the gender of children has been allocated alternately on the model.

The birth interval. Only during the Commonwealth period was the date of birth given rather than the date of baptism. Therefore we are forced into using baptisms as surrogates for births. At Kibworth,

---

* From the demographic point of view, it would be more interesting to know the number of children per mother. This is not possible at Kibworth, since wives are only designated by their Christian name, and too often successive wives shared the same Christian name.

baptisms were not confined to Sundays but took place singly throughout the week. Often a child was baptised and buried within a few days and, given the high infant mortality rate, it would have seemed a reasonable precaution to baptise children as soon as possible after birth (Schofield and Berry 1971: 453–63; Wrigley 1977: 281–312). Nevertheless, this is no more than a reasonable assumption for Kibworth and cannot be proved.

For each family the interval between baptisms was counted to the nearest whole week and the final average given in years and months. The intervals tended to be very regular; thus the spacing between Thomas and Alice Carter's children reads: 17 months, $30\frac{3}{4}$, $17\frac{1}{4}$, $23\frac{1}{2}$, $20\frac{1}{2}$, $20\frac{1}{2}$ months. If a child died before weaning, the interval between its birth and that of the next child was often shortened, and if an older child died it was often replaced by a Benjamin considerably younger than its siblings, which raises the average by giving an unusually long birth interval. A birth interval of 50–60 months recurs sufficiently frequently to arouse the suspicion that these are in fact double intervals: that a baptism has been omitted from the register. This suspicion is strengthened by the tendency already mentioned for the register to omit the baptism of a child subsequently mentioned in a will. In the period before 1616 there are frequently no entries in the register for the month of September, and thereafter for the month of October or September; this happens in roughly every third year, and one presumes that births, deaths and marriages were catered for in one of the neighbouring churches (although one would anticipate some reluctance to register births in an alien parish?). Whatever the cause, these fifty-month intervals tend to weight the average too high, at 32 months. As can be seen on the histogram (fig. 14), a distribution limited to the more common intervals has been employed, giving a birth interval of 29.67 months or $2\frac{1}{2}$ years, a figure which conforms closely to practice elsewhere in England and the Continent at this date (Wrigley 1969: 93–4; Goubert 1960: 32).

The age at which children left home. On a large holding, the age at which children left home was not a critical factor, since servants were substituted for children and the total household size therefore remained constant. But on a small holding, where the labour input of children did not compensate for the expense of feeding them the economic rationale would have dictated their early departure from home, or at least their entry into outside employment while continuing to reside in the familial home. However, if employment was not available locally, and the choice was one between long-distance

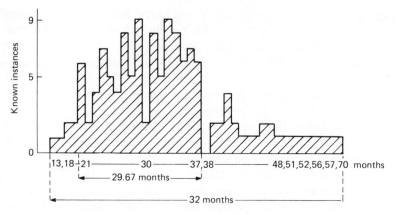

Fig. 14 Frequency distribution of birth/baptism intervals to the nearest whole month in the seventeenth century

migration and maintenance without income at home, the question of inheritance custom was drawn into the decision-making process. If, by a long period of absence, a child stood to lose his stake in that share of the inheritance which, however meagre, offered some security, the temptation to remain at home must have been a real one. Only if local custom did not give to every child the right to maintenance on the family holding could the head of a household dislodge a full-grown son. The age at which children left home was thus governed by a number of highly localised variables (the size of holding, the labour market, inheritance practice) which makes it difficult to generalise at a national level.

Nevertheless, this has been attempted in a number of pioneering computer studies based on census returns, listings, parish registers and depositions in church courts (in which the length of time certain persons had resided in the parish is recorded). The studies cover a number of parishes spanning a period from 1697 to 1841. The results show clearly that there was no general exodus at nine, twelve or fifteen years but, to quote Richard Wall, 'on the contrary, movement from home was a very gradual process, so that even in their early twenties as many as half of all children with parents still alive could be residing with them' (Wall 1978; 181–202). However, of those children who did leave home and enter into domestic service, the majority were aged from fifteen to twenty, most being over eighteen (Allison 1963: 91–103; Macfarlane 1970: 209).

Clearly, if we are to arrive at more precise figures for the Kibworth area we shall have to explore other avenues. The first is comtemporary comment.

A boy was sworn into tithing at twelve years old, and was sometimes taxed at twelve, though more usually at fourteen or sixteen. A girl could legally marry at twelve, a boy at fourteen; the son of a sokeman could inherit at fifteen, the son of a knight at twenty-one. In the eyes of the church, a child reached the age of reason at seven, and in the seventeenth century could take communion at sixteen. When Kibworth men left legacies to minors they generally stated at what age the children should inherit. With respect to girls, 18.75 per cent were to receive their portion when sixteen, 14.5 per cent when eighteen, 35.75 per cent when twenty-one and 30 per cent when they married. With respect to boys, 10 per cent were to receive their portion when sixteen, 26 per cent when eighteen, 52.5 per cent when twenty-one and only 5 per cent when they married. In two instances executors were charged with bringing up a man's sons until they were eighteen, but the boys were not to receive their portions until they were twenty-one. In another case a boy was to receive his legacy when nineteen, but was to be maintained until he was twenty-one. Two other boys were apprenticed at eighteen and nineteen respectively. By the seventeenth century it was not the custom at Kibworth for children to claim maintenance in the paternal household once they had reached adulthood: they received a generous portion and left. If the portion took the form of education or vocational training they received it while yet children, if in cash it was paid in instalments commencing at the ages indicated above. Therefore, there was no close correlation between the age at which they left home and the age at which they received their portion. Nevertheless, there is no hint in any of the wills of children being thought capable of fending for themselves at twelve or fourteen: sixteen or over seems to have been the commonly accepted minimum age.

This view is supported by the testimony of the wage schedules drawn up by Justices of the Peace, to which we have already had recourse (see above pp. 168–76). The schedules often include a scale for children – scales which reveal quite startling regional differences. In populous areas such as East Anglia, children could be employed at the tender age of ten and did not receive full adult pay until twenty-one. In less well-populated areas such as Rutland, a boy could command full pay at sixteen. The Norfolk schedules (1431, 1610) awarded a lower rate to boys under fourteen and girls between twelve and twenty; in Warwickshire, servants and apprentices between twelve and twenty-one and in East Sussex (1614) apprentices between twelve and twenty-one and servants between eighteen and twenty-one received less than full pay. At Ealing in 1599 most servants, as we have seen, were between eighteen and twenty.

Clearly, the nature of local labour markets affected the age and pay of child labourers.

At Kibworth, the small, 12-acre holding had virtually disappeared by the seventeenth century. In its place we find on the one hand relatively prosperous holdings of over 30 acres, and on the other a number of skilled craftsmen, carriers and tradesmen with little or no agricultural land, who were prospering at the beginning of the century, but in difficulties by the end. All these could make use of one or two children or servants in good times, but the artisans could manage without when times were bad. Unfortunately, it is impossible to take a head count of servants at any date in the early modern period, since the tithing lists and court rolls had become by this date little more than a register of landholders, while the parish register had little occasion to record even the names of young, landless, unmarried servants. Only in the wills do we find an occasional reference to a servant, and the cottages bought up by Sir Euseby Buswell and other absentee farmers were presumably intended for servants in husbandry (see above pp. 124–5, 135). The impression that there were few servants may thus be a false one; if not, then the inference surely is that children remained at home and undertook the function of servants until their late teens or early twenties, when many must have left the village forever, since only a tiny proportion married or took up land apart from heirs.

Only on a 12-acre holding or its equivalent in the craft sector would children have been sent into service at the early age of twelve. In such households the average household size could well have been reduced to as little as 3.34, as is shown in table 20. On a full yardland holding the size of the household would have been nearer 3.82, even more on some of the multi-yardland holdings. As Laslett once observed, there were not many large households, but 53.5 per cent of the population lived in them (Laslett 1969: 207). Some of the larger landholders, for example, make explicit provision in their wills for a son or a daughter to be maintained for life, or for an uncle or aunt to continue in the 'privilege' of maintenance in a nephew's household. The word 'privilege' suggests that the practice was not common.*

---

* 1568.   John Iliffe's daughter, Ann, to stay with his son and heir, Thomas, 'as long as she wishes'.

    1571.   Thomas Smythe leaves his property to his son and heir Henry, but his other son, Thomas junior, is to live with Henry 'during his life, with meat and drink and raiment' and to have £4 when he marries.

    1591.   Edmund Barnard's daughter, Agnes, is to live with his eldest son, John, 'all her natural life if she wishes' and is to have certain of the household goods.

The medieval period

Since the sources are so different, the evidence will also be different; strong on servants, very weak on all aspects of childhood. The key documents are the 1280 tithing list and the Poll Tax lists for 1377, 1379 and 1381. These capture the village community at two convenient points in time and serve as focal points around which to reconstruct the biography of each family in the village. These biographies have been extracted from the court rolls with occasional recourse to the rentals and are complete for the 1379 period but are more sketchy for the 1280s, since the court roll material does not pre-date the tithing list by a sufficient number of years.

The 1280 tithing list, drawn up on the back of a court roll,[1] lists the four tithings in the village, giving the name of each male head of household, his brothers and his sons over the age of twelve; thus '*Ive Godher, Wilhelmus fil' ei, Radulf fil' ei* and '*Ive Chapman, Robertus frater ei, Wilhelmus frater ei*' and so on. Where a mother's name is given in place of a father's, for example, '*Ive fil' Amice*', it has been assumed that the father is dead and Amice has accordingly been listed in table 21 as a widow. Some names have been crossed through and others added, but comparison with the court rolls shows this to have been part of the later process of updating. Therefore, for the purpose of obtaining a head count for 1280, names crossed through have been included in the count, except where names have been entered twice in obvious error; for example, *Ive frater Henrici filius Amice* is listed under Robert le Bonde's tithing, but appears again in the tithing of Robert Churt as *Ive fil' Amice* following the name of *Henricus fil' Amice*.

1605.	Robert Bryan's son and heir, Robert junior, is to keep 'my brother Christopher Bryan during his natural life'.
1641.	Thomas Carter instructs his son and heir, William, that 'my brother William Carter shall have the liberty and priviledge in my house and homestead as now and formerly he hath had during his life'.
1646.	Daniel Coleman's son-in-law, Richard Iliffe, had been living in the Coleman household and when Daniel died he was to remain and Daniel's wife and son were to depart.
1683.	Jane Iliffe (née Coleman) possibly the widow of the above Richard Iliffe, and mother of nine, left to one of her daughters, Luce, not only 40s and some household stuff but also one bay of building.
1692.	Samuel Clarke, blacksmith, left the shop to his brother, Daniel, until his son and heir, William, had completed his apprenticeship under Daniel. In addition, Samuel's sister, Deborah, was to have the 'continuation of her privileges' and his wife, Alice, was to 'keep my brother Benjamin as long as he and she shall live and after her death William [his son] to do the same'.

The 1280 list as it appears in table 21 has been edited to group members of the family together, rather than distributed in their several tithings, and the total amount of land held by each family group has been included in order to give some indication of the economic resources of each family in relation to its numbers. Men for whom no sons can be found in the records have been placed under the heading 'Marital status unknown'. They cannot be listed as celibates, since some may have had daughters and others may have been married but childless. Sons whose fathers were still living are listed as such and where known the heir has been indicated, which does not exclude the possibility that others also inherited land. Sons whose fathers' names appear in none of the records or whose obituary notices appear in earlier court rolls have been listed under 'Father dead'. Since no persons were listed as servants in the tithing list and no servants are recorded in the court rolls of the period, no heading has been provided in the 1280 table. By 'family' in this context is understood all persons with the same surname, since, from internal evidence, there is no doubt that in this small community persons with the same surname were related. In the cases where more than one branch held land, the failure of heirs in one branch resulted in the transfer of the land to another, as is so clearly illustrated in the Polle family descents (appendix 11), and if this could happen with respect to land it could, and almost certainly did, happen with respect to labour resources. The pattern is a common one in peasant societies and there is no reason to think of Kibworth as in any sense exceptional. Thus, although the budget tables have been based on the assumption that the production and consumption unit was the 'family' who shared the same board, table 21 serves as a reminder that on a wider level the production and consumption unit could embrace more than one household in a single unit.

The Poll Tax lists, 1377–81. The Poll Tax lists for 1377, 1379 and 1381[2] provide us with a second list of the adult male population of Kibworth, one hundred years after the 1280 list. Boys over fourteen were taxed in 1377 and boys over sixteen in 1379 and 1381. In theory, women were also liable to taxation, but in practice only wives or female heads of households were included in the Kibworth lists, so that we still have insufficient data with respect to women. The match between the names given in these lists and the names contained in the court rolls and rentals is very close indeed. No names from the tax list were absent from the court rolls. Only twenty-one names in the court rolls did not appear in the tax lists. Of these, William de

Table 21. *The 1280 tithing list for Kibworth Harcourt*

Family land	Adult members of the family		Children	
	Married	Marital status unknown	Father living	Father dead
½ virgate	Hugh Godwine		John Robert	
½ virgate		Roger Gilbert Robert Gilbert		
1½ virgates + *alia*	Ive Godyer		William (heir) Nicholas Radulf Hugh William John Henry	
?	Walter Brid'			
1 placea	Robert Brun Richard Brun			Nicholas son of Nich. Brun Robert son of Nich. Brun Roger son of Nich. Brun
1½ virgates		William son of Reginald Robert son of Reginald		
1½ virgates	Robert le Cuper		Reginald le Cuper (heir) Robert (heir)	
1 toft	Robert the Leech		John Robert Hugh Nicholas	
½ virgate	Robert Chop		Hugh William Nicholas	
½ virgate	Radulf Carter		Robert	
½ messuage (1295)	Alexander Mildus			
½ virgate	Ive Serrene	Robert le Serrene Walter le Serrene		John son of J. Serrene

Table 21. (*cont*)

Family land	Adult members of the family		Children	
	Married	Marital status unknown	Father living	Father dead
2 virgates + *aula*	Robert Sibile	Robert Sibile, jun. William Sibile Alexander Sibile Ive Sibile	William Roger	
1 cottage	Amice the Washerwoman		Henry (heir) Ive Roger Bonde	
1 virgate	Robert le Bonde	Robert Bonde Ive Chapman Robert Chapman } brothers William Chapman		
?				
½ virgate ?	Roger Johie	William Huralinebell[a] Nicholas Huraiinebell	Robert Johie	[b] Hugh son of Ive Hura' John son of Ive Hura' Robert son of Ive Hura' Radulf son of Ive Hura'
1 virgate		Robert Chure Robert Chure, jun.	Robert	
½ virgate land	Walter Yorte	Radulf		
½ virgate	Hugh Harcourt	John Harcourt Nicholas Harcourt } brothers	Hugh (heir)	

Holding	Holder	Kin	Heir	Descendants
2 virgates	Robert Polle	Hugh Polle; Henry Polle; John de Westerby (Polle)	Nicholas (heir)	Henry son of Nicholas Polle; William son of Nicholas Polle
1 virgate	Radulf Prepositus		William (heir)	Roger son of Robert, reeve; John son of Robert, reeve; Ive son of William, reeve
?				
½ virgate	Robert Wygerne		William	
2 virgates +	Roger Wade	Robert (brother)	Roger (heir)	
½ virgate	John Valendyn		William	
½ virgate	William Taylur		William (heir)	
1 toft	Roger Molend'		William	
1 cottage	William Molend'		John	
1½ virgates + domus,	Robert ad Fontem		John (heir); Roger; William	
½ virgate				Hugh son of 'Scolate'
½ virgate				John son of 'Scolate'
–				John (heir) s. of Hugh
?				Nicholas son of Hugh
1 virgate				Walter son of Hugh
–				Nicholas son of Hugh Man
?				William son of Mon'
1 virgate				Nicholas son of 'Alotte'
–				Robert son of Rob Arun
1 virgate				Roger son of Roger
–				Hugh son Alexander (Sander)
				Richard son of Walter

Table 21. (*cont*)

Family land	Adult members of the family		Children	
	Married	Marital status unknown	Father living	Father dead
½ virgate		Osbert Sutor		John son of Walter
1 cottage	John Honde			
Mill				
½ virgate		Hugh Leycester		
—		Ive Asteyn		
—		William de Aweston		
		Robert Textor		Robert son of le Textor
		Henry Textor		
1 virgate	Nicholas Faber			
½ virgate	Robert Nichol			
1 virgate		Adam de Burton		
½ virgate	Robert Silvestre			
½ virgate	William de Reynes			
1 cottage (Arun 1 virgate)		Robert de Missingden		
1 toft		William Gamelot		
1 toft		Alexander Godaron^c		
1 toft		Robert Pelleper^r		
½ virgate		Robert le brochar		
		the shepherd		
		William le (–)ole		

214

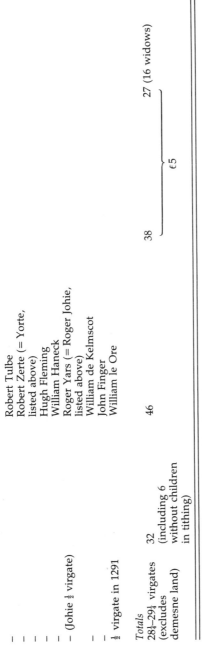

Robert Tulbe
Robert Zerte (= Yorte,
listed above)
Hugh Fleming
William Haneck
Roger Yars (= Roger Johie,
listed above)
William de Kelmscot
John Finger
William le Ore

— (Johie ¼ virgate)

½ virgate in 1291

Totals
28¼–29¼ virgates
(excludes
demesne land)

32   (including 6
without children
in tithing)

46

38   €5   27 (16 widows)

a 1282 pledge for the miller, together with other artisans.
b 1280 Messor.
c 1300 = Chaharon, later Arun or Sirrene.

Clipston was taxed at Gumley, John Asteyn and John Kynde at Smeeton Westerby, John Russell at Kibworth Beauchamp, Robert Palfreyman at Carlton Curlieu and William Clerke at Saddington. None of these villages lay more than a few miles from Kibworth Harcourt. This leaves only Valendine, Wright, Osborne, Parker and Michell as significant omissions. The Valendines had been holding land in Harcourt since at least 1280 and continued to do so for a few more years before becoming extinct for lack of heirs, the others had only recently taken land in the village. Since the remaining ten names did not appear in the court rolls again, or in any other document, they were certainly the names of transients.

Although the same names recur on all three lists, these lists are not identical. That dated 1381 supplies the Christian names of wives, occasionally provides an additional note on occupation, and at the foot of the roll lists all single persons, both male and female, in the village under the title *servientes*. The other two lists are not dated. Generally speaking, husbands and wives were *each* taxed 4d in 1377, but were taxed *jointly* at 4d in 1379. However, on both the undated Kibworth lists spouses paid 4d between them; therefore, one list at least must be dated to 1379. The other was either an alternative version for 1379 or is a copy of the 1377 list, implying that couples paid 4d instead of 8d at Kibworth in 1377. Happily, the precise date is not important, since all we need is a roll call of men and boys at a single point in time. Deductions as to the age of these men have been based on the court rolls; for example, a boy sworn into tithing in 1375 would have been fourteen years old in 1377 and sixteen in 1379, and if he married in 1390 he would have been twenty-seven at that time, whatever the dates of the tax lists. Since the 1381 list broke up family groups by introducing a separate category for servants, the undated lists were used for table 22, supplemented from the 1381 list. For convenience, the date 1379 has been ascribed to these lists, but the reader can substitute 1377 if required without disturbing the argument.

Table 22 provides a summary of the 1379 list on the same lines as that prepared for 1280. The total amount of land held by each family, as recorded in the rental for 1340–72, and verified and brought up to 1379 through the court rolls of 1340–80, is recorded under the heading 'Family land'. Since the tax lists are quite explicit on the subject of marital status, the category headed 'Marital status unknown' will be observed to have shrunk dramatically by comparison with 1280, when the status of so many men was unknown to us. Children were noted and taxed in the fourteenth century but their Christian names are not given: sons were indicated as *fil' eis* and daughters as *filiae eis*.

Table 22. *The 1377/9 Poll Tax list for Kibworth Harcourt*

Family land	Adult members of the family		Children i.e. sons and daughters over 14	'Servants'
	Married	Marital status unknown		
1½ virgates + 1 cot.	Rob. & Emma Gilbert (merchant)	Nicholas Gilbert & wife	(1391 Nich. sworn in to tithing)	John Tor Robert Alice (1381: Alice Gilbert, an elderly relative Will Gilbert
1 virgate + 1 cot. + *alia*		Mabyl, widow of Nich. Godwyne	William (inherited 1377)	(1381: Robert Godwyne, younger son)
3 virgates	Ric. Godyer & wife (1381 Nich. & Sara Godyer)		son	(John Godyer, son)
1 free messuage 1 mess., 1 cot. x acres, 5 rods	Will and Isabel Brown John & Joan Brown Rob & Margaret Brown		son (Will, inherited 1392) son	
2½ virgates + ¼ virgate +2 acres	Adam & Joan Brown (draper)		2 sons	servant
2 virgates	John & Amice Couper (son of Robert) Robert & Agnes Couper			Matilda, his mother
3 virgates + *alia*	John & Alice Peche (son of Roger Pek) Roger Pek & wife		son	
2 virgates + free	Robert & Matilda Carter (father of William)			(1381 Roger Pek widower) Robert (son) Anna (daughter)

Table 22. (cont)

Family land	Adult members of the family		Children i.e. sons and daughters over 14	'Servants'
	Married	Marital status unknown		
(land in Thorpe Langton and K.B.) 2 virgates, 2½ rods, 1 placea (aula) 2 mess (land in S. Westerby)	William & Emma Carter			John son of Will Carter & wife, Joan servant
¾ virgates + 2½ acres	Robert Scherman & wife		son (Robert) daughter	
1¼ virgates + 2 cots.	Robert & Emma Sibile		son	
	William Sibile & wife			
	(1381 Jn. son of John Sibile & Alice)			
	John Bonde & wife			
½ virgate	Ric. & Agnes Chapman, 'constabull'			
2½ virgates + alia	John Joye & wife		William	(1381 Jn. Joye retired)
1 cot.	Hugh & Beatrice Tory			
	Richard Polle & wife			
	Joanna Polle, widow			
½ acre	William & Emma Polle			John ⎫ Robert ⎬ sons? Emma ⎭ (1381 Emma Watlyng) servant (son)
	(1381 Nich. & Felicia Polle)			
½ virgate	Dionis' Wakynt			
1 cot. + ¼ virgate	John & Joan Tayliowr		daughter (son in 1367) (son in 1368)	
2 cots. + ¼ virgate	Amice Tayliowr			
	John & Agnes Scolas			
	John & Margery Mann	Robert Mann		
1¼ virgates	William & Amice Alotte		John (1383 inherited)	
2 virgates, 1 mess., 5½ acres	Robert & Agnes Smyth			Agnes Smyth (widow of Jn Smith)

Holding	Household		
1½ virgates 1 twodelrod	Henry & Millicent fitz Nicholas John Bordet & wife	John (son ?) 1381 (John Burdet – widower?)	
1¾ virgates, 1 mess. 1 placea, 4 acres	John & Agnes Heyne Adam & Isolda Heyne	(1372 John in tithing) (1373 son) daughter	(1381 Rob. Heyne, lived at Coventry)
(land in K.B.) 1½ virgates + 1 mess	John & Amice Wodher John & Dionesia Marram Henry & Alice Marram	daughter William took land 137- John took land 1375	
3 virgates	John & Alice Sander Robert & Margery Sander (m. 1361) Amice Sander (widow of Nich. died 1392, land to Robert)	(1378 Matilda) (1383 John)	(1381 Amice Sander grandmother) (1381 Amice Hychcok, daughter)
¾ virgate + 3 acres	William & Alice Hychcok	son son (Shangton) daughter (1369 William)	
1 virgates + 3 acres	William & Agnes Atte Cross Richard Pyper & Wife		(1381 Ric. Pyper widower)
¾ virgate	John Lod (Nogge) & wife	(1372 John into tithing)	William Nogge (1390 Recessit) Robert Nogge (1427 surr. 1 cot.) (both adult sons)
¾ virgate 1 mess. + 15 acres	John Thorpe (father of Agnes Atte Cross) Gilbert Swan		(1381 Juliana Swan relative)

Table 22. (cont)

Family land	Adult members of the family		Children i.e. sons and daughters over 14	'Servants'
	Married	Marital status unknown		
1 mess. + 4 acres + 6 acres free + land + share in 1 virgate ⎱	Gilbert Swan			
¾ virgate + *alia*	John Hildesle & wife			(1381 John Hildesle widower)
(land in K.B.)	John Boton & wife		(1370 Joan) (1376 John)	(1381 John Betsoun widower)
2 mess. + 25 acres + *alia*	John Maister			
?	Robert & Joanna de Langton			
1½ rods	Simon Lozkyn & wife, webster and miller			
Totals 1377/9	45 couples	15 sons	19 'servants' 1377	
38¾ virgates, 9 cots., odd acres	4 widows 4 widowers	5 daughters	[14 'servants' 1381]	

Persons omitted from the 1377 Tax list but mentioned in the court rolls c. 1377:

William de Clipston + servant (taxed at Gumley)
John and Agnes Asteyn (taxed at Smeeton Westerby)
John and Agnes Kynde (taxed at Smeeton Westerby and Kibworth Beauchamp)
John Russell (taxed at Kibworth Beauchamp)
William Clerke (taxed at Saddington and Gumley)
Robert Palfreyman (taxed at Carlton Curlieu)
William and Robert le Wright with a servant

Children	'Servants'
William and John Osborne	Stephen Glover
Avis, Matilda and Emma Osborne	John de Daventry
	John Custodus
William and Agnes Parker	Kitchener
John and Matilda Michell	Bed'
Adam Valendyn	Simon Milner
John Neatherd	John Chynden, miller
John Maxwelle, serviens	
William Glass, serviens	

In addition to sons and daughters, servants were noted in the Poll Tax lists in the following manner: *Rob' Carter et ux' eis 4d, Rob' s' eis 4d, Alic' s' eis 4d*. The Robert and Alice thus referred to are found in the court rolls to be the children of Robert Carter and his wife Matilda. The relationship of other so-called servants to the heads of their respective households is indicated in the table. Names interpolated from the 1381 list have been bracketed and have not been included in any counts.

Birth and childhood. On age at marriage and at death in the medieval period much can be learnt; so too on the age at which children left home; but on questions surrounding birth and childhood medieval sources are silent. Points three to five are therefore best discussed jointly. In the complete absence of evidence, we must assume a birth interval of two and a half years and, given earlier marriage, perhaps more than five children per completed family (for age at marriage see below p. 225). However, the infant mortality rate may well have been higher. The early fifteenth-century repair bills and lists of chattels reveal a pretty basic standard of living at Kibworth, but in view of the general improvement in the size and quality of peasant houses claimed for this century by medieval archaeologists, standards in thirteenth- and early fourteenth-century Kibworth may well have been even lower.* There is some reason to infer, therefore, a higher mortality rate, especially among the young, and a survival rate of perhaps only three or four per completed family. A higher infant mortality rate would give rise to greater irregularity in the birth intervals and high mortality in childbirth would have given rise to frequent remarriage, so that, in practice, many households would have been made up of two or more sets of step-children, whose ages were distributed over a longer timespan than that allotted in tables 26 and 27.

The average age of men at first marriage. Evidence for the age at first marriage for women is unfortunately too fragmentary to be of any use to us, but the age at first marriage for men can be approached by two methods. In the first, if we know the year in which a boy was sworn into tithing, and the year in which he first took land, then, assuming that he married just before or after taking land, one can calculate his

---

* Guy Beresford, 'The Medieval Clayland Village: Excavation at Goltho and Barton Blount', *Medieval Archaeology*, Monograph Series 6 (1975) – it is however possible that these sites were deserted in the *early* fifteenth century.

age at marriage. The other method is to assume that the average length of time for which a man held land reflects the interval between the birth and the marriage of the eldest son. Neither method yields precise results, but they serve the purpose of raising the age at marriage out of the teens and into the twenties, thus firmly placing the male marriage pattern within the Western rather than the East European tradition in thirteenth-century England.

Application of the first method was confined to the series of court rolls running from 1330–1440. The search yielded a dozen or so examples in which the date of swearing and the date of inheritance were recorded for the same youth. Mention is normally made of a boy being sworn into tithing only if he is twelve years or *over* and has not yet been sworn. Therefore, in some cases the boy may have been older than twelve, which would raise correspondingly the calculated age at marriage. Others inherited as minors and were thus in a position to marry as soon as they came of age, thereby depressing the age at marriage. However, the average age, as set out in table 23, was 22.8 years.

Before accepting this figure, we should check that the inheritance of land coincided with first marriage. The date of marriage is very rarely given, but if a son is sworn into tithing then the father can be presumed to have married at least thirteen years previous to that date. Similarly, if a son or daughter is mentioned on a tax list, then the father must have married at least fifteen years prior to that date. The approximate date of marriage thus arrived at can then be compared with the date at which the father first took land. Examples drawn from the court rolls between 1348 and 1370 have been set out in table 24 and indicate the degree of match which can be achieved by this method. It is unfortunate that the period was distorted by three serious mortalities which gave rise to a high proportion of men, often minors, taking land earlier than would normally have been the case. The method could, with profit, be extended over a longer period, preferably before 1348. Nevertheless, even the unsatisfactory dates of this pioneer study as set out in table 24 show perfectly clearly that marriage did not precede entry into the landed estate.*

The second method for arriving at the average age at first marriage is to argue that the number of years a man held land reflected the

* The case of William and Joan Carter (table 22), married but still living under the roof of William Carter, must surely be the exception required to prove the rule, and must reflect unusual circumstances. On the rare occasions when a Kibworth man retired before death the land was formally transferred in court from father to son. This had not happened in the Carter case and we must assume that William Carter senior had not retired.

Table 23. *Approximate age at marriage for men in fourteenth century*

Name	Sworn into tithing	First took land	Approximate age at marriage
Jn fil' Nich. Taylur	1332	1342	12 + 10 = 22
Will' fil' Nich. Polle	1333	1350	12 + 17 = 29
Will. Alot (a minor)		1349	His son was 14+ in 1377, so he must have married c. 1360. i.e. he inherited as a minor?
Nich. fil' Will. Gilbert	1349	1359	12 + 10 = 22
John Carter (a minor?)		1349	His daughter Emma married in 1391, which suggests that Carter married c. 1370 and inherited as an infant?
Jn fil' Rob. Couper	1375	1393	12 + 18 = 30
Nich. fil' Rob. Polle	1350	1365	He reached majority in 1365
Jn Man	1367 and again		
	1372	1376	12 + 9 = 21
Jn Marnham	1375	1400 (married)	12 + 25 = 37
Will fil' Jn. Sybil	1364	1375	12 + 11 = 23
Will fil' Rob. Carter	1369 & 1375	1377	12 + 8 = 20
Adam Polle de K.B.	1391	1400	12 + 9 = 21
Ric. Brown	1407	1421	12 + 14 = 26
Jn fil' Rob. Polle	(12 in 1441)	1448	12 + 7 = 19
Will. Smith	1433	1439	12 + 6 = 18

Table 24. *Coincidence of marriage with inheritance of land in fourteenth century*

Name	Children in 1379	Probable date of marriage	First took land	Inherited
W. Carter	Married son in 1376	Prior to 1356	1349	
R. Carter	2 children	Prior to 1358	1349	
H. Marnham	3 children	Prior to 1354	1349	
J. Marnham	1 daughter	Prior to 1362	1351	
N. Sandur	Son ordained 1371	Prior to 1351	1349	
J. Sandur	Son inherited 1372	Prior to 1352	1349	
	Daughter married 1378			
W. Brown	1 son	Prior to 1362	1358	
J. Brown	1 son	Prior to 1362	1361	
N. Godwin	1 son	Prior to 1362	1349	1349
R. Couper	1 son	Prior to 1362	1362	
W. Alot	1 son	Prior to 1362	1349	1349
R. Chapman	1 son	Prior to 1362	1361	
H. Nicholas	1 son aged 12 in 1376	Prior to 1363	1349	
J. Nogge	eldest son 12 in 1372	Prior to 1359	1351	
D. Boton		Prior to 1357	1351	
J. Sybile		Married by 1381	1375	
R. Sandur	1 son	Married in 1361	1361 from wife	
J. Sandur		Married in 1373	1372	
W. Atte Cross		Married in 1363	1363 from wife	
R. Smyth		Married in 1363	1362 from wife	
R. Langton		Married in 1361	1361 from wife	
J. Maister		Married in 1352	1349	1349
W. Sybile	1 son	Prior to 1362	1363	1364

interval between the birth and marriage of his heir. To provide this second counter-check, and also to reach some conclusions about the average length of life of a landholder in this period, the court rolls were searched once again and the findings set out in figure 15. One hundred and eleven examples were found where both the required dates were known, and the histogram shows the number of years each of these men held land. The method assumes that the firstborn was always a son and always survived. Therefore it will only indicate the *minimum* length of marriage: it could not have been shorter, but a father whose eldest child was a daughter or whose firstborn had died could have been married much longer.

Conclusions drawn from the histogram can be summarised as follows. The average number of years for which a landholder held land was 20.8 years in the case of those who are stated in the court rolls to have died of plague, but extends to 32.1 years in the case of those who did not die of plague. Since we are dealing with a period dominated by plague, plague casualties should not be treated as exceptions. If plague deaths are, therefore, included with other deaths we reach an average length of landholding of 27.9 years. Therefore, the interval between the birth and marriage of a man's heir would not, on average, have exceeded 27.9 years.

Thus the first method yielded an average age at first marriage of 22.8 years, the second a figure in the region of, but not more than, 27.9 years. Both take plague into account; the first is based on a limited sample from the period 1349 to 1363, the second covers a wider span to include fifteenth-century evidence and reveals no very noticeable fall in the age at marriage in the first half of that century. Neither method fosters the belief that men married between the ages of sixteen and twenty. For the purposes of tables 26 and 27 the compromise figure of 25 years has been used for the generation span.

The average age at death of landholders in the fourteenth century. Since we have no record of the date of birth of the men who appear in the court rolls as entering tithing, taking up land and later dying, our estimate of the average length of life of these men must be restricted to landholding men and must be based on indirect evidence. The simplest approach is to add age at marriage to the average number of years for which landholders held their land. We have already established that men held land for an average of 27.9 years and that they married, according to one method, in their twenty-second year and, according to a second method, before they reached their twenty-eighth year. Their average age at death then must have been

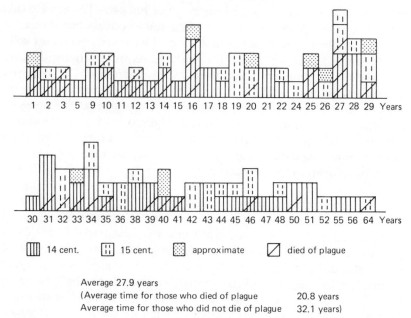

Fig. 15   Number of years for which landholders held land

between 50.7 and 54.9 years, as against 61 years in the seventeenth century.

The age at which children left home: sons and servants in 1379. The meaning of the term *serviens* as used in fourteenth-century England is not entirely clear to us today, but the Poll Tax returns shed some illumination on the subject.* Of the thirty-one servants mentioned in the Kibworth Poll Tax lists, thirteen were adult sons, eight were widows or widowers, two were grandmothers, five were relatives,

---

* P. D. A. Harvey (1965: 134–5) noted 'many references to the tenant's employees (ancille, famuli, manupasti)' at Cuxham before 1349, and he also observed that many families were extinct as early as 1352, which suggests a high emigration rate in this Thames Valley village even before 1349. It is not known if these *famuli* were related to their employees or not; if not, then we have an interesting example of the effect of migration upon the composition of the household in terms of blood relationships. It would lend weight to the view that the terms *serviens, ancille, famuli* were ascribed to any adult working in a household who was not the head of that household or his wife. It might include some wage labourers, but it also included relations who did not work for a wage. Professor Hilton (1975: 31, 312), commenting on the Poll Tax returns for Warwickshire, noted that 'persons described as servants could also be the offspring of the family' and that, for eighty Cotswold villages, 'one household in eight employed a servant' in 1381, a situation very similar to that described by R. H. Tawney in his study of early modern Gloucestershire, where he was able to add the further precision that the servants in households were nearly always relations, not wage-labourers. The distinction is essential to our understanding of the labour market of an area.

one was a 'foreigner' (who in the interval between 1379–81 changed his employer once) and of the remaining two nothing further can be learnt. We can therefore dismiss at once the idea that servants were necessarily wage-labourers. Kibworth servants were adult members of the family, dependent upon the same resources as the head of the family and contributing their labour insofar as they were still capable of doing so. Their presence in no way implies a larger or more successful farming enterprise, it merely records a household with a high proportion of dependent adults.

However, not all sons were classed as servants in the Poll Tax lists. Although thirteen were so classified, as many as twenty were termed *sons*. The *maximum* age of these twenty sons can be deduced from the date of their respective fathers' marriage, and for some from the date of their entry into tithing, and it was found that six were about fourteen years of age in 1379 (including one who had just left for Coventry), ten were over fourteen but under twenty-seven and of the remaining four little is known, since their fathers were freemen whose land transfers were not recorded in the court rolls.

Of the ten boys in the middle group some had been away from the manor and had but recently returned. The sons of Richard Godyer and Robert Scherman, for example, had just returned from Coventry. Further evidence confirms this impression of short-term absences from the manor in the 1370s: boys sworn into tithing in the early seventies do not feature in the 1379 tax list and some are reported to have left the manor; others are reported as having taken up land within a year or so of being sworn into tithing and appear in the tax list as married men. Yet others are sworn into tithing twice. Since the interval between the two oath-takings is irregular in length, it cannot have been that boys were sworn into tithing once at the age of twelve and again at the age of eighteen, so we can only conclude that a second swearing was necessary for boys who had been absent from the manor for some time. To cite but two examples: John Man was sworn in 1367 and in 1372,[3] and William Carter was sworn in 1369 and again in 1375.[4]

Sons seem, therefore, to fall into two groups: boys of little more than fourteen years, and men in their mid-twenties who had returned from an absence of some years and were on the point of taking up land. While away they were almost certainly wage-earners of some sort, but in the Kibworth context they were not servants but sons. Just precisely what the distinction was eludes us; the best we can do is describe, as we have done, the two categories, in the hope that evidence from some other community may shed light on the exact distinction: when is a son a servant?

Sons and brothers in 1280. The 1280 tithing list omits the category of
servants altogether, but in the process of listing the name of every
male over *twelve* it is as much concerned with brothers as with sons.
The brothers were the brothers of landholders, and since landholders
did not usually come into their inheritance until their early to
mid-twenties, their younger brothers could well have been in their
late teens or early twenties. The most marked difference in the
membership of households between 1280 and 1379 is the greater
number of young men and boys still dependent upon the family
holding in 1280. There were sometimes as many as three boys over
twelve in a household (in addition to daughters), and of these young
men only ten can definitely be shown to have been heirs (see table
25). The remainder are either known to have been younger sons, or
were sons whose subsequent history cannot be traced, which implies
that they died or migrated.

It is not possible to assign an age to most of these boys because the
court roll series begins only a few years before 1280, and we cannot,
therefore, check the year of marriage of fathers or the date when each
boy had been sworn into tithing. However, we can measure the time
elapsed between 1280 and the year of inheritance in a few cases. Of
these some inherited almost immediately; Roger Wade for example
took land in 1281;[5] others waited several years: William Taylur did not
enter his father's holding until 1294,[6] Robert le Couper took his
father's land in 1296[7] while John Sirrene took up his father's land in
1292, but was not enrolled in any tithing in 1280, although his
brother, Robert, was.[8] In John Sirrene's case we must suppose that he
was absent from the manor for some time in the 1280 period. If Robert
Sirrene was twelve or over in 1280 he would have been twenty-four or
over in 1292, which would make his elder brother, John, about
twenty-six or more. William Taylur would have been not younger
than twenty-six, Robert le Couper twenty-eight and Roger Wade an
unlikely thirteen, or over.

The fact that John Sirrene escaped registration in 1280 indicates that
migration was not unknown at this date, as does the disappearance of
many brothers and younger sons from the purview of the court rolls.
More impressive, however, is the continued *presence* of so many
young adults and the consequences of their presence: large households at a time when holdings were at their smallest in size, a
depressed labour market and a deep reservoir of brothers and sons
awaiting land. There were also of course other dependants: widows,
sisters, the old, the infirm. Table 25 contrasts the 1280 situation with
that obtaining in 1379, when the able-bodied had for the most part left
the village to seek their fortunes in a buoyant labour market. In

absolute figures there were 78 men, 16 widows and 65 boys working in the village in 1280, as against 49 men, 4 widows, 31 servants (including women dependants) and 20 sons in 1379. Moreover, as table 25 illustrates, as many boys were found in the households of tofters in 1280 as in the households of double yardlanders, whereas by 1379 sons or servants were rarely found outside the tenements of 1¼ yardlands or more.

The age structure in 1379. The two listings with a roughly hundred-year interval invite comparison with regard to the age structure of the community in 1280 and 1379. So far we have been considering sons and brothers, all of them single, and servants, most of whom were single though some were widows or widowers. Between them, they cover the non-householder element in the village. The remainder of the population were married couples or children under twelve/ fourteen. Of the forty-five married couples in 1379, 25.5 per cent had been married for more than twenty-five years and all their children had left home; 25 per cent had been married for sixteen to twenty-five years and had some children still at home, 45.4 per cent had been married for less than sixteen years and all their children were still under the age of fourteen.* Apart from these married couples there were four widows, four widowers, some five boys over fourteen and some ten sons in their twenties. To these can be added five daughters and nineteen adult relatives *alias* servants.

The high proportion of married couples in the Poll Tax lists for the country generally prompted Hajnal to suggest that a non-European pattern of very early marriage for males was the norm in England at this date (Glass and Eversley 1965: 101–43).† What he failed to make allowance for was the age at which children left home and for how long they remained away. We have just noted the high proportion of single males in 1280 at Kibworth and have discussed earlier the general problem of rural under-employment in the region. Even after the plagues, Kibworth men did not immediately venture very far afield, Stamford and Coventry being the furthest limits. Nevertheless, even in the 1280s some men did leave the village and return, as did John Sirrene, and others must have left, never to return. We are

---

* These figures are obtained by counting the number of years which had elapsed between the year of inheritance and the year 1377 (not 1379). The number of years naturally refers to husbands not wives.

† Sylvia Thrupp makes the similar assumption – that men married as soon as they reached the age of majority, which she takes to be sixteen. See her 'Problem of replacement rates in late medieval English population', *EcHR*, 2nd ser., XVIII (1965), 101–19.

Table 25. *Labour units per holding, 1280–1377*

| Land unit | Labour unit | | | Composition of the labour force | | | | | |
Size	Total no.	Total labourers	Average per land unit	Men Total	% of labour force	Widows Total	%	Boys Total	%
1280									
Toft	12	27	2.25	13	48.1	0	0	14	51.9
Half virgate	21	51	1.82	28	54.9	3	5.9	20	39.2
Full virgate	5	10	2.00	4	40	2	20	4	40
1¼–2 virgates	7	28	4.00	16	57.1	0	0	12	42.9
1377								Sons and servants	
Toft	3	3	1	3	100	0	0	0	0
Half virgate	3	6	2	4	66.7	0	0	2	33.3
¾ virgate	6	13	2.2	6	46.2	0	0	7	53.8
Full virgate	3	5	1.7	3	60	0	0	2	40
1¼–2 virgates	15	61	4	31	50.8	0	0	30	49.2

not in a position to put a figure on the proportion who left as against those who merely avoided trouble and kept out of the purview of the court; we can only observe that in comparison with 1379 the number of single men in the village was surprisingly high, and that from this high celibacy rate the figure drops to a low one in 1379 – which gives us a typical West European pattern for 1280 and an East European celibacy ratio for 1379. On the face of it, this seems unlikely, and a more acceptable interpretation of the low celibacy rate in 1379 is that the celibate element in the village was absent because young men had migrated in search of work, they had not rushed into matrimony in their teens. If boys left home at an early age and did not return unless to marry, then it follows that most men in the community would be married, but it does not follow that they married young. Moreover, if more sons married, and married young, the total number of married couples should have increased by 1379 and this did not happen. Which brings us to the question of age structure in 1280.

The age structure in 1280. The tithing list gives no indication of marital status, but from the court rolls we learn that at least forty-eight of the men in tithing were married, to which number we should add the tofters with secure jobs, such as the shepherd, the skinner, the brokers and the leech. This brings the number of married persons up to fifty or more including widows and widowers.

There was not, therefore, very much difference between the total number of married couples and widows in 1280 and in 1379: fifty as against fifty-three. An increase of three hardly supports the hypothesis that landless men were entering into marriage in their teens by 1379. This stability in numbers among the resident community is borne out by surname analysis and is illustrated in tables 21 and 22. The number had not grown beyond some sixty couples by the seventeenth century, a reflection of the same outward migration pattern which had become established in the late fourteenth century.*

* Apart from Arthur Redford's classic, *Labour Migration in England* (Manchester 1926), the subject of migration has lain virtually dormant for half a century. However, the 1970s saw a revival of interest particularly for the early modern period. See P. Clark, 'Migration in England during the late seventeenth and early eighteenth centuries', *P & P.*, 83 (1979), 57–90, which includes a useful bibliography. For the medieval period see J. A. Raftis, *Tenure and Mobility* (Toronto 1964), and 'Geographical mobility in the Lay subsidy Rolls', *Medieval Studies*, XXXVIII (1976), 385–403; P. McClure, 'Patterns of migration in the late Middle Ages: the evidence of English place-name surnames', *EcHR*, 2nd ser., XXXII.2 (1979), 167–82; and A. F. Butcher, 'The origins of the Romney Freemen 1433–1523', *EcHR*, 2nd ser., XXVII.1 (1974), 16–27. Kibworth was an exporter of labour and the goal was betterment rather than subsistence from the late fifteenth century onwards.

It is not possible to analyse the number of years each man had been married in 1280, because, as has already been observed, the court roll series begins only a few years before the tithing list was drawn up. However, it is possible to compare the number of children in the medieval and early modern period. According to the parish register, the average number of births per annum was in the region of 24, of which about 8 to 10 were born each year in Kibworth Harcourt. If we take the average age at marriage to be 25 in the fourteenth century, as against 29.9 in the seventeenth, and the average number per completed family to be about 5, then the 45 couples in 1377 would have produced about 9 children a year, or, if widows and widowers are included, then 10.6 children a year. Such a figure ties in with the 14 boys aged about fourteen taxed in 1377.

The size of households in 1280 and 1379. The data from which the size of the medieval peasant household in Kibworth can be deduced can now be summarised as follows. The average age at first marriage was between 22.8 and 27.9 years – taken as 25 in tables 26 and 27. The average lifespan of a landholding man was 50–5 years, making a three-generation male overlap rare, although mothers or stepmothers often survived to see grandchildren in the family. The average number of children per couple may well have been greater in the medieval period than in the early modern, that is to say, more than five, but the infant mortality rate may well have been higher, so that a total of four surviving children seems a reasonable estimate. The birth interval was probably the same as in the early modern period, to wit, two and a half years. Sons often stayed at home indefinitely in the pre-plague period, remaining as celibate brothers and uncles. The lack of rural employment which kept boys at home also kept daughters at home until they married, but girls may have married younger than men at Kibworth, since dowries were small, the mortality rate in childbirth probably high, giving rise to second and third marriages among men, and there was virtually no competition from landed widows before the plagues.* On the basis of this

---

* J. Z. Titow, 'Some differences between manors and their effects on the condition of the peasant in the thirteenth century', *AgHR*, X (1962), 1–13, and J. Ravensdale, 'Deaths and entries: the reliability of the figures of mortality in the Black Death in Miss F. M. Page's *Estates of Crowland Abbey*, and some implications for landholding', in *Land, Kinship and Lifecycle* (Arnold, forthcoming). Both found widow remarriage a vital element in the landmarket before the Black Death, but unimportant after it. At Kibworth, widow remarriage was almost unknown before 1348, but became relatively common after that date. This was because widows at Kibworth lost their right to dower if they remarried. After the plagues, if no heirs survived, they could keep the land and remarry. On the Somerset and Cambridgeshire fens, widows did not forfeit their dowry upon remarriage.

Table 26. Developmental cycle of the household in the pre-plague period, 1280–1349, for both 12- and 24-acre holdings
Average 4.84

Year	1	2	3	4	5	6	7	8	9	10	11	12	13	14	15	16	17	18	19	20	21	22	23	24	25
Grandfather	D																								
Grandmother	X	X	X	D																					
Husband	X	X	X	X	X	X	X	X	X	X	X	X	X	X	X	X	X	X	X	X	X	X	X	X	X
Wife	X	X	X	X	X	X	X	X	X	X	X	X	X	X	X	X	X	X	X	X	X	X	X	X	X
Sister	M																								
Brother	X	X	X	X	X	X	L																		
Sister	X	X	M																						
Brother	D																								
Daughter				x	x	x	X	X	X	X	X	X	X	X	X	X	X	X	X	X	X	X	M		
Son						x	x	x	X	X	X	X	X	X	X	X	X	X	X	X	X	X	X	X	X
Daughter									x	x	x	X	X	X	X	X	X	X	X	X	X	X	X	X	X
Son												x	x	x	x	X	D								
Daughter														x	x	x	X	X	X	X	X	X	X	X	X
Consumption units	5	5	5	3	3	3	3	3	4	4	4	5	5	6	6	6	6	6	6	6	6	6	5	5	5

D = dead   M = married   x = under five   L = left home

233

Table 27. Developmental cycle of the household in the post-plague period, 1371–1490, for both 12- and 24-acre holdings
Average 3.72

Year	1	2	3	4	5	6	7	8	9	10	11	12	13	14	15	16	17	18	19	20	21	22	23	24	25
Grandfather	D																								
Grandmother	X	X	X	D																					
Husband	X	X	X	X	X	X	X	X	X	X	X	X	X	X	X	X	X	X	X	X	X	X	X	X	X
Wife	X	X	X	X	X	X	X	X	X	X	X	X	X	X	X	X	X	X	X	X	X	X	X	X	X
Sister	M																								
Brother	L																								
Sister	L																								
Brother	D																								
Daughter				x	x	x	X	X	X	X	X	X	X	X	X	X	X	L							
Son							x	x	X	X	X	X	X	X	X	X	X	L							
Daughter										x	x	X	X	X	X	X	X	X	X	X	X	L			
Son												x	x	X	X	X	X	X	X	X	X	L			
Daughter													x	x	x	x	D								
Consumption units	3	3	3	2	2	2	3	3	4	4	4	5	5	6	6	6	6	4	4	4	4	2	2	2	2

D = dead   M = married   x = under five   L = left home

information, which is approximate in many areas, we can reconstruct a pre-plague household of three to six persons depending upon the age of the head of the household, which gives us an approximate average of 4.84 persons aged 5 or over where the father lived to be 50.*

The plagues of the late fourteenth century put an end to the crisis of under-employment. Households shrank to an average of 3.72 as youths and adults moved away in search of work and of vacant land. There is no sign of a sharp drop in the age at marriage to East European type levels, but there may have been a slight depression in marriage age reflecting the improved condition of the land market.

It should be stressed again that, whereas the seventeenth-century figures are well founded, those for the medieval period do not belong to the same class: the word 'probable' has entered into the discussion in certain key areas, and this detracts considerably from their accuracy without, however, rendering them valueless, not at any rate until more refined figures can be brought forward, since these figures are not in fact 'improbable', far from it. However, the lay-out of tables 26 and 27 makes it possible to adjust the figures for any regulating factor, so that the totals can be refined and improved should new material for Kibworth emerge or new approaches be developed.

Household size in Kibworth – general conclusions. At the beginning of this chapter we set out to discover three, on the face of it, quite simple facts: the average size of households in Kibworth in 1280, 1379 and in the seventeenth century. These three facts subsumed a number of elements the pursuit of which introduced more than a trace of convolution, not only to the argument but also to the hoped-for 'simplicity' of the three facts. However, we have emerged that much the richer for, in addition to three figures, 4.84, 3.72 and 3.34, which can be used in the budget tables, we can also make four inter-related observations of some importance.

The first is that among the factors affecting household size, the age at which children left home is as important, if not more so, as age at marriage or infant mortality, and the age at which children left home is determined by the labour market of the region and the nature and size of the family enterprise.

* No study has yet been made of another community directly comparable with Kibworth. However, for the densely populated salt-marsh and fen settlements of the Isle of Eloe, Hallam estimated an average household size of 4.68 (*EcHR*, X (1957–8), 340–61); for the Breckland manors of Redgrave and Rickinghall in Suffolk, R. M. Smith estimated a household size of 4.7 and 4.9 respectively, adjusted to 6.1 and 5.6; for a third pastoral region, Halesowen on the Worcestershire–Shropshire border, Zvi Razi estimated 4.7 adjusted to 5.8 before the plagues (R. M. Smith, unpublished Cambridge Ph.D. thesis 1975; Razi, unpublished Birmingham D.Phil. thesis, 1976).

Secondly, the natural developmental cycle of the *family* will only affect the size of the *household* if the family holding is so small as not to require the labour of more than a man and his wife. On holdings requiring a larger labour force, the absence of sons will be made good by the introduction of servants, and the household size will be maintained at a constant figure.

Thirdly, the very high mortality of the late fourteenth century did more than temporarily reduce the population and improve the prospects of wage-labourers. By extinguishing ancient peasant families with their long-established grip upon customary land, and by triggering off a period of intense geographical mobility which threw into confusion notions of servile and non-servile peasant status, the plagues swept away the established tenurial and tenemental structure. Although the distinction between demesne and customary land was later to reappear as leasehold and copyhold, for a period in the late fourteenth and early fifteenth centuries this distinction in tenures was largely ignored and not even freehold tenure was insisted upon. With so much land available and tenures irrelevant, new and larger holdings emerged, initially made up of half-yardland demesne and customary units thrown together, and later treated as single units measured in acres. Many of these new tenements comprised some thirty to one hundred acres by the late fifteenth century and required extra-familial help to run them, while the small, twelve-acre holding characteristic of the pre-plague period virtually disappeared. The nature of the tenemental structure at Kibworth had thus been profoundly altered and with it the size and composition of the household.*

Lastly, if we may anticipate the next chapter, alterations in inheritance custom will also affect household size. In a situation where *land* was distributed among all children in equal or unequal shares, the several branches of each lineage thereby established will necessarily remain in the same vicinity, but usually in separate houses, each constituting a separate household. But if, as in Kibworth, land was not so divided, only *stock and chattels*, children would not leave home if work prospects were poor, but if work was available and wages worth more than the share in the family chattels, children departed. Thus, where monogeniture was the custom and was commonly put into practice, the size of the household reflected the labour market more sensitively than in areas characterised by multigeniture.

---

* Failure to appreciate the full impact of the fourteenth-century mortalities led Alan Macfarlane to accept evidence derived from the fifteenth century to prove his case for the thirteenth. See *The Origins of English Individualism* (Blackwell 1978), chapter 5.

10

Inheritance strategies

> Custom, in truth, in regions where it is approved by the practice of
> those who use it, is sometimes observed as, and takes the place of,
> *lex*. For the authority of custom and long use is not slight.
>
> (Bracton 1968: 22)

In his enthusiasm for *lex* Bracton no more than touches on custom,
which for the student of peasant social organisation is particularly
unfortunate, since 'the custom of the manor is, in the villein's world,
at least nine points of the law' (Poole 1949: 15). With the exception of
England, collections of local customs have survived for most parts of
Europe and Scandinavia and central to their theme is the lineage and
family: the definition of the lineage, ranking within the lineage, the
distribution of resources within the lineage, the position of men who
have no lineage, the procedures by which land or other resources
may be alienated from the lineage (Goody *et al.* 1976: 113–15). These
have been most usefully described and analysed by B. S. Phillpotts
who was able to chart the demise of lineage as an active force in the
late medieval and early modern periods (Philpotts 1913). In an
exhaustive if unimaginative study the French legal historian, Jean
Yver, carried the investigation forward into the sixteenth century for
France, and once again the lineage, and methods of circumventing
the lineage, takes pride of place. By contrast, collections of customs
for English communities make no reference to lineage and confine
themselves for the most part to the description of the rents and
services owed by customary villein tenants to their lord. That there
were other customs, particularly customs concerned with rules of
inheritance, is not in doubt, since they are frequently alluded to in
legal disputes over inheritance, also in the enrolment of land transfers
in manorial rolls, and indeed are occasionally given a summary
description alongside the enumeration of rents and services (Clarke
1882: 89–130), but there is little or no evidence of an interest in lineage
as such. Are we to conclude that Bracton's allusion to the strength of

custom was a mere rhetorical flourish and that England was unique among her European neighbours in having no lineage-based corpus of customs? Seebohm has shown that even in North Wales the lineage had been reduced to a mere two-generation family by the thirteenth century (Seebohm 1902), and all the evidence for lowland England points to the disappearance of the lineage at a very much earlier date (Charles-Edwards 1971). Why the lineage disappeared so early in these islands is a fascinating problem which has not yet been systematically explored, but the nature of the societies which re-placed the lineage-based societies and the degree to which attitudes and values based on lineage systems survived into the late middle ages is a question upon which the records of Kibworth Harcourt shed more than a faint glimmer of light.

As with many other manors, the records for Kibworth include a list of customary services (see above pp. 22–4; MM 6370). The list was drawn up *circa* 1290 by which date the demesne was no longer in hand, so possibly the list was prepared in order to assess the value of the works to be commuted to money payments. This would explain the absence of reference to inheritance and other 'customary' matters, since these did not form part of the deal. But as we shall see, the rentals and court rolls tell us a great deal about family solidarity and family attitudes to land. The story they tell runs counter to the precepts and opinions of the common law and of jurists, which is interesting, not unexpected and deserves a digression. The story also contrasts quite sharply with the results of investigations along similar lines carried out for other medieval communities with rather different economic resources (cf. Smith and Wrigley, forthcoming; Jones 1979: 316–27). In this respect the Kibworth evidence is of particular value, since where one can find contrast we have a point of departure for the investigation of regional particularisms, which in turn cast light upon the factors which promoted such differences.

According to Glanvill, Bracton, and the legal thinkers of their times, the common law did not admit of villein inheritance, since the villein had no legal right to property of his own. Nevertheless, Kibworth villeins made wills, they inherited land, left land to heirs, and did so according to the custom of monogeniture (probably primogeniture). In this they were not alone: the Bishop of Winchester's tenants are recorded as taking up land *de testamento* and *de legato* at Waltham, Downton and Taunton in 1208/9 (Hall 1903), and Miss Levett found it commonplace for the villein tenants on the St Albans estates to make wills in which they devised land as well as chattels (Levett 1938). These wills were proved in the manor court rather than in church courts but with the approval of the church (Homans 1970: 134). It is not clear how far back ecclesiastical cognizance of wills extended: at least as far back as the Conquest (Levett 1938: 212–13; Hyams 1968: 123–6), but the church certainly encouraged the free disposal of land. Familiar with Roman law, it saw nothing outrageous in allowing the individual to alienate land from the family, but in this the church parted company not only with the *mentalité* of the lineage but also with feudal principles and with contemporary developments in the common law, which placed increasing restrictions on the freedom to alienate.

It would seem then, that in spite of the observations of Glanvill and Bracton, a villein's right to inherit both lands and goods was upheld both by custom and the church. Moreover, as Dr Paul Hyams has shown in his excellent study on the legal aspects of villeinage, the king's courts would uphold custom in those areas and places where custom took precedence over *lex*, and we may conclude with him that 'the gap between legal theory and practice is wider (here) than at any other point in the system' (Hyams 1968: 120; and 1980). In England, as on the continent, villeins could devise their land by will *de jure* as well as *de facto*.

Study of the rentals and court rolls of other village communities reveal in some cases rather different attitudes to land and inheritance to those found at Kibworth. On the Cambridgeshire fen-edge for example, where land was bought and sold in tiny parcels of little more than an acre, and where the opportunities for earning the purchase-money as fishermen, fowlers, watermen, reed-cutters and a host of similar enterprises, sons, and even daughters, could buy an acre or two and build up a viable livestock enterprise long before the death of their parents.* Inheritance, therefore, had not the same importance on the fen-edge as it had in Kibworth. A man could choose to sell his land or leave it to one or more of his children by his first or subsequent marriages, or to his wife, but if he died intestate local custom could be invoked, and local custom in this area was usually Borough English,† although in some villages it was partible

---

* This and following comparisons with fen- and wood-pasture economies in the medieval period are based upon my analysis of the tenemental pattern and family structure of the East Cambridgeshire fen-edge communities as recorded in the *Rotuli Hundredorum*, vol. 2, ed. W. Illingworth and J. Caley (HMSO 1818) and upon my analysis of the accounts and court rolls for the estates of Glastonbury Abbey on the Somerset Levels (Longleat House, Trowbridge, Wiltshire). This work has not yet been published.

† Borough English is the custom on the Somerset Levels today and was so in the medieval period; it was also very common indeed on the Essex marches and on the East Anglian fens.

inheritance* and occasionally primogeniture.[1] However, most sons held land, which land was acquired not by inheritance but by purchase.† In Kibworth, where there was no supply of tiny parcels of land for small-time purchasers, inheritance was the normal channel through which the younger generation entered into land: to Kibworth then we must return our attention.

Figure 16 shows the length of time each family remained in the village during the period 1280–1700 whether or not that family held land. Each millimetre square on the vertical axis represents one named village family, and the horizontal axis indicates how long each family remained in Kibworth and the decade in which it left the village or became extinct. Periods of plague (P) or high mortality have been indicated in order to show the cumulative effect of the late fourteenth-century plagues upon continuity of tenure. The data is derived from the tithing lists of 1280 and 1686, the Poll Tax returns of 1377/79 and the rentals, in addition to the court rolls which make possible a brief biographical record of each inheriting member of each family in the fourteenth and fifteenth centuries, and the Parish Register and probate records which provide an even fuller record for the sixteenth and seventeenth centuries. So rapid was the turnover in families between 1410 and 1440 that a separate chart had to be made showing the turnover at three-year intervals, and this has not been reproduced here. The second gap, that between 1540 and 1593, is due to lack of information.

The surnames of families which did not hold land have been distinguished from the rest and are conspicuous by their absence before the 1670s. Every family (with the exception of five single men) which was mentioned in the 1280 tithing list was also mentioned in the rental of that date as holding land.‡ Most of these families

* Partible inheritance is not in fact at all common, but is known to have been the custom at Richinghall and Redgrave on the Norfolk brecklands (see Yoko Miyoshi, 'A rental and inheritance case from the manor court rolls of a Suffolk village' and 'Inheritance cases and related documents from the manor court rolls of a Suffolk village', in *Jl. of Social Sciences and Humanities of Tokyo City University (Jimbun Gakuho)*, nos. 118 (1977) and 127 (1978)), at Terrington and Walpole in Norfolk, at Wisbech and Tydd in the Isle of Ely and at Sutton and Fleet on the Lincolnshire fens (Homans 1970).

† To infer, as Homans does, that where tenements 'were divided among kinsmen; (or) where more than one son regularly paid his relief in the manorial court for the father's holding' necessarily implies partible inheritance can be misleading (Homans 1970: 116) since free purchase on the land market would produce the same effect. The *post-mortem* custom on such manors was as often as not Borough English.

‡ Cf. Britton (1977: 11). Of late thirteenth-century Broughton Britton writes, '95% of families in the court rolls had clearly identifiable and quite stable surnames'. The same can be said of Kibworth, although some individuals were also known by their occupation. The use of patronymics was still common in the 1280s, but the combination of court roll evidence and rentals allows one to distinguish between individuals and between descent groups within a very small margin of error.

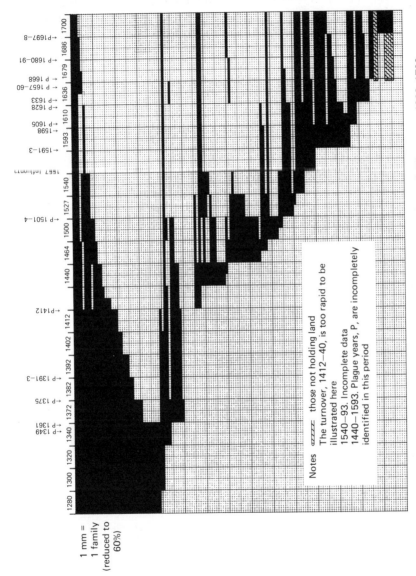

Notes   ▨▨▨ those not holding land
The turnover, 1412–40, is too rapid to be
illustrated here
1540–93. Incomplete data
1440–1593. Plague years, P, are incompletely
identified in this period

1 mm =
1 family
(reduced to
60%)

←P 1349
←P 1361
←P 1375
←P 1391–3
←P 1412
←P 1501–4
1557 influenza
←1591–3
←1598
←P 1605
←P 1628
←P 1633
←P 1657–60
← P 1668
←P 1680–91
←P1697–8

1280 1300 1320 1340 1361 1372 1382 1392 1402 1412 1440 1464 1500 1527 1540 1593 1610 1636 1679 1686 1700

Fig. 16   Chart to show the turnover of surnames at Kibworth Harcourt, 1280–1700

included adult brothers and sons without land of their own, but if and when these did inherit land the event was noted in the court rolls and eventually in a rental. The subsequent career of each landholder in 1280 can be traced in the court rolls, and of each new landholder as he took up land from 1276 to 1298, and from 1320 to the end of our period. It is thus possible to name the succession of tenants for each of the tenements noted in the rental for 1290 and its replacement in 1316. What is surely very striking is that no family left the village or ceased to hold some land between 1280 and 1340, and only five new families entered the manor. The court rolls which record for us this scene of massive immobility also record a steady trickle of fines, not for leaving the manor, but for entering it; an attitude not unknown elsewhere before the plagues. The contrast with the situation in Kibworth just fifty years later is equally remarkable, by then only about sixteen families had been in the village more than a few years, a number which had dwindled to eight by 1440. The cause of this dramatic shake-out was not just the plague of 1348/9 but rather the succession of plagues and epidemics which followed it.

In 1348–9, forty-four landholders in the village died. Only $4\frac{1}{2}$ bond virgates and $2\frac{1}{2}$ demesne virgates were not affected (see above pp. 42–4). By the end of 1349 only one-fifth of these holdings was still without a holder; all the rest had been taken up by sons, many of them minors, by brothers and by nephews.[*] There was no need for daughters to inherit. Here is a straightforward example of the phenomenon of which Professor Arthur Lewis has given the classic exposition:

> the phenomenon of an economy in which labour is so plentiful that its marginal productivity is negligible, or nil, or even negative; an economy in fact which has nothing to lose in productive power if its surplus manpower is removed, and indeed something, perhaps much, to gain.
>
> (Quoted by Bridbury 1973: 590–1)

In 1354 there may have been more deaths, certainly from this date onwards it was more difficult to find heirs, tenants were not finding it easy to keep up with rent payments and the first examples occur of villeins fleeing the manor. Eleven more died in 1361, an outbreak of 'pestilence' occurred in 1376 and the 70s and 90s were conspicuous for their high average death rate.

---

[*] Cf. P. D. A. Harvey, *A Medieval Oxfordshire Village. Cuxham 1240–1400* (Oxford 1965), p. 123. At Cuxham there was apparently no such reserve of heirs and tenements remained vacant until the 1350s when they were taken up by outsiders.

As plague followed plague at roughly ten-year intervals, one family after another became extinct in the male line. New names appeared on the court rolls, as land passed to sons-in-law or to adopted heirs. The size of households shrank from 4.84 to 3.72, while the average size of family holdings increased from twelve to twenty-four acres, and land in the hands of the lord was allowed to become *frysca et inculta*.

The medieval court rolls testify to monogeniture at Kibworth Harcourt, with the usufruct of the entire holding passing to the widow with reversion to the heir. The probate records of the sixteenth century confirm that monogeniture was still the custom in the early modern period and from the parish register it can be ascertained that the single heir was the eldest son, which was almost certainly the case also in the medieval period. Again, from the pre-plague court rolls we learn that land very rarely escheated for lack of heirs and rarely descended through daughters;* as figure 16 shows, the same surnames remained on the land for several generations. Yet it is exceedingly improbable that every eldest son who inherited land himself produced a male heir. It would seem then that, in the absence of sons, uncles or nephews inherited, then sons-in-law or adopted sons. It must be remembered that although inheritance by *descent* was gaining ground in the thirteenth and early fourteenth centuries (Phillpotts 1913), customs associated with inheritance by *ascent* lingered on, and just as in biological terms a son is no more closely related to a man than is his nephew, so, in a system of inheritance by *ascent* a nephew's claim was equal to that of a son, and the claims of both sons and nephews were subordinate to those of uncles.

The plagues of the post-1348 period administered the *coup de grâce* to the last traces of inheritance by ascent. By removing uncles, sons, nephews and sons-in-law alike, the plagues released vast amounts of hereditary, customary land into the hands of lords. Customs designed to apportion a rare commodity, land, among numerous members of a family were rendered redundant in a situation wherein claimants were rare and land available in abundance. Among the adjustments which had to be made were two which, with the benefit of hindsight, we can recognise as having been of considerable importance. The first was the question of equal division among heirs. According to Bracton, if there was land for only one son, then if primogeniture was the local custom, the eldest son should have it, but if there were two or more holdings, then the eldest son should

* J. Britton (1977: 49) notes a similarly low level of inheritance by daughters at Broughton, a fen-edge manor in Huntingdonshire: four cases in 60 years.

choose for himself one holding, the second son should choose another and so on until there were no more holdings, and the remaining children should rest content with the equivalent in movable goods (Bracton 1968: 220–1). In this, Bracton was enunciating a widely held principle, and one which was certainly followed by some families at Kibworth, the Polles for example. Many men in Kibworth around 1400 found themselves the possessors of more than one tenement. Had they decided to give one holding to one son, the other to a second son, within a generation or two the standard family holding would have been once again twelve acres. In fact, a significant number did not, they passed all their land to one son. This was almost certainly not a premeditated policy, but simply an *ad hoc* response to circumstances. There were fewer male heirs than usual, formerly inalienable, customary land was now on the market and high wages provided the capital with which to purchase extra-familial land. Therefore, younger sons could acquire new holdings for themselves.

The second issue was the question of land transfer from one family to another. Customary land was hereditary land, and how could *hereditary* right be conferred upon a man and his heirs? Surely not by the simple payment of a sum of money? Most of the Barbarian Codes have a good deal to say on this subject. The most detailed, to my knowledge, are the Gulathing Laws of Norway. According to them there are two types of land: hereditary or odal land and money land. Money land was a most unsatisfactory form of possession. At any time within 20 years of purchase, the seller's heirs could redeem it. After this initial 20 years the buyer's title became secure, but the land did not become hereditary land until it had remained in his family for five generations.* By contrast, land transferred by *gift* became immediately hereditary land. There were various types of gift: some, like the gift made by a king in repayment for service or hospitality, need hardly concern us in the peasant context, but the gift made in exchange for other land, the gift made to a son-in-law and, significantly, the gift made to a foster son, are extremely interesting. Adoption could mean the legitimisation of a bastard son with the consent of the heirs, but it could also take the form of a retirement arrangement in a case where there were no heirs. As the Gulathing Laws put it, 'when a man takes another into his keeping for good or for ill and maintains him to fire and pyre, as the saying goes' (that is, until death), that man becomes the foster heir of the other (Larsen 1935: §3; Beyerle 1972: 44–5, 124, 132).

---

* Larsen 1935, §270–94. It is also interesting to consider the *de donis* clause in the Statute of Westminster in this light.

Figure 16 shows a sharp decline in hereditary continuity between 1350 and 1412, as one would expect after the Black Death and subsequent plagues. In such circumstances one would anticipate a crop of retirement arrangements, if not with heirs then with foster heirs, as the survivors grew old and the enlarged holdings became too much for them.

Since Kibworth sons expected to inherit land rather than purchase it, members of the older generation were normally in a strong bargaining position and could expect heirs to work the land for them in their old age. Retirement contracts were therefore very rare in Kibworth but in the immediate post-plague period we find two straightforward contracts recorded in the court rolls, one with a son[2] and one with a son-in-law.[3] We also find tenements escheating to the college for lack of heirs and enquiries being set up by the college to search for possible heirs. There must, therefore, have been many elderly couples with no younger relatives to assist them on the land. With labour so scarce wages were exceedingly high, but an outsider might be prepared to maintain an elderly person or persons for life in return for immediate or future entry into the property.* The form of words used to record such an arrangement in the court rolls would vary from estate to estate and from steward to steward, but the grant of land from A *ad opus* B is associated not only with the two explicit retirement contracts at Kibworth, but also with retirement contracts in other parts of the country.† On closer examination the phrase *ad opus* was used at Kibworth only within the period 1359–1410, and then very frequently indeed. Furthermore, an *ad opus* transfer occurred only once within the history of any single tenement, on which occasion the tenement either passed out of an old, hereditary family to a newcomer, or the transfer formed part of a retirement contract between landholder and heir or foster heir. Once a tenement had

---

* Arrangements such as these were common in France and Norway to within living memory, and were standard practice in medieval England (see Homans 1970: 144–59).

† In addition to Homans (1970), see Yoko Miyoshi (1977 and 1978) *passim*; and F. W. Maitland, *Select Pleas in Manorial Courts*, vol. 2, Seldon Soc. (1888), p. 106. In her analysis of the court rolls of the Westminster Abbey manor of Launton, Miss Harvey noted that *ad opus* transfers were normally *inter vivos* and assumes that they were therefore sales. Nevertheless, she goes on to show that in the majority of cases these transfers *inter vivos* were between members of the same family. In an area where, as she points out, inheritance was strong and the land market poorly developed, it is a contradiction in terms to have members of the same family permanently alienating land to each other. An explanation more appropriate to the situation at Launton before the plagues would be that these were long leases, retirement contracts and similar intra-familial arrangements. Interestingly, the supply of heirs dried up after the plagues at about the same rate as at Kibworth (see B. Harvey 1977: 322–9).

escheated, that is, had become the responsibility of the lord for lack of heirs, it was never subsequently transferred *ad opus* by later tenants. Moreover, while the land which had escheated to the lord passed very rapidly from one holder to another, land transferred *ad opus* usually remained in the hands of the taker for many years, if not for generations. Lastly, the spate of *ad opus* transfers coincided not only with a period characterised by a shortage of heirs but also with a period when land was easily obtainable, especially vacant holdings in the hands of manorial lords who, in the hope of attracting tenants, were willing to waive entry fines and even to waive rents for the first few years. Why, one may well ask, did incoming tenants prefer to take land *ad opus* from other peasant families rather than vacant tenements from the lord?

A tenable hypothesis would be to suppose that an *ad opus* transfer conveyed an hereditary title to land from the holder of the hereditary land to his or her natural heir or adopted heir, in return for maintenance on that land for the remainder of the grantor's life. Once land had escheated it lost something of its traditional hereditary character and, although this did not become the case at Kibworth, might come to be regarded as demesne land which could be leased for a term of years only, and whose rents and entry fines could be altered in a fairly arbitrary manner (Harvey 1977: 246–51). If this was in fact the case then hereditary land *ad opus* was clearly preferable to leasehold, even if it entailed supporting the grantor for the remainder of his days. Although associated with retirement, the object of the transfer would seem not to have been primarily directed towards providing for the old as in conferring title upon the incoming tenant before the death of the hereditary holder. It must be remembered that at Kibworth land transfers were far from common and usually concerned either *leases* negotiated *inter vivos* or *post mortem* inheritance: the *permanent alienation* of land *inter vivos* was a form of conveyance that called for a distinctive form of words.

But why, one may ask, did the steward of a manorial court consider the phrase *ad opus* appropriate in the context we have been considering? In legal parlance the term *ad opus* (derived from the Old French *oeps*, which in turn was derived from the Latin word *opus*) signifies a 'use' – the device by which one person, or group of persons, held a parcel of land to the use of (*ad opus*) another who, in the legal French of the thirteenth century, came to be called the *cestui que use*. It is a sophisticated device arranged by lawyers and one which was unlikely to have been adopted by villeins on very small holdings in the fourteenth century. In fact the earliest known instance of a bondsman availing himself of this device occurred in 1504, by which date the tenurial basis of a bondsman's position had profoundly altered (*Statutes* II: 660 [19 Hen VII. c. 15]). J. M. W. Bean, however, makes several pertinent observations (Bean 1968: 129–32). He points out that the 'use' first became widely used in the late fourteenth and early fifteenth centuries, particularly in plague years. At this early date Bean found the legal usage of the term to be 'loose and ambiguous – in one case it covers an agreement to convey a marriage portion, in another security for a loan and in others some form of guardianship'. In tracing the legal concepts behind the development of the doctrine of 'uses', Bean discerned three trends. The first, the practice in Saxon and in early German law of transferring land temporarily to another trusted person, to a guardian for example, or to a friend, while away on pilgrimage. The second, the growth of a conception of trusteeship. The third and most immediate, the emergence of the executor in the late thirteenth and early fourteenth centuries as an agent who was responsible for the administration of the affairs of a deceased person after his death. The use came to be modelled on this institution.

> It is likely that it was the conception of the executor as the personal representative of the deceased person that led to an increasingly powerful realization among contemporary landowners and their legal advisers that those who had hitherto held land to the use of another during his lifetime could continue to hold it after his death and employ it or its revenues as he had directed them before he died.
>
> (Bean 1968: 157)

If we put ourselves into the position of Simon Pakeman, who was steward of Kibworth at this time, and was faced with a large number of hereditary village families who were in danger of extinction through lack of heirs, and who wished to adopt heirs in the traditional peasant fashion, it is not difficult to conceive of the phrase *ad opus*, with its undertones of guardianship, trust, conveyance of land by legal arrangement rather than by hereditary right, as the most appropriate phrase to adopt in the abbreviated entries of the court rolls. Pakeman came from one of those 'recognized professional families which supplied the official land-agent class of men both for the crown and its greater subjects' (Fox 1940: 72). He held land himself at Kirby Bellars, was Steward of the Honor of Leicester and also of Leicester Abbey, he represented the shire in the parliaments of 1333–4, 1346, 1347–8, 1364–5, 1366 and 1368, he was a Justice of the Peace, and was frequently engaged on royal business (*ibid*: 35). His duties under the Earl of Leicester would have brought him annually to Carlton Curlieu, Shangton, the Langtons, Smeeton Westerby,

Stonton Wyville, Glooston and Cranoe, all neighbours of Kibworth Harcourt, and it would be interesting to discover if *ad opus* transfers were introduced on these estates as well, or indeed, in Kibworth Beauchamp, since the Earls of Warwick (Beauchamp) made extensive use of the new legal device in their own affairs.

If adoption into a family and its heritable land was indeed common practice in the late fourteenth and early fifteenth centuries, this makes a strong case for the continued peasant preoccupation with hereditary land before the plagues, a preoccupation which carried over for a few decades after the Black Death until swept away by the massive changes which overtook the traditional tenurial pattern of medieval England in the first quarter of the fifteenth century.

The case against peasant attachment to land rests on the very marked turnover of surnames on many manors during the early fifteenth century (Faith 1962; also 1966: 77–95; Jones 1972: 18–27). A glance at figure 16 leaves one in no doubt that this was also true of Kibworth for the late fourteenth and fifteenth century, but a more careful scrutiny will reveal a return to something like the old stability by the seventeenth. Many of the short-stay surnames in the latter century were landless men and many of the new names were those of sons-in-law. The return to stability in the seventeenth century is more clearly seen if one follows through the tenurial history of the copyhold tenements. For example, of the fifteen tenements taken on 21-year leases in 1593–9, seven were in the same family in 1636, six had changed hands once, only one had changed hands twice and the descent of the last cannot be traced. Taking the same fourteen tenements for the 1636–79 period, eleven remained in the hands of the same family or in the hands of a son-in-law; the remaining three had all belonged to the Brian family, who moved back to the neighbouring village of Smeeton Westerby during this period and allowed their Kibworth lands to pass to in-laws, who were them- selves men of the blood of the village. In other words, there was no turnover among copyhold families between 1636 and 1679.

To return briefly to the period of maximum turnover – the fifteenth century – the average outsider held land in the village for not more than twelve years. To take the turnover of new names at even ten-year intervals would tend to underestimate the number of tem- porary landholders. Therefore, rather than try to estimate the degree of instability, I have attempted to measure the degree of continuity and stability by giving, in table 28, the percentage of surnames which survived each forty-year interval.

The sharp increase in the turnover of surnames coincided not only with the fall in the population level after the fourteenth-century

Table 28. *The percentage of surnames surviving each forty-year interval*

1280–1340	100%					
1341–80	80%	1280–1412	23.6%		
1381–1412	77%				
1413–40	60%				
1441–84	48%	1412–1527	27%	1280–1700	8%
1485–1527	51.5%				
1593–1636	69.2%	1593–1686	57.5%		
1637–86	75%				

plagues but, more significantly, with the extinction of hereditary landholding families. In such circumstances, either the land reverted to common land and was shared among surrounding villages or appropriated by the lord (a phenomenon to which the many deserted village sites bears witness*), or tenants who had no hereditary claim could be found to take up these holdings. The inflow of new tenants is reflected in the number of new names to be found on most court rolls during this period (Harvey 1965; Harvey 1977). Clearly, one cannot use the documents from this exceptional period to argue for or against peasant attitudes to hereditary land or the existence of a peasant land market in normal circumstances. But the documents of this period are crucial to the understanding of the legal position of landholders in the sixteenth and seventeenth centuries. At Kibworth, demesne land became leasehold *without* hereditary right, but customary land became copyhold *with* hereditary right. On many other manors in England, customary land was granted out on leases and without hereditary tenure, or demesne and customary tenements were thrown together and granted out with no clear understanding as to hereditary rights but, at a later date, were claimed to be leasehold without inheritance because they included demesne land.†
The question of customary tenures held 'at the will of the lord', which made their first appearance in the 1350s and were adopted for all customary tenements in 1439, has already been discussed in chapter four and will not be repeated here, although it is of course an essential element in the present discussion.

No discussion of peasant customs attaching to land and its descent can avoid the question of the existence of an active land market. The

* For example the five villages of Saxenton, Ardley, Cote, Tusmore and Bainton in Ploughley Hundred, Oxfordshire. See *VCH Oxon.*, vol. 6.

† See the contributions of Miss Harvey and others in the *VCH Oxon.*, vol. 6, for Ploughley Hundred. Also Harvey (1977).

argument for an active land market rests on the assumption that sales of odd acres and rods of land are sufficiently significant to constitute a land market within the context of an agrarian subsistence economy (Postan and Brooke 1960; King 1973; Hyams 1970: 18–31). Half an acre within an urban context represents considerable potential or actual wealth, either as building land or for market gardening. Half an acre within a fishing or pastoral area represents a useful supplement to a man's other sources of income: what the two-acre holding is to the modern Humberside steelworker. But half an acre in predominantly arable country was an anomaly; it could not possibly be thought of as a subsistence unit; it was of value only to the widow or the craftsman, both of whom had other means of support. Land to a subsistence *cultivator* meant an area sufficient to support a household; a land market only had meaning when the unit of exchange was at least a quarter or a half virgate. It is interesting to note, for example, that three virgates at Kibworth, which became ownerless in the early fourteenth century, and were subdivided to provide small plots for cottars, were reassembled within a generation by these same cottars into standard full and half virgate holdings; in other words into viable agricultural holdings which made sense within the village economy.

The fact that these sales of half acres were often accompanied by *cartae* serves to strengthen the case for the atypical nature of the transaction. A very small unit of land, the single acre, was being detached from a whole unit, a virgate, and added to another. This is one possible interpretation of the nature of the sale; the other, the more plausible, is that a small unit of land assarted from the waste, and hence the customary, hereditable, possession of no family, was being transferred, and since no village custom existed to sanction or uphold such transfers, recourse was had to the written charter, a form adopted from pre-Conquest times by church and state to give authority to agreements of an unusual nature, for which no time-hallowed procedure existed, and which might, therefore, be challenged and disallowed at some later date. It could be argued that the alienation of small units of land could lead to the amorcelisation of virgates by the process of steady erosion. The fact that these transactions required the drawing up of *cartae*, however, indicates that they were so rare that no normal procedure was ever developed to deal with them in the manorial courts. The freeholders at Kibworth were periodically called upon to show their *cartae*, when a relief was paid for example, or when a rental was being drawn up, the earliest extant record at Kibworth being the *Inquisiccio carta'* held in 1291.[4] The business of producing *cartae* was always surrounded by some confusion, since no record of their content or sealing was kept in the

Kibworth court rolls. The amount of land in question is consequently described as unknown, the services and rent as unknown and an enquiry ordered forthwith. By contrast, St Peter's Abbey, Gloucester, kept its peasant *cartae*[5] (Hart 1867), as did Peterborough Abbey (Postan and Brooke 1960). As Edmund King commented on the latter, the charters deal with very small holdings of one or two acres, often accompanied by a licence to build, and the list of charter holders reads 'like a register of daughters and younger sons' (King 1973: 124). Now the holders of the one-acre plots on St Peter's Abbey estates were also widows and younger sons. In other words these look like the dower holdings one comes across in most European peasant societies. At Peterborough and at St Peter's they were treated as separate from the chief messuage, at Kibworth and elsewhere they were not. According to the Kibworth wills of the early modern period, most widows held an acre in each field and house-space in the main house, but do not appear as separate tenants on the court rolls.

The second argument for the existence of an active peasant land market is based upon the interpretation of the numerous transfers which took place every year as being *sales*. Such an interpretation leads to some curious situations; the membership of the peasant community at Kibworth was closed, outsiders were not encouraged, and on average two transfers took place each year, the net result being that every man finished with the same land as his father had held before him (see above p. 48). Thus A inherits a virgate in let us say 1300, he surrenders it to B in 1305, to C in 1310, to D in 1314 and in 1320 he dies, leaving one virgate to his widow, who then comes and surrenders this in court to her son. Clearly, these transfers cannot have been sales, they must have been leases. Another look at figure 16 will again show how rare a permanent alienation was before 1349, in spite of an average of two transfers a year recorded in the court rolls for the 1280–1349 period. The practice of leasing land is perfectly compatible with the strong feeling that land should remain within the village community, and with the even stronger feeling that that land should not be alienated from the family. Yet it allows for the developmental cycle of the family, which at certain stages needs more land than at others.

So when we talk of a peasant land market, we must be sure that we are talking about complete subsistence units and about permanent alienations. The odd acre has significance for the townsman or the village craftsman or widow, but not for the peasant farmer. The lease made possible the retention of land within the family over many generations; the sale, on the other hand, destroyed this continuity.

But leases are the medievalist's nightmare! In fen- and wood-pasture areas characterised by an active land market in minute parcels of land, the subletting, exchange or sale of such parcels created an intricate tenurial pattern in which landholders were at the same time both lessees and lessors.* The situation created obvious administrative problems, not least of which was the drawing up of a rental. On some estates it was the practice to record lessees, but on many it was not, and in these cases it is necessary to examine other estate records, such as the court rolls, to ascertain the nature of the land market and the extent of subletting. The Kibworth records make no mention of lessees and the court rolls reveal a pre-plague land market almost entirely restricted to customary half-virgate units passing from one generation to the next by inheritance, which would suggest that subletting was not extensive. Furthermore, since no surnames other than those of landholders are to be found in the court rolls there appears to have been no group of 'undersettles' subsisting entirely on leases. This conclusion is supported by further strands of evidence. For example, between 1300 and 1310 or thereabouts three virgates became tenantless due to lack of heirs. It was a period of acute land shortage and so, very sensibly, the land was not offered to outsiders, but was broken up into small parcels and let to villagers. In subsequent rentals these odd bundles of two acres, five acres and so on, are always identified as part of 'Robert Holke's virgate' or one of the other three. No indication is given that this Robert Holke had been dead some seventy years. Had only the 1372 rental survived, one might easily have been tempted to argue the practice of extensive subletting, hidden leases, lack of attachment to hereditary land, economic and social mobility, the emergence of the kulak and so forth. In fact, so unusual was the existence of odd acre holdings in place of virgate holdings that this group was always given a special mention in the rentals, and their ancestry traced to the last full virgate holders.

But, it may be argued, if partition could happen to a vacant virgate, how do we know that holdings, recorded as passing from father to son, were not in practice sublet or subdivided to persons other than family members? Once again the documentary evidence answers this question simply and conclusively. In the first place, as has been seen, the rentals consistently distinguished between normal virgates and

---

* A typical example of the complexity of the landholding system can be found in the entry for Fulbourn, Cambridgeshire, in the Hundred Rolls for 1279, op. cit. pp. 430–432, 436–39, 443–46. See also A. Jones, op. cit. *EcHR* XXXII (1979); B. Harvey, 1977, pp. 212, 214; M. M. Postan, *Essays on Medieval Agriculture and General Problems of the Medieval Economy* (Cambridge 1973), pp. 121–2.

disintegrated virgates and name the present tenants of the latter. Secondly, in the fifteenth century, when holders of tenements frequently absconded secretly during the night, a body of supervisors was set up to inspect abandoned holdings and to report upon the condition in which they had been left. Damages were charged against the late holder, and the man's pledgers were called upon to find the money and to complete the ploughing. On no occasion did they call upon subtenants to pay or to plough. Lastly, when land in the lord's hand was let, never more than two or three acres were let from any one virgate. In other words, the subletting of the odd acre was a commonplace within the sytem of fixed family lands, which could not be permanently alienated whatever the present size of the family. But the alienation of entire virgates could only happen in very exceptional circumstances, such as the complete failure of heirs.

Up to this point the discussion of inheritance practice at Kibworth has been based upon the documentary evidence of rentals and court rolls. The discussion to follow will be based on the parish register and the probate records for Kibworth. The nature of the information yielded by these two very different types of source material is complementary rather than continuous. Therefore, it may be useful to sum up the data deduced from the late medieval documents before entering upon a new line of argument.

The village community of the early fourteenth century was remarkably stable. Land passed from father to son and supported other, landless, members of the family. There was often more than one branch of a family in a village, so that if one line failed there were usually close kinsmen to hand. In the exceptional circumstance of a family becoming extinct the family could 'adopt' an heir if it did not wish the land to escheat to the lord. Whether or not a lord could veto an 'adoption' is not clear; in theory he probably could, in practice he was probably glad to be spared the trouble of finding a new tenant acceptable to the village. Merton certainly favoured *ad opus* transfers in the late fourteenth century when tenants were very difficult to find.

The drastic culling of village families which took place during the plague period made possible the accumulation of two or more units of family land in the hands of one surviving line. This sudden increase in the size of holding, accompanied by a decrease in household size (since celibate adults and adolescent boys could now find work 'abroad'), made possible the accumulation of savings in the form of cash or capital equipment which had seldom hitherto been possible. Children could be endowed with cash portions in place of land or maintenance on the land. Consequently, these large holdings were not subdivided in the next generation to provide as many children as possible with a minimum smallholding. Instead, the large holding was preserved intact, but every effort was made to improve its profit so that larger cash portions could be distributed among the children.

The high turnover of surnames on the late fourteenth- and early fifteenth-century rentals can be attributed to the temporary dislocation of the hereditary descent of land, rather than to a decline in the peasant's attachment to land. By the seventeenth century the old stability had been regained.

The principal source materials for the sixteenth and seventeenth centuries are the probate records and the parish register. These shed abundant light upon the retirement arrangements of the Leicestershire smallholder, a subject which was as central to the economy and life style of peasants then, as it is in rural economies today. They also illuminate the related topic of marriage portions and child portions which had far-reaching repercussions on the regional economy.

The descents of some fifty families, extracted from the register, provide a framework into which the wills of these same families can be inserted, and against which they can be interpreted. For example, one can discover the age of subjects mentioned in the wills by consulting the register, and by this means can state with certainty that at Kibworth it was usual for the eldest son to inherit, a point which the earlier court rolls do not make absolutely clear.

Two hundred and seven wills were analysed. They all related to families either living in Kibworth Harcourt or who had at one time lived in Harcourt, and later lived in one of the other two villages of the parish, Kibworth Beauchamp and Smeeton Westerby. In the first stage of analysis the wills were grouped by family and examined under the following heads.

> Date
> Residue left to
> Special arrangements for wife, if any
> Number of children
> Were child portions equal or unequal in value
> If unequal, who was favoured
> Legacies left to brothers and sisters
> > affines
> > cousins or kinsmen
> > nephews and nieces
> > grandchildren
> > godchildren
> > friends
> > servants
> Specific mention of land
> Legacies in cash only

Legacies in cash and kind (excluding land)
Money to be put out at interest
Legacies contingent upon obedience, marriage, etc.
Remarks

With the resultant charts before one, it was possible to select the more significant lines of enquiry; in particular, the deployment of the family's wealth upon aged dependants, young dependants and persons who had a social but not an economic tie with the family, such as affines and godchildren.

The factual information thereby obtained for Kibworth could then be used to support a general discussion on the significance of dower arrangements in the life of the smallholder, the age of retirement and its repercussions on the age structure of the village and the composition of the household; the manner of disposing of movable wealth among the next of kin, and the effect this had upon the potential for capital accumulation among peasant landholders. And lastly, the implications of an increasingly cash-dominated economy, even among smallholders, upon the expectations of the younger generation, the majority of whom would migrate to other areas, taking with them a large portion of the hard-won wealth of the village.

No attempt has been made to distinguish between the attitudes of labourers, husbandmen and yeomen, the three groups represented in the wills, because it was found that practice varied from one generation to the next within the same family and economic group. The decisive factor was not class or family, but the age and family responsibilities of the testator at the time when he made his will.

Thus only those who had fulfilled their obligations, such as grandparents, widows, widowers, or those who had no such obligations, such as bachelors and single women, left legacies to the wider kin circle, for example to nephews, nieces, affines, cousins, grandchildren and godchildren, 'neburs' and servants.

The wider kin circle was thus relatively unimportant. By contrast, the distribution of land and goods between wife and children called for more detailed analysis, since the wills provided information on attitudes which could not be derived from the court rolls or the parish register. For example, it was the custom of the manor that the entire holding should go to the widow; from the wills we learn in what circumstances this custom was adhered to and when not. Likewise, it was the custom that only one son should inherit the land; the wills tell us in what sense he held the land, as sole owner or as family representative. Custom at Kibworth tells us nothing about the rights of the remaining children, the wills are primarily concerned with them. The information derived from wills goes far towards bridging the gap between monogeniture and partible inheritance.

Accordingly, the sample was reduced to 193 by selecting only the wills of married men. These were divided into four categories: those wills in which the land was left to the widow alone; those in which the land was left to the widow and a kinsman or son to be held jointly by them; those in which the land was left to a son or daughter, the wife being still living; and lastly, those in which the land was left to a son or daughter, the wife being dead.

In the first category, those who left land to the widow alone, there were 56 wills. Of these, forty testators left their property to their wife alone without any written condition safeguarding the interests of their heirs, and only fifteen of these were childless. The remaining sixteen inserted the type of limiting condition that one would expect: that their widows were to hold for life only, or for a term of years or until the heir reached his majority, and were to forfeit the property if they remarried.

In the second category, those who left property to the widow and a kinsman to be held jointly, there were 34 wills. Of these, all without exception laid down explicit conditions. The wife was to hold jointly for life or until the heir was twenty-one, after which the heir was to guarantee her maintenance, unless she remarried. All except seven of these testators left at least some children under twenty-one.

Thus the tendency was to leave the residue to the wife, or to the wife and a kinsman, if the couple was childless or the children were minors.

In the third category, twenty-eight testators left the land and residue to a son or daughter, the wife being still living. In every case specific arrangements were made for the maintenance of the widow; she was to have the use of a certain number of acres and/or maintenance in the house, while seven were left a sum of money in cash in the order of £20 or so. These legacies in cash are particularly interesting, and will be discussed below. This category belonged to an older age group; in only six cases were all the children under twenty-one.

In the last category, thirty-two testators made wills in which the wife was not mentioned. In every case it was found that she had predeceased her husband. Seven of these testators left children all under twenty-one, of these five left the property to the eldest son, the other two left it to be held jointly by all the children. Some or all of the children of the remaining testators were over twenty-one and the eldest son inherited. One case is significant. William Smith left four children and many debts. He instructed his executors to sell the copyhold in order to pay off the debts and to divide the proceeds equally among the two boys and two girls, giving to the youngest, a boy, an extra £5.

Thus there was a tendency to leave the land to the son if some or all of the children were over twenty-one, and to make the heir responsible for the maintenance of the widow according to prescribed conditions.

The results of this analysis of the wills within the context of family circumstances can be summarised as follows.

In the 33 cases where a man left children who were all minors:
>   42.4% left the tenement and residue to the wife alone
>   39.3% left the tenement and residue to a wife and kinsman (usually a son)
>   18.0% left the tenement and residue to a son alone (the wife being still alive)

In the 51 cases where some or all of the children were over 21:
>   29.4% left the tenement and residue to the wife alone
>   29.4% left the tenement and residue to the wife and a kinsman (usually a son)
>   41.2% left the tenement and residue to a son alone (the wife being still living)

In the 18 cases of a childless marriage:
>   83.3% left the tenement and residue to the wife alone
>   16.6% left the tenement and residue to the wife and a kinsman.

It has not been possible to trace, in a sufficiently large number of cases, the subsequent history of these widows, due to the convention in the parish register of merely noting 'widow' in the burial entries. One cannot be sure whose widow she was. Therefore, we cannot tell how long a widow remained a charge upon tenement, sometimes for over twenty years, or how soon she handed over effective control to the heir and 'went her way' as the wills and the old laws phrase it. The wills of widows seldom deal with land, and the court rolls show that widows often handed over the tenement to their sons after only a short interval, but we do not know in what proportion to those who did not.

It is quite clear, however, that provision for his wife was an important, one could almost say over-riding, consideration in a man's mind when he felt that his own days were numbered. This raises an aspect of inheritance custom which is easily overlooked, partly because, without the wills, there is little one can discover about retirement arrangements, and partly, perhaps, because it is so often assumed that the life of the medieval peasant was brutish and short, and that old age was consequently not a very probable eventuality.

The age at marriage in a region was determined by the age at which it was customary for a man to retire or, if retirement was uncommon, the age at which landholders tended to die. It was also influenced by the nature of the retirement arrangements in the region. For example, if it was customary for the heir to buy the land from his father, as in the Scandinavian countries and in nineteenth-century Ireland, then he had either to find some means of earning the necessary money, or he had to marry a woman with a large marriage portion. In such circumstances, the age at marriage tended to be high and fathers could only afford to provide one of their daughters with a suitable portion. The number of single women, in consequence, was large and the growth rate of the population was correspondingly reduced. This is not to say that the growth rate was necessarily low, modern Ireland being the classic example to the contrary (Williams 1956: 46–52; Frimannslund 1956: 65–6; Arensberg and Kimball 1968: 105–12, 135–6; Jutikkala 1964: 165–80).

In those parts of England which were characterised by an emphasis on livestock husbandry and by an active market in small units of land, it was common for sons to build up for themselves an independent enterprise during the lifetime of their parents. To do this there was an obvious advantage in marrying an heiress, and it is in these regions that it was normal practice for girls to inherit or purchase an acre or two which would serve as a marriage portion and as security in old age. By contrast, in regions where the younger generation inherited rather than purchased land, there was no pressing need for fathers to provide their daughters with very much in the way of stock or household goods, and still less with land. Retirement arrangements, therefore, cannot be entirely disassociated from marriage contracts and something should be said at this point about marriage portions. In modern parlance the word 'dower' is usually associated with the jointure or marriage portion which a woman brings with her to her marriage. The concept is derived from Roman and canon law and is relatively recent. The old word for this contribution was the *maritagium*, and the word 'dower' had an older and quite distinct meaning. It was money or land which a free man gave to his wife at the church door at the time of his marriage. He was bound both by the common law and ecclesiastical law so to endow his wife. According to Glanvill, a free man could not endow his wife with more than one-third of his lands; later lawyers held that the dower could be more, but not less, than one-third (Hall 1965: bks VI, VII). However, we get nearer to common practice if we turn to the church manuals and rituals. Here we find the familiar formula, 'Wyth þis ryng I wedde ye, and wyth þis gold and sylvere I honoure ye, and wyth my gyfts I dow ye' (York).

The last phrase varies regionally and a common alternative is 'with all my worldely catel I thee endow' (Norfolk, Wales) (Henderson 1875: xvi, 19, 167). Among villeins the dower was often quite literally 'all my wordlely catel', and the widow by right took the entire tenement and its contents; this was certainly the case at Kibworth, though in other regions she was endowed with only a half or a third of the lands (see also Homans 1970: 179–84; Britton 1977: chap. 2). Thus the dower custom in an area went far towards establishing the age structure of that region and the retirement custom. A girl's *maritagium* or marriage portion at Kibworth was the same as her child portion, and the child portions of all daughters were of equally little value, so that lack of a 'dowry', in the modern sense, was not the serious impediment to marriage that it was later to become.

However, the corollary of a modest *maritagium* was the absence of a substantial sum from a daughter-in-law in old age. A man had to put off retirement for as long as was physically possible in order to provide for each of his children and ensure an income for himself and his wife. Meanwhile his heir waited. On most manors in medieval England it was common practice for the lord to take a heriot from the family of a deceased landholder, usually in the form of the best beast or chattel. It was therefore in the lord's interest for the steward to note the deaths of landholders in order to facilitate the collection of the heriot. At Kibworth, if a man died while still in possession of his land the event was recorded in the rolls, together with the nature and value of the heriot, the name of the heir and a description of the land he had held and the rent (see above pp. 28, 32–3). But if the deceased had transferred his land to his heir during his lifetime then it was necessary to note no more than the fact of his death and the payment of his heriot.* Although such a record was kept in many cases, it is surprising how frequently it was not: land passed from father to son and some years later the father died, but none of these events was recorded, no entry fine taken and no heriot. We know that this was happening because the son's name replaces the father's on the rental as holding the land, and in the court roll as holding office, and eventually when the son comes to die he dies seised of the same lands that his father had held. For this reason, among others, court rolls can be a treacherous source from which to extract statistics. In the case of Kibworth the court rolls record more *post mortem* transfers than transfers *inter vivos*, whereas in practice transfers *inter vivos* were as common, if not more common. For example, in 1330[6] William

---

* Postan and Titow noted that on the estates of the Bishop of Winchester no heriot was demanded from young men when they alienated customary land, but that if an old man wished to transfer land then a heriot was taken (1973: 151).

Osborne, Robert (probably William) Reyne and John son of Walter
died. They had all held land at one time but had transferred it before
death (though Osborne had kept 3 acres and 1 twodelrod of free land
which passed to his wife). Their heriots were paid – Osborne's not
until 1347 – and nothing further is recorded of them. In the same year
John son of Reginald Sibile and Robert Bron died in possession of
land, the land was described, heirs found, heriots paid. But at about
the same time the landholder William Pek must have died, since no
more is heard of him and his son takes his place as juror. Similarly,
Robert Polle took over John Polle's land in the early thirties and
Robert Smith took over a virgate from William Smith, though his
father kept 3 acres and a *parva placea* of free land until his death in
1349. Both the Peks and the Polles often served as reeves and were
thus well placed to suppress certain facts from reaching the ears of
the steward and his court rolls, but the Sibiles and the Brons were
among the wealthiest freemen and should have been able to achieve
the same immunity: we shall probably never know why some heriots
and transfers were recorded in the court rolls and others were not.
The old in a household were sometimes referred to as 'serviens' (see
table 22) along with other dependent adults and they almost certainly
lived under the same roof as their children, since medieval retirement
contracts mention only food and clothing, not lodging[7] (cf. Harvey
1965: 123, 125; Hilton 1975: 29–30, 40), and by the sixteenth century it
was customary for the old at Kibworth to be given a room or a wing of
the family house. By the fifteenth century Kibworth houses were
often of four, sometimes even eight bays and this at a time when
derelict houses were available in abundance and could have been
brought into use for the old and for widows. The key factor may
have been fuel, which was in short supply in Kibworth to the extent
that the lord of the manor provided a common oven, even in the
sixteenth century when the wealthier families used coal for domestic
heating and cooking.

In the medieval period fathers seem to have relinquished control of
the land before death and therefore the old rule: no land, no
marriage, held good; sons were in possession of the land when they
married. But by the sixteenth century fathers tended not to retire and
sons, when they married, were not yet in possession of the land;
moreover the widow often remained in command for several years,
'and she to have the ruling of my house' until she retired and was
given house-space: usually a room with a hearth and storage space in
the yard.

For example, John Carter, when he died in 1690, had been
occupying seven rooms; his widow continued to occupy three of

these until she died in 1711, while her son occupied the remaining four rooms. The continuance of the widow in possession was nothing new; it had been the custom in the medieval period for the entire holding to pass to the widow if her husband had been in possession at the time of his death, it was just that more men were in possession at the time of their death in the modern period.

With no lump sum from a daughter-in-law in the form of a dowry, the old at Kibworth had to forego retirement or accept a dependent position in the households of their sons. In compensation a father did not have to find large child portions for his daughters and non-inheriting sons. However, he had to find *something* for them. In the sixteenth century, when a man died leaving minors he usually stipulated that his children should receive their portions when they were sixteen, eighteen, twenty-one or when they married. However, if one turns to the wills of older men or of widows, one finds that children in their late twenties had still not received their portions and that the heir had inherited the obligation to provide them. So the long generation interval did not necessarily mean that a man had thirty years in which to accumulate the savings from which he could endow his children; the first few years would be spent paying off his siblings. The total amount to be raised depended on his father's attitude towards the competing interests of his children as individuals, against those of the family inheritance.

In areas of land shortage, the equal division of *land* among all sons could rapidly lead to the subdivision of family holdings until the minimum viable unit had been reached, which it would be economically suicidal to subdivide. Younger sons could be expected to accept this as reasonable. But it does not follow that, because the land could not be divided among all the children, movables likewise could not be divided. We learn from the wills that the son who received the land did not receive the livestock and gear; these went to the remaining children. The heir could then either buy out his brothers and sisters, or could continue to support them on the tenement in return for the use of the livestock and the gear, at any rate for the first few years. In 1536 for example, Robert Smyth, who had only half a virgate and goods worth £13, left the land to his wife and eldest son and his goods to the other son and his daughters with the injunction, 'I will that my chyldren shall remain togyder in my house and live of my stok to the youngest be 16 years old.' In 1543, Thomas Stevenson of Smeeton, having made a similar division, concluded, 'If any of my children depart or be married, their part shall be parted among the others.' We have already seen how, when William Smith sold his land, he instructed his executors to divide the proceeds evenly between sons and daughters alike, giving £5 extra to the youngest. These examples could be matched by many others, and serve to illustrate one method of meeting the obligation to supply for many children without subdividing the land itself. In the days when most families in Kibworth held only half a virgate, this was probably the most common method of dividing the family inheritance. Seen in this light the sharp legal distinction between monogeniture and partible inheritance becomes somewhat blurred.*

It is possible in the case of a small number of Kibworth families to examine in detail the relation between the size of the holding, the value of the movable goods and the value of the legacies over a number of generations, to which one can add further refinements, such as the effect, if any, of current market prices on the value of legacies. Such an exercise can hardly be described as a short cut, however, and only one sample has been worked through, for the Carter family, as follows.

One branch of the Carter family held two and a half virgates of land from 1603–70, they then subdivided it among three sons. At the same time they may have leased three virgates from William Sheffield which had belonged to another branch of the Carters throughout the previous (sixteenth) century. Wills and inventories survive for 1603, 1641, 1670, 1690, 1697, 1707, 1709, 1718. The graph (fig. 17) shows the value of the movables as appraised for probate at these dates, against which is plotted the total value of the legacies to children at the same date. From 1603–41 the family invested heavily in cattle and horses, but always kept some 35 acres under the plough. Therefore, the market prices for mares and for barley at these dates have been added: these are Leicestershire prices derived from inventories covering the whole county.

Figure 17 shows a steep decline in the family fortune after 1641. No reason is given, of course, but one can hazard the guess that the Civil

---

* Too much perhaps has been made of Kentish gavelkind. The sixteenth-century lawyers were probably correct when they derived *gavel* from *gavella*, the Latin for *gweli*, which was the Welsh family holding of four generations, the Irish *gabhail* and the Yorkshire and Scottish *cavel* likewise meaning hereditary, family land. Such land was divided equally when possible but not beyond the limits of prudence. Similarly, Kentish gavelkind did not enforce imprudent division of land among all heirs, but permitted joint tenure. Since no work has yet, to my knowledge, been done on the marriage arrangements of Kentish parceners we do not know if all sons usually married. If only one married then the distinction between the stem family on partible land and the stem family on impartible land ceases to have any significance in economic and social terms. See C. I. Elton and H. J. H. Mackay, *Robinson on Gavelkind: the Common Law or the Custom of Gavelkind* (5th edn., London 1897); R. A. Butlin, 'Northumberland field systems', *AgHR* XII (1964), 107; the *NED* treatment of the word is quite inadequate.

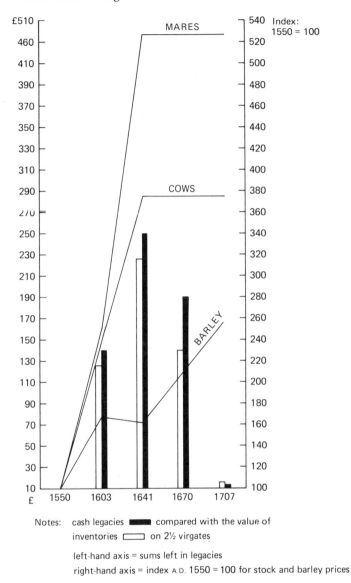

Fig. 17 Carter family: their cash legacies compared with the value of their inventories

War had something to do with it. The battle of Naseby was fought only a few miles to the south-west and tradition has it that Cromwell spent the night after the battle at Kibworth Beauchamp. Goodman Carter's cattle and particularly his mares would have been very much at risk. We shall never know, but his story may have read like the following for Mr Abberley of Stafford.

> Whereas Mr Abberley had eleven cows taken from him by the enemy it is ordered that he shall have two heifers and a white cow remaining in the Committee's hands and one other which was taken away yesternight if she can be found, if the right owner of the cow have not the same.
>
> (Pennington and Roots 1957: 182)

With livestock prices continuing very high it would be difficult to replace losses. In spite of this decline in fortune, William Carter, when he died in 1670, left legacies which far exceeded his income and were more generous than his father's had been thirty years before when the family fortune was at its height. The result was disaster. Unable to meet his commitments, the elder brother divided the land among the claimants. Robert mortgaged his share for £172 and lost it, but the remaining brothers farmed the land jointly and only one married.* The family survived as smallholders and carpenters until the twentieth century.

A simpler method, better suited for general surveys and regional comparisons, is to work through the wills and inventories for a given parish (if one works parish by parish one can be sure that at least within the parish the value put upon goods in the inventory is consistent, since the appraisors were drawn from the same group of men), noting the nature and value of the legacy left to each son and daughter. This method deals only with the portions of younger and unmarried children but yields quickly a large sample.

I have used this method for the parish of Kibworth in order to plot the changeover from legacies in kind to legacies in cash. The figures also allow one to chart the rise in the value of cash legacies and to compare this with the movement of prices in the Leicestershire area.

Figure 18 is based on the surviving wills for the whole parish of Kibworth over the period 1520–1720. The timespan has been divided into five forty-year periods and for each block of years the percentage of portions worth £1–£4 each has been tabulated against the percentage of portions worth £5–£8 each, and so on. Thus, in the period 1520–1560, 57 per cent of those who left legacies in cash left legacies worth only £1–£4, and only 3.57 per cent left a legacy worth more than £20. By contrast, in the period 1680–1720 only 14 per cent left legacies worth less than £5 each, 17 per cent left legacies worth over

---

* The temptation to over-burden the estate with excessively large portions for younger children was the undoing not only of yeomen but also of the old aristocracy and the nouveaux riches of the period. See L. Stone, *Family and Fortune* (Oxford 1973).

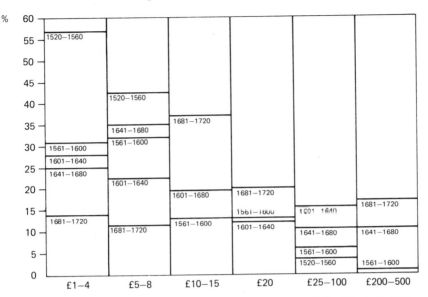

Fig. 18 Movement in the value of cash legacies over the period 1520–1720

Note: no legacies worth £10–15, 1520–1560; none worth £20, 1520–1560, 1641–1680; none worth £25–100, 1681–1720; none worth £200–500, 1520–1560 and 1601–1640

£200 each, while the majority, 37.13 per cent, left legacies worth £10–£15 each. No allowance has been made for inflation in the sixteenth century, but the figure shows an overall upward movement in the value of cash portions over the period 1520–1720.

Instances of a portion assigned wholly in kind are so rare for Kibworth in the sixteenth century that they can be disregarded, but figure 18 fails to indicate the value of legacies in *kind* which children received in addition to their cash portion. Hence the need for figure 19 which shows in the left-hand column the amount of surplus cash which could be accumulated in an average year on twenty-four acres, and in the central column the value of portions in cash as a percentage of the value of portions in kind, which is shown in the right-hand column. The amounts shown in the first column are taken from table 14 and serve only as a rough guide, since the dates, as can be seen, do not exactly coincide with the forty-year intervals adopted for the wills, and the column for 1636–41 antedates the Civil War. That the war was ruinous for some Kibworth graziers has already been exemplified in the case of the Carter family (fig. 17) and is also indicated by the falling off in cash legacies in the 1640s.

Thus figures 18 and 19 complement each other and should be studied as a pair. Figure 18 for example shows a rise in the proportion

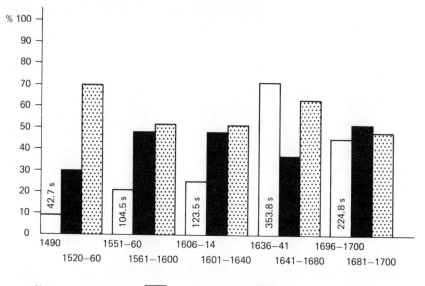

Note: portions in kind [:::::] to portions in cash ▮

Cash surplus per virgate per annum (showing the savings potential at each period, in shillings) is shown in the left-hand column

Fig. 19   Relative percentage of portions in kind to portions in cash, 1520–1700

of cash legacies between 1560–1600, followed by a fairly steady proportion in relation to legacies in kind of around 48 per cent, interrupted only by the Civil War. What the figure does not show is that the *value* of cash legacies continued to rise steadily, so that by 1681–1720 the 52 per cent of cash legacies were worth around £20 each as against the 48 per cent of cash legacies for 1561–1600, which were seldom worth more than £5 each. On the other hand figure 19 makes it plain that a hard core of poorer villagers continued to leave portions in kind supplemented by only very small cash sums (the conventional one shilling left to children who had already received their inheritance has been discounted throughout). Rich and poor alike will always leave gifts in kind: heirlooms, household goods, livestock; but in hard times the poor tend to leave only goods, and a higher proportion of these goods are left to younger children at the expense of the heir. No attempt has been made here to distinguish between basic goods and luxury goods, since this has been described in an earlier chapter, but figure 19 provides an indication of the general trend. Legacies in cash were worth more than legacies in kind and indicate a period of saving, of cash surpluses. For example, a plough in Leicestershire was usually valued at between 5s and 10s in the sixteenth- and seventeenth-century inventories, 12s being the average. Livestock was worth much more and prices rose sharply in the second half of the sixteenth century, from a minimum of 13s 4d to a maximum of 45s for a cow in 1600. In the same period the price of an ox went up from £1 to £3 13s 4d, and of a mare from 13s 4d to 33s 4d, and prices continued to rise steeply until the Civil War, by which date mares fetched £3–£4 and oxen £5.* Nevertheless, cash legacies kept ahead. When a cow was worth 45s only 28 per cent of legacies were worth less than £5, and 19 per cent were worth between £10–£20. In other words, when a father left his son a cash legacy, he was not leaving him the equivalent in cash of a cow and a cart, he was leaving him much more, in addition to which the cow and cart remained on the holding to the ultimate benefit of the heir. But this is not the same as saying that all sectors of the community forged ahead at a uniform rate, and it is my impression that over the period 1520–1720 the gap widened between those leaving few and inferior goods and those leaving high-grade stock and well-furnished homes. In the early sixteenth century 57 per cent of legacies were of between £1 and £4 and 42 per cent between £5 and £8: the difference in cash surplus between families was not very great. By the early eighteenth century 14 per cent of legacies were of less than £5 and 17 per cent were of between £200 and £500. The contrast speaks for itself.

Taken together, figures 18 and 19 allow one to make the following observations. By the sixteenth century, testators had begun leaving money portions to their younger children in place of livestock and gear, which were then left to the heir. These cash legacies were worth more than children would have received in kind and reflect the growing prosperity of yeomen and husbandmen during the inflationary years of the sixteenth century. A rise in the percentage of cash legacies relative to portions in kind would indicate a period of profitable farming, while a fall in the percentage would reflect more uncertain conditions. The poorer village families continued throughout the period to leave legacies in kind; only when prices fell could they afford to increase the amount of cash left to non-heirs. Not every family adopted the practice of leaving gifts in cash; some persisted over generations in distributing the entire surplus, including the livestock and gear, once in every generation, without ploughing any of the surplus back into the land. Ultimately, such families either recognised the error of their ways or perished. During these two centuries a marked polarisation took place which profoundly

---

* Prices are based on tables derived from the Leicestershire inventories, see pp. 149–50, 154, app. 7.

changed the character and appearance of the village. Whereas at the outset husbandmen and yeomen had been much of a muchness, by the dawn of the eighteenth century many of the husbandmen had lost their land and the suvivors remained of humble station, whereas the yeomen had gone on to adopt the title of gentlemen (cf. Spufford in Goody 1976). Thus the Parkers, the half-virgater family of the fourteenth century, the 'good nebur' and appraisor of wills of the sixteenth, had become the 'gentleman' at the Old House by 1679. And Robert Lount, whose father's goods had been worth £22 in 1627, was worth £274 in 1709, and left £400 to one grand-daughter, £300 to the second and £200 each to the remaining two. He had continued to run the farm personally during his lifetime but his son-in-law preferred to employ a bailiff.

Younger sons left home with up to £20 apiece; trade, the professions, the universities, lay open to them. If the matriculation lists of Brasenose College, Oxford or, the school for Puritans, St John's College, Cambridge, are reliable indicators, then these sons of yeomen, farmers and men of *mediocris fortunae* were not slow to take advantage of the opportunities thus opened to them (L. Stone 1964: 41–81; Simon 1963: 58–67; Everitt and Stone 1966: 16–55; Spufford in Thirsk 1970: 112–49). Kibworth boys went to Kibworth Grammar School, founded in the fifteenth century, and then to St John's, Cambridge (Elliott 1957). There was always an educated curate resident in the parish, even in the fourteenth century, and by the seventeenth century they had a 'schoolmaster' and, in addition, a nonconformist school, presided over in the eighteenth century by Philip Doddridge and by Dr John Aiken, the friend and biographer of John Howard. Other sons went into trade and commerce, and the village had strong links with Market Harborough, Leicester, Northampton and London. It was spawning a middle class, and itself became a comfortable closed village ruled over by the Rays and the Parkers, who had made their way in the legal profession, and by Haymes and Fox, who owed their prosperity to successful farming. Some of the other old families were less well off, but their sons inherited the skilled crafts of their fathers, and when they left home they took with them these skills. They were willing recruits for industry but they were not 'raw' recruits.

The effect of this shift from legacies in kind to legacies in cash not only ensured the continuance of large farms, but stimulated long-term improvements in agricultural practices, and provided the motivation for commercial, rather than subsistence, farming. Grassland management was brought to a fine art in south-east Leicestershire, so that it became one of the best fatting pastures in England without, as we have seen, finding it necessary to abandon open-field farming (Auty in Stamp 1937: 254–7).

It affected the quality of the migrants who left this area of impartible inheritance once in every generation. They were not recruits for the industrial proletariat: they swelled the ranks of the emerging English middle class (Habakkuk 1955: 1–12; Redford 1926). This is an important qualification of the formula; primogeniture generates long-distance migrants who will provide the raw recruits for industry. Very small holdings will send out penniless and unskilled sons, but large holdings and small craft businesses will send out educated or skilled sons to join the professional and managerial sector. From the wills we can learn the average size of money portion received by younger sons in a particular region, and this will probably give us a more reliable indicator to the pattern and quality of migration than the type of inheritance custom alone. So long as sons received equal portions in kind, the difference between partible and impartible inheritance was not very great, but once the shift had been made to cash portions, areas of primogeniture tended to become associated with large farms and large portions, areas of partible inheritance with dual economies, smaller or poorer farms and small portions. The migrants from the former joined the middle class, those from the latter joined the vagabond class of the pre-industrial era, for whom there was seldom sufficient employment, and the labour reserve for industry, once the industrial revolution had got under way.

To sum up: in regions such as south-east Leicestershire where land remained the sole source of family income, it was regarded as family property and was expected to support all adult members, either by supplying each with a share of land where possible, or by supporting one nuclear family and a number of celibate adults. The restricted supply of land in a period of population increase in the thirteenth century led to close regulation of inheritance strategies. A minimum of twelve acres seems to have been accepted as the limit beyond which subdivision would not be tolerated. Certainly one does not find holdings of less than twelve acres in Kibworth, except in the case of the eight demesne cottages and a handful of free parcels. The result was a pattern of holdings uniform in size, a uniformity which was characteristic of many other medieval villages in a similar economic setting.* Although grandparents were rare, celibate adult dependants

---

* To indicate but a few attested to in print: P. D. A. Harvey, 1965, p. 130, for Cuxham; B. Harvey, 1977, pp. 435–6, for Bourton-on-the-Hill (Glos.), Todenham (Glos.), Stevenage, Wheathampstead and Kinsbourne (Herts.), Ashford (Msx.), Sutton-under-Brailes (Warks.), Pinvin (Worcs.).

were all too common so that households were exceptionally large, labour well in excess of demand, and the failure of heirs rare. All this was radically changed by the severe drop in population levels brought about by the plagues and epidemics of the late fourteenth century. Land became abundant, heirs were in short supply and in consequence the size of holdings increased to between twenty-four and thirty-six acres and tenants experienced the novelty of cash savings: savings which could be used to endow younger sons. These same younger sons could also earn high wages outside the village and it became the norm for non-heirs to leave the family hearth and to acquire land elsewhere. By the sixteenth century conditions were less favourable to younger sons. Nevertheless, at Kibworth, they continued to take their child-portion and to depart, and significantly no return was made to the practice of leaving any land in excess of twelve acres to younger sons. On the holdings of over twenty-four acres non-heirs continued to receive a cash portion and to enter commerce or the professions, leaving behind them a three-generation nuclear family. On smaller holdings it was not always possible to provide cash portions and a return was made to portions in kind, which portions could not be removed from the holding. Younger sons could either leave with nothing to join the ranks of the Elizabethan vagabond class or they could remain as dependent celibates within a stem family. The wheel had turned full circle for these families, but the majority, those with over twenty-four acres, had escaped. From having been one of the poorer regions of subsistence agriculture in the medieval period, Kibworth and its region became one of the more prosperous regions of commercial farming in the sixteenth century, and remained so.* The nature and value of child *portions* is, I would suggest, as vital to our understanding of change in rural society and economy as is the type of inheritance custom governing the distribution of *land* among heirs.

---

* R. S. Schofield, 'The geographical distribution of wealth in England 1334–1649', *EcHR*, 2nd ser., xviii (1965), 483–510, ranks Leicestershire as seventeenth in 1334 and twenty-second in 1515 if lay and clerical wealth is combined. E. J. Buckatzsch, in 'The geographical distribution of wealth in England 1086–1843', *EcHR*, 2nd ser., iii (1950), 180–202, ranks Leicestershire against other counties as sixteenth in 1334 and eighteenth in 1503, rising to seventh in 1636 but falling to twenty-eighth during the Civil War, recovering to fifteenth by 1693 and sixth by 1803. Seventh place in 1636 may be an over-optimistic estimate for Leicestershire as a whole, but it may well lie close to the truth for south-east Leicestershire, which was by then already a highly specialised grazing area and one characterised by fat yeomen farms. What no survey based on tax returns can indicate is the amount of cash flowing from these farms into commerce and the professions outside the county.

Appendixes

APPENDIX 1

Burton's transcript of the 1279 Hundred Rolls for Kibworth Harcourt[1]

Dicunt quod sunt in eadem quinque carucatas terre de quibus scholares domus Walteri de Merton in Oxon' habent tertiam partem ville cum toto dominico unde tenent in dominico duas virgatas terre, in villenagio duas virgatas. Thomas de Wortinges tenet in dominico unam virgatam, in villenagio unam virgatam. Alanus de Portesmue in dominico unam virgatam, in villenagio unam virgatam. Magister Robertus de Pwelle (Ewelle) in dominico unam virgatam, in villenagio unam virgatam. Thomas Tayllard in dominico unam virgatam, in villenagio unam virgatam. Hubertus de Told duas carucatas et dimidiam quae tenentur in villenagio. Henricus Person dimidiam virgate et quartam partem unius virgate. Nicholas fab (Faber) dimidiam virgate. Willelmus de Reynes dimidiam virgate. Robertus Polle dimidiam virgate. Robertus Harin dimidiam virgate. Ricardus filius Rogeri dimidiam virgate. Mathildus filia Fabri unam virgatam. Johannes Boton dimidiam virgate. Johannes Sibile dimidiam virgate et tenetur de Ricardo de Harecurt et Ricardo de Comite de Warewike et Comes de rege in capite et dat eidem scutagium pro dimidio feodi.

[1] Bodleian Library, Rawlinson Mss B.350 f.21

APPENDIX 2
The dispersal of three virgates of free and Apetoft land among villagers c. 1316

Name	Acres	Arable rods/lands	Meadow/pasture	Buildings	Rent
Half virgate once held freely by William de Reynes[a]					
R. Swan	4 acres	4 rods	Meadow in Kerside	1 placea	6d
W. Heyne	½ acre				1½d
W. Atte Cross	1 acre				} ½d
R. Ferour		1½ rods			
W. Osborne		1 rod	1 twodelrod		} ¾d
Alice Heyne		1 rod			
A. Sybile	½ acre		½ rod pratum		} ¼d
J. Sybile		2½ rods			
S. & R. de Pek			½ pasture		¼d
J. de Reynes	1 acre	½ rod			} 1¼d
Amabil Heyne		1½ rods			
TOTAL	7 acres	12 rods	1 twodelrod, meadow, ½ rod, ½ pasture	1 placea	10½d
Adam de Kibworth's (Sybile) half virgate once held freely by William de Langton[b]					
Adam de Kibworth	5½		½ pasture		9d
R. Peke			1 twodelrod	1 toft	3d
R. Swan		9½ rods	1 twodelrod		3d
R. Hildesle		1½ rods	1 twodelrod		¾d
			1 pasture		
N. Polle		1 rod			¼d
Alice Heyne		2½ rods			¼d
W. Atte Cross			1 twodelrod		¼d
R. Polle			1 twodelrod		¼d
M. Bonde		1½ rods			½d
Dom. J. Godwin		¾ rods			¼d
TOTAL	5½ acres	16¾ rods	5 twodelrods, 1½ pastures	1 toft	17½d

One Apetoft virgate once held by Hugh de Harcourt @ 13s 3d p.a.[c]

	acres	rods			
R. Swan	6 acres			1 parva placea	3s 0d
N. Smith	3 acres			½ messuage	1s 10d
C. Sybile		3 rods			1s 9d
J. Chapman	1 acre				5d
A. Sybile	1 acre		7½ twodelrods meadow		8d
W. Atte Cross		4 rods			5d
R. Polle			1 twodelrod		1d
W. Osborne			1 twodelrod		1d
R. Harcourt			1 twodelrod		1d
J. Mann		1 land	meadow		5d
J. Smith		6¾ rods			8d
R. de Hildesle	3 acres		meadow	1 placea	2s 0d
J. Harcourt		1 rod		1 parva placea	2s 0d
TOTAL	14 acres	14¾ rods, 1 land	10½ twodelrods, 3 meadows	½ mess. 3 placea,	13s 5d

One messuage and 1 Aperoft virgate once held by Robert Holke for 13s 4d p.a.[d]

	acres	rods			
R. Swan	15 acres[e]			1 messuage	10s 4d
W. Heyne		6 rods			9¾d
W. Atte Cross		6 rods			9d
R. Polle	1 acre	1 rod			3¾d
N. Polle		2¼ rods			3d
W. Osborne		1¼ rods			2¾d
J. Sybile		1¼ rods			2¼d
N. Harcourt			1 twodelrod		1d
R. Hildesle	½ acre		meadow	meadow	4d
TOTAL	16½ acres	17¾ rods,	1 twodelrod meadow	1 messuage	13s 3½d

a MM 6373. a; 6242   *b* MM 6373. h; 6374. a
c MM 6374. b; 6242   *d* Ibid.   *e* MM 6372

Notes to Appendix 2 *(cont)*

In addition, the reeve in 1300 did not know who was responsible for the payment of the rent on the following parcels of land, about 4 acres in all:[1]

A. Sybile	1 rod super Colisbriggehull
R. Swan	1 rod iuxta Robert*[um]* Bronn
R. Hildesle	1 rod ad Flaxmedwe iuxta terra Ad*[ame]* Sybile
A. Sybile	½ acre super Litulhull iuxta Johan*[nem]* Heyn sone
N. Polle	1 rod ad Martinespoul iuxta Isabell*[am]* Polle
A. Sybile*	1½ rod apud Martinespol iuxta Robert*[um]* Swan
R. Heyne*	1 rod ⎫
R. Sybile*	aliam rod ⎬ super Holebrinks iuxta Isabell*[am]* Polle
A. Sybile	1 twodelrod iuxta Maymoor iuxta Isabell*[am]* Polle
A. Sybile	1 twodelrod subt' Nosthill iuxta Mabill*[am]* Heyne
A. Sybile	1 rod inco (sic) Nosthilsike iuxta Will*[elmum]* Allot
A. Sybile*	1 twodelrod iuxta Steamfordgat
R. de Reynes	alt*[io]*ra twodelrod iuxta eund*[em]*
A. Sybile	1 twodelrod Tr'umlsike iuxta Isabell*[am]* Polle
A. Sybile*	1 twodelrod in Barlicroft iuxta Matild*[am]* fil*[ia]* Rob*[erti]* de Westerby
A. Sybile	1 rod ad Carlemedwe iuxta Isabell*[am]* Polle

[1] MM 6373.b.

* William de Langton's land according to MM 6374. a

APPENDIX 3

How land made available by the dispersal of three virgates of free and Apetoft land c. 1316 was reassembled into viable virgate and half-virgate holdings

A The composition of Robert Swan's land
1 Held of William de Reynes, tenant of Alan of Portsmouth; 1 messuage plus 4 acres, 4 rods, 1 placea called Swaepit. Meadow in Kerside.
2 Held of William de Langton; ½ acre, 7½ rods, 1 twodelrod.
3 Held of Hugh de Harcourt; 6 acres.
4 Held of Robert Holke; 15 acres, 1 messuage.
5 Held of 'unknown tenant'; 1 rod.
6 1 virgate *quondam* John Lerane, held jointly with three others.

TOTAL: 25½ acres, 12½ rods, 1 twodelrod, 2 messuages, 2 placea.
Note: Swan held no land directly of Merton. The parcels he held amount to a full virgate, or two half virgates. The arable proportion is high. In 1333[1] Robert Swan of Kibworth Harcourt was taxed 2s 2d while William Swan of Kibworth Beauchamp paid 4s 0d, the wealthiest man in the village if the tax assessors are to be trusted.

B The composition of Adam Sybile's land
1 Land held of Hugh de Harcourt; ½ acre, 5½ rods, 5 twodelrods.
2 Land held of William de Langton; 5½ acres of pasture.
3 Land held of Hugh de Harcourt; 1 acre, 7½ twodelrods (6 of which were sublet).
4 Land held of William de Reynes; 2 rods, ½ rod meadow.
   TOTAL: 7 acres, 7½ rods, 12½ twodelrods, ½ rod meadow.
   In addition the Sybiles held ¼ virgate freely, and 2 customary virgates.[2] Adam Sybile did not have a share in these customary lands.

---

[1] PRO E.179 133/2.
[2] MM 6366, 6367, 6371.

APPENDIX 4

Explit references to by-laws in the court rolls for Kibworth Harcourt

(oblique references are very common but are not included in the following list)

Date	Roll no.	Date	Roll no.	Date	Roll no.
1430	6421.11	1502	6439.2	1601	6447.6
1432	6421.17	1504	6439.liii	1611	6447.2ii
1439	6424.10	1504–5	6439.liv	1679	6448 & 6449.2
1440	6424.11	1509	6439.3 i & ii	1686	6452
1450	6426.3iii	1510	6440		
1484	6434	1511	6440.2 i & ii		
1489	6435	1521	6441		
1492	6437	1525–6	6441–2		
1497	6438.1	1531	6441.3		
1499	6438.2	1539	6442.2		
		1539ᵃ	6442.3		
		1542	6442.6–7		
		1545–6	6442.8		
		1552	6444		
		1599	6447.1		

ᵃ The first written in English

APPENDIX 5

Land values in the probate inventories for Leicestershire

No manual of instructions for appraisors survives so we have no direct means of knowing the criterion by which appraisors put a value on an acre of land, nor do we know when they were referring to standard acres and when to measured acres.

However, the answers to these questions can be obtained indirectly. When the land values are plotted on a graph month by month and compared with the grain prices for the same months a marked correlation becomes apparent. If the land values had been based on rent or purchase value, estimates would not have varied from month to month. The variation in value cannot have been due to a variation in size only because in the first place land sown with barley is given twice the value of land sown with peas and secondly, appraisors would not always have estimated in standard acres in June and in customary acres in December. Therefore, it is clear that the criterion for evaluating an acre was the value of the crop growing on it.

The question of the size of the acre can be met as follows. Land described as fallow is given a standard value in the inventories: 6s 6d in the 1570s, 20s 0d in the 1610s and 1630s and a graduated system by 1700. Land explicitly described as 'land' rather than 'acre' is always given a value very considerably less than the fallow acre. Many so-called 'acres' have the same value as these 'lands' and must in fact have been customary acres, that is 'lands'. A standard acre once sown was worth more than a fallow standard acre but a customary sown acre was still worth less than a fallow standard acre. One can, therefore, treat all acres worth less than a fallow acre as customary and those worth more as standard acres.

For the purpose of estimating yields per acre one can ignore the lands and concentrate upon the standard acres. If the price of barley was worth 10s 0d per quarter and the value of a standard acre in the same month was also 10s 0d then its yield must have been estimated as 1 quarter, if it had been 2 quarters its value would have been 20s 0d and so on. If the harvest was very good the price of the quarter fell, as in 1606, and therefore, the value of the acre also fell while remaining two or three times the value of the quarter. If the harvest was bad, as in 1574, the price of the quarter rose and the value of the acre also rose while remaining of less value than the quarter.

Prices per quarter had a tendency to drop sharply before harvest due to the shortage of money. The expected value of the crop is therefore best seen in June before the drop occurs. The accuracy of the appraisor's forecast in June can be checked by the level of grain prices in the following autumn.

Using the graphs prepared from inventory data the following table has been drawn up and from this the figures on page 153 have been prepared.

Appendix 5 *(cont) Leicestershire barley prices and yields 1510–1700*

	Price per quarter in shillings	Price per acre barley in shillings	Yield per acre barley in bushels	Comment on harvest[a]
June 1570	6	7	5.6	very poor
May 1571	7.6	8	7.6	very poor
June 1573	5	10	16	good
July 1574	15	13 3d	9	poor
April 1575	6.4	7 5d	9.37	} poor
August 1575	6	8	6.6	} very poor
May 1606	26.7	37	11.08	} very good
June 1606	11	25	18.18	} very good
June 1607	19.2	28–31	11.6–12.91	average
June 1608	20	30–40	13.3–17.7	} average
August 1608	16.6	23.3–30	11.23–14.45	} average
June 1612	20	26.7	10.08	poor
May 1614	15	26.8–30	14.3–16	average to good
April 1636	20	28.6	11.4	} very good
August 1636	10.4	32.5	24	} very good
July 1638	15.8	52.5	26.58	very good
July 1639	21	42	16	good
June 1640	18	40	17.7	} excellent
July 1640	16	66	33	} excellent
July 1641	12	40	26.6	very good
August 1696	18	30.5	18.6	good
July 1697	21.8	30	15.6	average to good
July 1698	31	40	10.3	poor
July 1699	22.6	40	14.14	average
July 1700	23	47	16.3	good

Arithmetic mean of yields for barley in:
1570–5   8.8 bushels = 1.1 qtr
1606–14   13.6   = 1.7 qtr
1636–41   25   = 3.12 qtr   } 1.92 qtrs
1696–1700   14 bushels = 1.75

[a] My own comment derived from inventory data.

APPENDIX 6

Regional differences in sowing rates

1 Chalk soils, neutral to alkaline

Date	Area	Seed sown per acre in bushels		Authority
		Barley	Peas	
1208–1329	N. Wilts.	$2\frac{1}{2}$–4	$1\frac{1}{2}$–$2\frac{3}{4}$	Gras 1926: Appendix A
1329–1449	N. Wilts.	4	2	Gras ibid.
1310–30	Oxon.	3–4	–	Harvey 1965: 43
14 cent.	Wilts.	3.18–5.11	–	Titow 1972: Appendix B
1540–1650	Wilts.	3.83–4.1	4.2	Kerridge thesis: 133
1665	Dorset	3	2	Lennard EcHR IV: 23–45
1665	E. Gloucs.	3	?	Lennard ibid.

2 Clay soils, neutral to acid

Date	Area	Barley	Peas	Authority
1299	Worcs.	4–5	2–$2\frac{1}{2}$	Hollings 1934, 1950
1296–7	Essex	4	7	Midgley 1942, 1945
1452	Cambs.	4.4–5.2	4–5	Saltmarsh EcH III: 165
1534	Derby.	4	2	Fitzherbert 1534: 10, 11.
1562	Sussex[a]	8	–	Cornwall thesis: 118
1600–20	Leics.	4	–	Thirsk 1967: 654
1665	Devon	$2\frac{1}{2}$	$\frac{1}{2}$–$1\frac{1}{4}$	Lennard EcHR IV: 23–45
1665	Corn.	$2\frac{1}{2}$	$\frac{1}{2}$–$1\frac{1}{4}$	ibid.
1665	Yorks.	2–4	2	ibid.
1665	Kent	3	3–4	ibid.
1665	W. Gloucs.	3	2	ibid.
1973	Leics.	40	64	Mr Stops, Paddocks Farm, Kibworth Harcourt

3 National estimates

Date	Barley	Peas	Authority
Late 13 cent.	6	2	Lamond 1890: 67
1697	1/7 of the produce,		Cooper and Thirsk 972: 796
	i.e. 2.3	1.4	

[a] Heighton St Clair, light soil

APPENDIX 7

Prices in Leicestershire 1550–1700

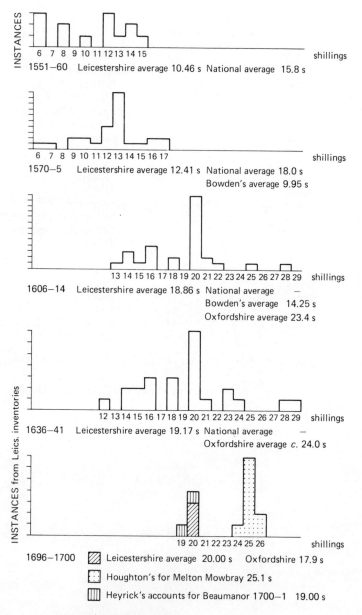

1551–60   Leicestershire average 10.46 s National average 15.8 s

1570–5   Leicestershire average 12.41 s National average 18.0 s
Bowden's average 9.95 s

1606–14   Leicestershire average 18.86 s National average   –
Bowden's average   14.25 s
Oxfordshire average 23.4 s

1636–41   Leicestershire average 19.17 s National average   –
Oxfordshire average *c.* 24.0 s

1696–1700   ⬛ Leicestershire average 20.00 s   Oxfordshire 17.9 s
⬛ Houghton's for Melton Mowbray 25.1 s
⬛ Heyrick's accounts for Beaumanor 1700–1   19.00 s

The price of wool per tod (28 lb)

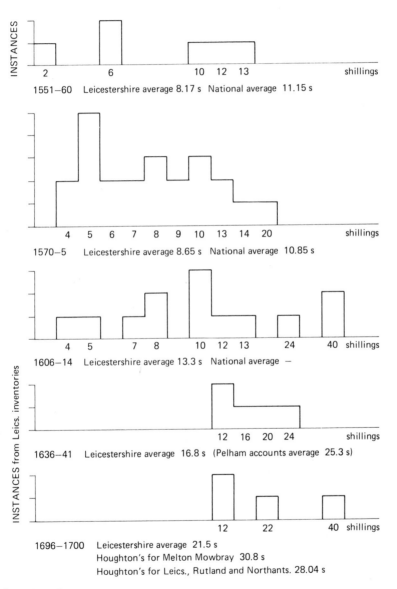

1551—60   Leicestershire average 8.17 s   National average 11.15 s

1570—5   Leicestershire average 8.65 s   National average 10.85 s

1606—14   Leicestershire average 13.3 s   National average —

1636—41   Leicestershire average 16.8 s   (Pelham accounts average 25.3 s)

1696—1700   Leicestershire average 21.5 s
Houghton's for Melton Mowbray 30.8 s
Houghton's for Leics., Rutland and Northants. 28.04 s

The price of peas per quarter

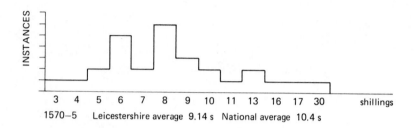

1570–5   Leicestershire average 9.14 s   National average 10.4 s

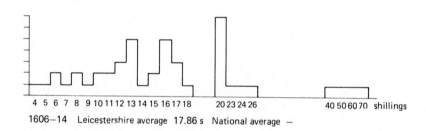

1606–14   Leicestershire average 17.86 s   National average —

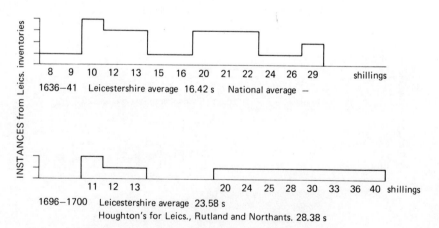

1636–41   Leicestershire average 16.42 s   National average —

1696–1700   Leicestershire average 23.58 s
Houghton's for Leics., Rutland and Northants. 28.38 s

The price of malt per quarter

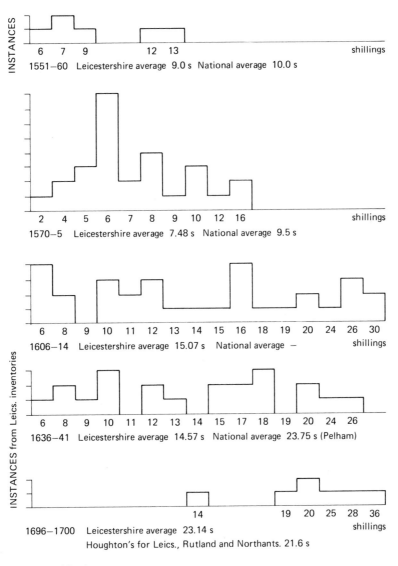

6   7   9   12   13   shillings
1551–60   Leicestershire average 9.0 s National average 10.0 s

2   4   5   6   7   8   9   10   12   16   shillings
1570–5   Leicestershire average 7.48 s National average 9.5 s

6   8   9   10   11   12   13   14   15   16   18   19   20   24   26   30
1606–14   Leicestershire average 15.07 s   National average —   shillings

6   8   9   10   11   12   13   14   15   17   18   19   20   24   26
1636–41   Leicestershire average 14.57 s National average 23.75 s (Pelham)

14   19   20   25   28   36
1696–1700   Leicestershire average 23.14 s   shillings
Houghton's for Leics., Rutland and Northants. 21.6 s

The price of barley per quarter

APPENDIX 8

Wills and inventories for Kibworth Harcourt

Kibworth lies within the Archdeaconry of Leicester whose records are now housed in Leicestershire County Record Office. The series of Kibworth wills begins in 1516 and continues without interruption to 1649. After the interregnum the series begins again in 1660 and continues to 1700 and beyond. They are usually written and witnessed by the curate and after the usual formula commending the soul to Almighty God and the body to be buried in the churchyard, they go on to make an offering to the mother church at Lincoln, and in pre-Reformation days to their parish church and often to other local churches with which they have some special connection – a useful indicator perhaps to short-distance migration. Both before and after the Reformation they leave money, malt or bread to the poor in their village, often naming each recipient and giving some indication of their condition, whether widow or servant or single man. Then, according to temperament, they either run through the list of kin leaving to each a carefully considered portion, or they run through a list of their goods allocating these to members of the family, followed by a list of after-thoughts. Both types have their contribution to make to the modern enquirer. The residual legatee is then named and the witnesses. By the 1530s an inventory of goods often accompanies the will and a supervisor was named and/or an executor, in accordance with 21 Hen. VIII c. 5.§.4.

In law, land held in socage tenure could be devised by will (32 Hen. VIII) and before 55 Geo. III copyhold was devisable or not according to the custom of the manor. Leases were chattels and could be devised by will. After the 1580s Kibworth copyholds were held by 21-year leases and so could be devised by will, though the custom of the manor held that land should pass first to the widow and then to the eldest son. So the only restraint upon a freeholder or copyholder at Kibworth was that of custom; the law offered no opposition or impediment.

An executor's duties were to pay, receive or acquit debts (Wentworth 1656: 43–4). He (or she) could pay off debts in whatever order found convenient and could pay himself first if he pleased. The executor could sell land to pay debts but not to provide money for legacies, portions and such like (Burn 1842: 303). Chattels, including corn growing on the land, could not descend to the heir; those which had not been devised became the residue and were held in trust by the executor for the next of kin. It is not surprising, therefore, to find at Kibworth that the executor was usually the wife or heir.

According to ecclesiastical law, debts owing to the deceased should be included in the inventory, though desperate debts need not be included in the total. Debts owing to others should not be put in the inventory because they do not belong to the testator. However, it was the practice in south-east Leicestershire to list debts in the will and credits in the inventory which allows one an interesting insight into the credit network of the countryside.

APPENDIX 9

The parish register

The first volume of the parish register runs from 1574–1725 and covers the three townships in the parish: namely, Kibworth Harcourt, Kibworth Beauchamp and Smeeton Westerby. There are no entries for the years 1582 and 1640–1 inclusive. Entries are incomplete for 1578–80 and for 1642–8, and on average about once in every two and a half years there are no entries for a complete month, the reason for which is not clear. Most of the clerical work was done by the rector's curate who can be identified not only from his signature in the register but also in the penmanship of the wills and his presence as witness to these wills. William Sawson was curate in 1574 and kept a perfunctory list of births, deaths and marriages on paper. Peter Sargiant succeeded him in 1581 and copied Sawson's lists into a handsome leather-bound book with parchment leaves. He continued Sawson's practice of merely listing names until in 1604 the new rector, Dr John Berridge, began to take an active interest in his pastoral duties (Woodford 1868: list of rectors and curates). From this date the name of a child's father is given and the register becomes more useful to the historian. Sargiant died in 1618 and Samuel Marshall kept the register for a few years until succeeded by Jacob Weston, curate, in 1625, who continued to keep the register in the same manner as his predecessors, though rather less neatly. The rector, John Berridge, was succeeded by Dr William Berridge BD in February 1639,[1] but in 1640 William Hunt BD replaced him until ejected in 1654 (Woodford: ibid.), with James Weston continuing as his curate. In 1634 the practice was begun of entering the names of both parents at a child's christening, which practice was kept up until 1660, and from 1648 onwards a note was made of the township to which the subject of the entry belonged: Beauchamp, Harcourt or Smeeton Westerby. It becomes possible at this point to reconstitute most Harcourt families and to give dates of baptisms and burials, though the date of marriage in many cases has to be inferred from the date of the birth of the first child. From the wills we can often discover the wife's maiden name. In 1654 John Yaxley MA was appointed minister and in December 1653 one of the leading men in Kibworth Beauchamp, William Coleman, was chosen as parish 'Register' in accordance with the Ordinance of 24 August 1653 (Tate 1969: 46). Apart from entering the date of birth rather than of baptism, Coleman continued to keep the register after the manner of his predecessors until September 1654 when he began noting the calling of banns before each marriage. This was a tedious and repetitive task and unfortunately he only kept it up for two years, but from the entries we learn not only the occupation and home town of the groom but also the occupation and home town of the bride's father and whether or not she had been married before. In accordance with the Ordinance of 1655 marriages took place before two witnesses in the presence of the local JP, in this case Thomas Brudenell, esquire, of Stonton Wyville. The experiment was shortlived, however, and by 1656 the ceremony had reverted to its traditional pattern. In April 1658 William Coleman

[1] Parish register fo. 32b. According to Nichols he was also lord of the manor of Kibworth Beauchamp.

delivered the register into the hands of John Yaxley and the period of secular administration was at an end. Yaxley, who was formally inducted into the rectory on 5 March 1659, introduced the practice of grouping all christenings together, followed by all burials, followed by marriages. This implies that he kept a working list of which the register is the fair copy. The heading 'marriages' remained blank until 1665, but otherwise entries remained detailed save in one important respect; the name of a child's mother was not noted. Robert Edwards BD became rector in 1662 and remained in this post until he retired in 1701. He signed the register himself and there is no mention of a curate in the wills, so it would seem that he performed the administrative duties of his office himself. The number of churchwardens was at the same time reduced from six – two from each township – to three. In 1676 he reported to the commissioners of the Compton census that there were no papists in the parish and no nonconformists in Smeeton Westerby, but that there were eleven nonconformists in Kibworth including five women.[2] Fortunately, therefore, the demographic record provided by the register is not seriously distorted by the non-registration of dissenters (Glass and Eversley 1965: 397, 379–93). (In fact, the children of nonconformists were probably always recorded, for we have in 1699 two entries to the effect that a child has been privately baptised and later brought to church, but the day and the month of the ceremony are not given.)

In the case of burial entries, the names of both parents were given from 1625 onwards, and in the case of married women, the name of her husband if still living. Widows are noted as such and the name of their late husband not given, bachelors are noted as such and unmarried women as 'singlewoman' or occasionally 'spinster', but spinster could also be used of a spinner, usually a widow. A man's name alone implies that he was or had been married and occasionally a guess is made at his age, for example 'about a hundred years old'.[3] Occupation is only consistently noted for the years 1636–7 and 1699, though the nature of a man's trade is mentioned in the odd case throughout the period.

From this description of the register it will be apparent that family reconstitution was only possible from 1604 until the thirties and for the fifties until the nineties. Every family which for any period of time, however short, was noted in the register as coming from Kibworth Harcourt was reconstituted and checked against the wills. Some men, buried in the parish, turned out to have had no family; other men, married in the village, left before their children were grown up, but for the majority an uninterrupted family tree can be recovered for the period 1604–1700. Fifty families were found in the last category, and most if not all of them left a will in one or more generations.

[2] Leics. Museum I D 41/43/48–97.

[3] Parish register fo. 48a. Richard West of Kibworth Harcourt, 26 March 1660.

APPENDIX 10

Letter of John Pychard to the Warden and Fellows of Merton College (c. 1447–8 at the latest)[1]

Moste wyrshyppefull and reverent lord y commende* me unto yowre worthe lordeshyp desyrynge to here of yowre prospertyte and bodyly helthe þe wyche almygthe godde preserve and susteyne unto hys plesans and† yowre welthe and welfare. And yf yt be plesynge to yowre worthy lordeshype þt y that am yowre owne pore servand and manne unto my power in watte‡ servyse þt lythe in me abyde uppon yowre lorde ye wyll wyth alle my harte. And forthermore syr y byggyd a place in þe der ʒere wanne y mygthe full ᵹvyll have done hytte, þe wyche byggyng coste me more than xl s′ and now fowle and wrongfully am [y] putt a wᵁy from hytt[by] recorde of heˢ Robard Polle[2] and all my neyburres. And yf yt plese yowre gracyuˢ lordeshyp þt yʳ mygthe have yowre gode wylle to have my cornmandis in þt place be rygthe os my truste bothe wasse wanne y byggyd hytte and ever hathe ben thorow you, y be seche you specyally os every y may deserve hytte oyder in dede or in preyer. Forthermore syr ye grauntyd me a cotage at leycetur before John Camden[3] þe bayle for xii d′ ʒerely þe wyche he takythe ʒerely ii s′ of me. For þt ys to saye thys ʒere and have no favor at all. And truly syr y wasse presonynd at Leycetur for youre love iiii dayes togeder and laye their and loste x s′ of mone or y mygthe gete thense. And thus vexyd and trobuld gretely for yowre love in diverse wyse bothe in penanse of body and losse [of] goddes preyynge yow ever more and besechynge you tendurly to consydur ther to. Also syr y laburd at þe¶ of yowre halle wanne no manne wolde labur ther but y. In no maner of warke y abode stylle uppon hytte alle weye and dysseyvyd yow nowgthe. And syr y beseche yow of yowre gracyus lordeshyp þt y mygthe have a lytull cotage lyethe even faste be þt at y have of ii s′ and vi d′ rent ʒerely for my sonne. And truly syr he shall truly pay ʒou ʒere be ʒere and þt y under take. And truly syr y shuld have hadde viii s′ for reperashon of my howse at furste comynge inne and ʒyt y hadde not a peny but sett uppon þe rente preyynge you þt y may have þe same scyle unto my costes be comyn uppe þt y have leyde ther over of þis mone þt y shulde have hadde. And forthermore syr we have a yonge manne wt us þe qwyche y[s] a godely scoler os for a grameryen after þe forme of þe cuntreye and a lyckely manne of person to doo you servyse. And truly syr he ys þe sonne of one of yowre tenandes þt ys to saye þe sonne of Agnes Powmer.[4] And truly syr the manne desyryd to have conynge over allthynge nowgthe wytstandynge he mygthe have maysters in þe kynggis howse and in dyverse places but he

---

* or *comawnde*. † two *ands* in ms. ‡ *watte*, transcription uncertain.

§ *he*, deleted on ms. ¶ a word has been omitted here in the ms.

[1] MM 3344.

[2] Robert Polle, bailiff 1406–43.

[3] John Caunden, bailiff 1446–8.

[4] William Palmer was aged 12 in 1439. His father, John, was last mentioned in the court rolls in 1448.

wolde evermore have conynge. And truly syr we prey you alle yowre tenandis everyche one þt ʒe wolde cheryshe hym for truly syr he shull be at you in haste and forsothe ʒe wyll lyke hys condysshons have ʒe asayde hym a wyle bothe for governans and person. Nomore at þis tyme but almygthe godde have you in hys kepynge. Wrytton at Kybworthe in þe feste of seynt Huge' mart'.

He yowre owne manne and pore servand John Pychard[5]

---

[5] John Pychard is first mentioned in the court rolls in 1426. He took up a messuage and half a virgate in 1437 for an annual rent of 7s 9½d. This was confirmed to himself and his son in 1439. John was a butcher and his quarrelsome tendencies earned for him frequent entries in the rolls. He married one Agnes and is last heard of in 1454. Stevenson dated this letter to *c.* 1500, but internal evidence would indicate a date around 1447–8 if not earlier.

APPENDIX 11

The Polle family 1280–1602

The movements described in chapter seven on inheritance customs and the conclusions reached can be usefully illustrated by the accompanying chart outlining the descent of land within the Polle family during the period 1280–1700.

In 1280 there were four landholding branches in the village. The chances of the family becoming extinct were therefore rather remote. Nevertheless, the plagues struck hard. Robert, Hugh and Nicholas died in 1349, two Williams and another Nicholas in 1361–6 and another William in 1376. Two branches were thereby eliminated and the land went to outsiders. Robert's line came to an end when Nicholas died without heirs. His land was leased to the Saundurs family from 1399–1417 and then passed to William Polle, a member of the Nicholas Polle branch. Of this branch only William survived by 1380, his two brothers and his cousin having died without heirs. Unfortunately, since no rental survives for the early fifteenth century, we have no complete list of his lands or those of his son, we have only a list of their acquisitions. By 1484, William Polle held three virgates. By 1527 John Polle held eight or nine, three of which were held by virtue of his position as reeve. By 1660 there were only two survivors in the male line, and no Polle children were born in the village after 1602. A yeoman branch flourished throughout the seventeenth century in Glen Magna and a leather-trading branch in Market Harborough. So we see the effect of plague upon a family, the lack of interest in land until after the settlement in 1439 and the subsequent policy of steady accumulation. John and Amicia lived in some style in the 1520s, but their decision to partition the land among four sons reduced their successors to the degree of husbandmen. This is the type of traditional action which, had it been practised on a large scale among peasant proprietors in the formative years of the fifteenth century, would have precluded the accumulation of cash and returned the countryside within a generation or two of the plagues to the patchwork of half-virgate subsistence holdings which characterised the pre-plague economy.

The chart also illustrates the amount of information that can be gained for each holder from the court rolls alone; when he was sworn into tithing, when he inherited, what acquisitions he made, when he died, to whom he left his land. It also includes the sole example of a purchase in the Kibworth records. The Russell family, who were resident in Harcourt in 1377 and in Beauchamp in 1555, were granted 'one house between the Greathallyard and the horsemill, and a garden and close adjoining called the Littlehallyard' in 1432 by Thomas FitzEustace of Kibworth Harcourt. William Polle purchased this two-virgate freeholding from John Russell in 1484 or therabouts. Part of this free land passed by marriage to the Clerke family and can be seen as Tenement 10a on the 1609 map, while the other remained in Polle hands as Tenement 10b.

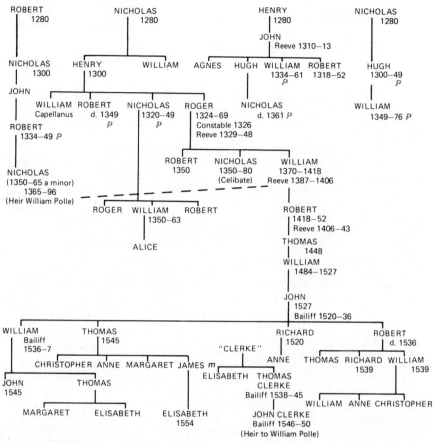

This family tree illustrates, among other things, the effect of pestilence (P) upon the family fortunes in the 14 cent., the accumulation of family land into the hands of one branch in the 15 cent. and its redispersal among four sons in the 16 cent. No Polles were born in Kibworth after 1602 and the land passed, through marriage, to the Clerke family.

The Polle family, 1280–1550

Notes

1. Kibworth Harcourt: its geography and early history

1 MM 1635 map of Kibworth.
2 MM 6402. *'Colisbrigge'* (1334) and Merton Maps.
3 Seminar held at Peterhouse, Cambridge, Feb. 1980.
4 PRO, SP 14.112.91.
5 Plans in the possession of the excavators; copies in the Leicester City Museum.
6 Catalogue of drawings made by Sir Henry Dryden (1912), p. 41, deposited at the Public Library, Northampton.
7 Pers. comm. from Mr G. C. Dunning 17 May 1972.
8 Pers. comm. from Dr Webster 1972.
9 MM 6212 (1303–4). The reeve accounted for 4s received from the sale of herbage *'in parvo monte'* over three years.
10 *Domesday Book*, ed. A. Farley (1783), II, fols. 377, 242, 225, 346, 234a.
11 MM 6376.
12 MM 6388.
13 PRO Cal. Inq. Misc. I. p. 102.
14 PRO, Cal. Pat. 1266–72, 264.
15 PRO, Cal. Pat. 1266–72, 150, 264.
16 Inference. No surviving deed.
17 MM 2876.
18 MM 2884.
19 MM 2877.
20 PRO, Fine. Trinity 55 Hen III (1271). This annual rent was surrendered by Saer in 1279. MM 2886.
21 MM 2871.
22 PRO *Inq. post mortem* Walter de Merton, 18/10 Vol. II, p. 145 (6 Ed I, 1278).
23 Ibid.
24 PRO Misc. Inquisitions no. 295.
25 MM 6366–6374.
26 MM 2857.
27 MM 2900.
28 MM 2902–2906, 2861.
29 MM 2901.
30 MM 2907, 2909, 2860.
31 MM 2911, 2871, 2944; PRO De Banco Rolls, 48 Hilary II Ed I (1283) m. 46d. Leyc.
32 MM 2867, 2893, 2895, 3017.

2. Land and tenants

1 MM 2867, 2869, 3017.
2 MM 2928, 2869.
3 MM 6377.
4 MM 6389.
5 MM 6366, 6367, 6370, 6373a-h, 6374a-c.
6 MM 6376.
7 MM 6383.
8 MM 3094, 6379.
9 MM 6367 and court rolls *passim*.
10 MM 2945, 3015, 6373; PRO, IPM Nich. Gryffen, 16 April, I Hen VIII (1510).
11 MM 2931–2, 2942, 2956, 2960, 2967, 2987, 3009, 3011–2, 2970, 2986.
12 PRO, IPM Richard de Harcourt 21/6 Vol. I, p. 111, 2 April 42 Hen III (1258).

3. Administration

1 PRO SC 5 Tower series. W. Illingworth and J. Caley (eds), *Rotuli Hundredorum* (Record Commission, 1818) 2, pp. 436, 445, 483, 484, 496, *inter al.*
2 Ibid., East Cambridgeshire vills, *passim*.
3 MM 2925, 2945, 3015, 6383; PRO Fine. Trinity 55 Hen III (1271).
4 MM 6421.12 (1430).
5 MM 6383, 6370.
6 MM 6198.
7 MM 6383 17 Ed I.
8 MM 6404 11 Ed III.
9 MM 6405 25 Ed III and *passim*.
10 MM 6383 17 Ed II.
11 MM 6452.
12 MM 6446.
13 MM 6447.5.
14 MM 6455.
15 MM 6408.13.
16 MM 6376.
17 MM 6196.
18 MM 6215, 2989.
19 MM 6219.
20 MM 6224.
21 MM 6240.
22 PRO E 179 133/1; 133/2.
23 MM 6202, 6205, 6217.
24 MM 6205, 6209.
25 MM 6218.
26 MM 6219.
27 MM 6230.
28 MM 6217, 6277, 6388, 6394, 6253.
29 MM 6402 8 Ed III.
30 MM 6378, 6405.
31 MM 6406, 6464.

32 MM 4122.
33 MM 3344.
34 MM 6196.
35 MM 6407.20.
36 MM 6243.
37 MM 6372.
38 MM 6230.
39 MM 6219.
40 MM 6217, 6222, 6228, 6230.
41 MM 6240.
42 MM 6199.

4, The plagues and their consequences, 1348–1450

1 PRO SC 2 183.76 f.5–9.
2 MM 6405 23 Ed III.
3 PRO E.179 133/29.
4 PRO E.179 133/109.
5 MM 2929, 2934, 2939, 2941, 3000, 3010.
6 PRO, IPM C series II, Vol. 13, 143, 985.
7 PRO, IPM C series II, Vol. 19 (70) (992).
8 MM 6372.
9 MM 6415.2
10 MM 6421.8.
11 MM 6425.1.
12 MM 6425.1 entry for John Hall.
13 PRO E.179 133/29, 35.
14 MM 6420.5.
15 MM 6302.
16 MM 6321.
17 MM 6408.8.
18 MM 6342.
19 MM 6465, 6324.

5. Kibworth in the early modern period, 1450–1700

1 MM 1373.
2 MM 6447b.
3 MM 6375.
4 MM 6443.
5 MM 6321.
6 MM 6340, 3355.
7 Leics. Museum. 46' 28/166.
8 PRO E 179/133 109, 125.
9 MM 6324, 6326, 6465.
10 MM 2784.
11 MM 3015.
12 MM 6443.
13 MM 6447.3.
14 MM 6448.
15 MM 6.1 Book of Leases 1578, p. 141b, also MM 6362ff.

5. Kibworth in the early modern period, 1450–1700 (*cont*)

16 MM 6354.
17 MM 6.1, p. 66b.
18 MM 6.1, p. 31.
19 Leics. City Museum 11 D 53/VIII/6/1.
20 MM 6448.
21 MM 6447.7 and 1609 map; 6.1, p. 41b.
22 MM 6375.
23 MM 5.17 and 1635 map.
24 NRO, Delapre Abbey, Northampton. ASR 562; 142.
25 MM 6448–9; 6451–2; 6455.
26 MM 1779 map.
27 LRO, EN/C/161/1.
28 Department of Environment. CPE/UK/1926, 16 Jan. 47, No. 4023 RS; 2175 FS.
29 PRO Cal. Pat. 1557–8, No 935 in 8–9.
30 PRO Cal. Pat. Rolls, 1557–8, No 929 in 25.
31 MM 6.1, p. 132.
32 Bodleian. MS Top Northants b.1. f.34.
33 LRO DE 526/126. See also chap. 7, tenements 45–46.
34 Bodleian. Idem. f.103.
35 MM 6362.1 ff and 6447.1.

6. The open fields and husbandry

1 MM 6424.15.
2 MM 6407, 6408, 6418, 6438.2.
3 MM 6420.7.
4 MM 6368.1.
5 MM 5.17.
6 MM 6368.1.
7 Brudenell Mss. NRO, ASR 142; see also M. Havinden, 'The rural economy of Oxfordshire, 1580–1730' (unpublished Oxford B.Litt. thesis 1961) who found 40 acres the safe minimum for Oxfordshire in this period.
8 MM 6368.1 and see above chap. I.
9 MM 5.17.
10 Leicester Museum, Archives Dept. 46'28/98.
11 MM 6219.
12 Communication from Mr M. Stops of The Paddocks Farm, Kibworth Harcourt, to whom I am most grateful.
13 The testimony of the inventories for probate, Kibworth.
14 MM 6405 23 Ed III.
15 MM 6425.2.
16 MM 2784. A list of encroachments dated 16 May 1609.
17 MM 6420 (November, 9 Hen V). Similarly, in the seventeenth century, barley ground was twice the value of peas ground.
18 MM 6411 (May, Hen IV, internally dated to 1401) until 6421 (November, 6 Hen VI).
19 MM 6421 (June, 1 Hen VI) until 6424 (May, 17 Hen VI).
20 MM 6421 (December, 1 Hen VI).
21 The inventories for the archdeaconry of Leicester have been indexed by H.

Hartopp, *Leicestershire Wills and Administrations 1495–1649* (Brit. Rec. Soc.
XXVII) and 1660–1750 (Brit. Rec. Soc. LI). The inventories themselves
have been mounted and bound into files according to the date of the
granting of probate. Some files contain the inventories for one year only,
others contain a group of years. The original methods of indexing have
been retained and these vary over the years as clerks replaced one
another; in some, the inventories are numbered, in others they are
arranged alphabetically by author, in others there is no index at all.
However, given the name of the testator, his village and the date of
probate, it is possible, with patience, to find the inventory. Therefore, I
have not given references to individual inventories cited in the pages
which follow, but have been careful to give the date.

22 Kibworth parish register 1574–1725 f.46b (1658).
23 Leics. Museum 4628/98.
24 LRO DE/526/126 Humphrey Papers. Indenture between Thomasine Coleman and William Sheffield, dated 16 May 1646.
25 MM 6.1 Book of Leases p. 282a.
26 MM 6448.
27 Bodleian. Ms Top Northants b.1.
28 MM 6452.
29 MM 5.17. Correspondence filed in the 1635 Survey Book.

7. Village morphology and buildings

1 MM 6375.
2 LRO QS/44/2/43.
3 MM 6418, 6419.
4 MM 6420.3.
5 MM 6421.8.
6 MM 6423.
7 MM 6425.
8 MM 6421.17.
9 MM 6436, 6447.1.
10 MM 6447.5, 6447.7.
11 *c.* 1662.
12 *c.* 1694.
13 Bodleian. Ms Top Northants b.1 f. 34.
14 MM 6375, the 1527 rental, under freeholders.
15 Leics. Museum 3D36/23 Abstract of the Parker titles 1674–1743.
16 MM 6375, the 1527 rental under freeholders. MM Book of Leases p. 141b
   refers to the lease of the windmill and a malt mill. Also Leics. Museum
   3D36/23 Abstract of the Parker titles 1674–1743.
17 Leics. Museum. Parker Deeds 46'28/177–188 and 3D36/21–23. Also LRO
   Humphrey Papers DE 526/126.
18 MM 6442.3.
19 LRO, DE 560/10. William Burgess of Harborough and of Turlangton also
   held land at Smeeton and Stamford 1653–1674.
20 Leics. Museum 42 D 31/168.
21 LRO DE 526 letter 13 April 1864; Bodleian Ms Top Northants b.1.f.21; F. P.
   Woodford, *History of Kibworth and Personal Reminiscences* (London 1868).
22 MM 6340, 3355.

7. Village morphology and buildings (*cont*)

23 MM 3323; PRO Cal. Pat. 895, 16 July 1555.
24 MM 6.1 Book of Leases, fos. 132, 141, 282–2.
25 Bodleian. Ms Top Northants b.1, fos. 58, 112, 124.
26 MM 6367, 6368, and see map 13.
27 MM 6465, 6324.
28 MM 2946, 2958.
29 MM 6421.1 (1423).
30 MM 6447.7.
31 LRO DE 526/126 Humphrey Papers. Deed dated 13 Sept., 9 James I.
32 LRO DE 526/126. Indenture dated 1764.
33 PRO SC 2 183.76, 77; SC Hen. VII. 1808 Bailiff's account.
34 MM 6425, 1373.
35 PRO Series II 683/199. IPM for Christopher Polle (died 1597) taken in 1616.
36 LRO DE 526/126. Humphrey Papers. Deed dated 1772.
37 MM 6448.
38 MM 6362.13.
39 LRO DE 242. The Enclosure Award.
40 MM 6412.
41 MM 6421.8, 6425.
42 MM 6446, 6447.1.
43 Leics. Museum 3D 42/23/1.
44 MM 6420.8.
45 MM 6448; heiress Mary Oswin married William Clerke.
46 MM 6407.18. John Sandurs built a cottage *in viam regiam*, 1369.
47 Leics. Museum 46'28/177. Parker Deeds.
48 Leics. Museum 3D 36/19 & 20; 42D 31/168; 73/30/11.
49 MM 2924, 2926, 2923, 2925, 2943.
50 MM 2983, 2985, also 6219.
51 MM 6407.2.
52 MM 6407.1.
53 MM 6408.7.
54 MM 3355.
55 MM 2784.
56 MM 6442.3.
57 LRO DE 442. Deeds dated 1733, 1750, 1766, 1768.
58 MM 6372.
59 MM 6407.19.
60 MM 6440.2.
61 MM 6442.3.
62 MM 6421.2. The whole village was amerced for not mending the common fold (1423); MM 6424.8. Common fold called the 'Pynfold'.
63 MM 6375.
64 Bodleian. Ms Top Northants b.1. fo. 54.
65 MM 6451.
66 MM pre-enclosure map *c.* 1780.
67 LRO. Will dated 7 Sept. 1723.
68 MM 6407.1.
69 MM 5.17.
70 LRO DE 242. Enclosure Award.

71 MM 6362.8. Also Bodleian. Ms Top Northants b.l. fo. 1.
72 Ibid.
73 MM 6447.7.
74 MM 6448.
75 LRO DG 24/72.
76 MM 2941.
77 MM 2934, 2930.
78 MM 6465, 6324.
79 MM 3355.
80 MM 6.1 Book of Leases p. 66b.
81 MM 6362 (1617–20).
82 MM 6362 (1621–27).
83 MM 6362 (1642–79) and 6448.
84 MM 5.17.
85 LRO DE 886. Bond. 1748.
86 Papers in the possession of Mrs Leslie-Miller, Crossbank House, Kibworth Beauchamp.
87 Leics. Museum 46'28/169–170, and Bodleian. Ms Top Northants b.l. fo. 91.
88 MM 2784.
89 Bodleian. Ms Top Northants b.l. fo. 103, and LRO DE 526/126. Humphrey Papers 1864.
90 MM 6407.1.
91 MM 2956, 2953, 2945, 2960, 2932, 2957, 2970, 2986, 2931, 2942, 2987, 3012, 3011, 3089, 2925, 2915, 2954, 3009, 2937.
92 MM 6372, 6405.
93 MM 6405, 6407.13.
94 MM 3009.
95 MM 1373.
96 MM 6447.2.
97 LRO 1516. Katherine Polle's will.
98 MM 6442.4.
99 MM 6373.3. The rector of the church land held $1\frac{1}{2}$ virgates for 32s p.a. in 1300.
100 Bodleian. Ms Top Northants b.l. fo. 7.
101 MM 6456.
102 Bodleian. Ms Top Northants b.l. fos. 19, 20.
103 LRO DE 526/126. Humphrey Papers. Conveyance dated 1772, but see also deeds dated 1635, 1639, and a will dated 1768.
104 MM 2916.
105 MM 6407.1.
106 MM 6408.9 (1390).
107 MM 6420.3, 6421.10–12.
108 MM 6424.2.
109 MM 6447.1.
110 MM 6447.1, 6448.
111 MM 6455.
112 LRO DE 526/126. Humphrey Papers. Abstracts of L. Humphrey's estate papers; Leics. Museum 3D 36/23 and 3D 46'28/177.
113 Idem.
114 Aerial photograph. Dept. of the Environment. CPE/UK/1926. 16 Jan. 1947. 4023 RS.

7. Village morphology and buildings (*cont*)

115 MM 6408.4, 6424.8, 6427, 6436, 6425.2.
116 MM 6426.3c; 6430; 6434; 6435.2; 6438.1; 6447.6.
117 MM 6421.2b; 6423; 6447.1; 6447.5.
118 MM 6421.3a; 6421.2; 6421.7, 11, 13, 15, 17; 6423.
119 MM 6408.11; 6407.11; 6407.21.
120 MM 6451.
121 MM 1609 Map of Kibworth Harcourt.
122 MM 6405 31 Ed III; 6242; 6421.18; 6424.1, 11, 13; 6465; 6341; 6323–27; 3126; 2819.
123 MM 6420.15.
124 LRO Inventory for Robert Standley of Knighthorpe (Loughborough), 13 May 1639.
125 MM 6465; 6324.
126 LRO Inventory dated 1568.
127 LRO Inventory dated 2 March 1673 f.74.
128 MM 1635 map of Kibworth Harcourt.
129 LRO Inventory dated 10 Sept. 1683 fo. 94.
130 LRO Inventory dated 20 Jan. 1686 fo. 151.

8. The economy of the small landholder

1 B.M. Add Mss. Pelham Accounts.
2 Housed in the Leicestershire Record Office.
3 For a collection of recent monographs see *Land, Kinship and Lifecycle*, eds. E. A. Wrigley and R. M. Smith (Arnold, forthcoming). The Cambridge Group is a unit of the Social Science Research Council and is based at 27 Trumpington Street, Cambridge.
4 MM 6405 23 Ed III; 6405 31 Ed III; 6407 33 Ed III; 6409 22 Ric II.
5 MM 6407 33 Ed III.
6 LRO Enclosure Award. DE 242. MM 6202, 6205, 6217.
7 MM 6372.
8 MM 6407.1.
9 MM 6424.14 (1442). See also MM 6401.1, 10, 25, 28, 29; 6408.12, 16; 6415; 6417; 6419; 6420; 6421; 6424; 6432.
10 This servant also appears on the Poll Tax list.
11 PRO E.179 133/35, 26.
12 PRO E.179 133/109, 124.
13 MM 6375; 6447. 6375 has been partially mutilated so that the list of names supplied is not a complete one.
14 MM 6451.
15 MM 6465, 6324.
16 PRO 179 133/35 (Gumley); 133/29 (Fleckney); 134/243 (Cheddingworth); 134/287 (Glooston); MM 6439.1.
17 LRO Inventories *passim*. Also PRO E.179 134/283 (1611) where Robert Carter, *Gent*, is listed as worth £3 in goods.
18 MM 6376 10 Ed I (1282).
19 MM 6421.1. And see above p. 126 and maps 8–10.
20 MM 6405 (30 Ed III), for situation see map 8.
21 MM 6350, for situation see map 4.
22 MM 6424.16.

23 PRO Cal. Pat. Rolls 1446–52. 10 Nov. 1451. See Farnham, p. 252.
24 MM 6434 *et alia*.
25 MM 6452 *et alia*. See chap. 7, Ten. 34.
26 MM 6441 ff.
27 MM 1373 (1485). For situation see maps 8, 9.
28 PRO E.179 133/35.
29 MM 6366.7; 6407.19.
30 MM 6421.1.
31 LRO Inventory of John Smith 1541.
32 LRO Inventory of Thomas Polle 1738.
33 MM 6446.
34 LRO Inventory of John Polle of Market Harborough 1639/40 (73).
35 PRO E. 179 133/35.
36 MM 6407.21; PRO E.179 133/35.
37 LRO Inventory of Richard Roworth 1584.
38 MM 6371.
39 PRO Cal. Pat. 6 Nov. 1558.
40 LRO Humphrey Papers DE.526.
41 PRO Lay Subsidy 251/4 Mich. 1664. Also see Farnham, p. 257.
42 LRO Humphrey Papers DE.526.
43 MM 6448; 6455.
44 MM 3094.

9. The size and composition of the peasant household

1 MM 6376, 8 Ed I.
2 PRO E 179 133/26 (AD 1377 or 1379); E 179 133/35 (AD 1381); Farnham, V, pp. 248–9.
3 MM 6407.15; 6407.22.
4 MM 6407.18; 6407.28.
5 MM 6376.
6 MM 6390.
7 MM 6391.
8 MM 6389.

10. Inheritance strategies

1 E.g. Swaffham Prior. Cambridge University Library. EDC. E.C./1.
2 MM 6405, 23 Ed III.
3 MM 6407.4, 34 Ed III.
4 MM 6389.
5 Gloucester Cathedral Library, Frocester Register B (1393) together with ten volumes labelled 'Deeds and Sales'.
6 MM 6396, 6398.
7 MM 6405, 6407.4.

Bibliography

A. Principal Manuscript Sources

Oxford, Merton College Muniments (MM)

Manor court records (AD 1276–1700): MM 6376–6457; 6373.4, 6.

Bailiff's accounts (AD 1283–1682): MM 6196–6362, 6445.

Rentals and Terriers: MM 6366–6375, 1373, 6447, 5.17
2928, 2935, 2945, 3094, 6425,
6326, 6448–6449, 6451–6452, 6455,
6365, 6.1 Book of Leases.

Tithing Lists: MM 6376 (8 Ed I, 1280), 6449, 6451.

Repair bills: MM 2819, 3126, 6312, 6324, 6405
(31 Ed III), 6421.1; 6424.1, 11, 12;
6465.

Administrative: MM 3094, 2784, 2908, 3322, 4122.

Maps dated AD 1609, 1635, 1779 and undated nineteenth-century maps.

Deeds: College dealings with the following families:

Harcourt:	MM 2928, 2870, 2920, 2890, 2887, 2886, 2944, 2989.
Apetoft:	MM 2959, 3094.
Ingwardby, Fodringeye, Candevere:	{ MM 2868, 2916–2921, 2919, 2935, 2984, 3017, 3021 and duplicates.
Tayllard:	MM 2871, 2911.
Clive:	MM 2857, 2900.
Ewelle:	MM 2861, 2902–2906.
Portsmouth:	MM 2901.
Worting:	MM 2860, 2909, 2967, 2907.
Wytside:	MM 2867, 2893, 2895, 3017.
Warwick:	MM 2920, 2989.
Walter de Merton:	MM 2871, 2876, 2877, 2884.
Boton:	MM 2897.
Parson:	MM 2869, 2896.
Caumpe:	MM 2915.
Clerke:	MM 3355, 3319.
Polle:	MM 3323, 6464, 6465.
Brown:	MM 2929, 2930, 2934, 2939, 2941, 3000, 3010, 3322.
Sybile:	MM 2923, 2925, 2926, 2943, 2945, 2983, 6373.5, 2924.

Leicestershire, in private ownership

St Wilfrid's Church, Kibworth: Parish register. Vol. I 1574–1725.
                                            Vol. II 1787–1812.
Mrs Leslie-Miller, Crossbank House, Kibworth Beauchamp:
                                      Haymes Deeds (1894).
Mr F. B. Aggas, 5 Springfield Close, Kibworth Beauchamp:
                                      Archaeological plans of the Mound,
                                      the windmill site, a section through
                                      Banwell Furlong. Also a photographic
                                      survey of every house in the parish
                                      and of alterations thereto.
Northamptonshire Central Library,   Abington St, Northampton NN1 2BA:
                                      Henry Dryden's sketches of his excavation
                                      of the Mound in 1863.
Northamptonshire Record Office (NRO), Delapre Abbey, Northants
                                      Brudenell maps and papers. Mss. ASR 142.

B. Primary Printed Sources

Allison, K. J. 'An Elizabethan village census', *BIHR*, 36 (1963), 91–103.

Archbold, W. A. J. 'An assessment for wages 1630', *EHR*, 1st ser., XII (1897), 307–12.

Barker, T. 'The rates of servants, labourers and artificers, set down and assessed at Okeham, within the County of Rutland, by the Justices of the Peace there, 28 April 1610', *Archaeologia*, 1st ser., XI (1794), 200–7.

Bateson, M. ed. *Records of the Borough of Leicester*. Vols. I–IV, Cambridge, 1899–1923.

Bergin, A. ed. *The Law of the West Goths according to the Manuscript of Aeskil*. Rock Island, 1906.

Best Robinson, C. ed. *The Farming and Account Books of Henry Best of Elmswell*. Surtees Society, XXXIII (1857).

Beyerle, F. ed. *Leges Langobardorum, AD 643–866*. Westgermanisches recht series. Witzenhausen, 1972.

Blagrave, J. *The Epitome of the Whole Art of Husbandry*. London, 1669.

Bracton, *De Legibus et Consuetudinibus Anglie*. 2 vols. Ed. S. E. Thorne. Cambridge, Mass., 1968.

Bradley, R. ed. *Collection of Letters for the Improvement of Husbandry and Trade by John Houghton* (1727). 4 vols.

Calthorpe, C. *The Relation Betweene the Lord of a Manor and the Coppyholder his Tenant* (London, 1635) ed. by The Manorial Society, no. 10. London, 1907. (Bodleian Viner 486).

Clarke, G. T. 'The Customary of the Manor and Soke of Rothley in the County of Leicester', *Archaeologia*, XLVII (1882), 89–93.

Coke, E. *The Compleate Copy-holder, together with the Form of Keeping a Copy-hold Court and Court Baron*. London, 1641.

Cooper, J. and Thirsk, J. *Seventeenth Century Economic Documents*. Oxford, 1972.

Defoe, D. *A Tour Through the Whole Island of Great Britain*. 3 vols. Everyman, 1928; *A Tour Through England and Wales 1724–6*. Harmondsworth, 1971.

Dormer-Harris, M. ed. *The Coventry Leet Book 1420–1555*. Early Engl. Texts Soc. nos. 134, 135, 138, 146.

Dryden, Sir H. *Catalogue of Drawings* (1912). Public Library, Northampton.

Farley, A. ed. *Domesday Book* (1783), vol. II.

Farnham, G. F. ed. *Leicester Medieval Village Notes*. 6 vols. Leicester, 1929–33.

Fitzherbert, J. *The Boke of Husbandry* (1534). [Bodleian. Douce XX 3 (2).]

Fussell, G. E. ed. *Robert Loder's Farm Accounts, 1610–1620*. Camden Soc., 3rd ser. LIII (1936).

Hale, Sir M. *De Successionibus Apud Anglos: or a Treatise of Hereditary Descents*. London, 1700.

Hall, G. D. H. ed. *The Treatise on the Laws and Customs of England called Glanvill*. London, 1965.

Hall, H. ed. *The Pipe Roll of the Bishopric of Winchester, 1208–9*. London, 1903.

Hallam, H. E. 'Some thirteenth-century censuses', *EcHR*, 2nd ser. X (1957–8), 340–61.

Hardy le, W. ed. *Buckinghamshire Sessions Records* vol. 1. *1678–1694*, Aylesbury 1933.

Harrison, W. *A Description of England in Shakespear's Youth*, ed. F. S. Furnivall. London, 1877 and 1881.

Hart, W. H. ed. *Historia et Cartularium Monasterii Sancti Petri Gloucestriae*, III. Rolls Series, 1867.

Harvey, P. D. A. ed. *Manorial Records of Cuxham, Oxfordshire 1200–1359*. London, 1976.

Havinden, M. A. ed. *Household and Farm Inventories in Oxfordshire 1550–1590*. Oxfordshire Rec. Soc. XLIV (1965). London, 1965.

Henderson, W. G. ed. *Manuale et Processionale ad usum insignis Ecclesiae Eboracensis*. Surtees Soc. 63 (1875).

Hollings, M. ed. *The Red Book of Worcester*. 2 vols. London, 1934, 1950.

Hudleston, C. Roy ed. *Naworth Estate and Household Accounts, 1648–1660*. Surtees Soc. 168 (1955).

Hughes, P. L. and Larkin, J. F. *Tudor Royal Proclamations*, II. New Haven, Conn., 1969.

Illingworth, W. and J. Caley ed. *Rotuli Hundredorum*. 2 vols. Record Commission 1812–18.

Kelsall, R. K. 'A century of wage assessment in Herefordshire 1666–1762', *EHR*, LVII (1942), 115–19.

King, Gregory. 'National and political observations upon the state and conditions of England 1697', in *Seventeenth Century Economic Documents*, eds. J. Cooper and J. Thirsk. Oxford, 1972.

King, P. I. ed. *The Book of William Morton*. Northamptonshire Rec. Soc. XVI. Oxford, 1954.

Lamond, E. ed. *Walter of Henley's Husbandry, together with an anonymous Husbandry. Seneschaucie and Robert Grosseteste's Letters* (1890). *A Discourse of the Common Weale of this Realm of England*. Cambridge, 1893.

Larsen, L. M. ed. *The Earliest Norwegian Laws: being the Gulathing and the Frostathing Law*. Columbia Univ. Press, 1935.

Luders, A. *et al.* eds. *Statutes of the Realm*. 11 vols. HMSO (1810–28).

McArthur, E. A. 'Prices at Woodstock in 1604', *EHR*, 1st ser., XIII (1898), 299–302.

Markham, G. *Countrey Contentments or the English Huswife* (London, 1623); *Farewell to Husbandry* (London, 1620); *A New Orchard and Garden* (1623).

Midgley, C. M. ed. *Ministers' Accounts of the Earldom of Cornwall 1296–1297*. 2 vols. London, 1942, 1945.

Miyoshi, Yoko, ed. 'A rental and inheritance case from the manor court rolls of a Suffolk village', *Jimbun Gakuho*, 118 (1977), 1–35; 'Inheritance cases and related documents from the manor court rolls of a Suffolk village', *Jimbun Gakuho*, 127 (1978), 1–131.

Nicholls, J. 'The rates of wages of all manner of servants etc. in Warwickshire. 36 Car II (1684)', *Archaeologia*, 1st ser., XI (1794), 208–11.

Norden, J. *The Surveyor's Dialogue*. London, 1607.

Oschinsky, D. ed. *Walter of Henley*. Oxford, 1971.

Postan, M. M. and Brooke, C. N. L. eds. *Carte Nativorum*. Northamptonshire Record Society, XX (1960).

Putnam, B. H. 'Northamptonshire wage assessments of 1560 and 1667', *EcHR*, 1st ser. (1927–8), 124–31. 'The earliest form of Lambard's "Eirenarcha" and a Kent wage assessment of 1563', *EHR*, XLI (1926), 260–73.

Rathbone, A. *The Surveyor in Foure Bookes*. London, 1616.

Reed, M. 'Early seventeenth-century assessments for the borough of Shrewsbury'. *Transactions of the Salop Archaeological Society*, LVII (1956), 136–42.

Rogers, J. T. *A History of Agriculture and Prices in England*. 6 vols. (1866–1900), vols. II and IV.

Salter, H. E. ed. *The Medieval Archives of the University of Oxford*. Vol. II, Clarendon, 1921, pp. 129–42, 182–3.

Slade, C. E. ed. *The Leicester Survey*. Leicester, 1956.

Smith, J. ed. *Men and Armour* (1608).

Stocks, H. ed. *The Records of the Borough of Leicester 1603–1688*. Vol. IV. Cambridge 1923.

Stocks, J. E. ed. *Market Harborough Parish Records 1531–1837*. London, 1926.

R. T., Gent. *The Tenant's Law, or the Laws concerning Landlords, Tenants and Farmers*. London, 1666.

Taylor, S. *History of Gavelkind* (1663).

Tingey, J. C. 'An assessment of wages for the county of Norfolk in 1660', *EHR*, 1st ser. XIII (1898), 522–7.

Tusser, T. *Five Hundred Points of Good Husbandry*. London, 1557.

Wentworth, Thomas. *The Office and Duty of Executors*. London, 1656.

Westgermanisches Recht series provides the latin text of the following *Barbarian Law Codes*:

  Salic. 5 vols. ed. K. A. Eckhardt (1953–56). 5 vols, Göttingen.
  Burgundian. ed. F. Beyerle (1936). Weimar.
  Ripuarian. ed. K. A. Eckhardt (1959). Hannover.
  Lombard. ed. F. Beyerle (1972). Witzenhausen.
  Merowingian. ed. K. A. Eckhardt (1935). Weimar.
  Saxon (Old English). ed K. A. Eckhardt (1958). Göttingen.
  Frisians. ed. H. K. Clausen (1941). Weimar.
  Alamanic. ed. K. A. Eckhardt. 2 vols, Hannover 1966
  Bavarian. ed. F. Beyerle (1926). Breslau.

Woodford, F. P. *History of Kibworth and Personal Reminiscences*. London, 1868.

C. Secondary Printed Sources

Appleby, A. B. 'Disease or famine? Mortality in Cumberland and Westmoreland 1580–1640', *EcHR*, 2nd ser. XXVI (1973), 403–31; *Famine in Tudor and Stuart England*. Liverpool, 1978.

Arensberg, C. A. and Kimball, S. T. *Family and Community in Ireland*. 2nd edn. Cambridge, Mass., 1968.

Ashley, W. *Bread of our Forefathers.* Oxford, 1928.

Aston, M. and Rowley, T. *Landscape Archaeology: an Introduction to Fieldwork Techniques on Post-Roman Landscapes.* London, 1974.

Aston, T. H. General ed. *The History of the University of Oxford.* Vol. I. J. Catto ed. Oxford (forthcoming).

Ault, W. O. *Open Field Farming in Medieval England.* London, 1972.

Auty, R. M. Part 57: Leicestershire, in *The Land of Britain,* ed. D. Stamp. London, 1937.

Baker, A. R. H. *Studies of Field Systems in the British Isles.* Cambridge, 1973; 'Some terminological problems in studies of British field systems', *AgHR* 17 (1969), 136–40.

Baker, T. C. *et al. Our Changing Fare: 200 years of British Food Habits.* London, 1966.

Bailey, M. W. *The English Farmhouse and Cottage.* London, 1961.

Barnes, J. A. 'Landrights and kinship in two Brennes hamlets', *Royal Anthrop. Institute,* 87 (1957), 31–56.

Bean, J. M. W. *The Estates of the Percy Family 1414–1537.* Oxford, 1958; 'Plague, population and economic decline in England in the later middle ages', *EcHR,* 2nd ser. XV (1963), 423–37; *The Decline of English Feudalism 1215–1540.* Manchester, 1968.

Bellairs, Col. 'The Roman Roads of Leicestershire', *TLAS,* VII (1893), 292–8, 357–64.

Bennett, M. K. 'British wheat yields per acre for seven centuries', *EcHR,* III (1935), 12–29.

Beresford, Guy. 'The medieval clayland village: excavation at Goltho and Barton Blount', *Medieval Archaeology,* Monograph Series 6 (1975).

Beresford, M. W. 'Ridge and furrow and the open fields', *EcHR,* 2nd ser. I (1948), 34–45; 'What is ridge and furrow?', *Country Life,* CV (1949), 472; *Antiquity,* 24 (1950), 34–55.

Berkner, L. 'The stem family and the developmental cycle of the peasant household: an eighteenth-century Austrian example', *American HR,* 77.2 (1972), 398–418; 'Inheritance, land tenure and peasant family structure: a German regional comparison', in *Family and Inheritance,* ed. Goody *et al.* Cambridge, 1976.

Beveridge, Lord. 'Westminster wages in the manorial era', *EcHR,* 2nd ser. VIII (1955–56), 18–35; 'Wages on the Winchester Manors', *EcHR,* 1st ser. VII (1936), 22–43.

Bishop, T. A. M. 'The Norman settlement of Yorkshire', in *Essays in Economic History,* vol. II, ed. E. M. Carus-Wilson. London, 1962; 'Assarting and the growth of the open fields', *EcHR,* VI (1935), 13–29.

Björkvik, H. 'The old Norwegian peasant community', *Scand. EcHR,* IV (1956), 33–61.

Bolton, E. G. 'Excavation of a house and malt kiln at Barrow, Rutland', *Med. Arch.,* IV (1960), 128–31.

Bowden, P. J. *The Wool Trade in Tudor and Stuart England.* London, 1962; 'Movements in wool prices 1490–1610', *Yorks. Bull. of Econ. and Soc. Research,* IV. 2 (1952), 107–24; 'The internal wool trade in England during the sixteenth and seventeenth centuries', Leeds Univ. D.Phil. thesis, 1952; 'Agricultural prices, farm profits and rents', in *The Agrarian History of England and Wales,* IV, ed. J. Thirsk. Cambridge, 1967.

Bowen, H. C. *Ancient Fields.* London, 1962.

Bowker, M. *The Secular Clergy in the Diocese of Lincoln 1495–1520*. London, 1968.

Bridbury, A. R. 'The Black Death', *EcHR*, 2nd ser. XXVI (1973), 557–92. *Economic Growth, England in the Later Middle Ages*. London, 1962.

Britnell, R. H. 'The proliferation of markets in England 1200–1349', *EcHR*, 2nd ser. XXXIV (May 1981), 209–21.

Britton, E. *The Community of the Vill: a study in the History of the Family and Village Life in fourteenth-century England*. Toronto, 1977.

Brodrick, G. C. *Memorials of Merton College*. Oxford, 1885.

Brunskill, R. W. *Illustrated Handbook of Vernacular Architecture*. London, 1971.

Buckatzsch, E. J. 'The geographical distribution of wealth in England 1086–1843', *EcHR*, 2nd ser. III (1950), 180–202.

Burn, R. *Ecclesiastical Law*. Vol. IV, 9th edn., ed. R. Phillimore. London, 1842.

Burnett, J. *Plenty and Want: the Social History of Diet in England, 1815 to the Present Day*. London 1966.

Burr-Lichfield, R. 'Demographic characteristics of Florentine patrician families from the sixteenth to the nineteenth centuries', *Jl.Ec.H.*, 29 (1969), 191–206.

Burton, W. *The Description of Leicestershire*. London, 1622.

Butcher, A. F. 'The origins of the Romney Freemen 1433–1523', *EcHR*, 2nd ser. XXVII.1 (1974), 16–27.

Butlin, R. A. See A. R. H. Baker, *Studies of Field Systems*; also 'Northumberland field systems', *AgHR*, 12 (1964), 99–120.

Campbell, M. *The English Yeoman under Elizabeth and the Early Stuarts*. New Haven, 1942.

Carus-Wilson, E. M. *Essays in Economic History*. 3 vols. London, 1954–62; 'Evidences of industrial growth on some fifteenth-century manors', *EcHR*, 2nd ser. XII (1959), 190–205.

Cecil, E. *Primogeniture. A Short History of its Development in Various Countries and its Practical Effects*. London, 1895.

Charles, F. W. B. 'Medieval cruck-buildings and their derivatives', *Med. Arch.*, monograph series, no. 2.

Charles-Edwards, T. 'A comparison of Old Irish with medieval Welsh land law', Oxford Univ. D.Phil. thesis 1971; also 'Kinship, status and the origins of the hide', *P & P*, 56 (1972), 3–33.

Chayanov, A. V. in *The Theory of Peasant Economy*, eds. D. Thorner, B. Kerblay, R. E. F. Smith. Illinois, 1966; *Peasant Farm Organisation*. Trans. R. E. F. Smith. Moscow, 1925.

Chibnall, A. C. *Sherington: Fiefs and Fields of a Buckinghamshire Village*. Cambridge, 1965.

Clark, H. M. 'Selion and soil type', *AgHR*, 8 (1960), 91–8.

Clark, P. 'Migration in England during the late seventeenth and early eighteenth centuries', *P & P*, 83 (1979), 57–90.

Clarkson, L. A. 'The leather crafts in Tudor and Stuart England', *AgHR*, 14 (1966), 25–39.

Cooper, J. 'Social distribution of land and men in England 1436–1700', *EcHR*, 2nd ser. XX (1967), 419–40.

Corder, P. ed. *The Roman Town and Villa of Great Casterton, Rutland*. Third Report 1954–58. Nottingham, 1951.

Cornwall, J. C. K. 'The agrarian history of Sussex, 1560–1640', London Univ. M.A. thesis 1953; 'Evidence of population mobility in the seventeenth century', *BIHR*, XL (1967), 143–52; 'The population of Rutland in 1522', *TLAS*, XXXVII (1961–2), 7–28.

Coulanges, Fustel de. *The Origin of Property in Land.* Trans. M. Ashley. London, 1904.

Court, W. H. B. *The Rise of the Midland Industries 1600–1838.* Cambridge, 1953.

Creighton, C. A. *A History of Epidemics in Great Britain from AD 664 to the Extinction of the Plague.* 2 vols. Cambridge, 1891.

Crowley, D. A. 'The later history of frankpledge', *BIHR*, XLVIII (May 1975), 1–15.

Curwen, E. C. *Air Photography and the Evolution of the Corn Field.* 2nd edn., London, 1938; *Plough and Pasture: the Early History of Farming.* New York, 1953.

Darby, H. C. and Terrett, I. B. *The Domesday Geography of Midland England.* Cambridge, 1954.

Davenport, F. G. *The Economic Development of a Norfolk Manor 1086–1565.* Cambridge, 1906 (Cass reprint, 1967).

Davis, R. H. C. 'East Anglia and the Danelaw', *TRHS*, 5th ser. 5 (1954), 23–39.

DeWindt, E. B. *Land and People in Holywell-cum-Needingworth: Structures of Tenure and Patterns of Social Organization in an East Midland Village 1252–1457.* Toronto, 1971.

Dodwell, B. 'The free tenantry of the Hundred Rolls', *EcHR*, 1st ser. XIV (1944–5), 163–71; 'Holdings and inheritance in medieval East Anglia', *EcHR*, 2nd ser. XX (1967), 53–66.

Dopsch, A. *The Economic and Social Foundations of European Civilization.* London, 1937.

Drummond, J. C. and Wilbraham, A. *The Englishman's Food.* Revised by D. Hollingsworth in 1958, London.

Du Boulay, F. R. H. 'Who were farming the English demesnes at the end of the middle ages?', *EcHR*, 2nd ser. XVII (1965), 443–55; *An Age of Ambition. English Society in the Late Middle Ages.* London, 1970; *The Lordship of Canterbury.* London, 1966.

Duby, G. *The Early Growth of the European Economy: Warriors and Peasants from the Seventh to the Twelfth Century.* London, 1974.

Dunning, G. C. and Jessup, R. T. 'Barrows', *Antiquity*, X (1936), 37–53.

Dyer, C. 'A small landholder in the fifteenth century', *Midland Hist.*, I (1971–2), 1–14; *The Estates of the Bishopric of Worcester 680–1540.* Cambridge, 1980.

Eden, P. *Dictionary of Land Surveyors and Local Cartographers of Great Britain and Ireland 1550–1850.* Folkestone, 1975.

Edwards, P. R. 'The horse trade of the Midlands in the seventeenth century', *AgHR*, 27.2 (1979), 90–100.

Elliott, B. *A History of Kibworth Grammar School.* Market Harborough, 1957.

Elton, C. I. and Mackay, H. J. H. *Robinson on Gavelkind: the Common Law or the Custom of Gavelkind.* 5th edn. London, 1897.

Emden, A. B. *A Biographical Register of the University of Oxford to AD 1500.* 3 vols. Oxford, 1957–9.

Everitt, A. 'The marketing of agricultural produce', in *The Agricultural History of England and Wales*, IV, ed. J. Thirsk. pp. 466–589, 396–465. Cambridge, 1967.

Everitt, A. and Stone, L. 'Social Mobility in England 1500–1700', *P & P*, 33 (1966), 16–55.

Ewart Evans, G. *The Horse in the Furrow.* London, 1960; *The Pattern under the Plough.* London, 1966; *Ask the Fellows who Cut the Hay.* London, 1956; *Where Beards Wag All: the Relevance of Oral Tradition.* London, 1970.

Eyre, S. R. 'The curving ploughstrip and its historical implications', *AgHR*, 3 (1955), 80–94.

Faith, R. 'The peasant land market in Berkshire during the later middle ages', Leicester Univ. Ph.D. thesis 1962; also 'Peasant families and inheritance customs in medieval England', *AgHR*, 16 (1966), 77–95; 'Freedom and villeinage and merchet', *P & P* 1983 (forthcoming).

Farmer, D. L. 'Some price fluctuations in Angevin England', *EcHR*, 2nd ser. IX (1956–), 34–43; 'Some grain price movements in thirteenth-century England', *EcHR*, 2nd ser. X (1957–8), 207–20; 'Some livestock price movements in thirteenth-century England', *EcHR*, 2nd ser. XXII (1969), 1–16.

Farnham, G. 'The Harcourt Family', *TLAS*, XV (1927).

Feavearyear, A. E. *The Pound Sterling. A History of English Money.* Oxford, 1931.

Fenger, O. 'The Danelaw and the Danish Law: Anglo-Scandinavian legal relations during the Viking Period', *Scand. Studies in Law*, vol. 16, pp. 83–96.

Field, R. K. 'Worcestershire peasant buildings, household goods and farming equipment in the later middle ages', *Med. Arch.*, IX (1965); 'The Worcestershire peasantry in the later middle ages', Birmingham Univ. M.A. thesis 1962.

Finberg, H. P. R. *The Agrarian History of England and Wales, Vol. I, Pt. II AD 43–1042.* Cambridge, 1972; and complete bibliography of his works in *Land, Church and People*, ed. J. Thirsk, Reading, 1970; *Lucerna*, London, 1964.

Finch, M. *The Wealth of Five Northamptonshire Families 1540–1640.* Northants. Rec. Soc., XIX. Oxford, 1956.

Fisher, F. J. 'The development of the London food market', *EcHR*, 1st ser. V (1935), 95–117; *Essays in the Economic and Social History of Tudor and Stuart England in honour of R. H. Tawney*, ed. F. J. Fisher. Cambridge, 1961.

Fitzherbert, R. H. C. 'The authorship of the Book of Husbandry and the Book of Surveying', *EHR*, XII (1897), 225–36.

Fox, Levi. *The Administration of the Honor of Leicester in the Fourteenth Century.* Leicester, 1940.

Frimannslund, R. 'Farm community and neighbourhood community', *Scand. EcHR*, IV (1956), 62–81.

Fussell, G. 'Four centuries of Leicestershire farming', *TLAS*, 24 (1949), 154–76.

Glass, D. V. and Eversley, D. E. C. *Population in History.* London, 1965.

Goody, J. 'The developmental cycle in domestic groups', *Cambridge Papers in Social Anthropology*, I (Cambridge, 1958); 'Strategies of heirship', in *Comparative Studies in Social History*, 15 (1973), 3–20.

Goody, J., Thirsk, J. and Thompson, E. P. eds. *Family and Inheritance in Rural Western Europe 1200–1800.* Cambridge, 1976.

Göransson, S. 'Regular open field patterns in England and Scandinavian Solskifte', *Geografiska Annaler*, XLIII (1961), 80–104.

Goubert, P. *Beauvais et la Beauvaisis de 1600 a 1730.* Paris, 1960; 'The French peasantry of the seventeenth century: a regional example', in *Crisis in Europe 1560–1660*, ed. T. H. Aston. London, 1965.

Gough, J. W. *The Rise of the Entrepreneur.* London, 1969.

Gras, N. S. B. *The Evolution of the English Corn Market.* Cambridge, Mass., 1926; *The Economic and Social History of an English Village.* Cambridge, Mass., 1930.

Gray, H. L. *The English Field Systems*. Cambridge, Mass., 1915; London reprint, 1969.

Griffin, N. 'Epidemics in Loughborough 1539–1640', *TLAS*, 43 (1967–8), 24–34.

Grimes, W. F. *Aspects of Archaeology*. London, 1951.

Gurevič, A. 'Representations et Attitudes a l'egard de la propriete pendant le Haut Moyen Age', *Annales*, 27 (1972), 523–47.

Habakkuk, H. J. 'Family structure and economic change in nineteenth-century Europe', *Journal of Economic History*, 15 (1955), 1–12; 'Economic functions of landowners in the seventeenth and eighteenth centuries', in *Explorations in Entrepreneurial History*, VI (1952); 'La Disparition du paysan Anglais', *Annales*, 20 (1965), 649–63.

Hajnal, J. 'European marriage patterns in perspective', in *Population in History*, eds. Glass and Lvorsley London, 1965, pp. 101–43.

Hallam, H. E. 'Some thirteenth-century censuses', *EcHR*, 2nd cer., X (1957–58), 340–61.

Hamilton Thompson, A. 'A corrody from Leicester Abbey AD 1393–4', *TLAS*, XIV (1925), 113–34.

Harley, J. B. 'Population trends and agricultural developments from the Warwickshire Hundred Rolls of 1279', *EcHR*, 2nd ser. XI (1958), 8–18; 'Population and land utilisation in the Warwickshire Hundreds of Stoneleigh and Kineton 1086–1300', Birmingham Univ. Ph.D. thesis 1960.

Harrison, Mead and Pannett. 'A Midland ridge and furrow map', *Geographical Journal*, CXXXI (1965), 366–9.

Harrison, C. 'Grain price analysis and harvest qualities 1465–1634', *AgHR*, 19 (1971), 135–55.

Hartopp, H. *Leicestershire Wills and Administrations 1495–1649* and *1660–1750*. British Record Society, XXVII (1902) and LI (1920).

Harvey, B. 'The leasing of the Abbot of Westminster's demesnes in the later middle ages', *EcHR*, 2nd ser. XXII (1969), 17–27; *VCH Oxon*, VI. London, 1959, pp. 205–19, 232–43; *Westminster Abbey and its Estates in the Middle Ages*. Oxford, 1977.

Harvey, P. D. A. *A Medieval Oxfordshire Village: Cuxham 1240–1400*. Oxford, 1965.

Hatcher, J. *Plague, Population and the English Economy 1348–1530*. London, 1977. with Miller, E. *Medieval England: Rural Society and Economic Change, 1086–1348*. London, 1978.

Havinden, M. A. 'The rural economy of Oxfordshire, 1580–1730', Oxford Univ. B.Litt. thesis 1961; 'Agricultural progress in open-field Oxfordshire', *AgHR*, 9 (1961), 73–83; *Household and Farm Inventories in Oxfordshire 1550–1590*. Oxfordshire Record Soc., XLIV (1965).

Henderson, B. H. *History of Merton College*. London, 1899.

Herlihy, D. 'Land, family and women in Continental Europe AD 701–1200', *Traditio*, 18 (1969), 89–120; 'Vieillir au Quattrocento', *Annales*, 24 (1969), 1338–52; 'Population, plague and social change in rural Pistoia AD 1201–1430', *EcHR*, 2nd ser. XVIII (1965), 225–44.

Hilton, R. H. *The Economic Development of some Leicestershire Estates in the Fourteenth and Fifteenth Centuries*. Oxford, 1947; 'Abbey leases of the late thirteenth century', *Birmingham Historical Journal*, IV (1953–4), 1–17; 'Kibworth Harcourt: a Merton College manor in the thirteenth and fourteenth centuries', *TLAS*, 24 (1949), 17–40; *A Medieval Society: The West*

Midlands at the End of the Thirteenth Century London, 1967; *The Decline of Serfdom in Medieval England* (Studies in Econ. Hist. series) London, 1969; 'Medieval agrarian history', *VCH Leics.*, II, pp. 145–200; *The English Peasantry of the Later Middle Ages*. Oxford, 1975.

Hindmarsh, N. 'The assessment of wages by JPs, 1563–1700', unpublished London Ph.D. thesis 1932.

Holdsworth, W. S. *A History of English Law*. 14 vols. London, 1922–52; *An Introduction to the Land Law*. Oxford, 1927.

Hollingsworth, T. H. *Historical Demography*. London, 1969; chap. 14 in *Population in History*, eds. Glass and Eversley. London, 1965.

Holmes, G. A. *The Estates of the Higher Nobility in Fourteenth Century England*. Cambridge, 1957.

Holmsen, A. 'The desertion of farms around Oslo in the late middle ages', *Scand. EcHR*, X (1962), 165–202; 'The old Norwegian peasant community, the introduction to . . .', *Scand. EcHR*, IV (1956), 17–32.

Holt, J. C. 'Politics and property in early medieval England', *P & P*, 57 (1972), 3–52.

Homans, G. C. *English Villagers in the Thirteenth Century*. Cambridge, Mass., 1941. Reprinted New York, 1970; 'The rural sociology of medieval England', *P & P* 4(1953), 32–43; 'The Frisians in East Anglia', *EcHR*, 2nd ser. X (1957–8), 189–206.

Hopkins, Sheila V. and Phelps Brown, E. H. 'Seven centuries of building wages' and 'Seven centuries of the price of consumables compared with builders' wage rates', in *Essays in Economic History*, II, ed. E. M. Carus-Wilson. London, 1962.

Hoskins, W. G. *The Midland Peasant*. London, 1957; *Provincial England*. London, 1965; *Essays in Leicestershire History*. Liverpool, 1950; *The Making of the English Landscape*. London, 1955; 'Harvest fluctuations and English economic history 1480–1619', *AgHR*, 12 (1964), 28–46; 'Harvest fluctuations . . . 1620–1759', *AgHR*, 16 (1968), 15–31; 'The deserted villages of Leicestershire', *TLAS*, 22 (1941–5), 241–64; 'The Leicestershire farmer in the sixteenth century', *TLAS*, 22 (1941–5), 33–94; 'Leicestershire yeomen farmers and their pedigrees', *TLAS*, 23 (1946–7), 29–62; 'The Anglian and Scandinavian settlement of Leicestershire', *TLAS*, 18 (1934), 110–47; 'Further notes on the Anglian and Scandinavian settlement of Leicestershire', *TLAS*, 19 (1935–7), 94–109; 'The fields of Wigston Magna', *TLAS*, 19 (1935–7), 164–97; 'The Leicestershire crop returns of 1801', *TLAS*, 24 (1949), 127–53.

Hughes, C. J. 'Hides, carucates and yardlands in Leicestershire: the case of Saddington', *TLAS*, 43 (1967–8), 19–23.

Hurst, D. G. and Hurst, J. G. 'Excavations of the medieval village of Wythemail, Northamptonshire', *Med. Arch.*, XII (1969), 167–203, and the series of reports on Wharram Percy in *Med. Arch.*, I–XV (1957–71).

Hyams, P. 'Legal aspects of villeinage between Glanvill and Bracton', Oxford Univ. D.Phil. thesis 1968; 'The origins of the peasant land market in England', *EcHR*, 2nd ser. XXIII (1970), 18–31; *Kinrs, Lords and Peasants: the common law of villeinage in the Twelfth and Thirteenth Centuries*. Oxford, 1980.

Ibarrola, J. *Structure Sociale et Fortune dans la Campaigne Proche de Grenoble en 1847*. Paris, 1966.

James, M. *Family, Lineage and Civil Society 1500–1640*. Oxford, 1974.

John, E. *Land Tenure in Early England*. Leicester, 1960; *Orbis Britanniae, and other studies*. Leicester, 1966.

Johnson, A. J. *The Disappearance of the Small Landowner*. Oxford, 1909.

Jones, A. 'Land and people in Leighton Buzzard in the later fifteenth century', *EcHR*, 2nd ser. XXV (1972), 18–27; 'Caddington, Kensworth and Dunstable in 1297', *EcHR*, 2nd ser. XXXII (1979), 316–27.

Jutikkala, I. 'The history of the Finnish peasant', summarised in a long review article by F. Skrubbeltrang in the *Scand. EcHR*, XII (1964), 165–80.

Kelsall, R. K. *Wage Regulation and the Statute of Artificers*. London, 1938. Reprinted in *Wage Regulation in Pre-Industrial England*, ed. W. E. Minchinton. London, 1972.

Kerridge, E. W. J. 'The agrarian development of Wiltshire 1540–1640', London Univ. Ph.D. thesis 1951; *Agrarian Problems in the Sixteenth Century and After*. London, 1969; *The Agrarian Revolution*. London, 1967; 'Surveys of the manors of Philip, First Earl of Pembroke, 1631–2', *Wilts. Arch. and Nat. Hist. Soc. Records Branch*, IX (1953); 'The movement of rent 1540–1640', *EcHR*, 2nd ser. VI (1953), 16–34; 'Ridge and furrow in agrarian history', *EcHR*, 2nd ser. IV (1959), 14–35.

Kershaw, I. *Bolton Priory*. Oxford, 1973; 'The great famine and agrarian crisis in England, 1315–1522', *P & P*, 59 (1973), 3–50.

King, E. P. *Peterborough Abbey 1086–1310. A Study in the Land Market*. Cambridge, 1973.

King, P. I. ed. *The Book of William Morton*. Oxford, 1954.

Kosminsky, E. A. *Studies in the Agrarian History of England in the Thirteenth Century*. Ed. R. H. Hilton, trans. R. Kisch. Oxford, 1956.

Krause, J. T. 'Changes in English fertility and mortality', *EcHR*, 2nd ser. XI (1948–9), 52–70; 'The medieval household: large and small', *EcHR*, 2nd ser. IX (1956–7), 420–32.

Lancaster, L. 'Kinship in Anglo-Saxon society', *British Journal of Sociology*, 9 (1958), 230–50, 359–77.

Laslett, P. with Wall, R. *Household and Family in Time Past*. Cambridge, 1972; with J. Harrison: 'Clayworth and Cogenhoe', in *Historical Essays 1600–1750 presented to David Ogg*, ed. H. E. Bell and R. L. Ollard. London, 1963; 'Size and structure of the household in England over three centuries', *Population Studies*, 23 (1969).

Latham, L. C. 'The decay of the manorial system during the first half of the fifteenth century with special reference to the decline of villeinage', London Univ. M.A. thesis 1928.

Laurence, P. M. and Kenny, C. S. *Two Essays on the Law of Primogeniture*. Cambridge, 1878.

Lennard, R. 'English agriculture under Charles II; the evidence of the Royal Society's "Enquiries"', *EcHR*, 1st ser. IV (1932–4), 23–45; *Rural England*. Oxford, 1959.

Levett, A. E. *Studies in Manorial History*. Oxford, 1938.

Levy, E. *West Roman Vulgar Law*. Philadelphia, 1951.

Lloyd, T. H. 'The movement of wool prices in medieval England', *Ec. H. Soc.*, supplement 6 (1973); 'Some aspects of the building industry in medieval Stratford-upon-Avon', *Dugdale Soc. Occ. Papers*, 14 (1961).

Lowry, E. C. 'The administration of the estates of Merton College in the fourteenth century with special reference to the Black Death and the problem of labour', Oxford Univ. D.Phil. thesis 1936.

McArthur, E. '"The Boke Longging to a Justice of the Peace" and the assessment of wages', *EHR*, IX (1894), 310–14; 'The regulation of wages in the sixteenth century', *EHR*, XV (1900), 445–55.

McClure, P. 'Patterns of migration in the late Middle Ages: the evidence of English place-name surnames', *EcHR*, 2nd ser. XXXII 2 (1979), 167–82.

Macfarlane, A. *The Family Life of Ralph Josselin.* Cambridge, 1970; *The Origins of English Individualism.* Oxford, 1978.

McFarlane, K. B. *The Nobility of Later Medieval England.* Oxford, 1973; *John Wycliffe and the Beginnings of English Non-conformity.* London, 1952.

Maddicott, J. R. *The English Peasantry and the Demands of the Crown.* Past and Present Supplement I. Oxford, 1975.

Maitland, F. W. *Domesday Book and Beyond.* Cambridge, 1907; *Select Pleas in the Manorial Courts Vol. II.* Seldon Soc. 1888. London, 1889.

Marshall, W. *The Review and Abstract of the County Reports to the Board of Agriculture from the Several Agricultural Departments of England.* Vol. IV. *The Midlands.* 1796. Vol. II. *Western Department* (1818).

May, A. N. 'An index of thirteenth-century peasant impoverishment: manor court fines', *EcHR*, 2nd ser. XXVI (1973), 389–401.

Mayhew, N. J. 'Numismatic evidence and falling prices in the fourteenth century', *EcHR*, 2nd ser. XXVII (1974), 1–27.

Mead, W. R. 'Ridge and furrow in Buckinghamshire', *Geographical Journal*, CXX (1954), 34–42.

Miller, E. and Hatcher, J. *Medieval England: Rural Society and Economic Change, 1086–1348.* London, 1978.

Milsom, S. F. C. *Historical Foundations of the Common Law.* London, 1969.

Minchinton, W. E. *Wage Regulation in Pre-Industrial England.* London, 1972.

Monk, J. *General View of the Agriculture of the County of Leicester.* London, 1794.

Morgan, M. *The English Lands of the Abbey of Bec.* Oxford, 1946.

Morris, W. A. *The Frankpledge System.* Harvard Historical Studies, no. 14. New York, 1910.

Naz, R. *Dictionnaire de Droit Canonique.* Paris, 1935–65.

Nichols, J. *The History of the Antiquities of the County of Leicester.* London, 1790. Vol. II, Pt II, Gartree Hundred: pp. 635–54.

Nightingale, M. 'Ploughing and field shape', *Antiquity*, 27 (1953), 20–6.

Oddy, J. and Miller, D. *The Making of the Modern British Diet.* London, 1976.

Osborne, F. M. 'The Manor of Kibworth Harcourt', *TLAS*, 2 (1870), 222–4.

Orwin, C. S. and C. S. *The Open Fields.* 3rd edn. Oxford, 1967.

Outhwaite, R. B. *Inflation in Tudor and Stuart England.* London, 1969.

Page, F. M. *The Estates of Crowland Abbey.* Cambridge, 1934.

Parker, L. A. 'Enclosure in Leicestershire 1485–1607', London Univ. Ph.D. thesis 1948; 'The agrarian revolution at Cotesbach 1501–1612', *TLAS*, 24 (1948), 41–76; 'The depopulation returns for Leicestershire in 1607', *TLAS*, 23 (1947), 229–89.

Payne, F. G. 'The plough in ancient Britain', *Arch. Jl.*, CIV (1947–8), 82–111; 'The British plough', *AgHR*, 5 (1957), 74–84.

Pennington, D. H. and Roots, I. A. *The Committee at Stafford 1643–44.* Oxford, 1957.

Phelps Brown, E. H. and Hopkins, S. V. 'Seven centuries of the prices of consumables compared with builders' wage rates', and 'Seven centuries of building wages', in *Essays in Economic History II*, ed. E. M. Carus-Wilson. London, 1962.

Phillpotts, B. S. *Kindred and Clan in the Early Middle Ages and After.* Cambridge, 1913.

Pingaud, M. C. 'Terres et Familles dans un Village du Chatillonnais', *Etudes Rurales*, 16, no. 42 (1971), 52–104.

Pitt, W. *A General View of the Agriculture of Leicestershire*. London, 1809.

Plucknett, T. F. T. *Concise History of English Law*. London, 1948; 'Bookland and Folkland', *EcHR*, 1st ser. VI (1935–6), 64–72.

Pocock, E. A. 'The first fields in an Oxfordshire parish', *AgHR*, 16 (1968), 85–100.

Poole, A. L. *Obligations of Society*. Clarendon Press, 1949.

Portman, D. 'The development of smaller domestic architecture in the Oxford region from the late fifteenth century to the early eighteenth', Oxford Univ. B.Litt. thesis 1960.

Postan, M. M. *Essays on Medieval Agriculture and General Problems of the Medieval Economy*. Cambridge, 1973; Ed. *Cambridge Economic History of Europe*, vol. I. Cambridge, 1966.

with Brooke, C. N. L. *Carte Nativorum*. Northants. Rec. Soc. XX. Oxford, 1960.

with Titow, J. Z. 'Heriots and prices on Winchester manors', *EcHR* 2nd ser., XI (1958–9), 392–413.

Putnam, B. H. *The Enforcement of the Statutes of Labourers during the First Decade after the Black Death 1349–59*. New York, 1891; 'Introduction on wage rates 1349–1445', in *Introduction to the Medieval Archives of the University of Oxford Vol. II*, ed. H. E. Salter. Oxford, 1921.

Raftis, J. A. 'Geographical mobility in the lay subsidy rolls', *Medieval Studies*, XXXVIII (1976), 385–403; *The Estates of Ramsey Abbey*. Toronto, 1957; *Tenure and Mobility*. Toronto, 1964.

Ravensdale, J. 'Deaths and entries; the reliability of the figures of mortality in the Black Death in Miss Page's *Estates of Crowland Abbey*, and some implications for landholding', in *Land, Kinship and Lifecycle*. Arnold (forthcoming).

Razi, Z. 'The peasants of Halesowen 1270–1400: a demographic and social study', Birmingham D.Phil. thesis 1976; *Life, Marriage and Death in a Medieval Parish*. Cambridge, 1980.

Redfield, R. *The Little Community*, 1955; *Peasant Society and Culture*. Chicago, 1960.

Redford, A. *Labour Migration in History*. Manchester, 1926.

Richardson, L. *Wells and Springs of Leicestershire*. HMSO, 1931.

Roberts, B. K. *Rural Settlement in Britain*. Folkestone, 1977.

Robinson, T. *The Common Law of Kent: or, the Customs of Gavelkind*, with an appendix concerning Borough English. London, 1822.

Rogers, J. T. *A History of Agriculture and Prices in England*. 6 vols. Oxford, 1866–1900; *Six Centuries of Work and Wages*. London, 1894.

Ross, C. D. 'The Estates and finances of Richard Beauchamp, Earl of Warwick', *Dugdale Soc. Occ. Papers*, 12. Oxford, 1956.

Round, H. *Feudal England*. London, 1909; 'The Domesday Manor', *EHR*, XV (1900), 293–302; 'The hidation of Northamptonshire', *EHR*, XV (1900), 78–86; contributions on *Domesday Book* for many volumes of the *Victoria County Histories*.

Roy Ladourie, E. le. 'The system of customary law: familial structures and inheritance customs in sixteenth century France', *Annales*, 27 (1972), 825–46; *Times of Feast, Times of Famine: A History of Climate since the Year 1000*. Paris, 1973, 1st edn. 1967. 'L'Amenorrhee de famine', *Annales*, 24 (1969), 1589–1601; 'Family structures and inheritance customs in sixteenth-century France', in *Family and Inheritance*, eds. J. Goody, J. Thirsk and E. P. Thompson. Cambridge, 1976.

Russell, J. C. *British Medieval Population*. Albuquerque, 1948; 'Medieval Midland and Northern migration to London, 1100–1365', *Speculum*, 34 (1959), 641–5; 'Effects of pestilence and plague 1315–85', *Comparative Studies in Society and History*, VIII.4 (1966); 'Demographic limitations of the Spalding serf lists', *EcHR*, XV (1962–3), 138–44.

Russell, P. 'Roads', in *VCH Leics.*, III (1955), pp. 57–91, map 60.

Sahlins, M. D. *Tribesmen*. New Jersey, 1968.

Salter, H. E. *Introduction to the Medieval Archives of the University of Oxford*. Vol. II, Oxford History Society Publications LXXIII. Oxford, 1921.

Saltmarsh, J. A. 'Plague and economic decline in England in the later middle ages', *Cambridge Historical Journal*, 1st ser., VII (1941), 23–41; 'A college home-farm in the fifteenth century', *EcH*, III (1936), 155–72.

Savine, A. 'Copyhold cases in early chancery proceedings', *EHR*, XVII (1902), 296–303; 'Bondmen under the Tudors', *TRHS*, NS XVII (1903), 235–89.

Schofield, R. S. 'The geographical distribution of wealth in England 1334–1649', *EcHR*, 2nd ser. XVIII (1965), 483–510.

   with Midi Berry, B. 'Age at baptism in pre-industrial England', *Population Studies*, 25:3 (1971), 453–63.

   with Wrigley, E. A. 'Infant and child mortality in late Tudor and early Stuart England', in *Health, Medicine and Mortality in the Sixteenth Century*, ed. C. Webster. Cambridge, 1979.

Scott, Sir Lindsay. 'Corn-drying kilns', *Antiquity*, XXV (1951), 196–208.

Searle, R. *Lordship and Community: Battle Abbey and its Banlieu 1066–1538*. Belgium, 1974; 'Merchet in medieval England', *P & P*, 82 (1979), 3–43.

Seebohm, F. *Tribal Custom in Anglo-Saxon England*. London, 1902.

Shanin, T. *The Awkward Class*. Oxford, 1972; Ed. *Peasants and Peasant Societies*. Harmondsworth, 1971.

Sheail, J. 'The regional distribution of wealth in England as indicated in the 1524/25 lay subsidy returns', London Univ. Ph.D. thesis 1968.

Sheehan, M. M. *The Will in Medieval England*. Toronto, 1963.

Shrewsbury, J. F. D. *A History of Bubonic Plague in the British Isles*. Cambridge, 1970.

Siegel, B. J. ed. *Biennial Review of Anthropology 1961, 1963, 1967* (California).

Simon, J. 'The social origins of Cambridge students, 1603–1640', *P & P*, 26 (1963), 58–67.

Simpson, A. W. B. *An Introduction to the History of the Land Law*. Oxford, 1961.

Slade, C. E. *The Leicestershire Survey*. Leicester, 1956.

Slicher van Bath, B. H. *The Agrarian History of Western Europe AD 500–1850*. Trans. Olive Ordish. London, 1963.

Smith, J. T. 'The evolution of the English peasant house in the late seventeenth century: the evidence of buildings', *Journal of British Archaeology*, 3rd ser. XXXIII (1970), 122–47.

Smith, R. M. 'English peasant life cycles and socio-economic networks; a quantitative geographical case study', Ph.D. thesis, Cambridge, 1975.

Smith, R. M. and Wrigley, E. A. eds. *Land, Kinship and Lifecycle*. Arnold (forthcoming).

Spufford, M. 'The schooling of the peasantry in Cambridgeshire', in *Land, Church and People*, ed. J. Thirsk. Reading, 1970; *Contrasting Communities: English Villagers in the Sixteenth and Seventeenth Centuries*. Cambridge, 1974; 'Inheritance and land in Cambridgeshire', in J. Goody, J. Thirsk, E. P. Thompson (eds.), Cambridge, 1976

Stamp, Dudley L. *The Land of Britain: The Report of the Land Utilisation Survey of Great Britain.* London, 1937.

Steer, F. W. *Farm and Cottage Inventories of Mid-Essex, 1635–1749.* Essex Rec. Office Publications, 8. Chelmsford, 1937.

Stenton, F. M. 'Types of manorial structure in the Northern Danelaw', in *Oxford Studies in Social and Legal History II*, ed. P. Vinogradoff. Oxford, 1910; introductory chapter on *Domesday Book* for numerous volumes of the *Victoria County Histories* including that for Leicestershire, *VCH Leics.,* I (1907), pp. 277–354.

Stone, E. 'Profit and loss accounting at Norwich Cathedral Priory', *TRHS*, 5th ser. 12 (1962), 25–48.

Stone, L. 'The educational revolution in England, 1560–1640', *P & P*, 28 (1964), 41–80; *Family and Fortune.* Oxford, 1973. with A. Everitt, 'Social mobility in England 1500–1700' *P & P*, 33 (1966), 16–55.

Stouff, L. *Ravitaillement et alimentation en Provence aux XIVᵉ et XVᵉ siecles.* Paris, 1970.

Stuckert, H. M. *Corrodies in the English Monasteries.* Philadelphia, 1923.

Styles, P. 'A census of a Warwickshire village in 1698', *Birmingham Historical Journal*, III (1951–2), 33–51.

Sutton, J. E. G. 'Ridge and furrow in Berkshire and Oxfordshire', *Oxoniensia*, XXIX (1964), 99–115.

Tate, W. E. *The Parish Chest.* Cambridge, 1969.

Tawney, R. H. 'An occupational census of the seventeenth century', *EcHR*, 1st ser. V (1934–5), 25–64; *The Agrarian Problem in the Sixteenth Century.* London, 1912; 'The assessment of wages in England by the Justices of the Peace', reprinted by Minchinton in *Wage Regulation.* London, 1972.

Thirsk, J. ed. *The Agrarian History of England and Wales 1500–1640 IV.* Cambridge, 1967; 'The common fields', *P & P*, 29 (1964), 3–25 and *P & P*, 33 (1966), 142–47; 'Agrarian history 1540–1950', *VCH Leics.,* 2 (1954) 199–253; *English Peasant Farming.* London, 1957; 'Industries in the country-side', in *Essays in Economic and Social History in Tudor and Stuart England,* ed. F. J. Fisher. Cambridge, 1961; 'The family', *P & P*, 27 (1964), 116–22; Ed., *Land, Church and People.* Reading, 1970.
with J. Cooper, *Seventeenth Century Economic Documents.* Oxford, 1972.
with J. Goody and E. P. Thompson eds., *Family and Inheritance in Rural Western Europe.* Cambridge, 1976.

Thorner, D. 'Peasant economy as a category in economic change', in *Peasants and Peasant Societies*, ed. T. Shanin. Harmondsworth, 1971, pp. 202–17.

Thrupp, Sylvia. 'The problem of replacement rates in late medieval English population', *EcHR*, 2nd ser. XVIII (1965), 101–19.

Titow, J. Z. *English Rural Society 1200–1350.* London, 1969; *Winchester Yields. A Study in Medieval Agricultural Productivity.* Cambridge, 1972; 'Some differences between manors and their effects on the condition of the peasant in the thirteenth century', *AgHR*, 10 (1962), 1–13; 'Medieval England and the open–field system', *P & P* 32 (1965).
with M. M. Postan, 'Heriots and prices on Winchester manors with statistical notes by J. Longden', *EcHR*, 2nd ser. XI (1958–9), 392–417.

Vaisey, D. G. ed. *Probate Inventories of Lichfield and District 1568–1680.* Staffs. Record Society 4th ser., Vol. 5 (1969).

Victoria County History of Leicestershire.
  Vol. 1. ed. W. Page (London 1907).
  Vol. 2. ed. W. G. Hoskins and R. A. McKinley (London 1954).
  Vol. 3. ed. W. G. Hoskins and K. A. McKinley (London 1955).
  Vol. 4. ed. K. A. McKinley (London 1958).
  Vol. 5. ed. J. M. Lee and R. A. McKinley (London 1964).
Victoria County History of Oxfordshire.
  Vol. 6. ed. M. D. Lobel (London 1959).
Victoria County History of Gloucestershire.
  Vol. 8. ed. E. R. Elrington (London 1968).
Vinogradoff, P. *Villainage in England.* Oxford, 1892; *English Society in the Eleventh Century.* London, 1908; *The Growth of the Manor.* London, 1904.
Wake, J. *The Brudenells of Deene.* London, 1953.
Wall, Richard. 'The age at leaving home', *Journal of Family History*, 3:2 (1978), 181–202.
Warriner, D. *Economics of Peasant Farming.* Cass reprint, 1964.
Watson, J. A. S. and More, J. A. *Agriculture: the Science and Practice of Farming.* Edinburgh, 1924, 11th edn 1962.
Webster, V. R. 'Cruck-framed buildings of Leicestershire', *TLAS*, 30 (1954), 26–58.
Wedgewood, J. C. 'Harcourt of Ellenhall', *William Salt Arch. Soc.* (1914), 187–210.
Welch, C. E. 'Early Nonconformity in Leicestershire', *TLAS*, 37 (1961–2), 29–43.
Westerfield, R. B. *Middlemen in English Business, particularly between 1660–1760.* Connecticut, 1915.
Whitelock, D. *Anglo-Saxon Wills.* Cambridge, 1930.
Williams, W. M. *The Sociology of an English Village: Gosforth.* London, 1956; *A West Country Village: Ashworthy.* London, 1963.
Wilshere, J. E. O. 'Plague in Leicester 1558–1665', *TLAS*, 44 (1968–9), 45–71.
Wilson, C. A. *Food and Drink in Britain.* Harmondsworth, 1976.
Wolf, E. R. *Peasants.* New Jersey, 1966.
Wood, M. *The English Medieval House.* London, 1965. (For its bibliography.)
Wrigley, E. A. *Population and History.* London, 1969; *An Introduction to English Historical Demography.* London, 1966; 'Births and baptisms: the use of Anglican baptism registers as a source of information about the number of births in England before the beginnings of civil registration', *Population Studies*, 31:2 (1977), 281–312; 'Age at marriage in early modern England', paper delivered to the XIII Congress of Genealogical and Heraldic Sciences, Sept. 1976.
Wrigley, E. A. and Smith, R. M. eds. *Land, Kinship and Lifecycle.* Arnold (forthcoming).
Yver, J. *Egalite entre Heritiers et Exclusion des Enfants Dotes.* Paris, 1966.

Index

abandonment of land, *see* land transfers
Abberley, Mr, of Stafford, 268
absentees from manor, 44–5, 227; *see also* migration
acres, *see* land units
Adam of Kibworth, 21
adoption of heirs, *see* inheritance customs
advowsons, 10, 25
Aelric, son of Meriet, 9
affeerors, 28, 30
aged, provision for, *see* family structure
aids, 26, 32
Aiken, John, 268
Alan of Portsmouth, 11, 13, 83, 91, 93
Albert Street, 138; *see also* Hog Lane
ale, *see* brewing
Allen, Abraham, 54, 66, 87
Alot family land, 141
Alwood family, 137; Margaret, 128; Richard, 141; Thomas, 141
amercements, *see* fines
animal husbandry, *see* livestock husbandry
Anonymous Husbandry, 101, 158, 159, 166
Apetoft estate, 11, 30, 41, 51, 64, 88, 126, 127; administration, 9, 2:–30; land dispersal (1316), 272–4, 275; in possession of Merton College, 13–14, 38; tenants, 19–24
Apetoft family: Laurence D', 13, 14, 24; Thomas, 14
apprentices, 177, 207
Arthur the Wiredrawer, 45
artisans, *see* craftsmen
Arundel, John, Rector, 46, 136
assart, *see* land use
Assizes of Bread and Ale, 27, 165
Asteyn, John, 216
Attelok, John, miller, 187
Audrey of Ingwardby, 13

aula, 19, 126, *see also* hall, chamber and stables
Aunger family: John, 54; William, 129
Avery, Edward, 109
Aylestone, 13
Ayre, George, bailiff, 124

bailiffs, 15, 27, 35, 67, 127, 131n, 141, 177, 186, 268; houses, 8, 124, 125, 144, 191; land, 64, 128, 130, 140; reeves as, 40; social status, 36, 64
Baker, Thomas, steward, 66
'Bakeyard', 140
baking, 6, 159, 164, 186, 189, 190, 193; bakehouse, 54, 58, 65, 68, 101, 135, 136, 188, 260
Bale, lessor, 68
Balkes, the, 65, 88, 139
Banwell Furlong, 2, 80–2, 83, 85, 86, 90–1, 123, 126
baptisms, 71, 285, 286; sex differential, 204; under-registration, 204, 205
Barkby, 20, 38, 112
barley, 54, 94, 96, 99, 103, 104, 105–6, 183, 196, 277; consumption, 157–9, 164; flour, 164; sowing, 150, 151; straw, 57, 96ff, 101; water, 165; yields, 98, 152–3; *see also* prices
Barnard family: John, 64; William, 113, 136
barns, 43, 55, 129, 143, 144
Barre, Philip, 54
Barrow (Rutland), 144, 188
Barrow on Soar, 186
barrows, 7, 8, 85
Bartholomewestyard, 43; Westyard, 123
Bartlett, J. E., 125, 144
'Bathyard', 140
Beaker burials, 3n
beans, 102, 164; straw, 101

319